0

KOKOSCHKA

Life and Work

1. SELF-PORTRAIT OF A DEGENERATE ARTIST (*1937*)

KOKOSCHKA
Life and Work

by

EDITH HOFFMANN

with two essays by
OSKAR KOKOSCHKA

and a foreword by
HERBERT READ

BOSTON BOOK AND ART SHOP INC.
122 Newbury Street
Boston, Mass.

Printed in Great Britain

FOREWORD BY HERBERT READ

Though he is undoubtedly one of the major artists of our time, the work of Oskar Kokoschka is not so well known in the United Kingdom and America as it should be. It is true that the Museum of Modern Art in New York has two superb paintings in its permanent collection, and most of the important art galleries in the U.S.A. possess one or more examples of his work. In England, the Tate Gallery has a portrait and a landscape, and there is a single example of his work in the National Gallery of Scotland. But in all these places considerably more space is given to artists of considerably less stature.

To explain this neglect might lead us into social undergrowths which cannot be explored in a short and would-be gracious preface. In a world of competing interests, of conflicting nationalisms, of the increasing commercialisation of art, the fame of any one particular artist is a counter, thrown into the game of wits. A poet is good if he sings the praises of the dominant party leader; a painter is good if he depicts the inevitable progress of the working-classes or flatters the vanity of the rich; and poet and painter sink or swim with the political fortunes of the country where they happen to be domiciled. If the country is a stable one, it may still be a question of the relative value of its exchange rate: for art is an export of potential value. The dealer plays a part, the press plays a part. What seldom gets a chance, in this sordid trafficking, is the unprejudiced sensibility of the people— of those people who can respond to the appeal of a work of art without the stimulus of fashion or fortune.

But even supposing we were back in a state of such innocency, and art was to be enjoyed for itself alone, it is idle to pretend that the work of Kokoschka would everywhere have an immediate appeal for the unsophisticated. That work does undoubtedly meet with uninstigated resistance in some quarters, and particularly in England. We feel abashed by such relentless realism. Even if we are not sentimentalists, we shrink from the exposure of nerves—our own nerves no less than the twitching nerves of the painter's victim. It is for this reason that a critic so typically

7

English as Roger Fry could not wholly accept Rembrandt—or Picasso. It is a Quakerish restraint in us. But then, we are not consistent. We accept El Greco, in spite of the quivering limbs, the distorted features, the fingers pointed with agony. We accept El Greco partly because we have been told to accept him by the critics, partly because his mysticism and masochism are expressed in Christian symbols. But there is no artist of the present time so near to El Greco as Kokoschka. I am not saying that the styles are related—stylistic comparisons are not part of my present purpose. It is the ideals that are related. Once we have discounted the symbols, which are useful conventions to which an artist may be driven by the circumstances of his time—then it is the essential humanism of the two artists which brings them together: they are both artists of love, of suffering, and of redemption.

Love is, of course, a soiled word. In Kokoschka it is instinctive identity; identity with the colour of the flower, the iridescences of fish scales and shells, the fluctuation of light over hills, or its splendour as it strikes the massed roofs of some city. It is the plastic artist's peculiar power of translating his sensations into living forms, and that power is effective in the degree that the love of the objects which arouse the sensations is pure and intense. There is no pride in such love, no judgement. The flayed carcass belongs to the same order of existence as the flower. But beyond love is suffering, and it is that perception which makes Kokoschka an exceptional artist in our age. His portraits reveal the mute suffering of the individual, of the person crucified on the codes of false social values. A few larger symbolic paintings resort to symbolism, not Greco's symbolism, but rather Goya's, to depict the suffering of oppressed peoples, the tortures of war.

And then beyond is the note of redemption. In this case it is not the divine redemption of the Christian religion, but a human redemption which Kokoschka takes over from his master and countryman, Comenius—redemption by education, by creative activity, by art. This theme is not, of course, explicit in Kokoschka's paintings. But it is the practical aspect of his humanism. It is implied in the love of man and in the belief that man can participate, through art, through creative activity, in the world of objective beauty—can become a part of that universal harmony which the great artist sees so clearly revealed in the world of objective fact.

HERBERT READ

PREFACE

The last comprehensive monograph on Oskar Kokoschka appeared in 1925, when the artist was thirty-nine years old. The following twenty years of his development have never been extensively recorded, nor have most of his latest works been reproduced. No book on Kokoschka has been published in the English language. As he has now spent five years in England, and in view of the fact that a number of works by him have lately entered public collections in this country as well as in America, it seems timely that an English publication should be devoted to him.

The story of Kokoschka's life, in its main features, is told here as he tells it himself. It is not possible, however, to rely on one's memory for every detail, particularly in relation to episodes of thirty years ago. There were no diaries, no letters, no private records of his works that could be used to fill the gaps. This book could therefore hardly have been written without the basis provided by Paul Westheim's biography, which has recorded and illustrated Kokoschka's work up to 1925. Westheim's dates have in some cases been reconsidered, but his work has made it possible to reconstruct Kokoschka's early years.

The fascination of Kokoschka's life—and of his work—consists to a great extent in the phantasy which he brings to play on mundane realities, and it is particularly difficult for a biographer to disentangle the plain facts from their colourful transformation in the imagination of the artist. History must inevitably be more prosaic than poetry, and Kokoschka himself would be the first to admit that some of his stories should be considered as significant fable rather than as sober truth. The artist alone has the responsibility for the passages which he has written.

Kokoschka's recollections have been supplemented by those of his friends. It is obvious that, out of consideration for living people, not all the available material could be used. The restrictions imposed by discretion are regrettable in the case of an artist whose work is most closely connected with the circumstances of his personal life.

9

Even with regard to Kokoschka's work completeness was excluded under the present conditions. Too many of his paintings on the Continent have been hidden for years, perhaps destroyed, or have secretely changed hands. A normal correspondence with their owners was impossible; many photographs were unobtainable; libraries were inaccessible. The material used had to be collected more accidentally than systematically. Nevertheless it is hoped that not too many serious omissions have occurred.

In spite of the unfavourable circumstances the attempt to catalogue Kokoschka's work was made while the collaboration of the artist as well as of some of his best informed friends could be ensured, which may be considered a compensation for lack of documentation. The list of paintings appended to the text aims at completeness, even though many dates and details of description could not be provided at the present moment. But while most of the oil paintings and lithographs could be accounted for, Kokoschka's drawings could not be systematically catalogued. Only those reproduced in the present or at least one other publication have been included. Those related to lithographs or published independently have been listed separately from the rest which are mere sketches or related to the paintings and catalogued among them.

It is evident from the above how many thanks are owed by the author. They are due to the artist for his collaboration; to the owners of pictures, both public and private, for their cooperation; to friends and colleagues for the loan of photographs and other material; and to Miss Margaret Senior for reading and correcting the text.

London, December 1943.

10

CONTENTS

CONTENTS

ILLUSTRATIONS

COLOUR

MONOCHROME

TEXT ILLUSTRATIONS

I. VIENNA AND BERLIN

BEGINNINGS

Vienna in the 1880's was the capital of over fifty million people: German-speaking Austrians, Hungarians, Roumanians, Czechs, Slovaks, Slovenes, Croats, Serbs, Poles, Ukrainians, Italians, Jews and Gipsies. Hitler has called Vienna a 'hotch-potch of heterogeneous nationalities',[1] and indeed its population was then a true reflection on a small scale of the many nations of south-eastern Europe. There were districts in Vienna in which almost as much Polish or Yiddish might be heard as German. The picturesque national costumes of some of the subject peoples could always be encountered in the streets of Vienna, and their national dishes contributed to the fame of Viennese menus. To visitors from the northern parts of Germany the Viennese themselves seemed southern in character, so easy-going was their temper, so naturally graceful and obliging their manners, so unbusiness-like their conduct of business affairs. The uncompromising Prussians, while they resented the Austrian lack of matter-of-factness, could not but admire and envy the charm of these people and their way of living. The Austrians themselves, although far from admiring their more efficient neighbours, looked with an ironical smile on all things Austrian: there was no society more sceptical, more disillusioned, than the Viennese *intelligentsia* when they discussed the state of affairs in their own country. This scepticism did not prevent them from being convinced of the peerless beauty of their country and of the superiority of Vienna compared with all other capitals. But they were conscious that the Empire's vitality was waning: they lived in a state of despondency.

It may be difficult now to visualise the Hapsburg Empire, which embraced one-eighth of the population of Europe, and to realise that not only was it a neighbour of the Germany which later swallowed the whole of Austria, but also that it bordered on Russia, Turkey and Italy. There could be no cultural—nor political—unity in this state, this 'meeting-place of Teuton and

---

[1] *Mein Kampf*, Chap. I.

B   17

Slav'; but its natural beauty was the greater for this extensive-
ness: a part of the Adriatic coast as well as the Eastern Alps
belonged to Austria, and so did the snow tops of the Tatra, the
wide Hungarian Puszta, the dark Bohemian forests and lakes.
Austrian cities, too, were rich in monuments of all the periods of
Christian civilisation: medieval churches, monasteries and
baroque palaces; other towns with their Mohammedan places of
worship had a predominantly oriental appearance. The beauty
of Vienna herself has often been praised. Yet that city could
never appear to a foreign visitor as she did to the native, who
knew all her moods like his own: the familiar cathedral of St.
Stephen rising black among the snow of mid-winter, stretching
its one spire towards the sky like a finger, and its darkness en-
shrining candle-lit altars; the magnificent avenue, the 'Ring',
which encircled the old city, so superb that even its nineteenth-
century monuments had dignity, bathed in the spring sunshine
that made Italy seem so close; the lilac in its gardens smelling
sweet like the mimosas in the avenues of Rome; the Danube
valley outside the city with its tiny, sleepy towns, a valley of
fruit-trees in blossom; in the early summer, the parks which
stretch from one princely baroque palace to the other, full of
statues and flowers: even the courtyard of the imperial 'Hofburg'
a forest of red-blossomed chestnut trees; and in the autumn, the
ground of the 'Wiener Wald' covered with many-coloured
leaves, its rivers swelling with rain.

The life of the Austrian capital was, of course, centred round
the imperial court. The Hapsburg dynasty, which had once ruled
over the greater part of Europe, had since 1848 been represented
by a lonely man, tired out by constant disturbances in his own
countries as well as by too many foreign wars, each of which left
his empire nearer the abyss into which it was finally to disappear.
Surrounded by the Spanish court ceremonial, the Emperor
Francis Joseph resided in the magnificent Hofburg in the centre
of Vienna; but he was separated by an infinitely elaborate bureau-
cracy from the life of his people. He was to be seen only on such
occasions as the visits of foreign royalties, when his bearded,
uniformed figure bowed from his carriage, or on Corpus-Christi
Day, when he headed the holy procession, carrying a candle in
his hand. The presence of the court had naturally a strong influence on the life of every-day Vienna: the aristocracy, returning
each year, when the hunting season was over, from their estates
in Hungary or Bohemia, were the only public for which the

brilliant opera, the glittering ballrooms, the famous Burg-
theater itself seemed to exist. The officers of the Vienna garrison
also played a part in the life of the city which has been described
in innumerable novels, plays and films.[1] They were the heroes of
the women who haunted the Prater[2] and the Heurigen[3] inns,
where all classes met, in suburban Vienna, drinking wine, half
gaily, half sentimentally enjoying the mild summer evenings
with congenial company and Heurigen songs. The officers of
the imperial armies were the spenders of money—as often won
as lost in an evening at the card-tables—the frequenters of the
Sacher Hotel and such famous establishments, and sometimes
the protagonists of such sinister tragedies as that in which the
heir to the throne, Prince Rudolph, lost his life.

But apart from these circles, which with all their splendour
made Vienna seem so brilliant, though in reality they only
marked her approaching decay—and, indeed, gave the capital of
the Hapsburg Monarchy an atmosphere reminiscent of Paris in
the days of Napoleon III—very different elements directed the
real life of the city.

In the realm of politics, two widely different movements had
developed at the end of the century, out of nineteenth-century
liberalism. The Catholic bourgeoisie and part of the academic
youth tended towards a doctrine called 'Christian Socialism',
which contained the germ of much that Hitler later incorporated
in his National Socialism—the cult of what we now call 'blood
and soil'—and an emphasis on the racial superiority of the
Germanic people; this movement was headed by the clergy; but
its most famous representative was Vienna's burgomaster Lue-
ger, who was also an outspoken anti-semite. On the other hand,
the working class and many of the intellectuals rallied around
Viktor Adler, a socialist in the Marxist tradition, intent on the
improvement of the workers' living conditions and education.
The struggle for supremacy between these two doctrines did not
cease until the *Anschluss* of 1938. They were powerful forces,
and it is natural that they were reflected in the culture of
the country. They impressed themselves on literature, the

---

[1] Arthur Schnitzler is the best-known author who, before 1914, made
these Austrian officers the centre figures of his short stories and plays, while
Joseph Roth has described them—in a more satirical way—in the period
between the two wars.

[2] Vienna's great amusement park.

[3] *Heuriger* is fresh wine.

fine arts and the drama and consequently on all receptive minds.

During the first years of this century, which concern us here, literature mirrored every fluctuation of local political life, though it came of course under the influence of the international movements which were revolutionising European literature as a whole. In Karl Schönherr's plays nationalist fanatics clashed with equally fanatical Papists; in others, the main characters were peasants, drawn as creatures of primitive and uncontrollable passions. Schnitzler wrote dramas round officers who deceived their lower-class sweethearts with ladies of their own class, with suicides following on duels. Decadent cynics were set against creatures of unreasoning impulse and emotions. Influenced by Ibsen and Strindberg, Zola and Baudelaire, Vienna's writers were for the moment preoccupied with social and psychological problems. But their individualism was merely a preparatory stage for the almost abstract generalisations of the next generation: it will be seen that the writings of the young Kokoschka, in which most characters were nameless (like those of Strindberg and some of Wedekind), while their problems were those of every man and woman of every time and place, grew out of the seeds of these years.

These Viennese plays may perhaps be only a minor contribution to the world's literature: but the poetry written in these years round 1900 has won international renown and is part of the great heritage of the German language. Hugo von Hofmannsthal's verses and lyrical prose gave expression to many moods characteristic of the old Austria: a melancholy longing for the past, a romanticised reflection of history; for the brilliance and grace of Baroque and Rococo; dreams of a visionary Italy, of an imagined Venice; admiration for all that is beautiful, in nature as well as in art; painted figures come to life, living persons behave like actors in a pageant; a world like that of Musset and Oscar Wilde, without their destructive irony. Hugo von Hofmannsthal wrote the text of Richard Strauss's operas and of some of Max Reinhardt's Salzburg festival plays: and so he reached even those who would never have read him for his poetry.

Hofmannsthal's works can be said to belong to an international tradition of poetry. There was another branch of writing more peculiar to Vienna: an analytical type of criticism, whose basis was purely ethical. Its last and most outstanding exponent was Karl Kraus, author of innumerable literary and political articles,

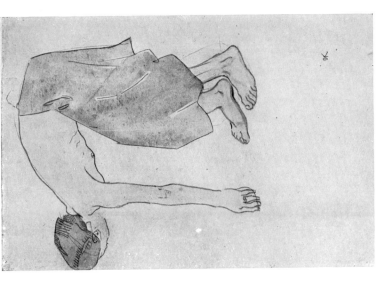

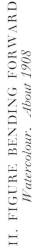

II. FIGURE BENDING FORWARD
Watercolour. About 1908

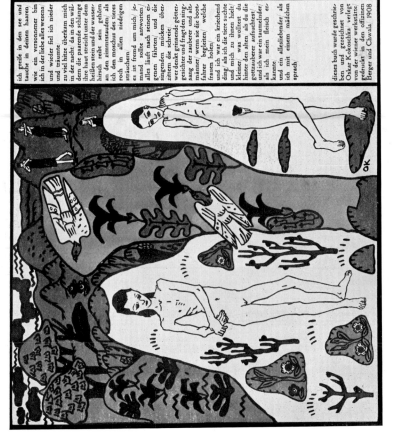

ich greife in den see und
tauche in deinen haaren/
wie ein versonnener bin
ich in der liebe alles wesens/
und wieder fiel ich nieder
und träumte

zu viel hitze überkam mich
in der nacht da in den wäl-
dern die paarende schlange
ihre haut streicht unter dem
heißen stein und der wasser-
hirsch reibt sein gehörn
an den rinnstrauden/ als
ich den moschus des tieres
roch in allen niedrigen
sträuchern

es ist fremd um mich/ je-
mand sollte antworten/
alles läuft nach seinen ei-
genen fährten/ und die
singenden mücken über-
zittern die schreie/

wer denkt grinsende götter-
gesichter und fragt den sing-
sang der zauberer und alt-
männer/ wenn sie die boot-
fahrer begleiten/ welche
frauen holen/

und ich war ein kriechend
ding/ als ich die tiere suchte
und mich zu ihnen hielt/
kleiner/ was wolltest du
hinter den alten als du die
gottzauberer aufsuchtest/
und ich war ein taumelnder/
als ich mein fleisch er-
kannte

und ein allesliebender/ als
ich mit einem mädchen
sprach

dieser buch wurde geschrieben und gezeichnet von
Oskar Kokoschka vertegt
von der wiener werkstätte/
gedruckt in den offizinen
Berger und Chwala 1908

I. DIE TRÄUMENDEN KNABEN
Lithograph. 1908

III. NUDE SEATED
Watercolour. About 1908

IV. NUDE SEATED
Watercolour. About 1908

who published in his own magazine, *Die Fackel*[1], a play in fifty-five scenes about the first world war, which he called *Die letzten Tage der Menschheit*,[2] as well as of other satirical plays and poems. He was, incidentally, a translator of Shakespeare's plays and of Offenbach's musical comedies. This is not the place to say more of Karl Kraus, though he played an important part on the intellectual stage of Vienna, for here we are concerned only with the Viennese background, and Kraus himself belongs to the actual story of Kokoschka' life.[3] For the same reason we need not speak here of Peter Altenberg, the most individual and yet perhaps most typically Viennese of all those poets who made the Austrian capital one of the centres of German literature.

Much more could be said of the immensely active intellectual life of pre-war Vienna, were this not a book on one Viennese painter. The names of Hugo Wolf, Gustav Mahler, Arnold Schönberg, who followed each other as Vienna's great composers and conductors, may be recalled; of Alois Riegl, Franz Wickhoff and Max Dvořak, who conceived an entirely new method of approach to the history of art; of Siegmund Freud, who at the same period was engaged on work that was to revolutionise the world of psychology. And in those same days an unknown, unemployed painter, selling his water-colours in the streets of

[1] The Torch.

[2] The Last Days of Mankind.

[3] Mr. Henry Wickham Steed writes of Karl Kraus in his excellent book, *The Hapsburg Monarchy* of 1914 (2nd edition), p. 192: 'No account of the Viennese press would, however, be even approximately complete without some mention of a biting, stinging, sometimes scurrilous periodical pamphlet called the *Fackel*, which keeps a vigilant eye upon the follies and failings of daily journalism and pillories them mercilessly. The editor, proprietor and staff of the *Fackel* consist of one and the same person, Karl Kraus, a Jewish writer of remarkable talent. The daily press maintains a conspiracy of silence in regard to his very existence but he has nevertheless a faithful public of readers who enjoy his mordant satire and find in his brilliant style relief from the pomposities and bathos of Austrian journalese. Occasionally he victimises the self-sufficient omniscience of the *Neue Freie Presse* by perpetrating at its expense some elaborate hoax. Kraus is a Viennese product, scarcely intelligible save in relationship to the Viennese press, though his literary style finds recognition beyond the frontiers of the Monarchy. He is an Ishmael, courting and requiting the hostility of his contemporaries but rarely allowing their shortcomings to pass unpunished. In one respect his efforts deserve specially honourable mention. He has encouraged by precept and practice the tendency of modern writers of German to react against the artificial clumsiness of the language and to prove that German can be written harmoniously. . . .'

Vienna, turned over in his mind the picture of this world—as he saw it—and brooded over the future—as he would make it: Adolf Hitler, in the days of his obscurity, walked these same pavements—a symbol of the darker side of Vienna's pre-war gaiety and culture.

To mention all these names in the introduction to the life of a painter is not so unjustified as it may seem: all these men had a more or less immediate influence on Kokoschka; they helped to form his life—and his work—as the scenery, the architecture, the many races of his country formed his character. Kokoschka is a true son of that lost Vienna—and one who found a path into the outer world, into the future.

★   ★   ★

Oskar Kokoschka was born in the small town of Pöchlarn on the Danube on the 1st March, 1886. His father had come to the capital from Prague, like so many Czechs who hoped to find a better existence there, and had married a woman from the mountainous province of Styria in the Alps. He came of a long line of artisans, mostly goldsmiths, and Oskar's grandfather, who was a friend of the Czech painter Manes as well as of the composer Smetana,[1] had taken part in the restoration of the jewelled medieval chapel of St. Wenceslas on Hradčany,[2] and had made a chalice for this chapel. A portrait that Oskar drew of his father shows him in his old age, his thick hair and beard still preserving their natural colour, his features serene and unrevealing.[3] The mother, as she lives in the memory of friends

[1] I owe this information to Dr. Palkovský, who had occasion to study Kokoschka's connection with Prague on the spot.

[2] The castle on the mountain where the kings of Bohemia lived and which was later the residence of the President of Czechoslovakia as well as the seat of many ministries.

[3] This is what Kokoschka writes about his father: 'My devotion to my father became evident in my early struggle for independence. The introduction of shoddy methods of production, the rise of new purely commercial values, destroyed the craftsman's human dignity and brought direct suffering to my father. From him I learned to endure poverty rather than to work slavishly at distasteful work. Furthermore, with the example of my classmates' parents before me, subaltern civil servants, shopkeepers and clerks, I realised how hopeless were the lives of my comrades who did not seem to dread their fate of growing up into an existence of monotonous routine work which offered them security but brought nothing creative before their eyes. In spite of the great affection uniting parents and children my father was very reserved. Only too often he had to tell my mother to

and in the portrait her son made of her, seems to have had the livelier temper, the more vigorous energy. Kokoschka himself says about her: 'I remember her pathetic efforts at times to fight for the family's survival, when I myself was too young to assist her. It is she I have to thank for a more direct understanding of my art than I gained from the refined mob that calls itself society. Born the daughter of an imperial forester in Styria who had many children and few worldly possessions, her childhood was rich and eventful; in the company of her brothers and sisters she had to trudge for many miles to acquire the secrets of the three

try to make the best of a miserable situation, until he secured regular employment in another town or country even. The family would then follow him. Often some little possession acquired in a favourable interval had to be taken to the pawnshop. Although my mother was robbed of most of the essentials of life, we children were neither unhappy nor neglected. One was born in this country, one in that, and to us it only seemed strange that other children should settle down. Perhaps that is why I still find it odd today to be treated as a foreigner in no matter what country. It was very different for my father who had been trained to practise his parents' art as a goldsmith in their family house in Spálená ulice in Prague. His had been one of the few patrician families in Prague. A true middle-class tradition of humanist interests had been handed over from one generation to another. Lessing's works were not merely something relegated to the library shelf, but principles of tolerance such as his took the place of the bourgeois *laissez faire*. In the evening Schiller's plays of freedom were read aloud. My father could still quote passages in his old age and was never more angry than when his memory failed him. The revival of the music of the people was perhaps due to the influence of Herder on the Czech composers, who were among the circle of my grandparents' friends, and this was perhaps the forerunner of the renaissance of the common peoples of the Slavonic family. The river of chauvinistic politics which soon swept over this idyll was not fed by such cultural tributaries; it was nurtured by machine-made civilisation announcing itself with the roar of Prussian guns over the battlefields of Bohemia. Yet before that the dethroned Emperor Francis I had to take up residence at Prague because the *Biedermeier* period at his capital had suddenly come to an end and in Vienna they were building barricades just as in Paris. In Prague he led the life of a citizen and sometimes liked to pay a visit to my grandfather's shop and, while selecting a new snuff-box or waiting for a loose stone to be reset, he liked to accept a cup of coffee from my grandmother. According to a portrait painted by Manes she must have been a beauty. My father remembered how he had boyishly tried on the ex-Emperor's high top-hat, handed over to him together with a *Biedermeier* walking stick of malacca cane, and how graciously the old gentleman had helped him out of his prison of pressed felt.

'The age of paternal absolutism had closed. In Vienna a constitution had been conceded to the nations which, uniting them under the crown of the

R's, whereas of their own secrets only the birds and beasts of the woods and lakes knew. Although the nearest school was many miles away, she was the best pupil and she could not help feeling resentful when at the school prize-giving she received only a little picture while the rich but lazy daughter of the village brewer was awarded a much coveted story book. In winter the forester's house was often snowed up for weeks on end and several times it was besieged by hungry wolf packs. At that period children were often stolen by gipsies, and once Romana's mother had to protect her brood rifle in hand against a band of vagrants. Her husband and elder sons, returning from one of Hapsburgs, had improved step by step until the parliamentary machinery resulted in the general voting right of true democracy. But the defeat on the battlefields of Bohemia had not only political but economic consequences with which no parliament could cope, its function being solely political. The machine had won the day and there was no planning of production. Who cared for the craftsman? Had he not now the constitutional right to seek his night quarters under the famous bridge or at choice to cross the bridge that led to the slavish fabrication of shoddy mass-products? At the beginning of the process of industrialisation, it is true, its begetters did not dream of the power inherent in it. Society had to wait for another generation to progress towards that deadly kind of production which today fosters in more and more people the illusory longing for a kind of democratic constitution capable of planning not only for war but for peace. During the Thirty Years' War the Czech humanist Jan Amos Comenius, adapting the law of cause and effect to the reform of politics, had been the first to try to humanise the warring nations by educating children. No government will put his method to the test for so long as the grown-ups can be convinced that everything is in the best possible state.

'But it is an unfortunate state of affairs when the ignorance of the fathers is visited on the children. When mass education had finally been accepted in practice by all civilised governments the universally humanist idea behind it was supplanted by one limited to mere national ends. Since then schooling continually gives a strange impression of being on the point of meaning enlightenment and then funking it. Could anyone anticipate that a normal day would open with the reading at breakfast about the "hamburging" of big towns and territories? Does it show human beings how to "make good", as the Americans say, after having discovered that the first world war had been a delusion? Do you think I am harping on the fuss made about the guilt of so-called war criminals? Certainly not. This only proves that the other side was not frightened by hell either.

'Shells are produced to go off whether they are intended for home consumption or for export. By all the accepted laws of nature it is reasonable to suppose that if people had been taught in school they would know at least that the physical laws of cause and effect impinge on human action. Society would have realised that education for the struggle implied in the law of the survival of the fittest is a boomerang returning to the thrower.

24

their inspection rounds, came to the rescue just in time. My mother was told that this happened just before she was born. It was from her mother she inherited second sight and its occasional manifestations were for strangers a little bewildering. Thus when visiting a relative she left abruptly because she could see that her younger son Bohuslav had injured his foot with an axe. She found this was so when she arrived at home an hour later. Her children accepted her strange gift as quite natural and attributed it only to their mother's superior qualities.'

There were four children, one of whom died during Oskar's childhood; a brother, Bohuslav, closely resembles Oskar and has

In my schooldays the quarrel between the central government in Vienna and the political parties standing for national self-determination had been extended into the educational field. Here it was called the conflict between reactionary and progressive tendencies, religion and science being at stake. Both sides were out for an era when Enlightenment should be rationed. As far as the rope-pulling concerned me, I suffered hell. My second-hand primers were turned down as no longer fitting in with the plan of progress by which one method of education was swopped for another while I was in midstream. School being compulsory I could not simply throw my bag on the floor and say to the teachers: There you are, sort it out among yourselves!

'But the very first book given me by my father before I could even read, Jan Amos Comenius's *Orbis Pictus*, has never ceased to be useful to me. As this classic encyclopedia of humanism has never been reprinted since the theory of the survival of the fittest was generally adopted, a few words may not be out of place to explain the popularity it once enjoyed. It pictured men of all nations as belonging to one family differing only in colour, language, religion, in their dwellings, habits, activities and sciences, and showed that these divisions were due to geography and climate. It described both the phenomena of the animate and the inanimate realms and put man in his true place in the cosmos. Words inscribed beneath the pictures in several living and dead languages, made it easy to learn the meaning when you could see the things and knew them to be true.

'I always think that the second-hand quality which is second nature with democracy today, is somehow linked up with this fact. People think what they are told to think by their authorities. Therefore they know about the essential things of their life only from hearsay evidence. Perhaps it is for such "dangerous thoughts" which the plan of the pedagogue Comenius might produce, that his *Orbis Pictus* had fallen in oblivion. Impatient young generations of this second world war, if dissatisfied with the restricted scope of enlightenment supplied today, may still catch up with the reasoning of the so-called dark ages. Saint Thomas Aquinas says "The senses are a kind of reason. Taste, touch and smell, hearing and seeing, are not merely a means to sensation, enjoyable or otherwise, but they are also a means to knowledge—and are, indeed, your only actual means to knowledge. . . ." Believe it or not, I do!'

25

done some painting which has led the famous artist to say that his brother is the better painter; their sister married a Czech and thus returned to the country from which the father came.

They had little contact with normal society and only one link with the world of art: an uncle who gave lessons on the piano. Oskar himself had a passion for music, and he was at last taught to play the violin. But his recollection of these lessons is limited to hours of waiting, until the luckier children, whose instruction was paid for, had finished and left. When he was older and a pupil at a secondary school, he began to spend his Sunday mornings in museums. He was not interested in the 'fine arts'. The stillness of the statues and pictures, as he passed through the collections in which Vienna is so rich, made him think of nothing but a graveyard. What did attract him were the ethnographical exhibits: the masks of South Sea primitives with their exotic colour and ornament excited him beyond measure. He learnt to understand the language of exotic colouring before the language of European painting. He remembers still his first favourite, a head from New Mecklenburg, adorned with shells and shark teeth, with ornaments like bundles of nerves painted in blue on its cheeks—painted freely, mysterious, and yet full of a familiar life—and so different from the classical ornaments with which he had been bored at school. It was this primitive art which influenced his own first creations: his early posters which were to evoke such horror among his contemporaries, were inspired by this barbarous mask. Long after, he liked to use masks in his own compositions (see Nos. 133, 164); and when, during the first great war, he encountered the Expressionists of the *Brücke*, who had made it their programme to embody elements of native art into their paintings, he could for a while believe that he was bound to them by a deep affinity. He had gone the same way as so many contemporary artists in Paris and in Central Europe. They consciously looked to exotic sources for inspiration, while he had gone that way by instinct.

The only living artist whom he credits with having made a deep impression on him in his youth is Stephan Romako, a once famous, since forgotten and, in Vienna, even rediscovered painter of great historical pictures. Romako's genius had fullest play in his sketches in oils[1], while his great painting, *Admiral*

[1] One of the best is now in a London private collection. It is a sketch for a curtain, commissioned by a Vienna theatre, which was never executed.

26

Tegethoff in the Battle of Lissa[1] (1866) was familiar to every Austrian. He may be called a nineteenth-century descendant of the Austrian Baroque: his compositions were dramatic in conception, crowded with figures that swept over the surface like a tempest. His canvases glowed with colour. His technique was impressionistic. In the same way Maulpertsch and Kremser Schmidt had been dramatic, passionate and impressionistic. Kokoschka was so impressed by Romako's colouring that he thought he found it again only in the reddest sunsets which he watched from the streets of Vienna; and so it was Romako who first opened his eyes to the beauties of the sky. He later discovered a similar colouring in the paintings of Turner, whom he loved at once because he reminded him of Romako—the first real artist whom he had known.

Kokoschka's early ambitions were by no means directed towards painting: he wanted to study chemistry. One might think that the charm of some old-fashioned pharmacy with its rows of many-coloured bottles, its smell of medicines and herbs, had attracted the highly imaginative boy, if Kokoschka himself had not always maintained that it was the mysterious reactions of the chemical elements that fascinated him, their melting together and their struggle against each other, symbolic, it seemed to him, of the complex human life around him. He may have imposed this interpretation on his early impulse later, when he came to think of his own life as laid out in a series of coherent patterns, and we have no means of checking its validity. But it is a fact that he wished to study chemistry. One of his old teachers who liked his drawings recommended him instead for a scholarship offered at the School of Arts and Crafts attached to the Österreichisches Museum für Kunst und Industrie. He accepted it, in the hope that this might open the way into the other field. But he never fulfilled his ambition.

★　　★　　★

Art in the early years of the new century showed many faces. The literary tendencies of the *fin-de-siècle* had been transformed but not completely submerged—they were in fact being absorbed into what was later generally called expressionism. At the same time those trends which aimed at purely visual effects were not only active but triumphant: they proved the primary importance of a

[1] The admiral had sacrificed his ship in this battle in order to destroy, by deliberate collision, the *Re d'Italia*.

painter's vision and of a sensual approach, in contrast to a predominantly intellectual imagination. It was these trends that made France the undisputed leader in art. In Paris the Impressionists were still at work; Gauguin, Toulouse-Lautrec, Seurat, had died young; but Matisse, Rouault, Vlaminck, Dufy, Dérain, Picasso, Braque, Utrillo, all born between 1880–90, were at the beginning of their careers and still under the influence of various established traditions. In England Sargent was at the height of his fame, Sickert, Brangwyn and John were well known. On the Continent, English art was mostly represented by book production and the works of Ricketts, Shannon, Beardsley, William Nicholson and Watts. In Germany, the romantic Klinger and the more realistic, naively poetic Hans Thoma were perhaps the two artists who best expressed the popular sentiment. But there were many cross-currents: the impressionism of Liebermann, Lesser-Ury and Slevogt; the more imaginative realism of Corinth, who favoured religious or mythological subjects; the harsher naturalism of painters of proletarian life, like Käte Kollwitz; the symbolism and *art nouveau* of Stuck and the Swiss Hodler; the blood-and-soil expressionism of Paula Becker-Modersohn and other Worpswede[1] artists; the more exotic expressionism of Nolde.

The school of Vienna was the equal of any other art centre east of Paris, but remained obscure internationally. German art historians, renowned for their thoroughness, have named very few Austrian artists in their monumental works on modern painting. It is true that, owing to the regional diversity of the Reich, the public of Berlin knew little even of what could be seen in the Munich or Stuttgart exhibitions, and still less of Vienna which was, after all, a foreign city. It is just as true that the cities of the South maintained the utmost reserve towards the artistic life of Prussia. This exclusiveness was extended also to Vienna: Berlin regarded the Austrian capital rather as a poor cousin, who might have some good qualities; and to Vienna, Berlin seemed a sort of *nouveau-riche* whose cultural achievements were hardly to be considered. As a result, the works of Viennese artists very seldom came into the Berlin galleries; and though Vienna was one of the first among the European capitals to have exhibitions of the leading French artists, she rarely showed the art of Germany.

Vienna had her centuries-old artistic traditions. Two of these

[1] A village near Bremen where Becker-Modersohn, Heinrich Vogeler, Hans am Ende and other painters lived.

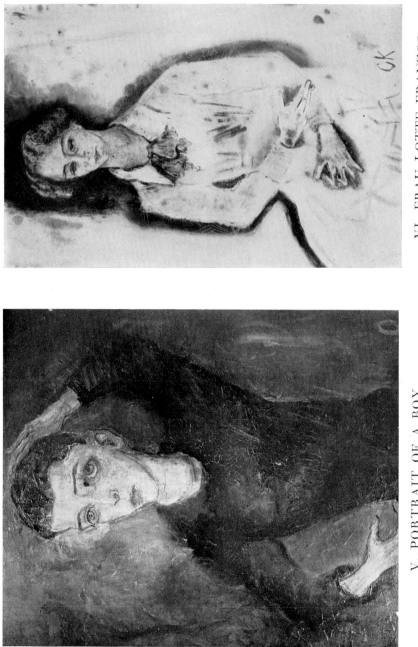

VI. FRAU LOTTE FRANZOS
1909

V. PORTRAIT OF A BOY
1908

VII. PROFESSOR HANS TIETZE AND FRAU ERICA TIETZE-CONRAT
1908-9

ruled her nineteenth-century painting: on the one hand, a realism inherited from Waldmüller and Rudolf Alt, the leading Biedermeier painters, which had been degraded by the following it had gained at the Academy, an institution as sterile and discredited in the eyes of all leading artists as in other countries; on the other hand, the Baroque, which had developed most fully along the Danube, covering with paintings the walls and ceilings of palaces and churches, and which underwent a revival at the hand of Makart and Romako. They were contemporaries of the middle and late Victorians, and Makart's name has in fact survived, suitably enough, in connection with those bouquets of artificial flowers which adorned stuffy Victorian drawing-rooms. In his time, however, he was a prince among artists and the idol of a society which sat to him in the nude, because they considered him a second Rubens.

In the Vienna of about 1900 the decorative arts flourished. Austria's Slav hinterland and oriental neighbours provided an unceasing flow of picturesque and colourful ornaments, and the city absorbed them with that receptiveness which derived from a prodigal mixture of races. Vienna was the capital of taste— taste in interior decoration, in the theatre, in fashion and in handicrafts. Not only the Balkan countries and the whole of south-eastern Europe, but even Germany looked to her for guidance, as western countries looked to Paris. And she held this position until the end of the first world war.

The centre of decorative arts in Vienna was the Wiener Werkstätte, at the beginning of our century headed by Josef Hoffmann, an architect of international renown.[1] This institute had a considerable influence on the whole of Austria and Germany, comparable only to the influence wielded by William Morris in England. Its materials, furniture and ceramics remained the best for a long time, even after the foundation of similar institutes in Germany.[2] By introducing good materials and sound craftsmanship these schools and workshops helped to form a better taste in well-to-do middle-class homes, even though their 'artistic' tendency dated them when, a few years later, pure functionalism became the fashion. In the first decade of the

[1] One of his most famous buildings is the Palais Stoclet (1905) at Brussels, important for the part it plays in *art nouveau* and the transition to modern architecture.

[2] Particularly the Münchner Werkstätten and the Deutsche Werkstätten at Hellerau near Dresden.

century, however, they were in their prime, and Josef Hoffmann, together with the leaders of the Kunstgewerbeschule, Kolo Moser and Alfred Roller, had the greatest influence on all young artists in Vienna. It must be said to their honour that these men were idealistic enough to further the cause of art whenever this was in their power. They were, indeed, always on the look-out for young talent. They organised exhibitions in which they encouraged beginners to take part, and young artists could under their ægis live and work in a congenial atmosphere.

The leading Viennese painter, famous well beyond the borders of his own country,[1] was then Gustav Klimt, an artist so typical of *art nouveau* that a more characteristic example of that international style could hardly be found. If *art nouveau* was an art of the surface—and a beautifully ornamented surface—of flowing curves and delicate figures, of ephemeral beauty and rich ornamentation, of poetical, sometimes symbolic subjects, a feminine and decadent art—Klimt was its quintessence. His subjects were women, of a fragile, yet proud beauty, whose pale colouring and reddish hair were reminiscent of the Pre-Raphaelites. Their anæmic heads were adorned with real gold and silver which Klimt, in imitation of Byzantine artists, applied to the surface. His love of splendour, as well as his strong eroticism, has often been attributed to Near-Eastern in-fluences. The garments of his women are brightly coloured, and spread out flat like meadows across the picture's surface, covered with jewels as if with flowers. The effect when the pictures were hung was that of almost abstract, yet blossom-like ornaments, and the figures, faces, hands could scarcely be disentangled from the magnificent robes. An æsthetically sensitive public revelled

[1] *The Burlington Magazine* of 1909 (Vol. XV), p. 388, printed the follow-ing praise of this artist: 'Gustav Klimt contributed but one canvas, the Portrait of a Lady seated; to my mind it is the most exquisite piece of art in the entire show. This kind of art is most emphatically caviare to the general, and it works upon the most refined of susceptible senses. The manner in which the modelling is effected, light in light, without the shadow of a shadow; the bewitching triad of old gold, pale rose and mother of pearl which strike the keynote of the colour symphony are fascinating beyond words. Those hands, with slightly interlaced fingers and a perfectly divine delicacy! All of it is unearthly, celestial in its beauty, and yet there is a power to suggest tissue and texture which has never been surpassed. I should call the portrait the evanescence of the very highest stage of culture to which the human race has yet attained.' (H.W.S. in 'Art in Germany, Austria and Switzerland'.)

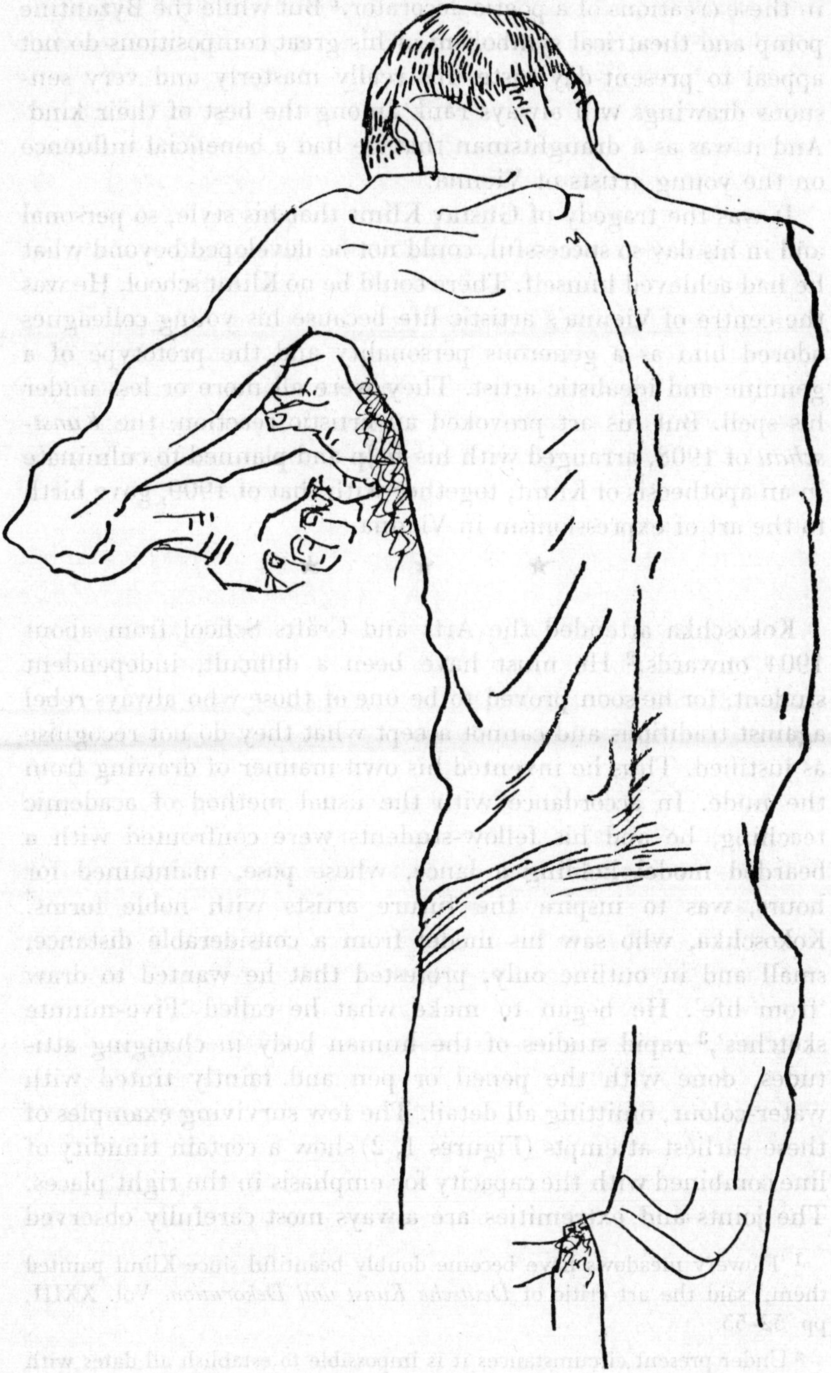

1. ACROBAT SEEN FROM BACK
About 1908

in these creations of a poetic decorator.[1] But while the Byzantine pomp and theatrical symbolism of his great compositions do not appeal to present-day taste, his really masterly and very sensuous drawings will always rank among the best of their kind. And it was as a draughtsman that he had a beneficial influence on the young artists of Vienna.

It was the tragedy of Gustav Klimt that his style, so personal and in his day so successful, could not be developed beyond what he had achieved himself. There could be no Klimt school. He was the centre of Vienna's artistic life because his young colleagues adored him as a generous personality and the prototype of a genuine and idealistic artist. They were all more or less under his spell. But his art provoked an artistic reaction: the *Kunstschau* of 1908, arranged with his help and planned to culminate in an apotheosis of Klimt, together with that of 1909, gave birth to the art of expressionism in Vienna.

★   ★   ★

Kokoschka attended the Arts and Crafts School from about 1904 onwards.[2] He must have been a difficult, independent student, for he soon proved to be one of those who always rebel against traditions and cannot accept what they do not recognise as justified. Thus he invented his own manner of drawing from the nude. In accordance with the usual method of academic teaching, he and his fellow-students were confronted with a bearded model holding a lance, whose pose, maintained for hours, was to inspire the future artists with noble forms. Kokoschka, who saw his model from a considerable distance, small and in outline only, protested that he wanted to draw 'from life'. He began to make what he called 'Five-minute sketches',[3] rapid studies of the human body in changing attitudes, done with the pencil or pen and faintly tinted with water-colour, omitting all detail. The few surviving examples of these earliest attempts (Figures 1, 2) show a certain timidity of line combined with the capacity for emphasis in the right places. The joints and extremities are always most carefully observed

---

[1] 'Flowery meadows have become doubly beautiful since Klimt painted them,' said the art critic of *Deutsche Kunst und Dekoration*, Vol. XXIII, pp. 52–53.

[2] Under present circumstances it is impossible to establish all dates with certainty. He may have begun his training in 1905.

[3] *Fünf-Minuten-Akte.*

VIII. CHILDREN PLAYING
1909

IX. CAT
1910

and accentuated. The thin bodies and large hands and feet which give these figures a pathetic appearance, probably not at first intentional, were soon to be exploited for their expressiveness. Kokoschka was to some extent under the influence of Klimt. But while the master and most of his followers sought to beautify and ennoble human beings, he would make them pitiable, even ugly: while others aimed at flowing outlines and a smooth surface he used angular contours to express a subdued melancholy—not unlike the work of his contemporary Picasso who was then passing through his 'Blue Period'—that seemed to reproach the older generation with superficiality. There is no explanation for this coincidental emergence of the same new mood in the work of both the Western and the Central-European artists, unless we accept as an explanation the well-known phenomenon that artists of one generation often solve formal problems in the same way: thus Picasso and Kokoschka both reacted similarly to the perverse moods of the *fin-de-siècle*. Kokoschka himself has another explanation: 'I was impressed by the Expressionists of the eighteenth century, Büchner's *Wozzek*, Heinrich von Kleist's *Penthesilea*, Ferdinand Raimund's moralistic plays, Nestroy's satirical works. To recount one man's literary experiences when he was born in the late nineteenth century, and in Austria, one ought to set out to face the finality of the moral and social struggle which had just begun. . . . It was the Baroque inheritance I took over, unconsciously still. Just as it offered itself to my dazzled eyes as a boy singing in choir in the Austrian cathedrals, I saw the wall-paintings of Gran, the Kremser Schmidt, and of the outspoken extremist amongst them, Maulpertsch. I especially loved the last artist's work because of the fascination of Maulpertsch's super-cubist disposition of space and volume. His emotions woke in me something of a conscious grasp of the problems of the art of painting. First becoming conscious of the near-ugliness of reality compared with the illusionist's magic colour, born in the master's unbound imagination, I soon became aware of and was caught by the Austrian Baroque artist's indocility to the classicist Italian conventions of harmony. It was my fate to share also their lack of appeal to my contemporaries who were repelled by "vision" in art, everywhere, all over Europe.'

Kokoschka's earliest drawings are reminiscent too of the work of yet another artist less remote in time, Ferdinand Hodler. The influence of this Swiss artist on expressionism has often been emphasised in general terms. It is particularly in the works of Gustav Klimt, Oskar Kokoschka and Egon Schiele that we find the most distinctive traces of the influence of this master of *art nouveau*. In fact Hodler owned not a little of his fame to his tremendous success in Vienna. He even had a close follower in Austria: Albin Egger-Lienz, a Tyrolean 'blood-and-soil' painter on a monumental scale. Hodler's symbolism could not fail to impress young men who were struggling for a means of expressing emotional values. The external characteristics of his works were at once imitated: particularly the expressive, large, bony hands of his figures are to be found in most works of the new Vienna school.

An unconventional approach was not taken amiss by the artists among whom the young Kokoschka moved, and his talent was encouraged by the school authorities. In his second year, while still a pupil, he was employed as an assistant master. He was also recommended to the Wiener Werkstätte where the arts were handmaids to the crafts and where Kokoschka's gifts were directed towards the creation of such objects as fans and postcards.[1]

It was in 1908 that Oskar Kokoschka was first introduced to the general public. This year was decisive for the young painter in two respects: he took part for the first time in an exhibition; and he published his first book.

The year of 1908 lives in the memory of all Viennese art historians as the date of the first *Kunstschau*. The leading artists of the Austrian capital, who had formerly exhibited in the *Secession* and who had been left by the closing of this institution without a gallery in which to show works of an advanced character, arranged the *Kunstschau* as a combined demonstration of all the arts. The organising committee consisted of Franz Cizek, internationally known for his discovery of the artistic productiveness of children; the architect Josef Hoffmann; the painters Gustav Klimt and Carl Moll; and the stage designer Alfred Roller. The works of masters and students were to be seen there side by side. The enormous success of the *Kunstschau* can be traced in the art periodicals of the time which were unanimous in their praise. It was an event, for not only did it offer a survey of the state of art in Vienna which was another proof of the leading position of that city in matters of taste—it pointed the

[1] Two of these are reproduced in *Deutsche Kunst und Dekoration*, Vol. XXIV, p. 244.

34

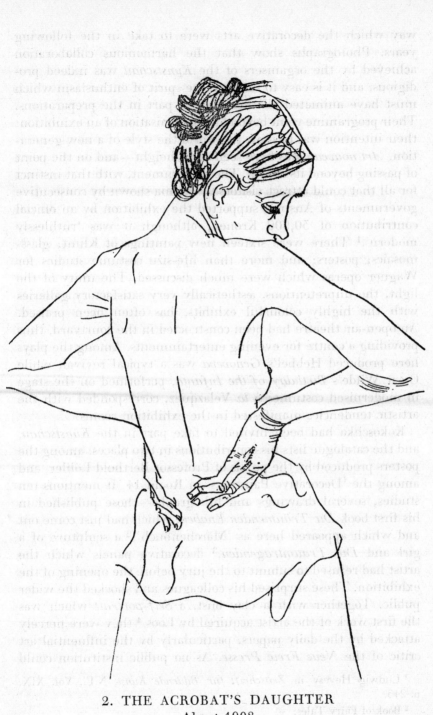

2. THE ACROBAT'S DAUGHTER
About 1908

way which the decorative arts were to take in the following years. Photographs show that the harmonious collaboration achieved by the organisers of the *Kunstschau* was indeed prodigious, and it is easy to imagine the spirit of enthusiasm which must have animated all those taking part in the preparations. Their programme went beyond the organisation of an exhibition: their intention was to show the world the style of a new generation. *Art nouveau* was here seen at its height—and on the point of passing beyond its zenith. The Government, with that instinct for all that could attract visitors to Vienna shown by consecutive governments of Austria, supported the exhibition by an official contribution of 30,000 Kronen, although it was 'ruthlessly modern'.[1] There were sixteen new paintings of Klimt; glass mosaics; posters; and more than life-size costume studies for Wagner operas which were much discussed. The unity of the light, the unpretentious, æsthetically very satisfactory galleries with the highly colourful exhibits, has often been praised. An open-air theatre had been constructed in the courtyard, thus providing a centre for evening entertainments. Among the plays here produced Hebbel's *Genoveva* was a typical revival, while Oscar Wilde's *Birthday of the Infanta*, performed on the stage in modernised costumes *à la* Velazquez, corresponded with the artistic tendencies manifested in the exhibition rooms.

Kokoschka had been invited to take part in the *Kunstschau*, and the catalogue lists his contributions in two places: among the posters produced by the pupils of Professor Berthold Löffler, and among the 'Decorative Paintings' in Room 14. It mentions ten studies, several drawings and lithographs—those published in his first book *Die Träumenden Knaben*, which had just come out and which appeared here as 'Märchenbuch',[2] a sculpture of a girl and *Die Traumtragenden*,[3] decorative panels which the artist had refused to submit to the jury before the opening of the exhibition. These surprised his colleagues and shocked the wider public. Together with a clay bust, a *Self-portrait* which was the first work of the artist acquired by Loos,[4] they were fiercely attacked by the daily papers, particularly by the influential art critic of the *Neue Freie Presse*. As no public institution could

[1] Ludwig Hevesy in *Zeitschrift für Bildende Kunst*, N.F., Vol. XIX, p. 245.

[2] Book of Fairy Tales.

[3] Those who carry a dream.

[4] This bust was not mentioned in the catalogue.

withstand such a concerted assault by the mouthpieces of the most narrow-minded and most powerful section of the population, and by those official circles which saw in each revolutionary art movement a political danger, the result was the artist's dismissal from the School of Arts and Crafts. *Die Traumtragenden* became the focus of one of those battles between the advanced minds of artistic Vienna on the one side, and the reactionary bourgeoisie and officialdom on the other, which not infrequently raged in the Hapsburg capital: even Klimt had lost one not many years before (in 1900), when a group of his paintings, officially commissioned by the University of Vienna, had been rejected as obscure and inappropriate, following upon the intervention of Parliament. But while the famous master had been able to make a proud gesture and retire, young Kokoschka could ill afford to lose his scholarship and employment.

We have no trace of *Die Traumtragenden*, which were bought by the Wiener Werkstätte; parts are said to have perished later in a fire, though some embroideries executed from them are reported to have been in the possession of one of Kokoschka's publishers, the book-seller Lanyi, and others in the house of a private collector. They have often been described as wildly fantastic, exotic and, to the uninitiated, offensive. According to Kokoschka's own recollection they must have resembled his drawings for *Die Träumenden Knaben*, the book published in 1908 (Plate I). Both were inspired by a young woman who 'wore a red frock' and came to see the young man in his studio, where 'she slept under a veil'. Her name was Lilith, and she was an art student like himself. Lilith was the heroine of all his earliest works, both painted and written. Her name appears also in the catalogue of the 1908 *Kunstschau* as one of the exhibitors in Professor Löffler's room. It is not unlikely that she was the subject of Kokoschka's sculpture in this exhibition.

Kokoschka's *Self-portrait* in plaster is only traceable in a reproduction.[1] It must certainly have been the most extraordinary object in the exhibition: only very vaguely resembling its model, it was a kind of caricatured skull, vividly coloured with blue veins ornamenting the cheeks, the tongue protruding between grimacing lips. We know that the artist had found inspiration in the ethnographical museum, and this horrible spectre was a kind of hybrid between a South-Sea mask and an anatomy prepara-

[1] *Kunstblatt*, January, 1929, p. 17.

tion.[1] It seems to have haunted his imagination for more than ten years, for it reappeared in a poster in 1912 as well as in a painting (*The Painter*, No. 164) shortly after the first world war. At that time, however, the public had grown accustomed to even more shocking sights, and no feelings were hurt by these extravagant creations.

Kokoschka's first introduction to the public had caused a stir which not only amounted to a scandal but also denoted an indisputable success. People began to talk about him. That this first fame was no mere notoriety the following note by the art critic of *Deutsche Kunst und Dekoration*[2] testifies: 'He is the prodigy of the *Kunstschau*. He reminds me of Arthur Rimbaud, who at the age of 17 wrote puzzling verses. . . . So I thought of Rimbaud, his drunken, unrestrained verses, which have a certain affinity with the colourful drunkenness of Kokoschka's puberty legends.' This comparison with Rimbaud points to the chief distinction between Kokoschka's works and those of his fellow exhibitors: where theirs were pleasant, his were disturbing; where theirs were pretty, his were awkward; where theirs were imitative, his were original, and their timidity was replaced in Kokoschka by an overwhelming release of the imagination.

Of all the works shown by Kokoschka in the 1908 *Kunstschau* there remain, so far as is known, only some drawings, fans, and the printed version of *Die Träumenden Knaben*. The Wiener Werkstätte had commissioned him to write and illustrate a book for children—a task considered suitable for a promising beginner. Again Kokoschka had done the totally unexpected. His book, although certainly not suitable for children, was the expression of a youthful mind, quivering with the urge to record a thousand experiences and observations, influenced by the most contrasting artistic impressions—early miniatures, medieval paintings, popular peasant art, Chinese scrolls, *art nouveau*, Gauguin's travel romanticism—yet strongly personal in effect. Like a child or a primitive, the young painter crammed every page with patterns and figures, with no consideration for unity of time and space or for perspective, and achieved a surprising similarity with the

[1] It should be noted that Picasso's corresponding works were not earlier, but rather later than Kokoschka's: thus the *Glass of Absinth*, a polychromed bronze in the New York Museum of Modern Art, dates from 1914. It is altogether unthinkable that either of the equally young and unknown artists should have had any direct influence on the other at that time.

[2] Joseph August Lux in Vol. XXIII, p. 50.

continuity of Chinese paintings. His text—a kind of lyrical prose —is printed in the narrow margin left by the tapestry-like pictures. These lines belong to a sphere familiar to children and poets alike, where animals and plants have the power of speech. Princesses ride on fishes, and sailors call across dark waters. These images are interwoven with an erotic symbolism as profound as it is picturesque. The pages are covered with birds and flowers, and with trees which have hands instead of leaves, or feet for roots. But the fishes that play in the waves have had their heads torn from their bodies—products of a cruel imagination which correspond to the slight perversity revealed here and there in the text. There is something almost Gothic in the broken outlines and thin, long limbs of the human beings in this world of imagery; of the men who lean against each other in a half awkward, half sentimental way (not unlike the St. John of some carved groups of the Middle Ages who rests his head on Christ's shoulder); who sail in archaic boats, or make gestures of prayer. The women, wreaths in their hair, sit in meadows like the Virgin in the Rose Garden, frail and noble creatures. All these scenes are represented in lithographs of deep, strong colours— blue, green, yellow, red—often on a black ground. But although the forms are reminiscent of medieval miniatures, the spirit of the whole work derives from the art of the *fin-de-siècle*. At the same time it is pregnant with something new: with the symbolism of the art of the new century. It is unlikely that any of the Surrealists of thirty years later have ever seen *Die Träumenden Knaben*; and yet, in this immature work they might have found some of those very elements of which their art is composed. The new symbolism, however, was still hidden under the ornament that in Kokoschka's first book pervades everything —the rampant ornament of *art nouveau*. *Die Träumenden Knaben* is dedicated to Gustav Klimt.

★　　★　　★

Die Träumenden Knaben was more generally accepted than any of Kokoschka's other works at that time—perhaps because the originality of this creation was less apparent at first sight than its obvious æsthetic merits. The rather precious edition of 1908, however, did not get beyond a very limited circle of connoisseurs. Much later, in 1917, another edition was printed at Leipzig, but this belated reminder of a half-forgotten phase never attained much celebrity, for by that time the book was no longer characteristic of a Kokoschka by then widely known as a revolutionary painter. Kokoschka himself, who naturally assesses this work by what it meant to him when he first produced it, values it highly.

Meanwhile the press attacks which had followed the opening of the *Kunstschau* had their effect. Since the Arts and Crafts School had dismissed him Kokoschka had no regular source of income. The Werkstätte continued to employ him sporadically, to paint more postcards and fans. A cabaret, which had advertised in the *Kunstschau* as '*Fledermaus:* Old Vienna Songs and Music, open from 10 to 1; after 1 o'clock no entrance fee', made use of his talents. This establishment, sponsored by the Werkstätte, represented an attempt to introduce something of the Montmartre spirit into Vienna. One of its programmes of 1908 contained the item: '*Das Getupfte Ei. Bewegliche Lichtbilder von Oskar Kokoschka.*'[1] Naturally such activities could satisfy neither Kokoschka's artistic ambitions nor his physical needs. He often went hungry. He began to play the part suggested by the name 'Bürgerschreck',[2] which the press had given him on the occasion of the *Kunstschau*. Almost any means was good enough to procure him the money which he could no longer earn in a decent manner. For a wager he would drink under the table opulent young Americans, whom he chanced to meet in cafés, and the money thus obtained he would squander spectacularly. After bouts of this kind he would have to return to his parents' home. His mother, like so many other mothers, suffered for her son and tried to help him; she fed him with whatever little there was and protected him from his father, who was convinced of his son's worthlessness. The misery of those months after his first exhibition must have been among the most painful episodes in the artist's life. Without help from outside he would hardly have recovered.

The help came from those few who recognised his talent. While the art critics of the daily papers burst into abusive attacks whenever the young painter's name appeared and called him a 'degenerate artist'—an expression which has acquired unpleasant familiarity since Hitler adopted it from the Vienna

[1] The Speckled Egg. Lantern slides by O.K. Reproductions in Vol. XXIII, p. 161, of *Deutsche Kunst und Dekoration*, show the same toy-like stags, wolves and trees as in *Die Träumenden Knaben*.

[2] Horror of the citizen.

press—who should be prevented from corrupting an innocent public, Vienna's *avant-garde* regarded Kokoschka as a most promising beginner.

The most important figure in Kokoschka's early years was the architect Adolf Loos, whose name should rank among the most famous in the history of modern art. He was the forerunner of those who have introduced modern building in all countries —it is, indeed, not too much to say that he was one of the originators of the modern style on this side of the Atlantic, not only in architecture, but in the whole art of living. Although he devoted an exceptional intellect and enthusiasm to questions of taste and culture, he shared the tragic fate of so many Austrians, of being persecuted in their own country and unrecognised abroad. While every student of architecture is now familiar with the names of Le Corbusier and Gropius, few have heard of Adolf Loos. Yet it was Loos who from 1898 onwards battled in articles, speeches and in practice against ornament, at a period when ornament was rampant. He was never deceived by *art nouveau* which he knew to be a passing fashion. He understood, at the end of the nineteenth century, that the style of the next generation would be formed by engineers and plumbers, not by stucco-artists and carvers. 'The lower the standard of a people, the more lavish are its ornaments,' he said, and an article of his which appeared in 1908 under the title *Ornament und Verbrechen*[1] is still well worth reading. He built his first houses on modern lines in the years round about 1900, and every one of them would pass as outstandingly modern today. They are clear, simple and cubic in shape, constructed on purely functional lines, avoiding all false pretences in the use of material, with comfortable as well as elegant interiors. They conform, in other words, to our present taste which, after passing through the phase of strictest functionalism, now prefers something less programmatic yet eschews the historical. The façade of the Haus am Michaelerplatz, which Loos built in 1910, so utterly unpretentious and only bent on fitting itself into an old square with a beautiful church, caused a storm which we can understand as little as the veto of the authorities who tried to stop the building before it was finished.

Loos was concerned with much more than architecture: he was equally interested in typography (for instance, the introduction of small initials for nouns throughout German writing, in

[1] Ornament and Crime.

41

conformity with the usage in all other European languages),[1] in fashion, furniture, ceramics, the fine arts. He explained to his fellow-citizens that to be well dressed is to be correctly dressed, to the degree that one's dress was quite unremarkable, even unnoticed. The Anglo-Saxon style of living was his ideal: he had been greatly impressed by the modern life of America, and England he regarded as leading in many matters of taste. He praised the comfortable English chairs and seats of all kinds; the English mail coaches (in 1898); the English love of nature; English mountaineering; the Englishman's underwear. 'The centre of occidental culture is at the moment London,' he said. As to interior decoration, he advised prospective clients that 'Neither the archæologist, nor the decorator, nor the architect, nor the painter or sculptor, should furnish a house.' With him functionalism was a necessity before it was a principle: 'The beauty of an object exists only in its relation to its purpose.' The writer Karl Kraus, who fulfilled a similar mission with regard to the German language, expressed it forcefully: 'Adolf Loos and I—he in deeds, myself in words—have done nothing but show that there is a difference between an urn and a chamber-pot, and that culture consists just in this difference. But the rest . . . can be divided into those who use an urn as a chamber, and those who use a chamber as an urn.'

It is characteristic that neither Karl Wœrmanns's *Geschichte der Kunst* of 1922, nor Richard Hamann's history of art, which appeared under the same title in 1933, even mention the name of Adolf Loos. The first edition of his collected articles was published in Paris (Editions Georges Crès et Cie) in 1921, because no German publisher could be found to undertake such a venture. But in 1930, when he was sixty years old, a group of people who recognised his greatness, including some who owed their first fame to him, contributed to a publication in his honour: the composers Arnold Schönberg and Alban Berg, the writers Karl Kraus, Else Lasker-Schüler, Maurice Maeterlinck and Karin Michaelis as well as Tristan Tzara, J. P. Oud, and Marcel Ray were among them. In 1931 they were followed by others, including Le Corbusier, who contributed to the French publication *Vient de paraître*. Loos's writings were at last published in

[1] "Apart from the German God we also have the German way of writing. Both are wrong." (Introduction to *Ins Leere Gesprochen*, Innsbruck, 1932, p. 5.)

3. ADOLF LOOS
1910

two German volumes, *Ins Leere Gesprochen* and *Trotzdem*.[1] They contain many more truths than can be quoted here, a rich fund of wisdom from which others have borrowed. In the year 1931 also Hans Hildebrandt paid him tribute for the first time in a German history of art; in *Die Kunst 19. und 20. Jahrhunderts*[2] he wrote: 'A friend of Altenberg, Karl Kraus and Oskar Kokoschka, Loos offered, both by the spoken word and in writing, the most determined opposition to the "Gemütlichkeit" (easy-going charm) of Old Vienna, on the one hand, and to the formal tradition of the Kunstgewerbeschule and of the Werkstätte. The natural result was a general ostracism from all sides and an almost complete boycott. . . . Loos, one of the wittiest writers and speakers, has given the most concise and convincing expression to all our demands of today. His main fault is that he came too early and that his perception, embracing all fields of culture, was far too disturbing to be forgiven.' And Dr. N. Pevsner, in his *Pioneers of the Modern Movement from William Morris to Walter Gropius,* of 1936, drew attention to his work in these words: 'Loos is one of the greatest creators in modern architecture. In spite of that, he never became known, during his lifetime, to more than a small circle of admirers.'[3]

Loos distinguished himself particularly by his great loyalty towards those whom he recognised as fellow artists. He protected the poet Altenberg as long as he lived, often saving him from starvation. He was one of the discoverers of Arnold Schönberg. He wrote triumphantly in 1910: 'I was banned, banned by the police, like Frank Wedekind or Arnold Schönberg. Or rather, like Arnold Schönberg would be banned, if the police could read the thoughts in his scores.'[4] And he could not fail to be interested in Oskar Kokoschka as soon as the young painter's reputation grew beyond the circle of his fellow-students. Loos was soon convinced that here was an unusually gifted artist worthy of support, moral as well as material. Himself possessed by a revolutionary spirit, he understood what the young artist needed for his development. It is likely that he even saw where his greatest

[1] Talks into the Void and Nevertheless. 1930 and 1931.

[2] One of the series *Handbuch der deutschen Kunstwissenschaft*, published in the Wildpark-Verlag, Potsdam.

[3] p. 192. Loos was previously mentioned by Raymond McGrath in *Twentieth Century Houses* (Faber and Faber), 1934.

[4] 'Zwei Aufsätze und eine Zuschrift über das Haus auf dem Michaelerplatz,' *Trotzdem*, p. 119.

gifts lay. In any event it was Loos who introduced Kokoschka, whom he met in 1907, to the people who could further his artistic career, and it was to Loos that Kokoschka owed every one of his commissions during his first years as a portrait painter. Later it was through Loos's efforts that Kokoschka's works were to be seen in the public collections whose keepers he had persuaded to acquire these unusual paintings. Loos sold some of the works he had commissioned Kokoschka to do, at once;[1] others he kept until his death.

It is easy to imagine what an enormous influence the clear-sighted, determined architect of catholic interests had on the immature painter, in whose mind the world must have been reflected in an oddly confused way. From an ideological as well as from a material point of view Adolf Loos acted the part of providence for Kokoschka throughout the seven decisive years of their association. If ever a man deserved the credit for having 'discovered' an artist, it was this Viennese architect who had the instinct and faith required for such an achievement. Kokoschka himself has written the following tribute to his late friend:

'To Adolf Loos I am grateful for the spiritual guidance I received from him in my youth. He had known from experience life in England and in the U.S.A. Western civilisation is the result of the conflict of interests of the poor, who do not feel in need of it because they lack the basis of culture, and the rich who use its possibilities to further their own interests at the expense of the poor. For this reason it looks as if culture would fail the rich as well. In England and the U.S.A. Loos found the greatest contrast between fabulous riches and abject poverty. In the U.S.A. he had passed nights, as a moneyless young emigrant, in doss-houses where a rope is fastened by both ends to the walls in order to support a row of wretched sleepers, who woke up when the rope was let down suddenly in the early grey of the morning. To realise that the luxury of the Western upper classes was not more than a dangerously thinning varnish which did not even cover the middle classes, one need not even go as far as to visit the bug-infested English slums. In the England of the period of industrialisation it would have been ironic to speak of housing in a civilised way. Therefore it seems likely that the Loos-house, which had become a notion in itself of world-wide importance, was created under the influence of the

[1] For the first paintings, which he sold to German museums before the first world war, he obtained about RM. 200.

Eastern civilisation. It is the worldly philosophy and culture of a Lao Tze and Li Tai Po, their humanism and practical common sense, which in Vienna he turned to popular account, often by making use of the demagogue's soap box. It is hardly comprehensible today that an architect, who had hardly ever been given the chance to build what he visualised, could fill at his will the great Viennese Music Hall, pack it full with 5000 bewildered listeners, whenever one of his classic Jeremiads *Ins Leere Gesprochen* was advertised. He stood for culture. But where he differed from a professed appreciator of the beautiful was that he rejected as a modern thinking man the belief that in the machine age social life must of necessity do without culture. To him social history was not an agglomeration of accidents, and consequently man's thoughts were the perfection of his social being, of his material life. Logically Loos became a reformer. He saw modern barbarism conditioned by the way the western man acts, earns, eats, sleeps, worships, copulates. The example of cheap modern housing which avoids filth, ugliness, darkness and stuffiness, was to him a Japanese house, where no accumulation of useless rubbish would be tolerated. He belonged to the very few in his time, like the Englishman Morris, the American Whistler, the Frenchman Toulouse-Lautrec, the Impressionists and Neo-Impressionists (whose art came to life when the painters saw for the first time the prints of the Japanese common people, which were used as wadding-material for the goods exported from Japan to Paris), to recognise that people, who in the West are called the lower classes, in Japan must be called an aristocratic people; if only for the reason that they created an art of their own, the Japanese wood-cut. In their creative power had originated what Loos already saw in its full bloom, the renaissance of Western art. In this context I may be allowed to quote an English authority, Laurence Binyon, from his standard work *The Japanese Colour Print*; he says: ". . . and it must for ever astonish us that a class of the population which in any other country of the world would have been satisfied with crude and gaudy productions, should have created and fostered and kept in eager and multifarious life for nearly two centuries an art of design as distinguished for delicate and fastidious taste as it is rich in creative power."—Unfortunately the gunboats of Commodore Perry had interfered with disastrous results, of which only today we are fully conscious. Loos used to tease me when I was still a shy young man: "In order to know

46

what culture looks like one must look at the wonderful Yoshi-
wara pictures by Utamaro, and afterwards see a Piccadilly whore."
How even an anthem can be transmuted from the usual tocsin
of warring peoples into a poem of profoundest magic, may be
seen from the following verses of the Japanese *God Save the King*,
which I hope for the sake of culture will continue to be sung
long after the Democracies have freed the Japanese People from
their artificially adopted western civilisation, used to such evil
ends in the waters of the Pacific.

> *Rule on, my lord, till what are pebbles now,*
> *by age united to mighty rocks shall grow*
> *whose venerable sides the moss doth line . . . .*'

As soon as Loos had made up his mind to take Kokoschka
under his wing he made himself responsible for everything.
Kokoschka was without means: so Loos found him an inn with
the attractive name of 'Griechenbeisel', the owner of which, a well-
known collector, could be persuaded to give meals in exchange
for pictures. Kokoschka was badly dressed—an unforgivable sin
in Loos's eyes: so he was introduced to the most exclusive tailor
of Vienna, the famous Ebenstein, who received the young man
among his aristocratic clients and not only made him perfect
suits, but also explained to him the secrets of anatomy from a
tailor's point of view—all in advance for a portrait, which was
to be painted later. But Loos's most important intervention was
his decision that, after the disaster of the 1908 *Kunstschau*, and
Kokoschka's dismissal, the painter should leave Vienna and see
the world.

Loos based his opinion of Kokoschka mainly on his oil paintings. Although at that time very few people had seen them, it
was here that the young artist's real character emerged and his
most serious intentions became evident. He had begun to paint
on canvas in or about 1907. His first attempts were mostly portraits. As so often later in his life, his closest friends were his
sitters: one of the actors who appeared in his first plays; one of
the young art historians who bought his drawings; his protector
Loos; the writer Kraus; the poet Altenberg; and some intelligent
bourgeois whom Loos had persuaded to have their portraits
painted. Kokoschka had had no schooling as a portrait painter.
He had little idea of perspective or composition, or how to place
a figure into a frame. But such minor deficiencies did not worry
him: he had watched his models with that peculiar sensitiveness

47

that was his own from the beginning, and he set out to render in colour what he had perceived of their personality. It did not even occur to him that what he saw might not be paintable: so strong was his impression of other people's make-up, physical as well as psychological, that he imposed his will on his material and never allowed himself to be overcome by technical difficulties. The results were staggering even to those who had some idea of what to expect. Most people found that these portraits did not resemble their sitters. The models themselves as well as other beholders complained almost without exception that these paintings could not be called portraits.[1] Even years later, when Kokoschka was at the height of success, art critics still used to apologise for him and to explain that, although not portraits in the usual sense of the word, they were nevertheless striking. They began to use the term 'psycho-analytical portraits' in contrast to the external likeness which they found lacking. With the passing of time such reservations have become superfluous. Everybody can now perceive the eminent truthfulness of these portraits: they live, almost more than paintings ought to live; they give psychological insight into men and women more convincingly than could faithful representations of all detail with academic mastery of technique; and even their external likeness is striking today, for in many cases they resemble their subjects as they now appear, aged by thirty years.

Kokoschka had also done a Still-Life (No. 4), very different from anything which the taste of the time had established as proper to that genre. In one canvas are united a dead sheep, collapsed in pitiful posture, with head and legs outstretched; a tortoise, with pointed head pushed forward, transfixed in that mysterious swinging movement characteristic of these reptiles; a white mouse, the only warm-blooded creature in this assembly, yet strangely ghoulish; a salamander floating in a glass basin. These unmistakable symbols of death are grouped round a flowering hyacinth which emphasises by almost shocking contrast the haunting death-scene atmosphere of the picture. The representation of carcasses had been admissible ever since the days of Rembrandt. But the inherent unpleasantness of the subject was here enhanced in a new way: the sweetness of the

[1] Karl Kraus wrote in *Die Fackel* of the 9th April, 1910: 'Kokoschka has made a portrait of me. It is quite possible that those who know me will not recognise me. But it is certain that those, who do not know me, will recognise me.'

XII. CHILD WITH THE HANDS
OF FATHER AND MOTHER
1909-10

XI. FRAU KANN (SKETCH)
1910

XIII. WINTER LANDSCAPE, DENT DU DIMI
1909-10

colours—the shimmering purples of the carcass, the radiant, brilliant white of the hyacinth—evoke an optical sensation comparable only to the sickly smell of death, an association readily produced by the image of the strongly scented flower. The effect was intended: the painting was but another expression of that pessimism and that perverted poetry which looked for subjects where nobody had hitherto suspected anything but horror and disgust. A more sophisticated painter might have called this work 'La fleur du mal'.

The year 1909 brought a repetition of the *Kunstschau*. Once again it was a sensation and a success. It contained several rooms full of works by Minne, Toorop, Van Gogh (first seen in Vienna two years before), Vallotton, Gauguin, Vuillard, Bonnard, Matisse (who was new to the Austrian capital), Munch, Liebermann, Corinth, Shannon, Gordon Craig and Bone. As usual, the greatest excitement was provided by Gustav Klimt, this time by a work entitled *Hope*, which the master had finished in 1903. '*Hope* is the object of hot rage, all cafés live on it,' wrote one of the critics.[1] He continued: 'Minister von Hartel, who sympathised with the young, entreated the artist not to challenge powerful sections of society by such daring.' The object of this controversy was the picture of a pregnant woman.

The only young Viennese artist to whom more than one word in the same review was devoted was Oskar Kokoschka, who was referred to as 'our talented terror'. The catalogue of the 1909 *Kunstschau*, like that of the 1908 exhibition, lists as well as some unidentifiable sketches by the artist and another sculpture, a white chalked clay figure of Lilith, the heroine of *Die Träumenden Knaben*, a *Portrait of the Actor Reinhold*, which later became known as *The Trance Player* (No. 5), and a text and illustrations for a book of the same kind as *Die Träumenden Knaben*, this one entitled *Der Weisse Tiertoedter*.[2]

No trace of the illustrations remains, for *Der Weisse Tiertoedter* was never published as a book. The text was later rewritten, and in 1913 it was published[3] with new illustrations, under the title of *Der Gefesselte Kolumbus*;[4] in 1920 it was included—in its final form, but without illustrations—in a

[1] Ludwig Hevesy in *Zeitschrift für Bildende Künste*, N.F., Vol. XX, p. 221.
[2] The White Animal Slayer.
[3] By Fritz Gurlitt, Berlin.
[4] The Fettered Columbus.

volume entitled *Die Gefährten*.[1] Between the years 1909 and 1913 Kokoschka's outlook had undergone profound changes. We may assume, however, that the main trends of thought remained the same and that, as in other cases, many lines had been literally transferred from the first into the final version. The chief motif of the poem is the dream-love of the mortal man for 'the Lady of the Moon'[2] whom he cannot attain, unless he achieves union with her in death. 'Lady of the Moon,' he says, 'now that I have cast off my body, can we remain together?' The sensual element that finds its expression in this work is as strong as the spiritual: on the one hand there are 'jars filled with warm cow-milk', bread loaves 'whose baking odour permeated the room', and 'small sweet fruit which her fingers arranged'; on the other hand the dialogue contains passages such as 'on land I am a shadow under the mirror of day, at night a liquid fire in which, in my dreams, you are drowned'. Allusions of a cruelly perverted character, similar to those in his first book, are not lacking: '**My** sides are bleeding from the thorns of your clumsy hands,' complains the Lady of the Moon.[3] And her lover, referring to events which are not otherwise described, reflects sadly: 'I hid my knife under the pillow. "Could you not have been saved?" I said to myself, as the girl's body was dead, while my thought of her was still alive.' Kokoschka was not alone in this conception of conflicting emotions in love. Among the greatest theatrical sensations created in the Germany of those days were performances of Frank Wedekind's plays, in which abound instances of 'cruel love', perversion and murder. In a cruder form, young Kokoschka was saying many things which before him Baudelaire had expressed in his subtler French manner. The beginning of

[1] The Companions. Published in Leipzig and Vienna.

[2] Die Mondfrau. It is worth noting that in German the moon is masculine and the figure in it habitually described as 'Der Mann im Mond' —The Man in the Moon.

[3] Compare this passage with Baudelaire's

'Ainsi, je voudrais, une nuit,
Quand l'heure des voluptés sonne,
Vers les trésors de ta personne
Comme un lache ramper sans bruit,

. . . .

Et faire à ton flanc étonné
Une blessure large et creuse. . . .'

(From 'A celle qui est trop gaie'.)

our century was intensely interested in perversions which were just beginning to be recognised as morbid variations of natural instincts and to be connected with social problems rather than with moral implications. In the case of Kokoschka these allusions are to be explained as the reflections of an immature young man on experiences not sufficiently absorbed and, at the same time, as attempts to follow the literary fashion of the day which he knew from second-hand. From the point of view of his later development several of his earliest motifs are noteworthy: one of them is the romantic search for the female companion, another the inevitable disillusionment which leads to the conclusion that death—spiritual if not physical—is the outcome of a union always represented as a struggle between lovers for domination. Bloodshed is the ever present symbol of this elementary strife.

The Trance Player (No. 5), which was shown at the 1909 Kunstschau, had, according to Kokoschka himself, been completed in 1907, as his very first oil painting.[1] It was obviously

[1] Paul Stefan, in his monograph of 1913, dates the picture 1907. Paul Westheim, five years later, dates it 1906, and Biermann, Heilmaier and Einstein as well as the catalogue of the Kokoschka exhibition held at the Galerie Arnold in Dresden in 1925 accept this date, probably on the authority of Westheim. Dr. W. Wartmann, in his catalogue of the Kokoschka exhibition which took place at Zürich in 1927, explains that the artist's friends, eager to make him appear even more extraordinary than he was, tended to ante-date his works; he quotes several instances to confirm this opinion. He dates the Trance Player 1910, thus proving that he himself is inclined to post-date Kokoschka's earliest works: the inclusion of the painting in the 1909 Kunstschau fixes at least the ante quem date. Here the painter's own recollection must be taken into account, and it is unlikely that he should be completely mistaken about one of his first canvases. Dr. Wartmann's remarks on the dating of Kokoschka's early works, however, deserve serious consideration, for he was the first to draw attention to a disturbing confusion in the literature concerning this subject. Kokoschka's biographers have all too easily accepted vague recollections as established facts. One instance of the disorder in the chronology of this artist's work is the portrait of Adolf Loos, which Westheim and Biermann date 1907, the catalogue of the Galerie Arnold 1908, while Stefan dates it 1909: the portrait is in fact inscribed with a large '1909' which Adolf Loos added with his own hand (this information is provided by the painter); Justi, in his catalogue of the Berlin Nationalgalerie, has duly taken this into account, although he believed that it was Kokoschka who had added the date. Wartmann also assumes that the date was added to the painting in later years by the artist, when he wanted to rectify the general pre-dating. More important seems to be the ante-dating of a whole group of pictures generally supposed to have been painted in Switzerland in 1908: the Winter Landscape, The Duchess of Rohan-Montesquieu, Count Verona, Bessie Loos,

an experiment—an attempt to find out how a human image could be built up in colours. The figure's pose, full face, erect, unmoved (except for the hands which are held at a right angle), with its straight verticals and horizontals as well as its position in the foremost plane, are reminiscent of the works of certain primitives. Even the odd fascination of the eyes derives from that rigidity and simplification which endows the empty stare of a mask, or even two symmetrical patches in a pattern, with life and meaning. All the more surprising, together with this primitiveness, is the instinctive sense of proportion manifest in the way the figure is related to the frame, the impression of monumentality it conveys and, above all, the quality of living substance evoked by colour and brush. The face with its flabbiness and its *blasé* expression has the unforgettable quality of some nightmare; the shirt, the light blue tie, are so solid and real, so distinctly perceived and rendered with such virtuosity, so far from the neatness of the purely decorative, that one can but wonder at such masterly strokes; the entire conception of the portrait is so daring in its direct translation from bodily substance into paint that one is forced to concede that the hand and the mind here at work had found their expression in the one medium most appropriate to them.

The Trance Player was the title later given to the painting. It is illustrative of Kokoschka's tendency to transform familiar individuals into fundamental human types—the same tendency as found expression in the nameless characters of his plays. But

Professor Auguste Forel. It is Forel's autobiography which gives 1910 as the undisputable date for his portrait and thus for the whole journey to Switzerland (see p. 59). We may have the greatest confidence in Forel's reliability, for it is obvious from his work as a scientist in general and from the innumerable exact dates in his autobiography in particular, that he was in the habit of making notes and, probably, entries in a diary. His reference to Kokoschka's visit to his house in 1910 explains the accomplished quality of his portrait. The fact that all the works painted in Switzerland were only exhibited for the first time in 1911 makes it even more probable that they were painted in 1909–1910. The artist himself, however, supports the established dating of 1908 for the whole series: 'On my first trip to Switzerland I arrived before Christmas in the winter of 1908 and painted first the *Winter Landscape*—the real name of this work is *Vue sur la Dent du Midi*—and *Bessie Loos*, for whose portrait I was sent by Loos to stay at "Les Avants"; then I did the portraits of her friends, the *Conte di Verona*, the *Duchess* and the *Duke*. I probably returned home after the New Year 1909 and before the winter season with tobogganing and ski-ing was over and the hotel closed.'

XIV. PETER BAUM
1910

XVI. SPOSALIZIO
1912-13

XV. ELSE KUPFER
1910

so penetrating was his perception that his types have all the complexity of the individuals who were his inspiration: in generalising he never needed to simplify. There were, however, periods during which he made more individual portraits—in fact his style was to change very soon in this direction—but basically he remained always a creator of types, always searching for the common factor in the human beings he came across. The interest these paintings inspire is to some extent based on this fact: in them we see not only the sitter, but ourselves and the painter.

The Trance Player has forehead, hair, eyes, ears and chin in common with the actor Reinhold, all characteristic of him. The nose is one which recurs in several portraits of this period. A few of his features, through their indistinctiveness, reveal the artist's inexperience. Not all the pictures that followed upon this one were equally successful, however. In fact, some of these betray much more timidity and uncertainty of aim. But they all have certain qualities in common: a fearless approach to the unusual; an inclination to reach into the sphere of the transcendental; restless searching for the real nature of human beings and of things; an urge to convey in paint what could hardly be put into words. As a result, all have the same queer, almost hypnotic power which, while it aroused wild enthusiasm in some, drove others to equally wild fury, as though they saw their own innermost secrets exposed to light.

Kokoschka's exhibits alone at the 1909 *Kunstschau* might not have given rise to undue antagonism among a public already more or less schooled in preparedness for the unusual. There were, however, two plays written and produced by the painter, which were to be performed on the open-air stage of the exhibition; and the poster which Kokoschka did for the occasion started an excitement that was only further enhanced by the performance. This poster was reproduced, with varying text, for several occasions in the following years.[1] The influence of certain works of *art nouveau* was still to be seen in it, but what had become of the gentle, æsthetic, and so poetic style! Like the plaster head, probably shown at the 1908 *Kunstschau*,

[1] Westheim, who illustrates it on p. 14 of his 1925 monograph, dates it 1911. His version refers to a lecture given by Kokoschka in the 'Akademischer Verband für Literatur und Musik'. The Berlin magazine *Der Sturm* advertised a poster in 1910; this was the same design with a different caption referring to *Der Sturm*.

the poster represented a kind of self-portrait, reduced to the form of a skull that showed its teeth and opened half-broken eyes. The head was unnaturally elongated—an ever-recurring caricature of Kokoschka's own skull—in three-quarter-profile above naked shoulders. The left hand pointed to a bleeding wound in the right breast—a modern *Ecce homo*. The figure was drawn with a few blood-red outlines and set against a blood-red shadow. Here and there the surface was marked by little irregular designs, like swollen veins outside the skin, or like mysterious hiero-glyphics on parchment. They enhanced the repulsiveness of this spectre, which was a hybrid of half-digested ethnographical recollections and of expressionism just emerging. It showed most of the characteristics of that style: the revolt against classical art; the desire to *épater le bourgeois* by means of violence, even dis-gust; the propagandist tendency; the emphasis on non-visual elements; the yearning for self-revelation, often bordering on exhibitionism. This poster was produced by Kokoschka for the special occasion of a theatrical performance. It became a mile-stone in his own development as well as in the history of paint-ing: it may rightly be called one of the earliest works of the expressionist school.

We, who are accustomed to the later Picasso, and more par-ticularly to the violent language of his *Guernica* period, can hardly imagine the stir which Kokoschka's poster created among the Viennese of thirty years ago. At any rate it drew excited crowds into the little theatre of the *Kunstschau*, eagerly antici-pating further horrors in store for them. They were not dis-appointed.

Of the two plays which Kokoschka produced one, *Sphinx und Strohmann*,[1] had been written in 1907 and performed in that year on the stage of the Arts and Crafts School, before Kokoschka's colleagues; the other, *Hoffnung der Frauen*,[2] had originally been written on little tickets handed out to a cast of pupils of a dramatic school at their first performance. After its publication in 1913 both were performed by the Dada-group in Zürich during the first world war, then by the Dresden Schauspielhaus in 1918 and in Reinhardt's Kammerspiele in 1919. By this time they had been re-written and re-named. In 1909 they were very short, hardly more than fragmentary scenes, but they already con-tained the main ideas of the later plays and many of their best passages. Like all his early works, painted as well as written,

[1] Sphinx and Straw Man.   [2] The Hope of Women.

they contained elements of amazing originality, wisdom and greatness. But in contrast to the paintings, the beauties in the plays are embedded in a mass of obscure stammering, through which it is hard to penetrate to the few precious lines. At the time of their first appearance, however, it did not matter how many pearls might be hidden in the litter: the plays were accepted or rejected in their entirety. They have been called the first expressionist plays.[1] There is no doubt that they gave expression to many problems, both theatrical and human, which were then in the air, and their particular form—or formlessness —was certainly characteristic of expressionist dramas.

The first to be performed was *Sphinx und Strohmann*, which had the sub-title *Ein Curiosum*. Kokoschka, whose circle of friends included dramatic students, had made a bet that he could write a play, and after having persuaded some of the young actors—Ettlinger and Rudolph Forster, who later became well-known stage artists, and the dancer Risch—to take part in the enterprise they began to work for a performance. The text was mostly composed during rehearsals. *Sphinx und Strohmann* might be judged on the level of an undergraduate joke, were it not for the fact that it contains some of the artist's profoundest convictions which he confirmed in later works. It was, in fact, but a fragment of a play, consisting of short dialogues between four characters of fantasy: Herr Firdusi, the Straw Man, who carries a pig's bladder, representing the human soul; the Rubber Man; The Female Soul, called Anima; and Death, described as 'a living, normal man'. A parrot's interjections contribute to the pathetically comic effect of Firdusi's entry. This sorry figure— obviously a caricature of Kokoschka himself, and at the same time of all men—explains in plain language that he had a wife whom he adored until she left him 'with a healthy muscle-man'; at first she had been a woman with whom he shared bed and table, but she had developed into an empty shell, and 'now she wanders from man to man'. Death must be his remedy. When Anima appears on the scene he gathers new courage. He can never really see her, for she has turned his head on his shoulders until its position remains at 180°. Unfortunately she falls in love with the Rubber Man, thus depriving Firdusi of his last hope. 'Oh never again will I believe in fairy tales.' But his final conclusion

[1] The *Encyclopædia Britannica* (14th edition, 1929, 475), in which Kokoschka is (erroneously) treated as a writer in the first line, takes them for the beginning of the expressionist theatre.

55

is that 'Passion must be filtered through the spirit, otherwise it pervades body and soul, inevitably leading to the pollution of both'.

Crude as the form of his play may be, the young author's purpose was not entirely frivolous. He gave expression to the same convictions as Strindberg had done before, and the same melancholic and defensive irony which we find expressed, for instance, in Paul Klee's earliest etchings, of the years 1904–6. It is the attitude of young idealists who, confronted with a corrupt, perverted world, exaggerate the vices which puzzle them rather than admit that they feel overwhelmed.

In *Hoffnung der Frauen* there is no hint of irony, no satire, no humour of any kind. The characters are as romantic in appearance as they are sketchy in delineation: a warrior and adventurer in blue armour, a bandage round his wounded forehead; a woman, described as tall, yellow-haired and wearing a red frock—most likely a memory of the red frock that Lilith wore when she slept 'under a veil' in Kokoschka's studio; and a chorus of men and women of wild appearance, carrying torches. The scene takes place under a night sky, and a red iron cage is the main feature of the set. The dialogue is from the beginning full of melodrama and symbolism; the incidents, cruel, even brutal, follow upon each other with dramatic speed. The man, who is addressed as leader and saviour by the chorus ('Our lord is the moon that rises in the East'), who performs miracles and commits murders, and the woman, who, though fearful of him, is evil herself ('She guesses what nobody understands; she feels what nobody hears: it is said that shy birds come to her to be caught'), are drawn together irresistibly from their first encounter. At first she feels hypnotised by his look. A minute later she is caught, stigmatised. She screams in pain, but hits back with a knife that wounds him, and he is carried away half-dead. Thereafter the murderess loves him whom she has struck, and can neither forget nor leave him. She gives her blood for him and as she lies dying, he goes off, victorious.

This drama of love, confusion and murder, this struggle between man and woman for love's sake, is as barbarous, passionate and nauseating as that of Siegfried and Brunhild. Since the days of the Nibelungen no such devastating passions had been represented in German art. Kokoschka introduced yet another perversion: that of love coupled with the lust for blood. This theme winds, a red thread, through all Kokoschka's early poetry, as do

56

the symbols of fishes, birds, the bleeding wound. The woman, whom he depicts, dreams dreams of desire; she is by nature unfaithful, cruel, ravaging, but nevertheless wonderful.[1] This world he shows is one of terrible conflicts rather than harmonies. It must be stressed again: these plays must be taken as symbolic. They represent a battle of the spirit: the young artist had half instinctively realised that in the struggle for domination the one who can spiritually subject the other will be victorious. It was to express this that he wrote his plays.

The citizens of Vienna were not inclined to examine his motives. They took the two plays for pure farce, especially written to outrage them, and so they were outraged. Havoc broke loose among the spectators, among whom were interspersed the author's friends, and in the end the two parties fought each other with umbrellas. The situation was aggravated by some Bosnian soldiers, whose barracks overlooked the small open-air theatre, and who had caught some glimpses of the spectacle across the fence: gasping at the sight of a half-naked young woman throwing herself about on the stage, excited by the murders committed before their eyes, and finally misled by the behaviour of the spectators who appeared more incensed than any Austrians they had ever seen before, these warriors broke through the barrier with drawn swords, yelling and quite prepared to turn the scene into one of real bloodshed. Calm was restored when the police arrived. But the outcome might have been very serious for the young artists, particularly for the author of the two plays, who were the obvious cause of the disorder. Fortunately Adolf Loos was there to stand up for them, and it is typical of the spirit ruling in the Austrian capital that he could avert any evil results by persuading the police, as well as the public, that the events of the evening were not meant as insults to decency, but had, in fact, given the signal for the triumphant restoration of culture in Vienna.

His intervention could not prevent the press from expressing their adverse verdict the next day. The scandal surpassed anything of the kind that had been witnessed in Vienna before. Officials, art critics and the public were agreed that the works of this young man Kokoschka were as dangerous to the public morals as they were offensive to æsthetics. No more of this sort

[1] For variations of this type in 19th-century literature see 'La Belle Dame sans Merci' in *The Romantic Agony*, by Mario Praz (London 1933).

of thing was wanted. The name of the artist was duly noted, but filed for the time being.

The practical consequences for Kokoschka were not as serious as they had been after his dismissal from the Kunstgewerbeschule in the previous year. He was now surrounded by friends who encouraged his originality and he had no need to fear starvation, for he started an evening class where he taught bookbinding; and after the Ministry of the Interior had forbidden this too he opened a course for lithographers. Nevertheless, the situation was far from easy. Kokoschka, not yet twenty-three years old, was ambitious, his talents were recognised by the most competent connoisseurs, and his life was rich in such excitements as are provided by artistic competition, the arguments of art students, love affairs and public scandals. But, considered from a realistic point of view, the circle of his admirers was limited to a few who equally were regarded as cranks, whose idea of the world around them was bounded by what they saw in the cafés where they met daily, and by their own polemics and speculations on a future which they believed to be theirs. Kokoschka's own name was as notorious as it could be—now more than ever he was the '*Bürgerschreck*', and no normal career was open to him. He was also as poor as ever. In this atmosphere of animosity, narrow-mindedness and cliquishness there was little scope for him to develop. He did not fit into the radiant Hapsburg capital with its social hierarchy, its cultural pretensions which were mainly based on an already distant past, and with its complacent citizens who dreaded nothing more than a mental upheaval, which would cut them off from that past. He felt that there must be another world, in which people were less afraid of a fresh wind, where he might say what he wanted, where he would not be an outcast. The pictures that had come to Vienna, from Paris and Berlin and Munich, had given him glimpses of such a world. Loos and his friends had told him about it. And they agreed that he should know it.

During this year Kokoschka had finished more portraits. He had painted a small child; a young boy; a friend of Loos, Janikowsky, and a young woman, Frau Hirsch. These portraits confirmed Loos in his opinion of the young artist. But he wondered whether Kokoschka could stand on his own feet. He was therefore glad that the painter saw the necessity to leave his native country and to measure his strength against that of his contemporaries.

For a young man in Kokoschka's position it was almost as

difficult to travel as it was to stay on in Vienna. Fortunately the resourceful architect knew what to do about it. His wife, who was in delicate health, lived at that time in a Swiss sanatorium, and he decided to take Kokoschka along on his next visit to her. Few preparations were needed for the journey.

Oskar Kokoschka was a good-looking young man, although not exactly handsome; his head, particularly the lower part of his face, was too long, his nose too broad, his whole face open and healthy rather than refined; and his tall, well-built figure bore witness to his mountain origin. He moved with the natural grace of an athlete; he held his head very erect on his broad shoulders; he had blond hair, which grew awkwardly into his forehead and was cut short, and wide-open, blue eyes; his skin breathed health, his broad hands had a strong, warm grip. His voice was soft, though masculine, and his frequent laughter burst out in gay, musical ripples. He had quickly learnt to be well groomed, to move freely, and to win affection, for he was not only attractive and charming, but also sensitive, observant, even clever. Genuinely naïve at first, he soon noticed that people liked him so. Original in his ideas and conduct by nature, he saw that that was what they expected from him. Something of a gallant, he discovered to his delight that he was attractive to women. It was not difficult for him to play up to all the parts that were ascribed to him: he just had to cultivate the gifts he had received from nature. And he learnt to conceal that he was intelligent when it was better to appear unsophisticated, to remain externally the modest, fanciful, unworldly, unbusiness-like, sometimes clumsy, but warm-hearted young man he had been when he first came to the Arts and Crafts School. He understood how to handle people—and he always succeeded in winning their approval, except when he met with matter-of-fact minds who could not appreciate his whims, or with characters not unlike himself, whom he resented as competitors.

Thus Loos found Kokoschka in some ways well prepared for his introduction to the world. And one day, in the second half of the year 1909, he took the hopeful, but also terrified young man to one of the world's fashionable resorts in Switzerland, and left him there to make his own way. It had been arranged that Kokoschka should live in a modest hotel room, and earn enough to pay half the fare and half the hotel bills. The painter consequently found himself under the same roof as aristocrats and adventurers of all nations. But he was at a disadvantage: for

59

he had no money apart from a golden ten-Gulden-coin given to him by his mother, which he carried tied in his handkerchief.

He had been told to paint for his living, and this he did, always horrified at the idea that Loos might forget to send the money for his room. This, in fact, happened soon enough. He had to leave the hotel at Leysin sur les Avants and move down to Montreux. There friends of Loos gave him shelter. His new room was grand enough, but his fare consisted exclusively of beans. He buried himself in his work and prayed for a miracle to save him. But in the long run the architect never deserted the painter, whose pictures he was meanwhile selling in Vienna. Nor did Kokoschka disappoint his protector: during his stay at the health resort he finished the portraits of Mrs. Bessie Loos, an Italian count who suffered from tuberculosis, a beautiful duchess and a marquis.

The greatest experience of this journey to Switzerland was Kokoschka's discovery of the majestic mountain landscape. He had seen photographs of Swiss landscapes on posters in Vienna which had always greatly impressed him. But the real thing was different. He was overwhelmed by its beauty, and even more by a feeling of space that was new to him. Standing at his hotel room window, which opened on to the snow-covered Dent du Midi, he saw a sledge, drawn by horses, pass below and travel smoothly across the wide valley, becoming smaller and smaller, until it was only a black point; yet it never reached the mountain which rose in the background. The young painter became acutely conscious of the third dimension. Here was something the posters had failed to convey, but that one had to recreate, if one wanted to paint a landscape. And when he painted his *Winter Landscape* (No. 26), he made good use of his new experience. This picture became one of his most famous works; it conquered at once those who saw it, so fresh, so convincing is its beauty. The horse-drawn sledge is there, and the fir trees, and the road leading into the depth of the valley. The mountains, close and clear at the foot, are veiled by a slight mist at the top, through which the sun's rays almost break. This is great composition, a forerunner of those pictures which made Kokoschka the greatest landscape painter of our time. Analysis of the painting reveals a closely thought out plan according to established rules. There are three distinct planes: the depth of the landscape; a telegraph post serves to close the composition on one side; the trees in the centre, with the sun above, form the focal point, the centre of

XVIII. THE DUCHESS
OF ROHAN-MONTESQUIEU
1910

XVII. PORTRAIT OF A MARQUIS
1910

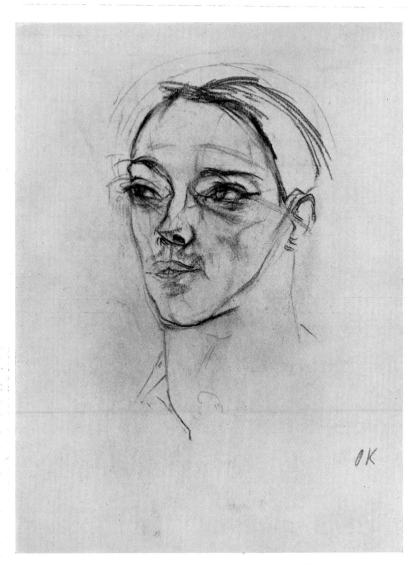

XIX. THE DANCER NIJINSKY
Drawing. 1912

gravity, as it were. This painting leaves no doubt that the young artist had not failed to take advantage of the lessons offered by the Vienna museum. He had obviously seen Brueghel's wonderful *Winter Landscape*, where human figures and bare trees stand out so picturesquely against the snow. Snow had moreover acquired a new fascination for painters since Monet and, above all, Edvard Munch had discovered new ways of painting it. But Kokoschka's *Winter Landscape* is so evidently the outcome of a genuine perception and experience, that it does not matter in the least whatever he may have seen of other snow paintings. Anybody who has experienced the incomparable, exhilarating and exalting sensation evoked by an alpine landscape in winter will find in Kokoschka's picture that sublimation of his own experience which an artist can only convey when he is most sincere.

★   ★   ★

After Christmas the artist again left Vienna with 400 francs in his pocket, given him by Herr von Ficker, a member of the Loos circle, as an advance payment for a portrait. Loos himself had given him a letter of introduction to Auguste Forel—'the most famous scholar in the world', Loos said—who lived in the Rhone valley and who, the architect thought, might have his portrait painted by Kokoschka.[1] When the painter, whom Loos in his letter described as 'the greatest artist of the future', arrived in the home of the scholar, who 'had millions of wrinkles' and lived very quietly with his family, devoting all his time to his researches, he was received in a friendly manner but with some slight surprise. Forel describes the episode in his memoirs: 'In January 1910 the modernistic painter, Kokoschka, then little known, came to me and asked if he might paint me. I told him that he could do so on condition that I did not have to buy the picture, and if I could work at my table as I pleased while he was painting me. This modern painter, who looked at me especially from behind and from the side, cared nothing for likeness, but only for the expression of moods! In point of fact, as the picture turned out, only one eye and the left disabled hand were particularly good and expressive—according to the opinion of experts. Kokoschka showed me other paintings, the products of imagination, which ought to have been regarded

[1] Forel had, at the beginning of the century, addressed a temperance meeting in Vienna and talked before thousands. It is probable that Loos had met him on that occasion.

61

from the standpoint of the psychiatrist rather than as works of art, and the same may be said, in my opinion, of the performances of many cubists, impressionists, anti-perspectivists and the like. I did not buy the pictures, but since the artist has achieved a very considerable success! *Mundus vult decipi, ergo decipiatur.*'[1] This statement of the great humanitarian and scholar,[2] welcome as it is as a first-hand comment from one of the painter's most famous models, is yet another proof that, while no artist or connoisseur would dream of passing judgment on a work of science, scientists and amateurs of any kind never hesitate to express opinions on works of art—and to do so in the most dogmatic way.[3]

The behaviour of the Forel family, however, did not make the painter feel uncomfortable. He spent several weeks with them, eagerly watching his model and working hard. He knew little of Forel, except that he was to paint him and that it was for Forel meanwhile to look after him. Many things struck him in this house, particularly the fact that the old man's food was always weighed on a scale in his presence. He tried in vain not to listen to the conversations at the dinner table which embarrassed him because of their intimacy: 'Minnie does not love him,' he could not help overhearing, and 'but he must establish a a family.' It took him some time before he understood that Minnie and her suitor were ants, the house pets. The old man himself often went to sleep in the course of their conversations. Only when Kokoschka had at last finished his portrait (No. 33) and was taking his leave did he learn, at least in part, what a strange position he had enjoyed in this house: 'Now that you are leaving us,' said the scholar, 'I wonder whether you would explain to me who this man Loos is who so pressingly introduced you.' 'The most famous man in Vienna,' said Kokoschka. For Loos knew only two kinds of people: 'most famous' ones and 'criminals'.

After his second return from Switzerland Kokoschka continued to paint portraits. It was now easier for him to find models

[1] *Out of my Life and Work.* Translated by Bernard Miall (London 1934), p. 273.

[2] Auguste Forel is the author of *The Ants of Switzerland; Le Monde social des fourmis; Hynotismus und Psychotherapie; Hypnotismus, Suggestion und Psychotherapie; Hygiene der Nerven; Die Sexuelle Frage*, etc.

[3] Adolf Loos, in his contribution to the Mannheim exhibition catalogue of 1931, describes how he offered the picture after its completion to the Berne Museum for 200 francs, and how the offer was refused.

who were not only willing to sit, but also to buy. It was still a small circle, however, in which Kokoschka moved and in which he inspired confidence. It is probable that the portrait of Herr von Ficker (No. 46), editor of the magazine *Brenner*, who had financed Kokoschka's second journey to Switzerland, was painted during the same months.

But the artist was now restless. A few months later he found his way to Munich, at that time an important seat of the arts. The counterpart of Gustav Klimt in Vienna was Franz von Stuck, an *art nouveau* artist on a monumental scale and an academic teacher. But Kokoschka was by that time little attracted to art masters: he had learnt to go his own way. He went straight to one of the most original men who then lived in Munich, the writer Gustav Meyrink, author of widely read novels and satirical short stories.[1] Meyrink's family came from Prague, as Kokoschka's did. A master of the fantastic and gruesome, he received the young painter as a kind of spiritual message from his friend Adolf Loos. He was just the sort of man to fascinate Kokoschka: extremely witty, even cynical, he was interested in occultism, without ever betraying how much of the ghost stories he told his friends he believed himself. On his mantelpiece stood a crystal glass containing a 'homunculus' with the help of which, he would explain, he had cured his paralysis. He also studied Buddhism, and Kokoschka, who could not quite penetrate this odd mixture of the occult and the rational, believed that he was mad. He did a portrait of Meyrink (No. 25), but all trace of it is lost. Meyrink had in his possession a copy of *Die Träumenden Knaben* which he introduced to all his friends. Apart from Meyrink, Kokoschka painted only one other portrait in Munich: that of the solicitor Dr. Caro (No. 29). His whole stay in this city lasted only a few weeks. He cannot have been more prosperous than he had been in Vienna, for he remembers having pawned the first watch he ever possessed, and one of the chief topics of conversation between him and the designer Alastaire, who lived in the same *pension*, was how, if need be, one could escape through the window by means of a rope.

★　　★　　★

From Munich Kokoschka went to Berlin. For four years, from 1910–14, he divided his time between the German and the

[1] *Golem, Das Grüne Gesicht, Walpurgisnacht, Des Deutschen Spiessers Wunderhorn*, etc.

63

Austrian capitals. It may be said that Kokoschka's first journey to Berlin was his first step to international fame.

The German capital was very different from that of the Hapsburgs and the greatest city in which Kokoschka had ever been. Four times the size of Vienna, Berlin was much more alive in every respect. Here too the centre was an imperial court, and although less than half a century had elapsed since the House of Hohenzollern had begun to rule over the whole of the Reich they seemed to be established on the throne for eternity. Their power was based on their army, which had grown with the dynasty ever since the seventeenth century. The military caste was the greatest power in Prussia, and the respect with which the ordinary citizen regarded all those wearing uniform was almost limitless. Officers could—and did—order civilians to step aside to let them pass. Military parades, bands, and manœuvres were features of the daily life which concerned every citizen. The army had won a victory over France in 1870–71 which had enhanced its prestige and brought great wealth to Prussia. The capital had grown enormously in those days, when money was lavishly spent on building, and had become not only one of the ugliest but also one of the most cosmopolitan towns. The style of the '*Gründerjahre*'[1] had spoilt Berlin for ever: long straight avenues had been cut, lined with huge blocks of flats the façades of which were hardly discernible under the rich masonry that covered their structure with cupids, wreaths, trophies, columns and balusters. From ancient Athens to medieval Nuremberg all cities on earth had lent their characteristic features to the buildings of Berlin. Even in the centre of the city, where here and there a few inconspicuous, but distinguished eighteenth and early nineteenth century houses could be found, the fine classicist cathedral was replaced by one many times bigger, more grandiose, more eclectic and incomparably more tawdry. Marble was lavishly displayed in churches, cafés, doorways. Private apartments were provided with the most up-to-date comforts and the largest rooms ever used by a town-dwelling middle-class. The wealth of those years, though transient, had laid the foundations of twentieth-century Berlin. At the same time the industrial quarters had grown, housing the millions of working-class people who had made the socialist party strong. But the inhabitants of the West End never went to the proletarian North or East. Until the first great war the working classes continued to be regarded

[1] Speculator years.

64

as an inevitable, sombre, rather unimportant background. Visitors
to Berlin hardly ever saw their dwellings which, although not
slums, had nothing of the brilliance of the fashionable quarters.
Even so foreigners seldom liked Berlin. There were too few of
those ancient monuments which make a city attractive; and
the Berliners themselves were dry, business-like people, who
showed no sensitiveness, although they had their own kind of
humour. Since Prussia had become the leading country within
the German borders and Berlin the capital of the Reich it had
lost its provincial character: made up not only of Prussian subjects of the Hohenzollerns but also of immigrant Bavarians,
Saxons, etc., it had become a cosmopolitan centre where foreigners, and particularly the inhabitants of the other German
countries, were welcomed, and their products, cultural as well
as material, eagerly absorbed. It soon became the ambition of
every German to show his goods, exhibit his works, produce his
plays in Berlin, which, like London for England, was the supreme
testing ground for everything produced. Berlin's cultural life
naturally profited from this state of affairs. Literature and the
art of the theatre particularly flourished now in this city as they
had flourished only once before in German history, at the beginning of the nineteenth century, when Berlin had been one
of the centres of the Romantic movement. The last years of the
nineteenth century brought the representatives of Naturalism
to Berlin. Ibsen's plays had been seen in the capital as early as
1878. August Strindberg had come to live near Berlin. Gerhard
Hauptmann, Germany's great revolutionary playwright, had
made his home there, and his plays, about the struggle of the
working men and about the new psychological problems which
were interesting the intellectuals of all countries, were constantly
performed in Berlin theatres. Arno Holz—a Prussian Walt
Whitman—was publishing his poetry inspired by the life of the
working masses, on factory chimneys and the lyrical associations
evoked by the noises of modern industrialism. A theatre devoted
especially to socialist workers (Volksbühne) had been founded in
1890. An imitation of Antoine's Théâtre Libre existed in Maxi-
milian Harden's 'Freie Bühne' which, protected by the status
of a private club, fought against censorship and the commercial
theatre; Ibsen, Tolstoy, and Hauptmann were the leading authors
of this stage. Idealist intellectuals of pre-war Berlin nursed every
kind of cause. Bruno Wille preached religious freedom, Wilhelm
Bölsche enlightenment and science for the people, others Chris-

tian socialism, and each had his disciples. Some were anarchists and vegetarians with equal conviction. Others talked of dionysiac ecstasy—a heritage from Nietzsche—and, following famous French examples, took drugs. In the last decade before 1900 popular themes of novels and plays which were wholly serious in their treatment, were the love stories of students and actresses, incest (Arno Holz), and mystic apostles who went among the people and became martyrs for the revival of faith (Hauptmann, Wille). Religious fanaticism, popular philosophy and individual conflicts played equally important parts on the intellectual stage. German sagas, Russian novels, Scandinavian plays and French poetry were the most important sources of inspiration. The workhouse was as popular a stage setting for the new theatre as the artist's studio. Russian women students, who wore their hair cropped, smoked cigarettes and discussed free love, were the muses of the new poets. The writers of Berlin were themselves as Bohemian as any group of artists. Peter Hille, for instance, one of the most famous poets of the day, is described by a literary critic who knew him[1] as 'the Verlaine of Berlin, who goes about in a shabby greyish-brown coat, with the beard of an apostle and hollow eyes; he spends his nights in the open air and in railway stations, his pockets and the bag which he carries from shelter to shelter, full of creased manuscripts'.

Some of this generation born in the 1860's, 70's and 80's—particularly Frank Wedekind and Carl Sternheim—appeared cynical rather than idealistic. Devoted to the satirical and the grotesque, they shrank from nothing which might shock the theatre-goer. Their plays were entirely devoid of all sentimental feelings. Nevertheless they were fundamentally moralists: they had made it their task to expose the insincerity in bourgeois morale, the perversions hidden behind a screen of convention, the degenerate instincts of certain over-civilised classes. As each of their first nights was accompanied by a public scandal, they were always in the limelight, always the centre of discussion and they had tremendous influence.

This was the intellectual whirlpool in which Kokoschka found himself on his arrival in Berlin. For quite naturally he made his way into the heart of Berlin's *avant-garde*: the 'Café Grössenwahn'.[2] We find this famous place described thus by a contem-

[1] Paul Wiegler in *Geschichte der Literatur*, 1930, II, p. 680.
[2] Café Megalomania.

66

2. THE CRAB (*1940-1*)

porary witness:[1] 'Men with long, curly hair, wild ties and "secessionist" socks, by their villainous, decadent, coffee drinking, bring German art near to the edge of the abyss. Kraus sends telegrams. The names of Ibsen, Hauptmann, Strindberg, Wedekind, Shaw and D'Annunzio, are bandied about on all sides. At midnight begins the great mutual congratulation and back-slapping: the gigantic shouting, the reading aloud. . . . And while menus and wine lists, daily, weekly and monthly papers, walls and marble table tops are covered with shameless, amorous contortions, Corinth sighs for disgusting subjects; Oskar Kokoschka brings in some dirt from the street, which he needs for his colossal painting. . . .'

However important the café may have been, it was not of course there that Kokoschka spent most of his time. He had come to Berlin to work. But he always needed an intellectual atmosphere to live in, to pick up new ideas and find congenial subjects for his art, and the company of other painters never had much attraction for him. Those of Berlin were different from the artists he had known, and there was much for him to learn in his own field. Berlin was never a painters' city, like Paris: but in the days before the first world war and even long after, the artists who were scattered all over Germany turned to the capital for intellectual encouragement and material support. They could count on a greater number of open-minded friends of art there than in their respective home provinces. Several of the city's numerous art galleries, although commercial undertakings, were directed by men with real artistic understanding and great enterprise, who attracted around them groups of artists of particular schools; thus Paul Cassirer, and later Alfred Flechtheim, brought to Berlin the best of the works then to be seen in Paris; the more firmly established French and German Impressionists were favoured by the cautious Bruno Cassirer, whose monthly magazine *Kunst und Künstler* was mainly devoted to their more conservative works; while the radical Herwarth Walden lent the *Sturm* galleries to the Futurists, and to German and Russian Expressionists whose works he constantly publicised in the *Sturm* magazine.

The names most prominent in painting in the Berlin of 1910 were those of the Impressionists, for whom Adolf Menzel's work in the 'sixties and 'seventies had paved the way. Among them was Max Liebermann, an admirer of the great Dutchmen and Manet,

[1] *Der Sturm*, October 1911.

67

whose style was more naturalistic than that of his French contemporaries, and more sober than that of most of his compatriots. Max Slevogt displayed a talent more brilliant, but more superficial, and will probably be longest remembered for his numerous illustrations to the *1001 Nights*, to James Fenimore Cooper, to Benvenuto Cellini and to *The Enchanted Flute*. And Lovis Corinth, a painter who, by his imaginative power, artistic temperament and vitality, far surpassed most artists of his age, was producing works which stand outside any particular group or school; realist and romantic at once, he was akin to both Rubens and Rembrandt; he belonged as much to the tradition of artistic heritage from the past as to the future; and like Kokoschka, with whom he had much in common, he formed a bridge between impressionism and expressionism. Liebermann, Slevogt and Corinth, supported by some other artists, had in 1899 founded the 'Sezession', originally a militant organisation for the defence of the tendencies of the generation born between 1850 and 1870. The Sezession later acquired an almost official status, and Liebermann became President of the Academy.

The year of Kokoschka's arrival in Berlin proved eventful in many respects. It was in 1910 that twenty-seven younger artists —most of them born in the 'eighties, but also including the much older Nolde, were rejected by the Sezession, and one of them, Max Pechstein, founded the 'Neue Sezession', which arranged two exhibitions of more advanced works in that year and one in 1911. The Neue Sezession grew into an important organisation and survived for many years. Its adherents were those artists who came to be called the Expressionists.

This name, though it covered a variety of divergent movements and tendencies, satisfactorily describes the one aim they all had in common: the expression of mental and emotional experiences as opposed to the production of impressions derived from the outside world. All were strongly influenced by the works of Hodler (first exhibited in Berlin in 1899), of Munch (known there since 1902), of Van Gogh (first seen in 1908), and of Gauguin, the only French painter who was of real importance for their movement. A quite conscious striving after emancipation from the French school was characteristic of these artists. This was also the barrier which prevented their becoming known in France or England, even while their reputation in other European countries and America was gradually spreading. The origin of the movement corresponded with that of post-impressionism in France: both were primarily motivated by reaction against impressionism. But while the western followers of Cézanne were most concerned with the recovery of shape and structure, the Germans were intent upon a new animation of the art of painting with emotional or spiritual values. The reason for this ambition will be more readily understood when expressionism is contrasted, not with the best of French impressionism, which by no means always lacked emotional appeal, but with the coldly objective works of Liebermann and with the theatrical flashiness of Slevogt, the exponents of impressionism constantly before the eyes of the young artists. Like the anti-naturalist intellectuals and writers of their generation they sought to make art reflect more than the mere appearance of things. Fragments of reality were to be represented only as symbols of the profounder reality which they believed lay behind the visible object world. Above all, the fruits of the artist's imagination were to find an outlet. Thus man himself became once more the central interest of all things artistic, although he did not necessarily appear as the object of a picture. Furthermore, all objects were individualised. Fantasy knew no bounds. Familiar things were transformed. Academic conventions were ignored. The only law recognised was that of composition. This new art was more anti-bourgeois than anything that had been seen before, and quite as much so as the works of Picasso's cubist period. But it was not anti-religious; on the contrary, the desire to express feeling and spiritual values gave birth to a new religious art which followed quite naturally in the tradition of the German Middle Ages and of the works of the Reformation. The expressionist painters fought against the materialism that had pervaded modern life, against mechanisation and decadence, and in their revolt they looked backwards and discovered the past and the primitive cultures. The members of the two main groups of expressionist artists varied slightly in their interests: those of Der Blaue Reiter[1] studied folk art, ancient glass panels, early wood-cuts, the art of children, and then also turned to the works of the Douanier Rousseau, Picasso, Matisse and other Paris artists in whom they recognised brothers-in-arms, not masters or guides. The artists of the Brücke[2] acquired the knowledge of primitive works in the ethnographical museum of Dresden. Several of them—Pechstein, Otto Müller and Nolde—even followed in Gauguin's footsteps and went to the South Seas. Barbarian, grotesque elements

[1] The Blue Horseman.   [2] The Bridge.

penetrated thus into expressionist art. Technically, the desire for an absolute art, no longer subject to the laws of faithful reproduction, led to the abandonment of detailed design and spacial depth. Monumental, flat constructions were the result. Outlines tended to become ornamental, like those of certain *Fauves*. Colour acquired a new value: it was made the most important vehicle of expression. Released from the duty of realistic representation, it ran wild: horses might be blue, cows yellow, skies green, just as figures might be misshapen, houses might dance and bodies fly. Above all the Expressionists sought to exploit the observation—suggested in Goethe's *Farbenlehre*—that certain colours evoke certain psychological reactions and are traditionally associated with certain—but not always with the same— emotions, as red with passion, yellow with jealousy or envy, blue with faithfulness and white with innocence. They spoke of 'dynamic' colours and introduced violent contrasts, without gradation and without any respect for the natural effects of light.

The origin of this movement can be traced back to the first meetings of these painters who became known as the members of the *Brücke*—Kirchner, Heckel, Schmidt-Rottluff, Nolde and Pechstein, later joined by Amiet and Kees van Dongen—in Dresden in 1902.[1] In 1908 the group moved to Berlin, and it did not dissolve until 1913. The *Brücke* represented the 'purest expressionism', so to speak. Measured by international standards, the individual works of its members—with the exception of Nolde, who will inevitably again come to be recognised as one of Germany's greatest artists and some of whose work ranks with the best of our day—will probably decline in æsthetic estimation. As a group, however, and from a historical point of view, the *Brücke* will always have to be accorded a place as one of the most important factors in post-impressionist art; what the *Fauves* were to western Europe, the *Brücke* was to all countries east of the Rhine, and if it often fell short of the æsthetic achievements of the Paris group it surpassed it in imagination and seriousness of purpose.

More international in character and in adherents than the *Brücke* was the group *Der Blaue Reiter*, founded in 1911 by the

---

[1] The date for the official establishment of the group is given by Einstein in his *Kunst des 20. Jahrhunderts*, p. 132, as 1903; by Woermann in *Geschichte der Kunst*, Vol. VI, p. 491 and by E. v. Sydow in *Die Deutsche Expressionistische Kultur und Malerei* as 1906; by Sauerlandt, in *Die Kunst der letzten 30. Jahre*, p. 147, as 1905.

Russian Kandinsky, the Bohemian Kubin and the South-German Marc. The Russian element, which further included Chagall and Jawlensky, was the strongest in this group, which was particularly influenced by Kandinsky's abstract inclinations, a factor that made the works of *Der Blaue Reiter* more acceptable to the public west of the Rhine than that of the *Brücke*. The main point in the programme of *Der Blaue Reiter*, frequently emphasised by Franz Marc in his letters, was to discover and reveal the laws which rule the universe, to reach beyond the individual and enter into metaphysical spheres. Art, in other words, was to represent objects as symbols standing for ideas. It must be said that these painters were most successful when they were furthest from the realisation of these abstract ideas. Marc himself, for instance, had a remarkable decorative talent, and in his animal pictures immense vitality; in his last pictures, however, he too approached abstract art, though his purely geometrical shapes are animated by the same grace and have more transparency than his earlier animals. The group, which originated by seceding from the *Münchner Neue Künstlervereinigung*, had its permanent seat in Munich, but its works were, of course, well known in Berlin. Its publication, *Der Blaue Reiter*, of 1912, the initial and only volume of a planned annual, is one of the basic documents of expressionism.

The *Brücke* and *Der Blaue Reiter* had obviously much in common: they had a common attitude towards painting, an approach more active than the traditional, reproductive aim: both were intent upon a reformatory participation in the intellectual life of the time; both were revolutionary, in mental attitude as well as in technique. An analysis which Herwarth Walden published with reference to *Der Blaue Reiter* might apply equally to both: '. . . the object is recognised at once as an element in, not as the essence of the picture. The pictures are painted acording to relations of shapes and colours, ruthlessly, without the intention to imitate, with regard for the picture itself only, as the unity of a painted surface. The pictures are not to be considered playful (or, as has been said less correctly, merely decorative), they are the expression of a vision, the visualisation of a revelation, the realisation of an emotion by the means of painting: shape and colour. Emotions are expressed immediately, not indirectly by way of the object.'[1]

[1] *Einblick in die Kunst; Expressionismus—Futurismus—Kubismus*. Berlin, 1917, p. 18.

The reception accorded to the Expressionists was as bad as could be expected. One instance may suffice to demonstrate their treatment at the hands of the art critics of those days; the following lines were written on the occasion of an exhibition of the *Brücke* in Leipzig:[1] 'One can bear such things calmly for a while, but the number of these prophets is ever increasing—which is very understandable, as it is not difficult to adopt such methods —and in the end they will turn people's heads.' What this pessimist had foreseen in fact happened: the Expressionists gained ground slowly but surely, and at the end of the first great war their triumph was such that, their early labours forgotten, they were often regarded as a post-war phenomenon. Every leading museum and many private collectors bought their pictures, and countless exhibitions of their works were held, while the bibliography of books and articles analysing their achievements grew yearly. Yet Marc and his companion Macke had been killed in the war, Nolde was an old man, more moderate now but never weak, and the others were no longer young. The fate the Expressionists suffered at the hands of the new regime, which purged Germany's culture soon after 1933, is well known: they were labelled un-German, *kulturbolschewistisch*, blamed again for the same things which had earned them reproaches thirty years before, their works were removed from the public galleries, destroyed or forgotten. When all this happened, however, they had long become a part of history: there had already been reaction; the members of the groups had themselves modified their methods; and new schools had arisen. Nevertheless they cannot be wiped out as though they had never existed: for expressionism is one of the inherent characteristics of German art. It has always been so and it will be so anew as soon as there is a German art again.

Although he was not immediately influenced by the art of the Expressionists, there is no doubt that Kokoschka was greatly impressed by their programme, as indeed any young man as eager as he to absorb all the elements of his time must have been. They were of his age and they had developed in a similar cultural atmosphere; the same *art nouveau* heritage, dominated by the same international masters, was the background of his work and of theirs, and he as well as they shared the new interest in primitive art; like them, he too had come to the conclusion that it was the reality behind the appearance that mattered;

[1] *Zeitschrift für Bildende Kunst*, N.F., 1910–11, Vol. XXII, p. 205.

XX. SELF-PORTRAIT
1912

XXI. PORTRAIT OF THE PAINTER POINTING TO HIS BREAST
1913

XXIII. DER GEFESSELTE KOLUMBUS
Lithograph. 1913

XXII. DER GEFESSELTE KOLUMBUS
Lithograph. 1913

XXV. BACHKANTATE
Lithograph. 1914

XXIV. BACHKANTATE
Lithograph. 1914

they were equally unconcerned about the conventions of taste and, like him, they were the *enfants terribles* of their age; moreover, they fought a common battle, for his enemies were their enemies. Nevertheless, he was not yet one of them. While his own brush at that time was only, half involuntarily, revealing the sores hidden behind the façades of convention, they were consciously reformers. Nor did he, at that time, adopt their artistic tenets. Only after the war, when he had finally broken with Vienna and made his home in Germany, did his work reveal his acceptance of many of their principles. When he first came into contact with them, they formed a part of that general picture 'Berlin' which for him represented an active and varied intellectual life, an atmosphere of revolutionary enthusiasm and a freedom from interfering authorities unheard of in Vienna.

Berlin on the whole was very different from the Austrian capital, but the café which he frequented, with its discussions and arguments, was rather like his own circle of friends in Vienna. It was, in fact, through his old friends that he had found his new ones: for one of Berlin's intellectuals, Herwarth Walden, had heard of the young artist when visiting Loos and engaged him to work on his fortnightly magazine, *Der Sturm*.[1] For nearly a year this was his main employment: all through 1910 he did a drawing for the title page almost every week. And during this time Walden assumed, to a certain extent, the role previously played by Loos.

Kokoschka's new protector was, however, quite a different type—a natural product of the hot soil of Berlin. 'Critic, artist, prophet and—business man,'[2] he was one of the leaders of the expressionist movement. In 1910 he had founded his fortnightly, in which he published the works of those artists whom he desired to introduce to Germany: among them Chagall, who through Walden became known in Berlin long before he was ever heard of in Paris; Archipenko; Severini; Leger; Picasso; Delaunay; Max Ernst; Kubin; the Artists of *Der Blaue Reiter*, Klee, Kandinsky, Marc and Campendonck, and many others who are now forgotten. For these, the members of *Der Sturm*, he opened galleries under the same name, in which he arranged fifty exhibitions of their works in the period from 1912 to 1917. He sent these exhibitions on tour through the most important

[1] The Tempest.
[2] Eckart von Sydow in *Deutsche Expressionistische Kultur und Malerei*, 1920, p. 131.

cities in Germany, and some of them were even shown in London, Brussels, Copenhagen, Helsinki, in Norway, Sweden, Holland, Austria, Switzerland and Japan. The 'Erste Deutsche Herbstsalon' of 1913, also arranged by Walden, contained representative works by the foremost *avant-garde* artists of Europe. As publisher too Walden encouraged the *Sturm* artists, producing series of reproductions of their works and books dealing with these. And at the same time he was director of a school for the fine arts. A man of boundless initiative, Walden exercised a profound influence on the art and the artists of pre-war Germany. Yet he cannot be said to have possessed the integrity nor the clear-cut intellectual aims of a Karl Kraus or an Adolf Loos: he dabbled in too many activities at once—always with an eye to good business, and his taste was not so commendable as his energy. The artists to whom he extended his protection had one thing only in common: that they were among the most advanced. No other factor united the members of the *Sturm* group. When, in 1917, Walden published a record of his activities,[1] he gave it the characteristic sub-title 'Expressionismus—Futurismus—Kubismus'. To him, one was as good as the other. If he had any personal predilection, it was for futurism because it was 'dynamic', and he always wanted to see things move. He was fascinated by the repudiation of all effort to imitate and reproduce in the new art movements—for in those days it seemed that art's emancipation from nature was complete and final. He was always eager to provoke the philistine. His gifts were not those of a leader, but he was a perfect manager, and he could write readable articles to introduce his artists, rather in the style of a political pamphleteer explaining a new programme. Walden's intellectual capacity was considerable; it was in the field of æsthetics that he was unreliable. During the first years of his activity he succeeded in drawing into his net the best artists of his day, who were naturally attracted by his initiative; later he took up very minor talents with the same vigour, but less success. Consequently his influence waned with his reputation; his fortnightly had by 1917 become a monthly; his gallery and art school closed down a few years later; and in the late 'twenties Herwarth Walden was but a lonely picturesque figure, often seen in art exhibitions and cafés, thin, grey, with long hair and thick, strong glasses, a bird-like head on a thin neck, poor, old and withered, a living relic of the past. He was last heard of when

[1] *Einblick in die Kunst.*

74

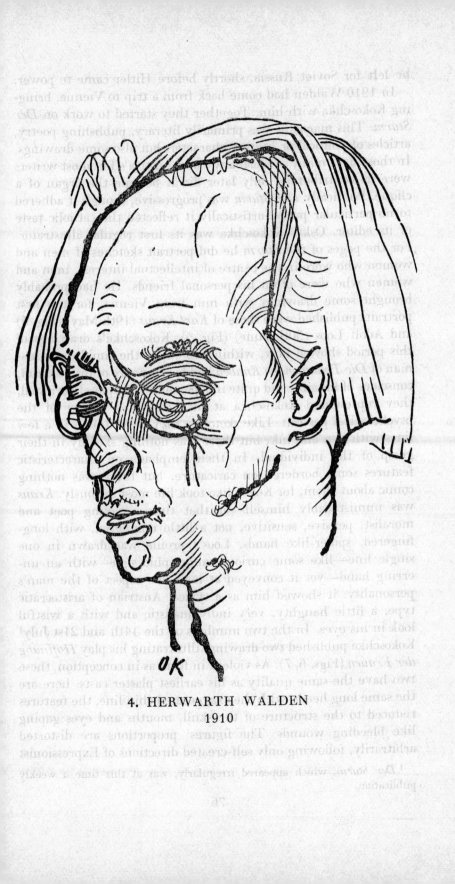

4. HERWARTH WALDEN
1910

he left for Soviet Russia, shortly before Hitler came to power.

In 1910 Walden had come back from a trip to Vienna, bringing Kokoschka with him. Together they started to work on *Der Sturm*. This magazine was primarily literary, publishing poetry, articles of political or literary character, but also some drawings. In those days many of Germany's and Austria's foremost writers were its contributors; only later did it become the organ of a clique. Politically *Der Sturm* was progressive, though it adhered to no particular party; artistically it reflected the catholic taste of its editor. Oskar Kokoschka was its first regular illustrator. For the pages of the *Sturm* he did portrait sketches of men and women who were in the centre of intellectual interest, men and women who were often his personal friends. He had probably brought some drawings with him from Vienna, for the first portraits published were those of *Karl Kraus* (19th May) (Fig. 5) and Adolf Loos (30th June) (Fig. 3). Kokoschka's drawings of this period showed how, within two years, the timid draughtsman of *Die Träumenden Knaben* had become sure of his medium, conscious of his aims and quite independent. Completely original, they represented Kokoschka at his best—as a master of the psychological portrait. Like sketches, they were drawn in a few lines with pen and ink; but there was nothing sketchy in their grasp of the individual. In their emphasis on characteristic features some bordered on caricature, but there was nothing comic about them, for Kokoschka took life most seriously. *Kraus* was unmistakably himself—at that time a young poet and moralist, pensive, sensitive, not a little mannered, with long-fingered, spider-like hands. Loos's profile was drawn in one single line—like some curious calligraphic sign—with an unerring hand—yet it conveyed at least one aspect of the man's personality: it showed him as a typical Austrian of aristocratic type, a little haughty, very individualistic and with a wistful look in his eyes. In the two numbers of the 14th and 21st July[1] Kokoschka published two drawings illustrating his play *Hoffnung der Frauen* (Figs. 6, 7). As violent in form as in conception, these two have the same quality as his earliest plaster casts: here are the same long heads, with the exaggerated chin line, the features reduced to the structure of the skull, mouths and eyes gaping like bleeding wounds. The figures' proportions are distorted arbitrarily, following only self-created directions of Expressionist

[1] *Der Sturm*, which appeared irregularly, was at this time a weekly publication.

76

5. KARL KRAUS
About 1910

emphasis. Anatomy is not completely given up, but subservient to the artist's determination to emphasise what interests him most: the movement of a hand is stressed by a few strokes of the pen around the wrist; others point to a woman's navel, a man's genitals. Although some of these rudimentary graphic signs appear in the most unexpected places—on one arm, for instance, or around the arm-holes—they create the desired illusion of roundness, of a living surface, of animated figures. One of the most remarkable facts is that hands and feet are reduced to the same essential shapes and spread out flat in the same way as is to be found in the works of Picasso, in his *Guernica* period, twenty-five years later. The effect is the same: that of something barbaric, elementary, but inescapably expressive, appealing not to our sense of beauty, but to our emotions. There is another feature in Kokoschka's drawings of 1910 which makes one think of Picasso: the divided faces, containing profile and full face in one. But while Kokoschka had discovered—perhaps by chance—and sometimes used the mysterious effect of this technical trick, it remained for Picasso to exploit it fully, exploring all its possibilities. And this is a key to one of the fundamental differences between these two artists who, although often interested in the same problems, represent two opposite poles of European art: while Picasso is always searching for theoretical solutions to problems of technique, for Kokoschka his subject has always been the point of departure.

For the last July number of the *Sturm* (1910) Kokoschka did a portrait of *Herwarth Walden* (Fig. 4). With helpless eyes behind thick glasses, long hair and no chin, every inch a pseudo-genius, the painter's new employer was mercilessly exposed. August brought another illustration for *Hoffnung der Frauen*, and a drawing representing *Sacred and Profane Love*, with a new, grand gesture of pathos. But the same number of the 25th August contains an anti-climax in the comic figure of an *Athlete* swinging on the trapeze, and some enthusiastic notes by Kokoschka on 'Archie A. Goodale and his Gymnastic Evolutions', displayed in Berlin's variety theatre, the Wintergarten. The painter's impressions of 'The 12 Sunshine Girls' were most movingly reflected in these words: 'A mild but weakening rain of sweet little arms and legs. 12 chaste pairs of knickers flutter in the wind. The English euphony of the lisping twelve Sunshine Girls is a hymn of thanks, for the preservation of the virgins. I was the only one to hear it.'

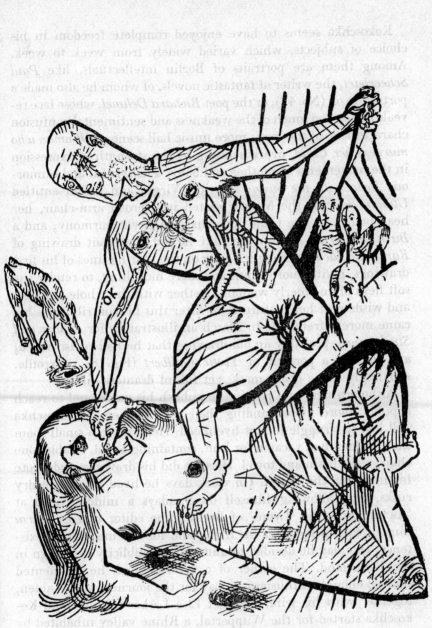

6. HOFFNUNG DER FRAUEN
1910

Kokoschka seems to have enjoyed complete freedom in his choice of subjects, which varied widely from week to week. Among them are portraits of Berlin intellectuals, like *Paul Scheerbart*, the writer of fantastic novels, of whom he also made a portrait in oil (No. 47); or the poet *Richard Dehmel*, whose face reveals almost too much of the weakness and sentimental confusion characteristic of the man; more music hall scenes; a *Woman who murders her Child*, overwhelming by the strength of expression in the movements of mother and baby; a delightful and humorous *Leda with the Swan*; a lyrical Virgin and Child, entitled *Utinam delectet*, the Mother seated in a broad arm-chair, her head bent over the Child in a curve of sweet harmony; and a *Birth of Christ*; in January 1911 he did a portrait drawing of *Karin Michaelis*, relying less now on the sparing lines of his first drawings, giving more depth and more modelling, to render the soft flesh of an elderly woman together with the whole kindness and wisdom of her mature face. After this his contributions became more infrequent. In March an illustration for *Sphinx und Strohmann*—probably an old drawing that he had rediscovered; and in July a portrait of *Yvette Guilbert* (Fig. 8) in profile, startlingly like a death mask, yet full of dramatic life.

Although now in a position to publish his works and to reach a public more understanding than that of Vienna, Kokoschka still had to struggle for his livelihood. He lived in a small room that Walden had vacated for him, containing a bed, a table, one chair, wash basin and towel. Here he did his drawings and wrote his notes for the *Sturm*. On week days he lived mostly on dry rusks, only allowing himself on Sundays a midday meal at 'Aschinger's', the 'Lyons' of Berlin. The editor of *Der Sturm* himself had to fight for his living and for the magazine's existence. One day he decided to undertake a publicity campaign in the Rhineland. The owner of a tavern which he frequented showed enough enthusiasm to pay for the journey, and Walden, together with his wife, the poet Else Lasker-Schüler, and Kokoschka started for the Wuppertal, a Rhine valley inhabited by a purely industrial population. Else Lasker-Schüler was one of the most famous of Berlin's Bohemians who, under the name of Jussuf, Prince of Thebes, wrote poems in a style to match her pseudonym. She wore her black hair cut short, velvet trousers and pointed shoes. Walden, on the other hand, had very long hair of a yellow colour, and he wore a most formal but old-fashioned morning dress. Kokoschka, for his part, was the

7. HOFFNUNG DER FRAUEN
1910

smartest of the trio, for he was still dressed by Ebenstein. The three went from house to house, from one mining village to the other, putting a free copy of *Der Sturm* into each letter box: the magazine was a revolutionary organ, in which all that was new and young was published, and they accordingly expected the mining population of the Wuppertal to be interested. It was no wonder that the police showed a most lively interest in their activities.

It was in the Rhineland, too, that Kokoschka first found official acknowledgment as a painter: in September, 1910, the Folkwang Museum in Essen showed his paintings in a one-man show. Probably the paintings exhibited on that occasion were the portraits of Altenberg, Loos, Kraus, Stein, a new one of Walden, and those he had painted in Switzerland: of the Duchess of Rohan-Montesquieu, Count Verona and Forel.[1] And it may have been at this date that the Folkwang Museum acquired the portrait of the Duchess of Rohan-Montesquieu.

On the whole Kokoschka found much more encouragement in the Reich than he had ever enjoyed in Austria. While even Kraus's *Fackel* still printed uncomplimentary remarks about the painter like the following by L. E. Tesar in March, 1910: '. . . the paintings and other works by Kokoschka do not appeal to any of us, or at any rate only to a very small minority . . . ,' Else Lasker-Schüler in *Der Sturm* described him enthusiastically as 'a young priest, with broad shoulders resting on a slim stem, with his doubly domed forehead thinking two-fold'. And of his portraits she said that he 'uncovered the roots'. Recording a visit to his studio, she praised the portrait of the Duchess of Rohan-Montesquieu, which she described as the picture of 'a glass-house miracle, a princess, a blood-sucking plant', she also mentioned the portraits of Janikowsky, of Count Verona, of Kraus whom she called 'the Dalai-Lama', and of Loos, whom she said she recognised from his 'malicious gorilla pupils'; the *Winter Landscape* she compared with a Dürer or a Grünewald.

Although he had a home under his editor's hospitable roof, where he kept house in an attic, together with a young actor, Rudolf Blümner, Kokoschka's material difficulties were not at

[1] It is impossible at this time to obtain a catalogue of this exhibition in England. The above-mentioned pictures, however, were shown in an exhibition arranged by Cassirer in Berlin in the same year, which was reviewed by Kurt Hiller in *Der Sturm*, 7th July, 1910, and they had been on view in Karlsbad in the previous year.

8. YVETTE GUILBERT
1910

an end. At times he experienced real hunger. He has since written a story[1] in which he describes how he and Blümner, in their poverty and isolation, began to suffer from hallucinations, in which figured not only the richest kinds of food but also a dream-girl they had invented and whom they brought up together. She was called Virginia, and of course she was the loveliest creature any poet could imagine; she was fed, clothed and educated by the two hungry bachelors, who surpassed each other in care and attentions, until Virginia was so grown up that they both fell in love with her most violently. Naturally this touching story ended in tragedy. Virginia, however, although only a child of imagination, fulfilled her mission: she kept the two young men above water until they found, in one way or another, something more substantial to live on. And now—thirty years later—she has even become the heroine of one of the most charming pieces of German writing.

Meanwhile Kokoschka continued to paint portraits. Besides those of his employer, *Herwarth Walden* (No. 40), and of the writer *Paul Scheerbart* (No. 47), drawings of whom had already been published, he painted his companion *Blümner* (No. 28) who was conveniently at hand, some of his colleagues among the contributors to the *Sturm*, the sculptor *Wilhelm Wauer* (No. 41), and the actress *Tilla Durieux* (No. 32). This lady, who was more interesting, exotic and famous than beautiful, was also the subject of a portrait by Renoir.[2] She was the wife of the great art dealer Paul Cassirer, who later took charge of Kokoschka's affairs. He showed Kokoschka's works for the first time in June 1910.

This exhibition was a great event in Kokoschka's career; it proved that he had inspired in a man renowned for his dis-crimination sufficient confidence to win his active encourage-ment. Therewith Kokoschka entered the ranks of those artists whose works are a matter for speculation—material as well as intellectual. For Paul Cassirer, who had displayed great initiative and earned much success by introducing the French Impres-sionists to the Berlin public, an active interest in Kokoschka was a risk: it was still impossible to say whether the young artist

[1] Read by Kokoschka at a meeting of the 'Free League of German Culture', in London, 1939.

[2] Dated 1914. In the possession of Mr. Stephen C. Clark. Exhibited in the Renoir Exhibition of the Metropolitan Museum, New York, 1937. Reproduced in the catalogue, pl. 60.

OK

9. DIE SCHÖNE ROLLSCHUHLÄUFERIN
1910

would fulfil the expectations of his few admirers, and it meant hard work for a dealer to gain the interest of an unwilling public for his work. But Cassirer was powerful as well as enthusiastic; having once taken a young artist under his wing he could convince collectors and museum officials of his talents. In this way several artists' works had found their way into the museums of hesitating directors. At first Kokoschka's existing pictures migrated from Herwarth Walden's bohemian sitting-room and the colourful disorder of the *Sturm* offices into Cassirer's smart gallery. Soon after Cassirer gave him a contract which must, at that time, have seemed to him like a heavenly blessing. The great firm was from now on to see to the sale of his works. He was suddenly—and for years—relieved of material worries, for Cassirer was generous with regard to advance payments. It was a long time before the necessity of painting a certain number of pictures a year became irksome to the painter and before he came to resent his obligations towards his agent. Eventually, however, this situation led to an open conflict. Whoever may have to be blamed for this, Cassirer must be credited with having given Kokoschka his support when he most needed it.

★   ★   ★

At the beginning of the year 1911 Kokoschka went back to Vienna. The immediate reason for his journey was an exhibition of paintings and sculpture by young artists, to be opened in February, 1911, in the rooms of the Hagenbund, where twenty-five of his paintings and some of his drawings were to be shown. It was the greatest exhibition of his work yet presented in his native city, and he doubtless looked forward to it with keen expectations. So did all those who had previously condemned him and had watched his successes in Germany with bitterness. Every one was prepared for a new scandal, and the anticipation of a repetition of the events of previous occasions was enhanced by the announcement that a new play by Kokoschka was to be performed. But the storm that broke this time was worse than anything Vienna had seen for many years. At the private view the heir to Franz Josef's throne, the Archduke Franz Ferdinand, declared that 'this fellow's bones ought to be broken in his body'.[1] The press took their cue from this utterance and con-

[1] The historic words were: 'Dem Kerl sollte man die Knochen im Leibe zerbrechen.'

tributed their share to the uproar. One of Austria's most famous art scholars, Josef Strzygowsky, called Kokoschka 'a mangy creature', his works 'disgusting plague-sores', and 'puddles of foul stink'; he wrote further: 'This Oskar Kokoschka, who penetrates with his Koko-rays those persons whose ill fortune it is to come under his brush, should apply his talents to the decoration of brothels with warning pictures of syphilis and paralysis.'[1] This furious attack not only demonstrates the rage of Kokoschka's adversaries, but also points to those of Kokoschka's gifts which were most praised by his admirers: his penetrating eye and his faculty of exposing the ills from which modern man is suffering. Even those who were not prejudiced against him spoke of his art as of something unpleasant, some sympton of decay. Thus we read in Kraus's *Fackel*: 'Nobody can stand before his pictures without seeing at once that the people he represents look as though they had experienced serious illness, or several years in jail, as though they were suffering from repulsive physical and, of course, mental diseases. . . . It need not be denied that the way in which Kokoschka attains the effect of his pictures is not one that also leads to the beautification of his subjects: another goal is aimed at by other means.'[2] This was written in defence of an artist understood only by a small minority of advanced people. But even if we consider that embittered fights were frequent in the art world of those days and that Kokoschka's pictures were unusual, we wonder today whether there was cause for so much excitement. At least two aspects of this question have changed since 1911: we have no doubts left about the faithfulness of Kokoschka's portraits, and we find an absolute beauty in most of his works of that period.

The shock caused by this first cross-section of Kokoschka's works nevertheless is understandable. In a room hung with his earliest paintings the visitor would find himself surrounded by ghost-like figures emerging from coloured mists, unsubstantial and yet possessed of a mysterious life of their own. Distorted, yet intensely expressive, these sad, forlorn people with large eyes and gesticulating hands have a peculiar fascination. Like the very prototypes of modern man emerging from chaos, or like visions of an unknown world inhabited by unhappy spirits, they

[1] Quoted from *Die Zeit* by E. L. Tesar in his article 'Der Fall Oskar Kokoschka und die Gesellschaft', published in *Die Fackel* of the 1st April, 1911.

[2] Franz Grüner in 'Oskar Kokoschka' on the 28th February 1911.

are doubly haunting because they are reminiscent of something familiar without being familiar themselves. Quite unconsciously the painter had reversed a normal process: while the starting point of paintings is usually a material subject and the resultant pictures only rarely suggest the immaterial, the spiritual, Kokoschka started from the incorporeal, the evanescent, which he expressed as directly as he could with brush on canvas, often only suggesting material forms and leaving the spectator to identify them and to draw on his own experiences for their elaboration and definition. The spectator's task of appreciation was complicated by the fact that each picture was a vehicle not only for the sitter's personality, but also for the artist's own strong emotions with which he saturated the subject. Only a public that had learnt something of Kokoschka's personality through encountering his work at successive stages and through its reflection in the works of other artists could, in later years, look back and fully understand these works of his early years.

Some of the indignation produced by these paintings can be inferred from a comparison with the other 'advanced' works at that time to be seen in Vienna. Klimt's portraits, although imbued with the same seriousness of purpose, appear quite conventional by comparison. His ladies are always most exquisite, and adhere to the accepted code of beauty; they are dignified, graceful creatures, harmoniously presented. Their souls—seldom unconventional—are expressed only through their melancholy attitude. Beside these fashionable women Kokoschka's figures are shapeless, awkward, almost unpleasantly individual. But while Klimt's portraits have through the course of time come to be regarded merely as period-pieces, Kokoschka's works have after thirty years been admitted to the class of the masterpieces of painting.

Various factors had converged to produce in so young a man the impulse to paint such unusual, unprepossessing pictures. As a young artist of Vienna, who wished to emancipate himself from the preceding generation, he naturally paid heed to the desperate warning: 'Our art is being ruined by good taste!'[1] Sincerity, an approach to the essence of human life, fearlessness in the rendering of reality could be learnt, not in the art schools of Central Europe, but from the Old Masters in the museums as well as from western artists of the recent past: Van Gogh, Toulouse-Lautrec, Edvard Munch were more impressive than anything

[1] Otto Stoessel in *Die Fackel* of the 13th July, 1908, referring to that year's *Kunstschau*.

Kokoschka's immediate surroundings offered. Intellectually, he and his contemporaries were fed on the most pessimistic literature and philosophy that Europe had ever produced: Zola, Ibsen, Strindberg, Dostoievsky and Wedekind were the prophets of his generation, whose admiration was divided between the doctrines of the highly ethical Eastern Europeans and the cynicism of the western decadents. Most important in his development, however, were Kokoschka's own experiences. At the time when most of these early pictures were painted he had been poor, much ridiculed, driven out of the posts he had secured after much strenuous work, punished for his most sincere efforts, a stranger to security, and the men who surrounded him were in a sense outcasts like himself, although the best among them had been voluntary exiles from a society they despised. Whatever may have been their qualities in their particular fields, they were all slightly abnormal: they lived in an atmosphere of permanent tension, bristling with revolutionary ideas; and they indulged in those personal eccentricities which so often accompany artistic gifts. Neither conventional nor even balanced works could be expected from a beginner under those circumstances. But the extraordinary could thrive and it did so, happily, in the case of Kokoschka.

Apart from their artistic independence Kokoschka's exhibits were also sensational for a different reason. There was an element of *succès de scandale*, for most of them represented people very well known in Vienna. There was *Herr Ebenstein* (No. 11), the fashionable tailor, standing upright behind a chair, on the back of which his two hands were resting, a severe expression on his face, his body and clothing of the same massive construction as those of the earlier *Trance Player* (No. 5), also exhibited on this occasion. There was *Karl Kraus* (No. 7), not melancholic and delicate as in the *Sturm* drawing (Fig. 5), but seated awkwardly in front of a plain wall, his head supported with difficulty on his narrow shoulders, the skeleton-like hands, second in importance only to the face, prominently placed. The head alone is drawn distinctly, the square forehead and chin, eyes, eyebrows and slightly opened mouth clearly outlined with the brush, while the rest of the figure, contourless, dissolves into the surrounding space. The ghost-like appearance which results from this submerging of the body into the indefinite background, was enhanced by the fixed gaze of the large eyes and further emphasised by the predominating colour, a vivid yellow. This was not Karl Kraus the fighter, whose pen was equally feared and hated by press, officialdom and all slack writers of the German tongue, the authority to whom purist and moralist fanatics looked for guidance in matters of their artistic and political conscience. Nor was it the prophetic writer, who had the courage to stand alone and work in almost complete isolation, to battle for truth and justice in small as well as in great matters. This was Karl Kraus as seen through the eyes of his enemies: it was the portrait of an unhealthy man, deserted, unhappy, certainly frightened, perhaps abnormal. Yet the deformity and physical weakness expressed by the painter were not pure invention, and believers in Kokoschka's insight will say that the fear which makes the subject of this picture so pitiable, was probably really there, at the bottom of Kraus's courage. We know that Kraus himself did not welcome the painting. But if Kokoschka did not do him justice, the reason was probably a lack of common ground between the two unusual men, one of whom was purely intellectual, a man of principle and absolute integrity, while the other was primarily impulsive, always open to new impressions and influences, driven by an artistic imagination that was stronger than any self-imposed rational purpose. Kokoschka never pretended to be a great friend of Karl Kraus's. He admits quite frankly how little they had in common. 'My education was acquired through reading under my school desk,' he says, 'therefore my intellect resembles the Tibetan desert, with a few pagodas here and there. For this reason I was even allowed not to read the *Fackel*.'

The case of Kokoschka's *Peter Altenberg* portrait (No. 16) was quite different. Here the human contact which the artist needed was easily established, for the painter in many ways resembled the poet. Altenberg had for many years been Vienna's most famous Bohemian, and his friends considered him a poet of the first order. His sketches, which were collected and published in several volumes,[1] are like *poésies en prose* transplanted into German, but at the same time they express a human attitude not unlike the Russian. They are extremely personal, many of them autobiographical fragments often reminiscent of periodpieces. In *Wie ich es sehe*[2] he writes for instance: 'I was born in

[1] S. Fischer, Berlin, published eleven volumes, a selection from which was published by Verlag Anton Schroll & Co., Vienna, in 1932. This volume was edited by Karl Kraus.

[2] As I see it.

90

1862, in Vienna. My father is a merchant. He has one peculi-
arity: he reads only French books. For forty years there has
hung above his bed a wonderful picture of his god, "Victor
Hugo". In the evening he sits in a dark red arm-chair, wearing
a blue jacket with large velvet collar à la Victor Hugo, and reads
the *Revue des deux Mondes*. No, idealists like him are no longer
to be found in the world. Once he was asked: "Are you proud
of your son?" He replied: "I did not take it much to heart that
he was a good-for-nothing for thirty years. So I am not very
flattered if he is now a poet! I gave him liberty. I knew it would
be a gamble. I reckoned with his soul!" [1]

Altenberg was an Impressionist with heart. He could write
about the colours of the flowers he saw every day in the park,
or about the most delicate human relations, which he would
express in short realistic dialogue. He loved women whose weak-
nesses he untiringly described, and children, whose grace and
freedom from self-consciousness he admired above all, and he
understood the poor and the wretched. Encounters with children
of nine, or conversations with hotel maids gave him subjects. He
was a reproachful moralist like Kraus, but less severe in his
judgments, recognising more the poor sinner in himself. It is
true that we have today less faith in Altenberg's greatness than
had his contemporaries, for we see better how much he was
limited by his time: his flowers were those of a Monet, his interiors those of an Oscar Wilde or a Whistler—all 'in blue and
brown'—while his prostitutes, like those of Tolstoy, were burdened with a soul. We may resent his admiration for the purity
in children when we find it intermixed with a sensual appreciation that made him speak of the sweet odour of their bodies.
We suspect affectation in his women who turn pale when excited, and in his children who become speechless with emotion.
Altenberg was perhaps at his best when paradoxical, witty,
philosophical. And if he was somewhat pretentious in acting the
poet, who sees and experiences things differently from other
people, it was perhaps his defence against a public which ridiculed
him. For he was an unusual, somewhat ridiculous figure: bald,
with an enormous moustache, always untidily dressed, and too
poor to appear dignified. This is how he describes himself shortly
before his death: 'On the 9th March, 1919, I shall be 60 years
old. I go without a hat, with bare feet, which I never dry after

[1] P. 58 of *Peter Altenberg Auswahl*, edited by Karl Kraus, published by
Anton Schroll, Vienna, 1932.

a foot bath, in wooden sandals; I own neither underclothes nor
night shirts. . . .'[1] Naturally his habits were considered eccentric.
He had a meagre income but always found somebody to pay for
his room which became quite renowned in the course of years.
'My small attic room with one window on the 5th floor of the
Grabenhotel is my nest, built up during 20 years. The walls
are covered with photographs. The Princess Elisabeth Windisch-
grätz in her fifth year of life: the same with four angel-children:
Franz Schubert and Hugo Wolf, Beethoven and Tolstoy, Richard
Wagner and Goethe, Japanese birds, the mountain Fushji, a
great crucifix from the Tyrolese school of wood carving, Gustav
Klimt's *Schubert-Idylle*, Orth Castle in winter, Ciseri's *En-
tombment*: photographs of Bertha L., Klara P., Nabaduh from
Accrà, Paula Sch., Greta H., Kamilla G., Frl. Mayen, Frl.
Mewes; and my beloved earthenware vases and 64 Japanese
bric-à-brac objects, obtained by begging from female "admirers":
briefly, everything to correspond with my being, my taste, my
internal life. A nest!'——Altenberg's evenings were spent in the
circle of his friends in the famous Café Herrenhof, where he,
Kraus and Loos sat through the night. His relationship to Kraus
is best explained by himself; in a feuilleton entitled 'Wie ich
mir Karl Kraus gewann'.[2] It begins: 'I was then, in 1894, a
mere nobody, although I was already as eccentrically dressed as
today. We met at Ebensee, and on the way to Traunkirchen I
began, out of boredom, to sing "Heini von Steyer", the words by
Gottfried Keller, with music by Engelsberg. This was the way I
won the interest of a man so inaccessible. Later he sent, behind
my back, the manuscript of my first book, *Wie ich es sehe*, pages
of which had been scattered in beds, tables, drawers, cupboards,
etc., to Germany's first publisher *in modernibus*, S. Fischer of
Berlin. I do not know whether he did it only to prove that all
the others were not genuine. It is a possible explanation, in view
of his aggressive mentality. He favoured me because I was
"genuine".' Loos was Altenberg's protector, as he was Kokoschka's. There is no doubt that Kraus, Loos and Altenberg influenced each other constantly, and although the architect had
the most constructive mind, they all shared the same interests
and opinions, and they all lived according to their common
principles. It is not surprising that, after many years of continuous interchange, they came to see themselves in contrast to

[1] 'Sunt certi denique fines,' p. 508 of Kraus's anthology.
[2] How I won Karl Kraus.

their surroundings and to overestimate each other. All three detested and publicly castigated insincerity, pompousness, banality, just as all three admired everything that was progressive, real and brave, and made a cult of anything coming from England, be it the teachings of William Morris or the performances of touring acrobats. They were like three companions on the war path, always supporting and defending each other. The names of Karl Kraus and Adolf Loos occur frequently in Altenberg's sketches. Kraus spoke the last words at Altenberg's grave and later edited a volume of his selected works, which he prefaced with a poem to his dead friend.

Kokoschka's portrait of Altenberg was inspired by a particular, very characteristic occasion. He had often seen the poet, whom he considered one of the most graceful people he had ever met, and he had wanted to paint him. Altenberg was, however, not to be found during the day-time, when he used to lock himself into his hotel room; only in the evening he appeared and could be found in the Herrenhof, among his friends, surrounded by a curious public, who visited the café especially to stare at him from neighbouring tables. When Kokoschka came there one evening to meet him, Altenberg was sitting in his usual place, his eyes fixed on a burning candle in front of him. His friends arrived one after the other, and as usual the poet, who was out of pocket, asked them to lend him some money. Each one of them showed him a ten-Kronen-note without, however, handing it to him. 'Write something,' they teased him, 'and you will get it.' This game they continued as long as it amused them. Altenberg, who could go half mad on such occasions, poured out insults. Fury changed the colour of his eyes, made them glow with fire. The spectacle reminded Kokoschka of a cuttle-fish he had seen in an aquarium where, for payment of a trifle, one was allowed to tease the creature and make it eject its black fluid. He saw at first an entreaty for peace, then anger, finally rage in the victim's eyes. And so he painted Altenberg, his small hands lifted, half imploringly, half in defence, his eyes protruding, his moustache hanging down sadly, his neck collarless in accordance with his principles ('Only waiters, who are condemned to it by society, wear stiff collars!'), creased and wrinkled. The portrait, which expressed Kokoschka's whole sympathy, is one of his best works, and it was more moving than anything that had gone before. Altenberg was so delighted with it that he stood Kokoschka a schnapps and a pair of Vienna sausages. This is said to have been the only time the poet ever played the host. There is no doubt that Altenberg exercised some influence on the young painter. The circuses, coloured women and English dancers which were the common subjects of his daily talk as well as of his sketches, were to play their part in Kokoschka's career. The whole fantastic atmosphere surrounding the poet, in fact, left its imprint on Kokoschka's mind.[1]

Kokoschka's motives in painting the portrait of *Herr von Janikowsky* (No. 23) were similar to those which had moved him to paint Altenberg. Janikowsky was a writer belonging to the same circle; when Kokoschka first saw him he was interned in a lunatic asylum to which Loos took the young painter. The haggard face with the sad eyes and the frowning brow reflected and evoked the greatest misery. Once more there was an expression helpless and reproachful to an almost unbearable degree.

But while the faces of Altenberg and Janikowsky really bore

[1] There is, for instance, a sketch called 'La Zarina' (p. 92 of Kraus's anthology), quoted here for its closeness to Kokoschka's story of Virginia, which he wrote in 1939: 'A.L. and P.A. saw her for the first time in the window case for the display of photographs in Kohlmarkt. Silently they gazed on her perfection, and conceived at once a hatred for all women who had thus far crossed their path and despised themselves for having been so tolerant. La Zarina!

'Relieved of the terrible deception in which they had lived till now they walked away. They had had a sight of perfection, and they knew at last where they were.

'One night they sat in the Café R. and gazed at La Zarina drinking wine with three gentlemen of the aristocracy and behaving with indescribable charm, radiating more gracious kindness towards everybody. When she left they remained there like men intoxicated, transported, as it were, to another sphere! After this they did not see her again for some time; they only read in newspaper advertisements that she was to be seen at Ronacher's in *poses plastiques*. They never went there. They felt: "In your dress, you sweet, perfect one, we saw you naked. Authorised, censored nakedness, however, by the grace of flesh-coloured silk! A dress is an adornment of the truth. But a sheath of silk is a falsification!"

'Then P.A. saw her once more, all in white, in the box of a theatre. This he announced to his friend. He was much moved. The two of them, deeply grieved, sat at supper, tears of enthusiasm and regret in their eyes. As a result of all this they deserted their faithful and sweet girl friends, writing to them infamously, brutally: "The imperfect kills us," they wrote, "adieu . . . !" etc. etc.'

This sketch shows clearly the kind of nourishment Kokoschka's imagination found in his intercourse with the two friends, and that when he, together with Blümner, lived for months with a girl of their invention they followed an established tradition.

94

all the marks of unhappiness and disintegration with which Kokoschka was reproached in those early years, there was no trace of such features in his portrait of *Frau Lotte Franzos* (No. 18; Plate XVIII). In trying his hand for the first time on a young, attractive subject the painter had evidently been able to cast off his usual overshadowed, depressed outlook. Although the manner in which the figure is seated is still slightly awkward and self-conscious, her hands still of an odd, bony shape with stiffly outstretched fingers, her shoulders not yet quite in the right perspective, there are passages of a new, unexpected beauty. The delicate face, though serious in expression, seems to hide a smile; the forehead is high and smooth, partly hidden by light, waved hair; the eyes are timidly cast down; the nose is narrow, the cheeks round, the mouth small. The head, gracefully poised, is carried by a strong neck, which links its gentle inclination with the curve of the shoulder, as though a harmonious rhythm ran through the whole slim, coy figure. The high-necked dress with the bow underlines the girlish appearance of the young woman. Kokoschka had here succeeded in catching the youthful, romantic quality of a human being who inspired neither pity nor melancholy. In this picture he had proved that he was not a painter only of the sick and the poor. Yet here again he shows his particular gift for the rendering of 'personal attitude'—in this case youthful coyness, the reserve of a middle-class woman who neither could nor would let herself go, and perhaps the pensiveness of one who has unexpectedly discovered that respectability is not everything. Technically, too, Kokoschka had made progress: the shadow surrounding the figure is evidence of a new effort to enliven the background of his paintings; and the poise of the delightful head is so deliberate, so sure, that it foreshadows new possibilities for the painter's development.

In contrast to the portrait of Peter Altenberg, that of *Adolf Loos* (No. 19) represents an unexpected detachment: there is no dramatic gesture here, nor a lyrical transcription. The architect is treated objectively as a model who excites the painter's interest but not his emotions, well observed, studied, but not too much interpreted. He is seated with his hands joined, fixedly staring with eyes cast slightly downwards, like one listening intently or deep in thought. His eyes are asymmetrical—a feature common to most of Kokoschka's early pictures, and which considerably added to their vitality—and set in deep hollows; one of his eyebrows is raised as though in wonder, and its curve finds a swift continuation in the finely cut nose; the tight-lipped mouth and the square chin connote purposeful energy. The deep-set eyes and wavy hair give the portrait a quality of dreaminess, while the pose of the massive arms and the grip of the fingers create an impression of firmness and vigour. The painter describes his recollection of Loos's appearance at the time of this portrait as that of a man 'looking like Byron at Missolounghi'. In 1932[1] this portrait was still reproached with lacking resemblance to its model, at least in the ordinary sense of the word, by the director of the Berlin Nationalgalerie who, however, at the same time spoke of the painter's 'second sight'. It certainly bears witness to Kokoschka's gift of unusual penetration, for it appears to us today as a most realistic likeness: a comparison with a photograph[2] and a sketch which Kokoschka made of Loos in later years leaves no doubt as to its faithfulness. Apart from this it is masterly in composition, the oblong shape of the canvas being counterbalanced by the polygon which is formed by the sitter's arms and shoulders. The treatment of the surface reveals how free from the conventions of his art the painter had by that time become: the canvas is hardly covered in some places, while in others the colour is thickly applied; strong brush-strokes emphasise the outline, model the folds of the suit with calligraphic signs, animate hair and hands with a nervous vitality. The picture is dated 1909.

The portrait of *Bessie Loos* (No. 24) was obviously painted as a companion piece: the size of the canvas corresponds with that of her husband's portrait, and the model is seated in a similar pose, but this time the figure is leaning slightly to one side. Like some of Kokoschka's most attractive models the young woman is painted less with fervour than with delicacy. Only the treacherous spots on the cheeks, the lustrous lips in the pale face let one guess her morbid condition: one year after this portrait was finished she died of phthisis. The simplicity of her attire could hardly be surpassed: the greenish frock is close-fitting, long-sleeved, its severity broken only by the white collar, and the demure bow which covers the throat carries down the line of her centre parting. The seriousness of the face as well as the unpretentiousness of the dress hardly conform to the popular conception of a stage dancer: there is no glamour, no trace of

[1] Ludwig Justi in *Von Corinth bis Klee.*

[2] Reproduced in Adolf Loos: *Ins Leere Gesprochen*, Innsbruck, 1932, frontispiece.

XXVI. TEMPEST
1914

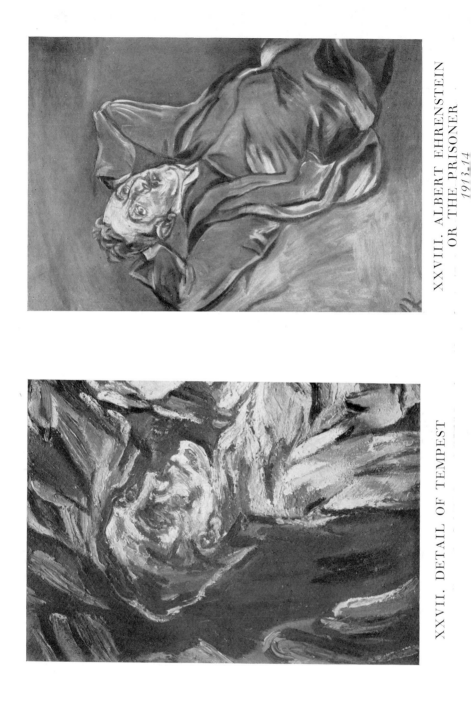

XXVIII. ALBERT EHRENSTEIN
OR THE PRISONER
1913-14

XXVII. DETAIL OF TEMPEST

frivolity, no feature that would not become a young school-mistress—except, perhaps, the fluffy hair that surrounds the face like a cloud. There is no violent brush-stroke in this picture, only subtle drawing and tender modelling. The sureness with which the slim figure is fitted into the broad oblong like a diagonal, dividing the surface into a lighter and a darker half, is proof that the young painter had a natural instinct for composition as well as a gift of psychological insight.

Painted in the same Swiss sanatorium as Bessie Loos was the portrait of *Count Verona* (No. 39). The critics who have con-demned the gloom of the artist's pictures may not always have remembered that some of them, to be sincere, must necessarily have borne the mark of despair: their subjects were sick men who were suffering, if not doomed to death. The Italian count with his large, lustreless eyes and underdeveloped chin might well be an illustration to Thomas Mann's novel *Der Zauberberg*, which describes the pathetic and grotesque inhabitants of a cos-mopolitan sanatorium for tubercular patients. But apart from physical marks of wasting decay there is no expression of suffer-ing in the painting; the artist had, unusually, been more struck by a certain picturesqueness in his sitter's appearance than by his psychological condition. The picturesqueness derived from the patient's ugliness, from the incongruity of his physical cir-cumstances and his background: the head, decadent and hollow like a skull, contrasted with the fat, ringed hands of a rich man, and with the exaggeratedly pointed finger tips. His hair was smoothly brushed, but his tie disarranged. The background of this picture is covered with light and dark patches, mysterious signs, mostly purely decorative, but forming in one place a pattern like the red print of a blood-stained hand. The attempt to enliven the background had here, as in several later pictures, given scope to the artist's playful and always symbolically inclined imagination.

Kokoschka's pictures of children probably enraged his critics more than anything else he did. There was one which he called *Newborn Child, held by the Hands of its Parents* (No. 22; Plate XII), in fact representing a child at the age of some months. From the mysterious way in which the child emerges from a nebulous background, from its large eyes and old expression this picture acquires an atmosphere of unreality. The soft structure of the face, on the other hand, the baby-like hands and the movement of the arms are rendered with that amazing sense of the characteristic with which the artist was endowed. The protective gesture of the two parents' hands, which do not really support the child, is purely symbolic.

Children Playing (No. 17; Plate VIII), the picture of the two children of the bookseller Dr. Stein whose own portrait was also exhibited, exemplifies a new method of composition: contrary to all convention the boy and his younger sister are lying on the floor, he absorbed by one of those moods which can make children appear so serious, the little girl looking straight out of the picture, with a curiously wistful expression. Nothing more child-like than these two faces, the four thin legs, the girl's straight, untidy hair and short frock can be imagined. Yet it is easy to visualise the horror caused by the painting, if one compares it with any of the pictures of children of the same period: for there is not the least effort here to make the models appear charming, pretty, or well-groomed; no beautiful flow of line, no mellow textures; yet there is no doubt that this is the way children behave at play when left to their own devices and on the nursery floor, leaning on one elbow or rolling on their tummies, when one happens to surprise them.

The *Portrait of a Boy* (No. 9; Plate V), the son of Oskar Reichel, one of the earliest collectors of Kokoschka's work, has a poetic rather than a realistic quality. The queer attitude of the boy, with one hand on his hip, while the other is held high up behind his head, may have no other purpose than to fill the square canvas; at the same time it repeats the broken lines of his *Dreaming Boys*, and it can therefore be assumed that it was painted very early in the artist's career. Although not one of his most successful compositions, the fine shape of the head and the expression of the over-large eyes imbue the picture with a peculiar beauty of its own.

It is difficult to establish exactly which other portraits by Kokoschka were exhibited at the Hagenbund on the same occasion. The catalogue mentions six further portraits of men and two of women. The men may have included the lawyer *Hugo Caro* (No. 29), whom he had painted in Munich; the *Painter Harta* (No. 20), whose portrait dated back to his earliest Vienna period; the *Marquis* (No. 37; Plate XVII), painted in Switzerland; *Dr. Rudolf Blümner* (No. 28), with whom he shared his attic in Berlin; or *Dr. Schwarzwald* (No. 56), whose portrait is inscribed on the back 'Etatis (*sic*) suae 40 AD 1911', so that it must at any rate have been finished some time during the year of the Hagenbund exhibition. The women represented may have included *Frau Hirsch* (No. 1), a young woman with unnaturally large, oblong eyes; or the actress *Else Kupfer* (No. 36; Plate XV), who was seated with a dog in her lap, her infinitely sad, and so very soft, feminine face gently echoed in the face of the animal —one of Kokoschka's most beautiful and most human portraits, more plastic than any other works of his of that period; or possibly one of them was *Frau Dr. K.* (No. 43), a bourgeois lady in a dark dress, her hair piled up high on her head and her neck enclosed in a high collar, a certain hardness in her features repelling our sympathy.

The catalogue further mentions the *Winter Landscape* (No. 26; Plate XIII), and a *Still-Life*, most likely that of the hyacinth and the tortoise (No. 4). Certain important pictures had, however, not been included in the exhibition, for one reason or another. In the case of the double-portrait of *Professor Hans Tietze and Frau Erica Tietze-Conrat* (No. 15; Plate VII), for instance, the owners never agreed to exhibit their picture; this was perhaps just as well, as this work, which is now regarded as one of Kokoschka's most impressive paintings, would only have caused the unsympathetic crowd of Vienna to jeer yet more loudly. The art historian, painted in profile, is depicted severely featured, with the moustache affected by the young intellectuals of those days and slightly bent as if labouring under some burden; his wife, whose main attractions were her beautiful dark eyes, full face, an erect and dominating figure: thus the two were drawn sitting at right angles, while their four hands, even more prominent in this painting than in most of Kokoschka's works, seem to form an almost mystical bridge between them—as if invisible currents ran between the fingertips of the man and those of the woman. The concentration of these two figures is so intense, the grouping of the hands so strangely significant that it is almost embarrassing to have to look on: this is a scene which has no need of witnesses. Yet the picture has a great appeal: its composition, the coordination of the two figures within so unusually long an oblong, is extraordinary, quite the young painter's own. The picture is noteworthy too for its background, which is covered with innumerable tiny figures scratched into the pigment, covering the surface with a network of little suns, rays, wires, dots and shadows functioning as the colour skeleton of the three-dimensional space. Obviously invented to defeat a sense of *horror vacui*, they seem to form a whole organic world in themselves, fore-

99

shadowing in fact some creations of Paul Klee who, years later, found in similar images both the subject matter and the formal starting point of whole pictures. In Kokoschka's painting they merely fill the background behind his figures, contributing to the mysterious atmosphere whose other components evade human perception.

Neither was the portrait of *Auguste Forel* (No. 33), which might have convinced some of the painter's adversaries of his capabilities, included in the Hagenbund exhibition. The portrait hardly does justice to the mental and moral powers of that great scholar and humanist, that religious free-thinker who had shown himself a hero in the fight against metaphysical dogma, who had introduced a new ethical conception of sexual problems and had made a unique contribution to the study of the brain, social hygiene and the evolution of society. Kokoschka had, however, produced a picture of a highly spiritualised human being, at the same time evolving to a very high degree the characteristic frailty and helplessness of old age. Forel was in reality only sixty when Kokoschka painted him; while this is the portrait of a man twenty years older, characterised by the stubbornness as well as the dignity of great age. When we remember the lack of personal understanding between subject and artist that comes out so clearly in Forel's comments on the picture, we realise how the portrait became what it is: the painter sensed a reluctance, a mistrust and a slight maliciousness in the demeanour of the scientist who sat to him, though he missed its real significance. The additional twenty years with which he burdened the old man were his unconscious vengeance. But as a composition the picture is perfect. And one feels at once that the gesture with which Forel is arranging his cuff with his thumb must have been a highly characteristic one.

Another picture not mentioned in the Hagenbund catalogue was the portrait of *The Duchess of Rohan-Montesquieu* (No. 38; Plate XVIII). Painted in Switzerland, it had been included in the exhibition of the Folkwang Museum, which later purchased it, and it is most probable that it was never taken to Austria. In composition it resembled the *Portrait of a Boy* (No. 9; Plate V) with the same long, narrow forms and broken outlines—the same angular contours as Modigliani, influenced by cubist painters, came to use after the war. The artist had been fascinated by the aristocratically sensitive, the almost ethereal quality of this foreign woman, whom he endowed with a strong intellectualism

100

rather than with emotional capacity. The face had the transparent quality and the delicate outlines of some old Flemish portrait; the butterfly, in sharp contrast to the black dress, scintillates with all imaginable colours. The obvious frailty of his model may have been due to her state of health—she was a consumptive like Bessie Loos.

Lastly, among Kokoschka's works which are likely to have been completed at this date but which were absent from the Hagenbund exhibition, is the whole series of Kokoschka's new group compositions. *The Flight into Egypt* (No. 49), *The Visitation* (No. 52), and *Knight, Death and Angel* (No. 35), had all been left behind in his studio. Had they been included they would have greatly added to the completeness of the survey offered here of the painter's development. The full story of the course of that development would have been revealed for all to read: how he had begun with such clumsy, almost shapeless figures as the so-called *Trance Player* (No. 5), solidly built up in front of sweetly coloured, rather Ensorian backgrounds, the most important features somewhat primitively emphasised by distinct outlines; how he later gained in psychological insight, became inclined to dramatise his subjects, but also began to model certain parts—eyelids, for instance, or cheek-bones—more roundly in order to explore the third dimension; how, at the time of his journey to Switzerland, he started to extend his compositions over the whole canvas, instead of concentrating it in one mass, filling it in with brush-strokes more like graphic signs than modelling accents, and how his work gained consequently in balance and decorativeness, while retaining his earlier depth—as exemplified by his *Winter Landscape* (No. 26; Plate XIII), the *Auguste Forel* (No. 33), and *Frau Lotte Franzos* (No. 18; Plate VI); how he achieved plasticity, most perfectly in the picture of *Else Kupfer* (No. 36; Plate XV), a portrait which at the same time represented a culmination of his power to paint without any visible effort a state of mind as naturally as a Renoir or a Manet rendered a colour-scheme; how gradually he acquired, as in his Berlin portraits of *Herwarth Walden* (No. 40), and *Paul Scheerbart* (No. 47), distance from his models. And finally one would have seen how he had begun to attach more importance to surface treatment, merging the figures into the background by a system of lines covering the whole like a net —a method that made his pictures of the 1911–13 period look almost like compositions built up in crystal, pale in colour, and iridescent as mother-of-pearl. His first group compositions, *The Visitation* and the *Knight, Death and Angel*, were thus half hidden behind a nebulous system of lines. It would have been apparent that he had gradually become interested in movement and gesture, and that he had simultaneously been seized by the dual ambition to follow in the footsteps of the old masters and to paint religious subjects. The *Knight, Death and Angel* was an obvious paraphrase of Dürer's *Ritter, Tod und Teufel*, an engraving which could always be found in almost any German house. Kokoschka's version of the subject repeats the strongly expressive gesture of one of his own drawings, *Gesindel in der Sternennacht*.[1] In the *Visitation* the same gesture recurs once more, this time even more musical, almost audible and strangely evocative. This painting was an instance of the daring which Kokoschka brought to his interpretations of traditional sacred subjects. He was probably the first artist ever to represent one of the two women naked or to make of their meeting a subject for such startlingly dramatic treatment.

The interval between the artist's first appearance in public and this exhibition was but three years. His development within so short a space of time could be called considerable. It was not, naturally, a smoothly continuous progress; its irregularity, in fact, accounts for the confusion evidenced in attempts to date certain of his pictures for many years. *The Duchess of Rohan-Montesquieu* (No. 38; Plate XVIII), for instance, in spite of its exotic quality, looks like a very early work: but we know that it was painted in Switzerland, that is, in the winter of 1909–10; the *Forel* portrait, finished in the beginning of 1910, seems infinitely more mature; while the *Rudolf Blümner*, though it appears to be the work of a comparative beginner, and might be ascribed to the *Trance Player* period, cannot have been painted before 1910–11, when Kokoschka first met the actor in Berlin.

In 1911 the time was not in any case ripe for an objective consideration of Kokoschka's work. Opinions were sharply divided, and the painter was defended by his friends and attacked by his detractors with equal fervour. Dr. Tietze, for instance, writing in 1919, said: 'The Hagenbund exhibition of 1911, in which a small group of Austrian artists made their first appearance, has remained one of the strongest artistic impressions and recollections of many a member of my generation. . . . Through this exhibition, in which the works of Kokoschka, already grown

[1] Rabble in a Starry Night. See *Der Sturm* of September 15, 1910.

102

out of his first, wild unsteadiness, were to be seen . . . I became a writer on modern art. . . . Not all have kept what they seemed to promise in that hour . . . but Kokoschka's mastery, the sign of which was then already imprinted upon his work, visible to all those who could see, is today no longer seriously disputed.'[1]

A long article on Oskar Kokoschka by Franz Grüner was published in the friendly *Fackel* of the 28th February 1911, containing a searching analysis of the artist's principles of composition. Grüner says, for instance, of Kokoschka's use of colour: 'The harmonisation of the colours is attained by means of the strongly prominent contours which separate them: to put it crudely and schematically, the colours in many, and in some of the best, pictures are applied in stripes which run from the top to the bottom . . . they are light and thin, and by this linear system they are divided into strokes and dots in such a way that none of them appears as a unified, heavy mass.' Here too we find the following description of the *Children Playing* (No. 17; Plate VIII): 'The theme of the picture is a rhythmical fluctuation between red and brown. . . .'

But the day had not come yet when critics, referring to Kokoschka's achievements, would speak of 'second sight', 'magic', 'vivisection', 'X-rays', 'the eyes of the Hypnotist', or 'demoniac powers'. People were repelled by the unusual in these pictures, the origin of which they did not recognise: but it was sympathy and, one may say, a fraternal feeling towards a suffering humanity, which inspired the young artist. He had discovered what, even though rarely noticed, lies open in the faces of so many twentieth-century men and women: their restlessness, uncertainty, anxiety, self-consciousness, fear and loneliness. Once he had realised what the faces of his friends expressed, he was filled with fear for them; but at the same time was seized by an indomitable urge to relieve his own fears and uncertainties by fixing theirs on his canvas. This was the essence of his relationship to people: that he wanted to paint them. The circle of his friends, or rather their faces, was his microcosm. This is why he was satisfied for many years to represent nobody but his intimates, the few people who surrounded him. It was sometimes a cause of real suffering to him to be so haunted by familiar faces, and there was no other remedy but to reproduce them in colour on canvas, to give form to their spirits. The young Kokoschka was never primarily interested in æsthetic problems. It

[1] *Die Bildenden Künste*, 1919, p. 136.

was this that distinguished him from all previous painters with the possible exception of Munch—which chiefly constituted his originality. What colour combinations, light and textures were to the Impressionists, his model's human experience and foibles were to Kokoschka. Compared with him even Van Gogh might be said to have rendered human beings as though he were painting still-lifes, while Cézanne's portraits might seem mere experiments in structure. But Kokoschka knew no *nature morte*. He approached mankind not in the way typical of most Western artists, but more like a Russian or a Scandinavian: his perception was that of Dostoievsky,[1] Ibsen or Strindberg. Had he not been obsessed by the brush which he came to handle with great mastery, and had he not inherited that sense of colour which seems, mysteriously, to be second nature in the upper Danube regions, his gifts of observation and his imagination might have found an outlet in psychological writing. A literary tendency remained, in fact, always alive in Kokoschka, and this bent has even to be considered as one of the most important components in his make-up as an artist. But this is how Kokoschka himself reflects on his relationship to his art: 'A student's tendency always remained alive in me since my first public speech in 1911 in the Musikvereinssaal on the theme *Bewusstsein der Gesichte*. My curiosity was directed towards the ways in which human beings, on their way from the cradle to the grave, are transformed into an ill-at-ease specimen of an average grown-up of this century. I found a wrongly managed mass-education to be a possible explanation of the phenomenon that modern men do not know the origin of their malcontent, do not even know how to find it. Still I am compelled to agree with the government of these masses, whose attention I tried to draw to this problem, that the time is not yet ripe for considering the merits attributed to rational education. During the Thirty Years religious war, 300 years ago, the inventor of the method of rational mass-schooling, the pacifist Jan Amos Comenius, received the same answer from the governments then in power. As in this book my individual experiences in life shall be told (rather to my discomfort) to a large audience, I cannot resist mentioning that they must not be understood as adventures of a bravado, but rather as a

[1] The fact that Dostoievsky played a part in the art history of Central Europe is well established: Erich Heckel, for instance, painted *The Brothers Karamasov* in 1912, and the Czech artist Vlastislav Hofmann produced a series of imaginative portraits in charcoal of figures from the writer's work.

104

student's way to put his own nature to the test for the sake of a more direct control over the experiment. The device of an ancient Greek philosophy "Know thyself" was guiding me as soon as I was mature enough to realise that it was all I had received from the hands of the Gods. I was following up primarily two motives, which I saw reappearing like threads in the weft of modern society: to what limits will individual nature flexibly accommodate itself and how rigid is the framework of modern society. For instance, when I became a soldier in the first World War and when I asked myself, how did I come into the situation of being ordered to kill other people, entirely indifferent to me, something fundamentally foreign to me, I simply discarded complicity with society for the reason that these grown-ups had become man-slayers. So I offered my body to the kill! Was it not the original form of sacrifice? Obviously they acted according to the law that senility links up with infancy. Thus in avoiding complicity in the common crime I felt guiltless and free from the consequent remorse in the Christian sense. Since I grew up a second World War bids me argue against a repetition of my former attitude. The sense of being "unclean" had been successfully allayed through my former psychological situation in which I even meant to expiate the evil done by others, due to my isolated case. This way of thinking leaves me with doubts today. The question is, are there still restrictions (and of what nature?) being obeyed in war to make the white man feel "clean"? Are we still allowed to pose the question whether the unchristian break of all human rules in modern warfare is felt to make us "unclean"? It is at this point in the development of group life that the white man's path gradually leads him beyond the primitive conception of society. To observe this phenomenon needs more than the average democrat's wit, more than the expert's profound analysis of myth, more than an individual life's potential instincts: what our generation does so far is turning around like blind mice. In the main we avoid human life, with the alternative of committing suicide or becoming a robot.

'The man I meet in life is my problem. It will remain so and therefore it makes no difference to me whether I paint or write about him. He is the central figure in my thoughts because there are no egoistic interests to blur my vision. I myself am only interested in myself when I am human as the others are.'

Once more, as in the year of the first *Kunstschau*, it was a play that crowned the scandal of the Hagenbund exhibition of 1911. Its title was *Der Brennende Dornbusch*.[1] It was like a continuation of the first one, or like another, maturer version of the same theme: the relationship between man and woman, or the polarity of the spirit and the flesh. Such problems were very much in the air at a time when Strindberg and Otto Weininger, the author of *Geschlecht und Character*, were so heatedly discussed. Once more, as in his earlier plays, there is no plot, not even a situation, only a dialogue. The greater part is spoken by the woman; the language is an expression of passion rather than of thought. The old story of the two sexes, their mutual attraction and repulsion, is compressed into its most elementary form. The woman, lonely in a moon-lit night, yearns for the man who is to redeem her; 'during the day I am a doubtful being akin to man; only at night-time man blows his breath into me . . .', and she dreams: 'Oh miraculous men who, out of ghosts, made women who bear life.' By the strength of her desire she draws man to her, and their first encounter is sweet: 'Close thine eyes, thy wounds—I have found thee . . . now kindle thy light at my love, and thy body will sustain it. Tired of the quest as thou art, thou hast given thyself to me. Even so thou hast become thyself. . . .' But she, who has become dependent and submissive, does not want him to leave; and when he tears himself away, she becomes a destructive force crying for revenge: 'A white bird is fluttering through my room, it has hacked my eyes . . . a red fish has drunk my blood. . . .' The first curtain falls while an onlooking 'professor' remarks: 'Earthly love is but an agony, a rose thorn in the path that leads to the door of Golgotha.' But the stricken woman cannot forget the man: 'Woe to me! He lives somewhere with my strength—I am sore—I am weak—' A chorus of men and women, as in the first play, helps her in her search for the man. In their choruses he has become 'a metallic man' and she 'an animal who ate of his heart'. The second meeting of the two is full of discord, but still blessed with moments of happiness: 'My body is a burning fire-bush; thou, man, art its nourishing wind. . . . My hands are hot wings, my feet burning coal—white and red—white and red I burn; in a fire garment of long pain, glowing with shame I burn but do not perish. Come to me, extinguish and redeem me.' But she is also reproachful; 'Why art thou not good—man who crushed me with desire? I know thou wilt be my wooer and

---

[1] The Burning Bush.

liberator—I, who am impure, unknown—And thou art my enemy, my jailer.' And seized by sudden fury she throws a stone at him. While he falls she calls out: 'I know thee no more!' The man, wounded and weakening, now takes the beggar's part: 'Have mercy! Thou who hast loved now injurest me. See my life escape with my blood! The earth can hardly drink up the strength which runs from me. Now thou leavest me to perish. . . . Sister, dry my brow!' And she can now say: 'I suffer with thee.'

Like *Hoffnung der Frauen* this is a drama of man and woman who yearn and search for each other, meet and separate, reunite, hurt and curse one another, steal each other's strength and at last cause each other's death. But while the first play ended on a note of destruction and discord, *Der Brennende Dornbusch* resolves itself in a harmony only reached through common suffering and common guilt.

The two plays, produced at an interval of two years, had much in common: apart from the fact that they were both composed in the form of a continuous dialogue only intermittently broken by the voice of the chorus, they were written round the same problem and in the same rhythmical prose, only now and then changing for a few lines into formal verse. The language of both was that of poetry and symbolism. In *Der Brennende Dornbusch*, as in *Hoffnung der Frauen*, the unspeakable was spoken, with a simplicity that lifted it beyond any suspicion of obscenity. It should have been at least acceptable to a public that revelled in the more equivocal cabaret jokes. But directness was more feared than ambiguity by the false modesty of those sheltered pre-war days; all the efforts that were made by artists, here and there, to penetrate to the roots of human action were fore-doomed to lead to those scandals which marked the development of artistic life in the period before and after the turn of the century. The reception accorded to Kokoschka in Vienna was in the tradition of the outbreaks of public fury that had been let loose on Ibsen and Strindberg and which had been the cause of Gustav Klimt's retirement into private life. The events of the last few years had made the authorities of the Hapsburg capital particularly circumspect; the police demanded to see the notorious Kokoschka's new play before it was publicly performed, and the inevitable happened: it was stopped during the dress rehearsal. *Der Brennende Dornbusch* was never shown in public until the German revolution of 1918 had displaced many conventions.

Kokoschka's works, written as well as painted, had always been reflections of personal impressions. But *Der Brennende Dornbusch* had given immediate expression to an experience which was to leave its mark on him for a very long time. It must have been shortly after 1911 that he first met the person who was to have a greater influence on his life and outlook than anyone—except for his mother and Adolf Loos—whom he had known before. During the next ten years, the same figure appeared again and again in his drawings and paintings: a tall, fair woman with large, dark eyes, a strong chin, regular clear-cut features and proud bearing. This woman was well known in the Hapsburg capital: she was the widow of one of Austria's most celebrated artists and herself a famous beauty. She had married when she was a very young girl, and had become a kind of queen of artistic Vienna, for she was not only the attractive wife of a famous man in a high position: she was intelligent, highly cultured, strong-minded, so gifted as to challenge comparison with those women of the Renaissance who, by beauty and intelligence, had ruled over their age. After she became a widow she had continued to play her part as a woman of society and as a member of an artistic circle which thrived in close relation with the wealthy bourgeoisie. She was in fact one of the most brilliant of hostesses Vienna had known in modern times. In her *salon* one met outstanding people in every walk of life: ministers, politicians, artists, æsthetes, financial magnates and foreign visitors were her guests. To Kokoschka, who had spent his life among the poorer Bohemians or moved among a clientèle to whose standard of living he did not aspire, she seemed to belong to a different class: but he was more dazzled by her beauty and the fact that she had chosen him, the poor painter, as her closest companion, than by the style in which she lived, her knowledge of the great world, her expensive clothes, her apartment, the box she occupied in the opera, her horse-drawn carriage. He was conscious that 'she belonged to him when their eyes met for the first time'. Yet it was probably the woman who first felt drawn to the young man—the focus of so much public attention—because she recognised the stamp of genius in him. In Kokoschka she must have found a personality measurable against her own. She and Kokoschka had more in common than is usual between a man and a woman; they were indeed so similar in character, that violent conflicts were inevitable. In the beginning Kokoschka, who was the

108

younger of the two, was willing to acknowledge in her a person equal to himself. He learnt more from her about the world, society, and human relationships than any man could ever have taught him. They travelled to Tyrol and Italy. He painted her, and himself with her. To please her he went back to an art which he had not practised since his Wiener Werkstätte days: he decorated six fans telling their story, showing himself and his friend like two actors on a miniature stage. She was the heroine of three plays which he wrote during the next few years, as well as of all his graphic cycles, and the pivot on which turned all this thoughts and emotions. Yet this relationship was from the beginning fated to be one of discord rather than of harmony. Both were distinguished by the most brilliant gifts that the gods might be said to give. But they behaved too much as if they were gods themselves: their liaison was reminiscent of the tempestuous intercourse of the Olympians who were none of them ever ready to forgo a privilege, or to renounce precedence even in favour of the most illustrious of their fellows. Both watched jealously over their independence. The tension between man and woman, which at the time of his first play he had more guessed at than known, became terribly real: he lived with the fear of losing himself, his strength and his creative power under her influence, without being able—and without really wishing—to free himself. In the Naples aquarium, when he took her there, he saw an insect overpowering its victim by a sting in the nerve centre, paralysing it ready to be devoured: at once he associated this drama with himself and the woman at his side. He began to fear and hate her, though he could not give her up. She too was in a similar dilemma: she was afraid that this young man whom she had honoured with her affection would outgrow her influence and become more indispensable to her than she was to him, and to a woman like her death would be preferable to such a fate.

Admiration, love, happiness, humiliation, quarrels, anger and paroxysms of fury did not hinder the artist's work. On the contrary, it was during his closest intimacy with this friend that Kokoschka matured as an artist and finally found himself. He painted, drew and wrote. It was during these years that his fame was firmly established. In 1911 he had illustrated *Tubutsch*, a new book by a young poet, Albert Ehrenstein (Fig. 10). The same year he had taken charge of the Austrian section of *Der Sturm*, where his name was always in evidence, either under one of his drawings or as the subject of some critical note. But in

1912 Herwarth Walden arranged a second exhibition of Kokoschka's work in Berlin; on this occasion even the journal *Kunst
und Künstler*, which was almost entirely devoted to a cult of
French and German Impressionists, had to take notice of him.[1]
In the same year he was invited to take part in an international
exhibition arranged by the Sonderbund at Cologne. Hung here
side by side with Picasso, a new discovery to the German public,
and with the German Expressionists, Kokoschka appeared among
the pioneers. The recognition which he had already found in the
Reich became more general. Although his reputation could not
penetrate to a wide public before a politicial revolution—that of
1918—had made it ripe for the acceptance of a new cultural life,
Kokoschka was steadily gaining ground. The acclamations of the
most authoritative publications proved it. The art critic of the
Zeitschrift für Bildende Künste wrote: 'The Austrian room contains a great surprise for many: Kokoschka is a most original
young man, is the first Viennese painter in whom one can say
there is genius. He is by no means to everybody's taste, for he
possesses exceptional individuality. Probably Germany has seen
nothing so wild and fantastic expressed in colours since the death
of Grünewald.'[2] In 1913—five years after the first *Kunstschau*—
the first monograph on Kokoschka was published, Paul Stefan's
Oskar Kokoschka: Dramen und Bilder;[3] it contained three plays
—*Hoffnung der Frauen, Sphinx und Strohmann* and *Der Brennende Dornbusch*, at that time still called *Schauspiel*, for want of
a title—and a selection from Kokoschka's paintings and drawings.
This was the final confirmation of his prominence. From then
onwards reproductions of his more important works appeared
frequently in the leading art journals, and the comments which
accompanied them had quite a new tone. When his works were
shown, together with those of Munch, Picasso and the Swiss
Karl Hofer, in the Berlin Herbstausstellung of 1913 the critic
of the old-established magazine *Kunst und Dekoration*[4] wrote:

[1] Kokoschka's name appeared for the first time in *Kunst und Künstler* in
1910, when Franz Servaes reviewed Vienna's young artists and wrote:
'Kokoschka is the only one for whom one would sincerely wish that he
may find the way to Klimt: that he might awake from his barbarian in-
toxication with ugliness, to a purified feeling for form.'

[2] Paul Ferdinand Schmidt, in Vol. XXIII (N.F.), p. 229.

[3] Published by the Kurt Wolff Verlag, Leipzig. 64 pages accompanied by
27 plates.

[4] Vol. XXIII (1913–14).

10. TUBUTSCH
1911

'Oskar Kokoschka stands out by the noble calm and by the characterisation of his portraits. . . .'

The painting of portraits was still Kokoschka's most frequent task, and his sitters were always members of the artistic or bohemian circle in which he moved. In the period between his return from Berlin and the outbreak of the first world war he painted *Karl Ettlinger* (No. 59), the actor; *The Singer Ennehjlem* (No. 58); *The Actor Sommaruga* (No. 66); the composer *Anton von Webern* (No. 68, 97), who was a friend and pupil of Arnold Schönberg; and another modern musician and music historian, *Egon Wellesz* (No. 53); he did a new drawing of *Karl Kraus* (No. 60), as well as one of the dancer *Nijinsky* (No. 61; Plate XIX), who appeared at the Vienna Opera. Kokoschka began to approach his subjects in a new way. He concentrated less on their idiosyncrasies, and was less intent on making an emotional appeal; instead he was becoming more interested in the surface-treatment of his pictures; he filled his canvas lovingly, caressed it, adorned it, wasted no inch of it. He had been seized by the fascination which material and tools can exercise on the craftsman who has learnt to get the best out of them. Now that he had surmounted the initial stage of being overwhelmed by his vision, whether or not the means of execution were at his command, technical experiments had begun to play a greater part in his work. He had bought himself a prism with which he studied the colours of the spectrum; those colours he used in his canvases to create the impression of depth and shadow. The opaque colouring of Kokoschka's pictures in this period was the direct result of these experiments with his prism. He no longer scratched lines into the colour surface, as he had done from 1908–10 or a little later, in order to overcome his *horror vacui*; nor did he in these years between 1911–14 endow faces with those thinly drawn wrinkles which followed the lines formed by characteristic facial movements; concentrated where nerves and veins lie close under the skin, they had made his earlier works so expressive—and often so old. He modelled every head as a whole, emphasising the main outlines rather than the details. He still preferred to include both, or at the least, one hand in his portraits, to accentuate his characterisation; but he now was capable of portraying a sitter in a study of the head and shoulders only.

From the point of view of composition the most important innovation of this period which began with Kokoschka's return

112

XXIX. KNIGHT ERRANT
1915

XXX. SELF-PORTRAIT
1917

from Berlin in 1911, was the double portrait. He had made two attempts at this type of picture at the outset of his career: the portrait of *Dr. Tietze and his Wife* (No. 15; Plate VII), and *Children Playing* (No. 17; Plate VIII); ingenious as these had been, they bore the stamp of inexperience. This can hardly be said of the *Sposalizio* (No. 71; Plate XVI) which Kokoschka painted in 1912 or 1913. Although it clearly sprang from the artist's own observation, in composition this picture of his two friends is reminiscent of certain impressionist works which are also portraits in the setting of a café and which we know from Renoir, Degas and Toulouse-Lautrec. The inevitable table and glass which figure in all the French paintings are here too; but the parallel does not go beyond externals and the emphasis is quite different. In the works of the French Impressionists the setting is still so important as to make portraits into genre-pictures. In the *Sposalizio* the setting has gone, but for the table with a glass and a book on it to suggest the scene. They have no background, yet the two figures, suspended, as it were, in immaterial space, are complete in themselves. The woman has all the tender delicacy so beautifully manifest in the earlier portrait of *Frau Lotte Franzos*. The man, who wears the unconventional dress affected by some artists, is chiefly characterised by the firm grip of his big hands as he presents his future wife, and at the same time demonstrates that he is taking possession of her. The young woman's gesture, pointing to her engagement ring, is an example, in a simple form, of a device often found in Kokoschka's work: the symbolism which was to be at times the content of his paintings. Although the *Sposalizio* was first and foremost a portrait, Kokoschka's tendency towards symbolism is illustrated both in this pointing to the ring and in the title he gave the picture.

Another experiment in a similar direction is his *Two Nudes* (No. 70): two women, one kneeling and supporting the other, are depicted in a hardly discernible landscape. This study is so obviously an exercise in technique that it retains little value as an artistic conception. But it foreshadows a new development in the artist's 'hand-writing'. Long, vigorous brush-strokes draw together the parts and emphasise movement and form. The painstaking and minute application of colour is a thing of the past, and so is its distribution in crystal-shapes.

The same technique is more advanced in the *Blind Mother* (No. 75). The subject is one which might have attracted Kokoschka in his earliest years of absorption in psychological and humanitarian problems; but both composition and the new technique are proof that it belongs in the immediate pre-war period. The old manner has gone, but the expressiveness of the *Blind Mother* demonstrates that Kokoschka's dramatic power was by no means impaired: the wide open, blind eyes, the peasant simplicity of her appearance, her grey blouse, her worn, hard-working hands, the one deep line that runs from her mouth downwards, and the way she sits, firmly holding and rocking the child in her lap, are unsurpassed in realism as well as in their emotional appeal—an emotional appeal which yet makes no concession to sentimentality. This picture of a mother, holding her embryo-like child in her arms enclosed as though it were still part of her own body, was the first of a series on the 'Mother and Child' theme to which Kokoschka has reverted again and again during his career.

★   ★   ★

1913 was the date of Kokoschka's second *Self-Portrait* (No. 80; Plate XXI). Comparison with the first, which he had finished one or two years before, reveals the great progress the painter had made in these years. In composition it harks back to that early poster in which his head was shown as a kind of barbarian mask: both are three-quarter profile portraits of head, breast and shoulders, one hand—in the poster the left and here the right—pointing to his breast, as though to draw attention to himself. Only the eyes are turned in a different direction. As in the first *Self-Portrait*, the head is exaggeratedly elongated, and the expression one of very youthful seriousness. But while in the earlier painting the face had been half hidden behind a network of lines and so delicate that it resembled a reflection in a dimmed mirror, the features are now clearly outlined and the whole figure vigorously modelled: the head rests firmly on the strong neck, the forehead is bulky, the nose broad and flat, the abnormally long chin cleft by a deep furrow down the middle; and the hand is so plastic as to attract the beholder's attention in the same degree as the face itself. The first picture had been built up with the pale, iridescent crystal shapes of the period immediately following Kokoschka's return from Berlin; in the second work he abandoned that manner completely, in favour of a more direct approach to the subject, closer to the spontaneity of his earliest paintings; but his former concern with psychological problems had now yielded to a conscious search for a congenial form of expression. In this second *Self-Portrait* can be seen the renewed beginnings of his struggle with a new task that was never again to lose its fascination for him: that of creating an impression of spatial depth on the picture surface. His experiments with the prism, although undertaken with the same purpose in view, had resulted in images like phantoms, transparent but somewhat shapeless. His new technique of applying local colour enabled him to create several planes, to emphasise elevated parts, and to indicate highlights as well as shadows. There was now hardly any trace of line drawing left in his painting; the roundness and feeling for the structure of the body, on the contrary, endowed his figures with the quality of sculpture. At the same time this *Self-Portrait* was filled with a new spirit; the poetic youth of one or two years before had become a temperamental, strong-willed young man, no longer a dreamer, but more than ever dramatising himself and the world around him. The softness of the large eyes and the slightly opened lips give the picture a romantic interest that is enhanced by the intense blue of its colouring. This was the first painting in which Kokoschka used the blue, somewhere between the shade of the Mediterranean sky and a mist-grey, which always remained his favourite colour and which so often reappeared in his self-portraits.

Close upon the *Self-Portrait* of 1913 followed Kokoschka's *Double-Portrait*, showing himself and the woman he loved (No. 76). This painting was perhaps his most extraordinary achievement up to that date. From an iconographical point of view it belongs to that series of self-portraits of artists with their wives which begins with Israhel van Meckenem's engraving of about 1490 and leads up to Rubens's and Rembrandt's double-portraits in Munich and Dresden. But while the Rubens is a representational, almost formal picture, and the Rembrandt a manifestation of exuberant happiness, the Kokoschka is a much more intimate and, at the same time, more abstract work: for though it represents Oskar Kokoschka and his friend in a relationship so personal that one can hardly believe it to have been destined for public view, the two figures seem to stand also for man and woman in general, just as the men and women in Kokoschka's plays are always abstractions rather than individuals. The painting can, in fact, be called an illustration to the plays, just as the plays can be considered as a background to the painting. 'She and I' were the two poles around which the artist's thoughts and

115

emotions persistently centred; he saw them now united and in harmony, now separated, in contrast to one another. They were the subject of his works as well as their inspiration. It was the case of a complete interpenetration of an artist's life with his art: nobody could say where the one ended and the other began.

The man and woman in the *Double-Portrait* are represented facing each other, but both looking out of the picture, the man one step nearer and therefore lower on the canvas than the woman. They are both dressed in loose coats, which seem informal as well as somewhat indefinite; the man's is of that blue colour which Kokoschka liked to wear in his self-portraits, while the woman is dressed in a pale coral red. In their long, square jaws and their large, dark eyes is a certain likeness as between a brother and sister, while the evident closeness of their relationship is rather that of man and wife. There is a dignity and emphasis in their attitude suggestive of classic drama rather than of modern life. There is no detail, no immaterial feature to detract from the grandeur of these two figures which are unique in the history of painting. Yet both portraits were peculiarly realistic in their own way: the woman appears as the magnificent and powerful creature she was known to be in real life, while the painter, even compared with his *Self-Portrait* of earlier in the same year, looks older, more haggard, his eyes no longer searching, but sadly knowing, his whole figure more set than before.

A portrait of the woman (No. 78) alone was painted in the same year. At a first glance it is suggestive of another portrait, famous in the history of art: Leonardo's *Gioconda*. Kokoschka never hesitated to draw his inspirations from any source available to him; for in contrast to most of his contemporaries he placed himself with full consciousness into the tradition of European painting. There is no doubt that he had the Louvre picture in mind when he began to portray his friend, and that the resemblance was an intentional, meaningful one. The woman is seated in the same position as Mona Lisa though her hands are not included; her loose hair covers her neck and shoulders with fair waves, and she wears a dress with the same neckline as that worn by the Italian model; the resemblance is carried into her features, her eyes, eyebrows, nose, lips and chin: and even a mountainous landscape is indicated in the background. Yet the imitation was not a slavish one: it was a deliberate experiment, one of those acts of symbolism to which Kokoschka has always been addicted. A painter who had a modest opinion of himself would not have attempted a paraphrase that might be taken almost as sacrilege; but Kokoschka had by then been acclaimed as a genius by his friends and had found followers among the younger artists; and he was still young enough himself to aim very high. Those whom an experiment of this kind might annoy will observe with satisfaction that the sin brought its inescapable punishment: the Viennese lady, in spite of her renowned beauty, was no Gioconda, and Kokoschka was too good an artist to falsify nature for the sake of a significant but playful parallel; Mona Lisa's serious, knowing and evasive smile is exchanged for a wary, even a hostile, look. There is more than a hint of malice in the sweetness of the smile. In spite of these unpleasant features, which might easily have turned the picture into a parody, some of the mysteriousness and of the innate beauty of the prototype is preserved in the modern painting.

Three landscape paintings which originated during these last pre-war years are the remaining documents of Kokoschka's travels with his companion. One of these had taken them to Naples. A view of that city (No. 79)—the first of Kokoschka's extensive series of 'townscapes'—revealed how even the peace of a Mediterranean panorama could not calm the storms which were incessantly raging in the painter's mind: not only the waves of the sea and the sky flickered with disquieting lights; even the buildings, and particularly the cupolas of two churches, seemed to rock under the percussions of an earthquake. The wide landscape, built up in three spheres—land, sea and sky occupying three well-balanced zones—was a piece of most accomplished painting. This work, which has been much illustrated, was irretrievably lost in the fire which destroyed the Munich Glaspalast together with its contents in the summer of 1931.

The *Alpine Landscape* (No. 74) and *Tre Croci* (No. 90) were done in the Dolomites. The latter is of a meadow enclosed by fantastically rugged mountains, with a grazing horse and a horse-drawn cart that moves towards the pine-trees in the distance. For the first time the painter has here renounced all the usual structural aids, such as *repoussoirs*, all artificial division into fore-, middle- and background and thus gained a complete unity of composition. There is the same restlessness as in the *Naples* picture; soil, trees and mountains all seem to quiver under the hectic

117

emotions which guided the brush. Like all such dynamic land-scapes this one, of course, could hardly exist without the pre-cedent of Van Gogh. But there is no doubt that Kokoschka, who certainly knew the great Dutchman's work, only came to paint in a similar vein because he was at that time in a similar state of mind. That the art of Van Gogh should strike a chord in the breast of the most gifted painter of the generation just born when he died[1] was one of those historic coincidences from which movements may often arise; in this case the result was the school of expressionism. Van Gogh's style has been so greatly trans-formed by Kokoschka, however, as to prove that he had merely pointed the way. At that time Kokoschka's palette too contained only a very limited range of colours compared with the Dutch painter's variety, particularly of light pigments. Deep blues, greens and greys dominated in his pictures instead of Van Gogh's bright yellows, reds and greens. That both painters had the flame-like brush-stroke in common may have been due to the fact that they both poured all the fervour of their emotions into an art that was the only thread which bound their unruly natures to an indifferent, unmanageable world.

The most significant picture that Kokoschka painted during this decisive phase of his life was the *Tempest* (No. 98; Plates XXVI and XXVII). No prototype, no tradition had inspired this composition which sprang from the artist's most personal experi-ences alone, from his feverish imagination and his unique power to translate thoughts and emotions into pictorial form. It shows a man and woman reclining in a boat—the woman peacefully resting on the man's shoulder, while he is alert and wears the expression of one who is aware but powerless. These two seem to be driven along as the angels and saints of baroque paintings are wafted through the skies by some irresistible force. In the world of modern painting this depiction of passion, at once con-crete and symbolic, was new: there is no other painting that attempts so direct a representation of human destiny. It has often been proclaimed that the Expressionists sought to represent the metaphysical world which they assumed to lie behind visible phenomena, to represent, in other words, things that can be made visible by symbols only. The *Tempest* has always been re-garded as one of the main works of that school. Yet, like all of Kokoschka's works, its character is so individual that it can hardly be claimed by any school or movement; symbolism is only

[1] Kokoschka was born in 1886, Van Gogh died in 1890.

one of its elements, while realism is the other, and of no less importance.[1]

The portrait likenesses in the *Tempest* have always been recognised. But there is little detail in this composition which is, more than anything else, a fixation of movement on canvas and, as such, an achievement never surpassed by the contemporary Futurists who regarded themselves as the painters of movement. The colours, among which greys and blues predominate, serve to render the mood which is one of complete abandonment. The picture is a hymn, a song of love and of glory in life which is here accepted in its entirety—a compound of terrors and joys. The woman in this picture might appear beautiful to some, and witch-like to others: to the painter she was both. The picture represented his Walpurgis night. Imagination and reality are so closely combined in this work that any attempt at exact interpretation will inevitably fail. But it certainly demonstrates that the artist had, at the moment of the greatest turbulence in his personal life, achieved the artistic powers which enabled him to exorcise the chaos of his own emotions by transferring them to a general, more abstract plane.

In the same year 1914 Kokoschka painted a *Still-Life with Cat* (No. 96). This was the first picture in which he let his imagination go further than he could justly expect general understanding to follow. The painting is a pictorial riddle, each of its three figures having a symbolic meaning. The cat is the clue: she has a human face which is turned mockingly towards the sulking boy with the man's head in the left corner—and one has to know that Kokoschka liked to compare his friend's face with a cat's before one can interpret the enigma. The setting is a landscape with a mountain, a castle and a river—vague reminiscences of a journey. The white rabbit in the centre watches the two like a looming spectre. In the background appears a ghostly figure in a boat—a vision of the past that would not recede, or a messenger from that abode of departed spirits which had begun to occupy the painter's mind at the time of the outbreak of war and which, four years later, was to be the theme of his next play, *Orpheus*.

While the most important works which Kokoschka created during the last pre-war years were those in which his personal experiences were reflected, he also painted some pictures of the

[1] The German title, *Die Windsbraut*, while standing for 'gale' or 'tempest', contains also a poetical allusion: literally translated it means 'the wind's bride'.

kind which had made him famous: portraits of such friends as the painter *Carl Moll* (No. 88), *Dr. Schwarzwald* (No. 107), whom he had already painted in 1911; the poet *Albert Ehrenstein* (No. 84; Plate XXVIII), whose *Tubutsch* he had illustrated in 1911; a double-portrait of *Brother and Sister* (No. 94), the saddest picture of two children he ever did; and some commissioned portraits: one of the writer *Victor von Dirsztay* (No. 83), and another of the wife of a champagne dealer, later often called *Lady with Feather Hat* (No. 95). They all show that new technique which Kokoschka had adopted and developed in the last year or two: a nervous but decided brush-stroke, applied in heavy *impasto*, broadly outlining the main features in the face and the folds in the garments, and sweeping across the background without leaving room for the meaningful hieroglyphs which had animated his earliest works. The portrait of *Albert Ehrenstein* particularly gives proof of a newly acquired virtuosity. Leaning back informally on a bed or couch, with his hands folded behind his head and his eyes looking pensively before him, the figure cuts diagonally across the picture like the couple in the *Tempest*, and the composition shows, in its own way, the same boldness as that other work. The modelling of the bulgy suit with a few strokes of colour is as masterly as the characterisation of Ehrenstein's arrogant and intelligent features.

★   ★   ★

During the three years between Kokoschka's return from Berlin and the outbreak of the first world war his productiveness seemed almost unbounded. Oil paintings alone could not satisfy his urge to give form to the manifold pictures which his imagination created with such overwhelming swiftness; he began therefore to experiment more persistently in the field of graphic art. A request from Karl Kraus to illustrate Albert Ehrenstein's *Tubutsch* (Fig. 10), a peculiar and melancholy piece of prose writing, was enthusiastically granted by the painter. *Tubutsch* was a witty product of the pre-war litterateur's *Weltschmerz*. It consisted of the man Tubutsch's complaints about the unbearable uniformity of a life in which nothing happened. The twelve drawings which Kokoschka made in 1911 to accompany this text, not particularly congenial to his temper, were but loosely connected with it. While Karl Tubutsch, for want of any other distraction, meditated on the absurdity of a policeman who smelt

120

XXXI. LOVERS WITH CAT
1918-19

XXXII. LOT AND HIS DAUGHTERS
1923

XXXIII. THE PAINTER—I
1923

XXXIV. LAKE LEMAN—II
1924

of rose perfume, the artist, interpreting vague associations, represented the sorry fate of Aristotle with Phyllis astride his back; the casual mention of a lion-tamer encouraged him to revive in a delightfully humorous vein his recollections of the vaudeville he had frequently attended in Berlin; an allusion to the flirtations between Czech nurse-maids and Bosnian soldiers on the park benches of Vienna inspired a most charming drawing of an evening idyll the angular grace of which surpasses the most ingenious Feininger fantasies; an encounter between a beggar and a bulldog, although taking place in a Vienna court-yard, became a *chinoiserie* through its play with space and volume, rendering movement as something slightly comical; Tubutsch's ill-humoured allusions to the other sex were taken as welcome pretexts to draw magnificent nudes in varied poses; while the poet's thoughts on suicide gave rise to a queer, and most characteristic, portrait of Ehrenstein with a little Death riding on his shoulder. All these drawings were done in the style which had marked Kokoschka's last *Sturm* illustrations and which corresponded with the crystal-shaped structure of his paintings of that period: thin pen strokes were used in even hatching, or radiating from certain points like bundles of rays to produce an effect now reminiscent of a spider's web, now of splintered glass. In contrast to the intensity of all those works in which Kokoschka gave expression to his own experiences and emotions they expressed a sense of ridicule, a humorous grace or graceful absurdity which suited the romantic irony of the text. The lyrical element was strongest in the portrait of the poet; the representation of a man with Death looking over his shoulder was, of course, a traditional subject in German art: Böcklin's *Self-Portrait with the Fiddling Death* of 1872 in the Berlin Nationalgalerie and Lovis Corinth's *Self-Portrait with a Skeleton* of 1896 were famous prototypes. The strength of Kokoschka's drawings, however, lay in their movement. Done at a time when the artist was still fighting for recognition, the *Tubutsch* illustrations were attacked as had been all his earliest works: the *Münchner Neueste Nachrichten*, for instance, printed a review of the book[1] which said that the drawings looked 'like the scribblings of a beginner suffering from the furies of genius'. Nevertheless, the work was reprinted in a popular edition of 1919, when Kokoschka was at the height of his fame.[2]

In the year of his second *Self-Portrait* and of his portrait of

[1] Quoted in *Der Sturm* of December 1911.

[2] Insel-Verlag, Leipzig (Insel-Bücherei, Nr. 261).

his friend, 1913, Kokoschka devoted a series of lithographs to the drama of which he and 'la femme fatale' were the chief actors. He prepared a new publication of the text before called *Der Weisse Tiertöter*, which he had slightly altered, and this he illustrated with twelve drawings to be reproduced from stone. The whole work was published under the title of *Der Gefesselte Kolumbus*.[1] In a more consummate form than Kokoschka had ever achieved before in a graphic work, this cycle of pictures represented the problems which moved him most passionately during these years, and it ended on a note of unanswered query. The frontispiece (Plate XXII) shows the familiar features of his friend, but very different from her oil portrait: the drawing is less representational, less sweet, but more characteristic. More than any other portrait that Kokoschka ever did of her, it gives an impression of the really overpowering beauty of this woman whose face reflected her masterful character without, however, losing in robust femininity. This profile is an individual portrait and at the same time a general personification of 'Woman'. It is strong and energetic in expression and yet naturalistic enough to render the softness of the flesh. In structure the head has something of the superhuman finality of an antique sculpture. The next plate shows the new Columbus, with the painter's own features, on his knees, his arm lifted to show his fetters; behind him appears the gracious figure of St. George—another symbol, expression of his own dual personality which Kokoschka liked to represent. In a third picture a dancing Death embraces an open coffin, with a skeleton in it—an allusion to the shadow of the dead rival. The whole scenery looks like a prophecy of the first world war which was to break out in the following year. The next plate shows the couple of the *Tempest*, this time in a chaotic landscape; this drawing of 1913 is the first published version of a composition which was to be taken up again by the painter one year later, and then considerably enlarged, elaborated and transposed to quite a different place. The same couple reappears in the following picture, this time in a room, the woman seated on a couch and protecting a burning candle from the current of air caused by his entrance, while the man looks on in wonder, his face expressing a strong emotion in which delight is not unmixed with anguish (Plate XXIII). The next plate shows the two kneeling in a landscape, the woman holding out the apple of Eve, the man lifting his hand to his eyes as though to protect

[1] The Fettered Columbus.

122

them from too much light. Later the man is seen prostrate on the ground, forlorn and opening his arms in a helpless gesture of inquiry; this same pose was to appear again two years later in Kokoschka's painting *Knight Errant*; in the lithograph it is accompanied by a figure of Death. The ninth sheet represents the man and woman, both nude, walking towards each other in a landscape: or perhaps rather they are moving in a circle, driven around an invisible axis; no picture more expressive of the polarity of man and woman can be imagined than this drawing, in which the man's body is of a darker shade than the woman's, and both seem at once to strive towards each other and to avoid each other, simultaneously attracted and repelled; they are in a permanent state of suspense, a unity and yet two opposed parts. After this comes a *Pietà* which might also be interpreted as an embrace. The woman, who is here soft and full of devotion, reappears in the eleventh drawing, upright and pitiless as she steps over the bier with the body of the overwhelmed man. Finally, there is a picture of the woman, less portrait-like this time, supporting her head on her hand as in meditation, and with the large eyes of an unearthly beauty—an idealised picture out of the artist's imagination—perhaps a triumphant angel contemplating the fateful troubles in which two mortals are hopelessly involved (Fig. 11).

From a stylistic point of view these lithographs represent a stage of transition from a purely graphic to a more painterly method: the figures are no longer veiled by a spider-web of thin lines, but seem much closer to the surface and are softly modelled. While the *Sturm* drawings of two years ago, with their hard and sparing outlines, had betrayed the scratching of a hard pen and the *Tubutsch* illustrations were built up in strong black-and-white contrasts, the softness of the chalk which Kokoschka employed for the *Kolumbus* drawings had led him to form larger, more roundly modelled shapes with less rendering of detail. A very varied application of hatching which, however, still consists of but one layer of parallel strokes, results in a wide variety of shades of grey and black. Those bundles of rays so characteristic of the *Tubutsch* illustrations still appear here and there in the *Kolumbus* lithographs. But on the whole the drawings merge more completely with the background than those of *Tubutsch*, which stood out against it. Where the distinct outlines are preserved they are used to emphasise movements and those wide gestures which would well befit a biblical or mythological subject. In expressive power and dramatic impetus *Der Gefesselte Kolumbus* corresponds completely with the paintings of this most successful period.

The next graphic work, undertaken by Kokoschka in 1914, was illustrations for Karl Kraus's *Die Chinesische Mauer*.[1] Inspired by the sensational murder of a white woman in Chinatown, this was one of those pieces of writing which displayed Kraus's clear and precise prose as well as his highly ethical spirit, here preoccupied with the sexual aberrations of a degenerate age. Kokoschka illustrated it with the two figures which almost alone populated his works during those years. Familiar motifs appear here again in new combinations: the Aristotle-Phyllis scene, which he had represented in *Tubutsch*—it had for centuries stood for the humiliation and destruction of man through the lust of the flesh, and Kokoschka must surely have seen the popular woodcut by Hans Baldung Grien of the same subject—recurs here; in another drawing a couple is shown in very much the same pose as that of the *Tempest*, but joined here by a gracefully dancing Death; most lovely, however, is the woman, who very closely resembles Botticelli's *Primavera*, and is led by Cupid through a landscape which hides a loving couple in the background.

Kokoschka's graphic work of this period culminates in the *Bachkantate*, a series of eleven lithographs illustrating Bach's 'Oh Ewigkeit—Du Donnerwort, So spanne meine Glieder aus'.[2] It was finished in 1914 and has become much more widely known than *Die Chinesische Mauer*. *Die Bachkantate* (Plates XXIV and XXV) speaks the same language of pictorial symbolism as *Der Gefesselte Kolumbus*, and the figures in both series are the same. Again a man and a woman move through a cosmic landscape adorned by skulls and cross-bones and, even more clearly than in the earlier work, it is the woman who takes the lead. But the portrait-likeness of both man and woman had become fainter, and there is a new tendency to sacrifice the appealing beauty of the Kolumbus figures to an even greater emphasis on expression. At the same time the strongly personal character of the earlier work has given place to a more general representation of almost mythological grandeur. The title page shows a female figure on a globe—a subject later repeated in an oil painting (No. 100).

[1] The Chinese Wall.

[2] Published by Fritz Gurlitt, Berlin, in 1914, shortly before the outbreak of the first Great War, and again in 1918.

11. DER GEFESSELTE KOLUMBUS
1915

This is followed by a self-portrait in three-quarter profile, showing the painter, brush in hand; this is the only purely personal representation in the whole work. Next comes a picture of an apocalyptic animal, shaped like a dragon, over a burning candle. The third sheet represents the man as a wanderer, leaning on his stick like a new St. Christopher, in front of a background of sea and a sky torn by lightning. Bach's 'Oh schwerer Gang zum letzten Kampf und Streite' is illustrated by a picture of a man and woman, she leading forward with comforting, encouraging gesture, he following with an expression of fear. 'Ich weiss vor grosser Traurigkeit nicht wo ich mich hinwende' is translated into a kind of Gethsemane in which the kneeling, praying figure is that of a woman. The sixth sheet shows man and woman naked in a landscape, the male figure gesticulating excitedly as though in some argument. Upon this follows a picture of 'Fear and Hope', the woman fearfully turned away, while the man is this time the bearer of courage and consolation. She takes the lead again in the eighth sheet, as they walk across open graves and grinning skulls. 'Selig sind die Toten' is represented by a magnificent eagle, who cries triumphantly across a strangely Leonardesque landscape, thus described by Kokoschka: 'The central motive is a mountain, first seen from afar, swimming in light, luring the wanderers and again disappearing before their eyes, like a mere reflection, changing into an arid conglomerate of rock and falling stone when the pilgrims reach their goal, a hole under its summit where the man is to be buried.' In 'Wohlan, soll ich von nun an selig sein' the man lifts his head out of a grave over which the woman is seated thinking, as if trying to understand Death, which in its very nature is foreign to her: for Kokoschka the woman is the symbol of everlasting life. Lastly, 'Es ist genug' is represented as a *Pietà*, very consciously gothic in spirit, and in expression surpassing the despair and facial distortion of the most realistic Madonnas. The work ends thus on a most pessimistic note, without the reconciliation which is implied by Bach's text as well as by his music. As always, Kokoschka had here again proved himself to be a most individualistic illustrator, who used an original text only as far as he could mould it to his own ideas. In the *Bachkantate* he found that fear of death, that doubt about his destiny which moved him most profoundly; hope as well as fear were personified by the figure of the woman, while the man was the wondering, in the main passive and powerless victim; and the end was a tragedy of pity and regret.

126

This work was unique in its inter-relation of personal and general symbolism. Graphic cycles of this kind were frequent in German art of that period. Max Klinger had etched a *Brahms-phantasie*. Slevogt's illustrations to the *Magic Flute*, though they belong to the post-war period and are in character much more works of graphic decoration, may be recalled as another cycle that was inspired by a musical composition. Much closer to Kokoschka's cycle, however, were certain works by Lovis Corinth, particularly *Das Hohe Lied*, a series of coloured lithographs published in 1911. Certain types, certain gestures of the *Bachkantate* are even very reminiscent of Corinth's figures, which sometimes also have that curious grin characteristic of Kokoschka's faces. Furthermore, both artists share the same sensualism, and in matters of technique they were probably subject to mutual influence.[1] The older artist was usually distinguished by a rare gift for transforming his subjects into living, tangible scenes. Kokoschka, on the other hand, was able to lift his themes into the sphere of the purely symbolic, or abstract. There is only one artist who was Kokoschka's predecessor in spirit as well as in style: Edvard Munch, in certain passages of his University frescoes at Oslo, had anticipated what Kokoschka expressed in *Die Bachkantate*.

[1] It is usually assumed that Kokoschka was influenced by Corinth in his paintings as well as in his graphic work—an assumption that seems convincing enough as Corinth was the elder and one of the Berlin artists with whose work Kokoschka was well acquainted. Kokoschka's style, however, can be regarded as developing quite naturally, from his own beginnings, without any interference by external influences, at least up to his Dresden period which begins in 1916-7, while Corinth had belonged to a very different art tradition—that of the nineteenth century—until he suddenly succumbed to expressionist influence. It is interesting in this connection that Hans Hildebrandt, in *Die Kunst des* 19. *und* 20. *Jahrhunderts* (1931), p. 344, speaks of Kokoschka's unrecognised influence on Corinth.

II. THE WAR AND DRESDEN
EXPRESSIONISM

Kokoschka's private life had latterly become so difficult, so overcharged with complications that, when the war broke out in 1914, he rushed into it as though it might bring him relief. Paradoxical as this may sound, he escaped into the war. Vienna, with her constant scandals, had now definitely become too narrow for him. Everything he did only provoked the embittered enmity of the most influential people. In 1913 his friends had made a new attempt to establish him—this time as an art master at a girls' private school, which was directed by a well-known figure in Vienna life, Frau Dr. Eugenie Schwarzwald. The first thing that Kokoschka did here was to introduce the principles of Komensky whose *Orbis Pictus* was still to play a great part in his later life. Enthusiastically he had absorbed the ancient pedagogue's idea that education ought to be less burdened with theoretical knowledge and more derived from visual experience. But the parents of his pupils could not be persuaded to follow him in such matters; they feared that the activities of a young man as notorious as Kokoschka had become in Vienna could hardly be a beneficial influence on their daughters. Public attention was soon drawn to his presence at an institution which had already been suspect for its many reforms, and the authorities, who had never forgiven him the disturbances he had caused in the past, banned him altogether from teaching in Austrian schools. Kokoschka was now sufficiently independent to resist such a blow. But his feelings towards the authorities of his native country grew so embittered that he decided to turn his back upon them as soon as possible. He was never entirely to get over these experiences of his early years; it is owing to them that he became extremely sensitive to unreasonable criticism, and has always been activated by the desire to prove to everybody—and most of all to himself—that he could do everything he wanted, everything that anybody else did, rather better than anybody else could do it; his argument with the authorities has, so to speak,

128

XXXV. PARIS, THE OPERA
1924

XXXVI. MARSEILLES—II
1925

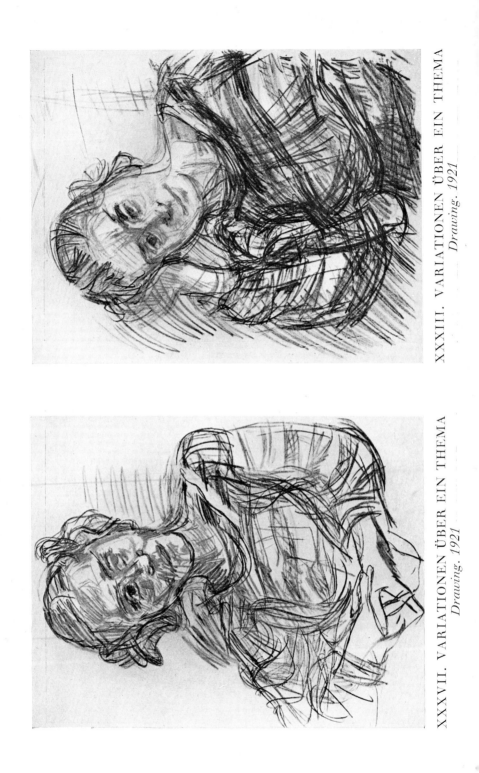

XXXVII. VARIATIONEN ÜBER EIN THEMA
Drawing. 1921

XXXIII. VARIATIONEN ÜBER EIN THEMA
Drawing. 1921

never come to an end, and in spite of all success and official recognition, he has never been free of the suspicion that he might
at any time be once more the subject of philistine attack. In his
own eyes he remained and still is the powerless youth of thirty-
five years ago, misunderstood by the majority, persecuted by
those in power, and grateful for the devotion of a few tested
friends.

Not only Kokoschka's personal friends, but all those who had
eyes to see resented the treatment he received and unceasingly
warned the public of Vienna that the city was about to lose one
of her best sons. Vienna's creative geniuses had always been in
a difficult position. Hermann Bahr had written in his book *Wien*
(p. 9): 'A real man in real life, the Viennese have never tolerated;
neither Beethoven nor Hebbel nor Kürnberger nor Hugo Wolf
nor Mahler. Real men are kept in the cage of an immense
solitude. The Viennese never let them enter their beloved light
and lusty life. Hence the great silence of Vienna. Nothing moves,
nothing can happen. The boldest, the greatest acts have no effect,
they remain hidden.'[1] And with reference to Kokoschka—among
others—Hans Tietze wrote in 1919: 'Just as in the past we had
a case of Beethoven, a case of Grillparzer, a case of Feuerbach and
a case of Hugo Wolf, we have in these last years made cases of
Klimt and Mahler, Schönberg and Kokoschka, instead of regard-
ing them as beneficial intensifications of our own nature, which
may not recognise itself in the unfettered genius, but should at
least feel a certain foreboding. Cases, in which judgments, dictated by frivolity and indifference, live on in the cultural history
of the city as painful accusations. . . .'[2]

Kokoschka's personal ties had also become unbearable in the
course of time. His daily life was increasingly composed of scenes
which resembled those of his plays, with their tensions and ex-
plosions. He had exhausted all that an extremely complicated
relationship could offer him. 'Without knowing it my friend, by
the very fact of belonging to the well-to-do society, lost her hold
over me. As soon as the romantic atmosphere of the early days
had frozen into the pathos felt at the death of happy possibilities
the magic spell was broken. We both wanted to regain our independence.'

The war seemed to offer the freedom for which he longed and

[1] The translation is taken from Wickham Steed's *Hapsburg Monarchy*,
2nd edition, p. 204.

[2] *Die Bildenden Künste*, 1919, p. 247.

opportunity for new adventure—the prospect of which he was still young enough to relish. In spite of the sceptical attitude of his friends, who were pacifists, he was, to a certain degree, the victim of his curiosity. Adolf Loos gained him admittance to a most exclusive regiment of dragoons, which he chose to spite those who had snubbed him for snobbish reasons, and also because he found its uniform, consisting of red trousers, blue coat and golden helmet, irresistible. As soon as he was allowed to wear it Loos ordered a photograph to be made of the young artist as a dragoon, which was sold in Vienna as a postcard to be cherished together with the pictures of the favourite actors of the Burg-theater. He still needed a horse, and to enable him to buy one as well as to manifest his independence he sold the picture that must at that time have meant more to him than he would probably have admitted: the *Tempest*. This was a symbolic act which should cut him off from a past during which he had been torn between his passion and the struggle for undisturbed work, from a period in which his mood had swayed intolerably between extremes and his self-respect had almost been destroyed. By selling this painting he bought his liberty. The deal was his revenge, his final triumph over his own emotions and over all attempts to suppress his freedom-loving nature. The sale of the *Tempest* broke the spell which had held him for four years. And never again did he allow himself to be entirely lost to anything but his work.

Before he left for the front, however, he gave as a last token to the woman who had played such a predominant part in his life, who had fascinated, educated and stimulated him, six fans which he had painted for her. A more beautiful present from an artist to a woman could hardly be imagined. These six fans, which have been miraculously preserved, tell the story which the two had in common, in a most original and delightful manner. Like some of Kokoschka's paintings, they are full of profound symbolism and at the same time realistic enough to depict familiar figures and localities. Regarded from the point of view of Kokoschka's art, they give the most convincing proof of that incessant flow of imagination, that incomparable ability to raise features of reality into the sphere of fantasy and to experience artistic visions with the same intensity as physical sensations to which he owes his unique position among his contemporaries. They show Kokoschka's connection with the tradition of his country's baroque art more conclusively than anything else that he has done. Their pictorial wealth, their variety and their richness of colour find their only parallel in the frescoes of the eighteenth century which cover the walls of Austrian and South-German buildings.

The order in which these fans were painted cannot now be established with certainty. One of them, which may have been the first,[1] shows in the centre, grouped as in the *Double-Portrait*, the woman radiant with a beauty more striking than in any other portrait that Kokoschka did of her; on the left they are represented resting in each other's arms, while the right shows Kokoschka carried by a bird which wears a crown. The design of this fan is stylised in the manner of *art nouveau*, ornaments covering the whole surface, and the figures beautifully drawn, with emphasis on the magnificent physique of both figures. The flesh is tinted with a light yellow, while the dominant colour of the ornamentation is pink. Interspersed among the ornamental designs are fishes and other small animals, like those of *Die Träumenden Knaben*.

Another fan is similar in composition. On the left are two boats, one occupied by the woman, the other by the man; in the middle the young man is seen on his knees before the woman and, on the right, she is carried off by a horse. These three scenes are separated by two ornamental columns. The design has a certain calligraphic quality which, together with the delicate colouring of the background—pale shades of pink, green and yellow prevailing—produces a Far Eastern effect.

A third fan shows the motif of the *Tempest* in the centre with Vesuvius in the background; on the left the two are seen in a carriage, behind prancing horses; on the right Kokoschka appears as St. George. None of the six fans tells as much of the couple's real story as this one: it records, in Kokoschka's best pictorial and symbolic fashion, the delights and torments of their association as well as the scenes of their daily life, and the romantic rôle which the painter ascribed to himself in his relationship to the woman he loved. The colours of this fan were more glowing than on any of the others—the mountain is deep green, a theatre curtain purple—and its designs are most closely related to Kokoschka's oil-paintings. Each one of the three scenes is a complete picture in itself.

Another of these fans, like the reflection of a confused, tormenting dream, represents psychological situations rather than

[1] According to Kokoschka's recollections, done at Christmas, 1912.

131

actual circumstances. Kokoschka appears here reclining on the ground, in front of a tree trunk, sleeping; before him stands an angel with his friend's features; in the centre the two are seen half naked in a mountainous landscape, the man on his knees, the woman threatening him, her arm menacingly raised, her eyes flashing dangerously; on the right, however, she receives him lovingly, like a repentant rebel, while a burning candle between two beds indicates that a peaceful night will harbour the reconciled couple. This fan, probably painted in a stormy mood, is less clear in design than the others, while it displays all the colours of a rich palette.

The next fan is more mysterious in its conception. On its left two girls in a field are milking cows; in the centre the woman, holding a small sphinx in her arms,[1] is seen hovering over a burning bush—*Der Brennende Dornbusch*; by her side Kokoschka appears, again as St. George, on a horse, his lance piercing a monster with three heads; on the right, war scenes are represented. It seems most likely that this fan was meant to depict the contrasts of peace and war, while the centre shows the painter's private struggle against some evil power. The style of this fan is that of a work of folk art; the design is simple and clear, supported by strong body colours.

The last of these six fans is, owing to its poetic vision, the most beautiful of all. It bears the date of 1914 and Kokoschka's initials. Painted under the shadow of war, it reflects the painter's reactions to the events of that year in a simple, yet imaginative manner. On the left, a woman with the familiar features feeds two children; the scene is a wood consisting of trunks like those which remained standing, monuments of desolation, after whole areas had been devastated by bombardment; in the centre a gunner loads a cannon, while sailors are seen storming ahead; further, the painter is prostrate on the ground, a lance piercing his body; his forehead is bandaged; in the middle he appears again, wrestling with a bearded warrior—obviously a Russian—whom he looks straight in the eye; on the right women walk among graves, carrying a cross and weeping, while Kokoschka

[1] The symbolic meaning of the sphinx, according to Mario Praz (*The Romantic Agony*), one of the attributes of the *femme fatale*, had already been exploited by Kokoschka in *Sphinx und Strohmann*. The ease with which Kokoschka used symbols of this kind is explained by the fact that the literature of the 'Decadents' had made them familiar to the whole of Europe.

kneels on one side. The artistic form of this fan is perhaps the most satisfactory of all six; its rich blues and purples are strongly reminiscent of the baroque paintings whose influence on the artist is so clearly to be seen in the whole series; the lyrical flow of the lines, on the other hand, again recalls the grace of Japanese woodcuts; but the intensity of expression in such scenes as that of the woman feeding the children—a modern version of the old 'Charity' motif—or of the wrestling men, whose fight seems to be decided not by force of arms but by the power of the human eye, is peculiarly Kokoschka's own.

The fashion of painting fans had not for a long time been so popular as in the eighteenth century, but it was still now and then practised as a kind of artistic hobby. Thus Charles Conder painted fans, and in Vienna Makart had decorated fans which rank among his best works; some of these are preserved in the Berlin Nationalgalerie. Kokoschka had learnt to paint these decorative objects in his early years, when he worked for the Wiener Werkstätte. And although his fans are mainly of a delicate prettiness of which even his most ardent admirers would hardly have suspected his brush to be capable, they are as original of their kind as any of his other works. They are poetic and expressive, like some medieval book illuminations. Following the same impulse that had made Schubert sing 'Ich schnitt' es gern in alle Rinden ein', he had poured his feelings into the colours with which he covered the folded paper, making these dainty objects into vehicles of his violent and changing emotions. It is obvious that, had he had walls at his disposal, to cover them with huge pictures of his story, he would eagerly have done so. As he had to compress it into miniature format he transformed it into a series of love letters written in images instead of characters, lyrical and graceful. These fans were invented as gifts of a very personal character, and they have all the flavour of intimacy; at the same time they rank among the most valuable documents of his art which has too often—and many times unjustifiably—been reproached with fierceness and brutality.

* * *

In the light of later events Kokoschka's last fan had given proof of a curiously prophetic vision. Soon after its completion the realities of war were brought home to the painter in the most decisive way. He joined up in 1915. If he had had difficulties in his civilian life, those of his military career were much worse.

133

He was an insubordinate soldier who could not submit himself. He was afraid of mechanical things, such as guns and aeroplanes; but, paradoxical as ever and in order to overcome his fear, he volunteered for the most dangerous reconnaissance patrols. 'I had pledged myself never to kill a so-called enemy, and I kept my word.' A few months after his arrival at the eastern front he was gravely wounded by a Russian cossack who, according to Kokoschka's recollection, strangely resembled the bearded warrior with whom he had represented himself wrestling on the fan. With a shot in the head and a bayonet wound in the lung he became a prisoner of war; but he was rescued by advancing compatriots. 'I did not forget to recommend to the care of my own riders my Russian guards with whom I had made friends and who were only too willing to lay down their arms.' He lay between life and death for weeks in a field hospital and then he was finally sent back home. Transported in an open carriage across the endless plains of the Ukraine and Poland, with nothing but the sky before his eyes whenever he awoke from feverish unconsciousness, he tried in vain to get hold of something stable; the train was incessantly moving, and so was the sky which was sometimes interminably blue, and then again flickering with stars. His thoughts were confused and his memories heavy; past, present and future seemed equally obscure and painful. But he wanted desperately to find his way through the maze of physical and mental sensations that oppressed him; so he held on to the only thread he could reach: his recollections of the last period in Vienna. And his mind, eager to gain control of the situation, set to work. Kokoschka invented a new version of the eternal drama with which he was always preoccupied, although he had already twice written it down and even produced it. Helplessly prostrated in the roofless railway carriage, unable to use his right arm, with serious wounds, delirious thoughts and dry lips, he declaimed to himself the verses which, reshaped and completed, he published in 1918 under the title of *Orpheus und Eurydice*. This was his summing-up, his statement of the new attitude which he had wrung from the past. It took him three years finally to formulate his thoughts and to give clear expression to his feelings. When at last the play came to light it had become his first written work which can be called complete and successful from a technical point of view: it was less obscure and less improvised than its two forerunners; it was arranged in three distinct parts; apart from the man and the woman who had before been his only actors,

134

there were now the additional figures of Hades (Pluto), Amor, Psyche, three furies and the usual chorus; the scene, quite un-defined in the past, now changed from the house of Orpheus to the Orcus and back again; and, most important of all, there was a logical sequence in the construction of the play, which makes it possible to appreciate it by the traditional standards of drama.

Equally new was the gentle key-note of the first scene, which describes the idyllic love of Orpheus and Eurydice. To express the harmonious affection which binds these two together the poet has found pictures of the same original imaginativeness as those with which in the past he had more often described opposite feelings. Thus he makes Eurydice recall Orpheus's departure in these words: 'Your carriage became smaller and smaller, until it was a point. That point hid your face from me which—yet—did not grow smaller for me!' And the enamoured Orpheus ex-claims: 'O, what grace is yours! My madness! No, let me speak —I love you, love you more than happiness!' But this bliss is of short duration. In accordance with ancient traditions the three furies arrive, to carry off Eurydice. Although these phantoms squabble with each other in Viennese dialect, the course of the play has so far followed the Greek legend from which its title was borrowed. The beginning of the second part is still faithful to the original story: Orpheus appears at the gates of Pluto's abode to claim his Eurydice. Only some allusions in the ensuing dialogue strike a new, more personal note: Psyche warns Orpheus not to frighten Eurydice with inquiries. The past—her years in the home of the dead—must not be evoked. But his curiosity cannot be silenced, and significant events remind him again and again that she has a secret which he cannot share: a human skull is thrown by the waves into their boat like a message from the underworld; he dreams that they have a child together, but she kills the fruit of their love with a hair pin—just as the murderess in one of his *Sturm* drawings[1] had stabbed her baby with a hair pin. He begins to torment her: 'Will you not speak? Perhaps I shall feel easier when I know all and need no longer imagine everything blacker than black.' And at last he comes out with the real cause of his self-torture: 'Do you see—Him—when I am with you?' Him, that is Pluto, whom she left behind; it is also the dead man who for four years overshadowed the young painter's life and whose name was conjured up so often to hurt him. Eurydice begs: 'Why do we awake memories? From you I

[1] See *Der Sturm*, 20th October 1910, p. 267.

want firmness. . . .' But then she loses patience; she takes her vengeance: 'I see the dead one's smile again! You are seeking your own undoing. Beat me—the other will protect me.' In deeply moving words she describes how she resisted the temptations of Pluto for five years, 'and like a burning flame was my desire'. At last Pluto released her, defeated by her faithfulness to Orpheus; she, touched by his noble act, had now suddenly been willing to follow him—and at that very moment Orpheus had appeared to rescue her. Ever since she has been divided, not knowing where she belonged. Hearing this confession Orpheus understands that everything is lost. With a brutal gesture he relinquishes his and her happiness: he gives her and himself up to the waves. In the third part he—or his ghost—is back in his home country, at the ruins of his destroyed house. The introduction of a new motif underlines the poet's identity with the hero of the drama. 'I am the most famous', he boasts, 'for I have shed most blood.' This attitude towards the war, which presented itself in a new light to the wounded man in the open carriage, was the first manifestation of Kokoschka's later pacifism; it corresponded with the general change of ideas which in 1918 turned the soldiers of the German army into disgusted rebels. The bacchanalia performed by the farmers and soldiers in the last scenes of the play gave expression to the same apocalyptic mood, and they were inspired by what Kokoschka had experienced at the front. More reminiscences from the war turn up in this third part of the tragedy: a dead man lies in a ditch, and horses break loose in order to escape from their burning stables. In the middle of this witch sabbath a woman's voice is heard from above: 'You are alive?' The years before the critical period in which he was wholly absorbed by one unique relationship come for the first time back to his mind: it is his mother's voice to which he replies: 'I am no longer a child . . . I am awake now . . . I must put out the fire. . . .' Then follows one of those self-accusations of the returning warrior: 'I am a devil . . . who splashes blood about when you touch him.' And he bursts out: 'What have I done?— I have exhausted what life has to offer—happiness and unhappiness. I know all I want to know about it.' Undeterred by this disillusionment Eurydice reappears, to find out whether she still has power over him. 'There must still be a way to his heart.' He replies: 'No, if there were I would still be the curious child. . . .' He scorns the ghost, whom he calls a stranger, as well as the past for which he has no more affection: 'What tie binds man and wife together? Our imagination. . . . When I thought of you my heart stood still, my throat contracted, I turned pale.' She kneels to him: 'Once more let me embrace you.' But this time he has finally freed himself: 'I confess with devilish joy that I hate you.' He falls into madness, confusing his wife with his mother and his individual troubles with those of his generation: 'Mother, how does it say—Thou shalt not do murder?' In the end it is the woman who is liberated; she silences the madman by throttling him and sighs: 'Thus, embracing you in a last struggle I free myself—at last redeemed. . . .'

★   ★   ★

To cure his injuries, Kokoschka was taken to a hospital in Austria. As soon as he was more or less recovered he was sent a second time to the front, but not for very long: his lungs would not heal properly, and the wound he had received in his head affected his sense of equilibrium; although he regained the use of his right arm and leg, there were times when he could not walk straight owing to an injury of the inner ear. 'If it is by mere coincidence that in my early youth I suffered the same disturbances, but of a hallucinatory nature, affecting my sense of equilibrium, it is rather strange that each time my art benefits from what the observed phenomena allowed me to discover. An especially characteristic feature of my art is my gift to create in the onlooker the illusion of space while ignoring the ordinary means of geometric perspective.' After renewed treatment in hospital he was at length released as incurable but nevertheless not discharged from the army. Every month he had to undergo the ordeal of painful medical tests, as an effect of which he often felt madness obscure his mind. In 1917 he was sent to Sweden to consult a brain specialist. He stayed a few months in Stockholm where he began to recover. A wonderfully blue picture of the city's harbour (No. 111) and lithograph portraits of *Selma Lagerlöf* and *Svante Arrhenius* showed that as soon as he felt better, the urge to work in him was stronger than any physical impediments or psychological depressions.

'Because the famous specialist in Stockholm could not free me from the tag labelling me as unfit for an unlimited period, I decided to go for the third time to the front, this time to make an end to an existence, which gave me no alternative but either to desert my country or continue being a mere number in the roll of heroes who themselves felt more like gun-fodder in that senseless, mechanical war in which only governments continued to believe, because they did not know how to get out of what they had knavishly entered upon. It was at night at Dresden station where I waited for the Vienna train, that a stranger introduced himself to me on the request of the poet Albert Ehrenstein, from whom he had heard about my proposed journey. This man, Dr. Neuberger, of whose identity I never gained positive knowledge, who had lived in India and whose days were numbered as he obviously was in the last stages of consumption, not only helped me to restore my morale by not letting me out of his sight till the war ended, but in similar ways saved the lives of many people doomed to be sacrificed in the holocausts which marked the end of the war. He knew in a mysterious way everything the governments were hiding from the people who were doing the fighting. He explained to me the origins of the war, the character of the armistice that was to follow, and the social landslide resulting from it. It was miraculous how he gained approach to big people like General Ludendorff and the managers of the I.G.F., when he needed the influence of big bankers and industrialists. Although he himself was always very poor and needed very little, he was the most influential person I ever met, if he chose to put his hypnotic power on the scales in order to save the life of one protected by him. I think he was somehow mixed up with the organisation which succeeded in bringing Lenin back to Russia, because he made allusions to that effect before the famous sealed transport had even started, and because he was in those days in a strange state of hilarity and suddenly departed on a mysterious voyage returning only when everything was over. He played a decisive part in the organisation of the German revolution, to my own knowledge, as far as the movement was voiced from the stage, in looking for the authors of the day, helping them to formulate their ideas and to rise to their task, and, last but not least, convincing the big theatrical managers to voice these dangerous thoughts. He died soon after the armistice in the Berlin-Dresden train, unfortunately on an errand for my sake. Before that he had succeeded in moving me from the army sanatorium to a small house where he lived together with some friends whom he had saved, people famous in the Germany of that time, of whom the name of the playwright Hasenclever has been brought into the memory of a large public when he committed suicide in a French concentration camp when Hitler invaded France!'

The small house here referred to stood in a suburb of Dresden, where Kokoschka spent the next seven years of his life. This town in the Elbe valley, which its inhabitants like to call 'Elb-Florenz', was at that time the capital of Saxony, a country that ranked third in importance among the German states. With its beautiful historic buildings, its ancient bridges that span the wide river, and encircled by gentle hills, Dresden was one of the loveliest cities in Germany. The Elector Frederic August III, who was also King of Poland, had in the first decades of the eighteenth century made it one of the centres of architectural activity, and to him the city owed its characteristic panorama with the silhouettes of graceful baroque spires, the domineering cupola of the Frauen-kirche and the airy courts of the Zwinger, so well known through Canaletto's paintings. From the same period dates the world-wide fame of Dresden as the city of the porcelain which owes its origin to the initiative of the same monarch. Not even the age of industrialisation could change the serene character of this quiet residential town. While other, more active cities grew into noisy agglomerations, Dresden's historic splendour ceded to a peaceful sleepiness. The last King of Saxony was a simple man of great common sense, whose only royal pursuit was hunting for which he had a passion; he did not interfere with the cultural life of the city which, particularly owing to an influx of artists and intellectuals from other parts of Germany and from abroad, developed considerably in the years just before and after the war. The opera and the two great theatres were so well managed that they came to be counted among the best on the Continent and attracted visitors from all countries. The celebrated Dresden Gallery was directed by a most efficient and broad-minded man, Hans Posse, who had a great share in bringing art, modern as well as ancient, before the public. In one of Dresden's suburbs, the garden-city of Hellerau, the Deutsche Werkstätten produced modern interiors of admirable quality. Social experiments were conducted in connection with this undertaking, which guaranteed a house and garden to every one of its workers. The most prominent inhabitant of Hellerau was the Swiss musical peda-gogue Jacques Dalcroze, for whom a school—one of the first modern buildings in Germany—had been built in 1910, where he trained many citizens even of the most distant nations in gymnastics and music. Dresden was also one of the centres of the youth movement as well as, in the last years of the first world war, a hiding place for left-wing politicians. But one of its craziest and most notorious sets during those years was the circle of people to whom Kokoschka had attached himself when he settled at the Weisse Hirsch.

This was a kind of artists' colony, a group of men and women who were more or less of the same age as the painter and equally detached from the surrounding bourgeois world. Their faces are familiar from the portraits which Kokoschka soon began to draw and paint of his friends, while some of their names were once well known among German intellectuals. Fritz Neuberger, a black-bearded writer and philosopher, of whom mention has been made, seems to have exercised, as some people do, a mystical influence over those around him: it is to him that Kokoschka ascribes his final recovery from the psychological wounds of the war. Ernst Deutsch was an ascetic-looking actor, who had come from Prague to play under Max Reinhardt and for whom a miraculous career was predicted; he became in fact one of Germany's prominent stage and film artists. Iwar von Lücken was a Baltic aristocrat disowned by his family because he preached—and practised—Tolstoian principles; a poet and a man of great knowledge, whom poverty had reduced to a Don Quixote-like appearance; while all the others cultivated a conscious dissimilarity from other people but were in fact very comfortably connected with the bourgeois world which provided for their needs. Lücken, with his unworldliness, his extreme modesty, his love for children, his classical quotations, his old-fashioned politeness, his weakness for the bottle and his disreputable suits, was probably the last real Bohemian. Walter Hasenclever was a young playwright whose *Sohn*, a drama of conflict between the young generation and its parents, had caused much excitement in 1916; in the same year he had written *Antigone*, a protest against war and absolute monarchy in classical disguise. Käte Richter, lastly, was a good-looking actress of garçonne-type, tall, dark, temperamental and intelligent, who was employed by the more advanced of the two big Dresden theatres, the Albert Theater, and who was to be the woman in Kokoschka's next pictures. In his lithographs she appears under the name of 'Katja'.

The general mood of those years was one of despondency. It was the third year of the war; the casualty lists increased all the time, and men on leave found their life at home disappointing; the food situation grew more and more desperate: for a whole winter the main dish had consisted of swedes, and it was obvious that the bread contained large pieces of straw and bran, while the more attractive kinds of food had almost wholly disappeared. In Dresden the revolution, which broke out in the autumn of 1918, consisted mainly of isolated acts by the mob, who once stoned and drowned a Minister of Finance, of strikes and some shooting. The King resigned with a disdainful *bon mot*. As the revolts and changes of government did not happen simultaneously in the various states of the Reich, there was a constant exchange of political refugees, of rumours and experiences. The changes which finally came about in the life of the ordinary individual were not considerable. But the intellectual revolution, prepared for the last eight or ten years, was spectacular: all those ideas and their realisations on the stage, in books and pictures, which had caused so much consternation, were now suddenly officially accepted, had wide circulation and state protection. Everything could be said in public—in fact, nothing could be too strong, new, and even revolting. The pacifism, which had had to be held back for four years, came out into the open.[1] 'Nie wieder Krieg!' was the most popular slogan—'No more war!' The generation which had spent four years in the trenches and had known terrible experiences was filled with an indomitable desire to make up for lost time. Their works were no longer individualistic or sceptical like those of the pre-war period: the writers, like the expressionist painters, showed a strongly ethical tendency and an urge towards unity with the rest of a suffering humanity. Moral and social questions were the issues that occupied their minds, the war and revolution were their subjects. War profiteers, cripples, workers, and prostitutes were the figures most frequently represented on the stage—figures that have become

[1] There is plenty of actual proof of the pacifism latent in Germany's artists in the first world war. The Berlin Sezession, for instance, in 1915 published 48 lithographs under the title *Krieg und Kunst* (War and Art) which, far from extolling the war, described its horrors and contained sheets with such significant titles as *Kain*. The authorities were innocent enough not only to permit these publications, but even allowed them to be posted to soldiers at the front. In Austria, Karl Kraus wrote his most terrible accusations against the military caste and those intellectuals who regarded the war in the light of a new boom for themselves, *Die Letzten Tage der Menschheit*, in 1915–1917. Two lithographs by Kokoschka were issued illegally, through the press of the photographer Ehrfurt at Dresden, 'one showing soldiers fighting each other with crucifixes, the other one representing a condemned man being lifted to the gallows by soldiers, in the presence of a hypocritical judge. This was in the days of spy fever, when official culprits had to look for scapegoats because defeat was in the air.'

so familiar through the satirical drawings of George Grosz. Just as in the fine arts, cynicism pervaded the new language of the stage only as a means of stirring the public into self-defence against social evils and parasites. The writers of those years, who were at all concerned with the life of their time, had to choose between two possible attitudes: they could continue to cultivate a patriotism which was out of favour with the war-weary majority and add to the sagas of the war, or they could identify themselves with 'the people', the working class who was fighting for its future. This last was what most of them did. Naturally the battle-cry *'épater le bourgeois'* was louder than ever. The ordinary conservative citizen who would not follow the new slogans was treated with the most biting mockery. Workers and artists alike were far too partisan to foresee that the middle-class whom they ridiculed would, after a quarter of a century, take a terrible revenge.

Kokoschka had great sympathy for the revolution for which he entertained expectations that were never fulfilled. He had from the beginning been 'anti-bourgeois' in outlook. Official authorities he had learnt to dislike more than to respect. Since he had seen the war with its obliteration of the individual and its wasteful destruction, he had become a convinced pacifist. Moreover, his personal state of mind coincided with the general state of things: like the people around him he had decided to break with the past. They wanted a new social order; he yearned to become independent of Vienna, to forget the personal ties that had held him so close. A new world would liberate him and give his art its place. It is a fact that during those years of Germany's military collapse, of constitutional changes and of an intermittent violence, more notice was taken of the activities of intellectuals than will readily be credited or understood by anyone who is merely a distant observer; the explanation will have to be sought in the enormous prestige which, up to the days of the Third Reich, the written word enjoyed in Germany; as in the days of the Napoleonic wars the nation's writers and intellectuals were quite naturally expected to take a leading, stimulating part. Apart from this, Kokoschka had always been an *enfant terrible par excellence*, and the new atmosphere suited him. The revolution, as it manifested itself in Dresden, was his element, more even than the Café Central of Vienna or the Café Grössenwahn in Berlin, where battles had been fought with words. There he had been one of many, who had been regarded

142

as insignificant by those in influential positions. Now, in this excited provincial capital, he was one of few who were in the centre of public attention. Everything he did could only add to his fame. He could even, in his own way, participate in the political life of the town. He drew posters and published manifestos.[1]

At this time the painter became known as 'der tolle Kokoschka.'[2] The Scandinavian writer Karin Michaelis bestowed this title on him in an article which appeared in *Das Kunstblatt* of December, 1918. There is no doubt that he deserved it. In the same year he conceived one of his most fantastic ideas, never to be surpassed by the most grotesque surrealist efforts. This adventure

[1] Here is the wording of one of these, followed by Kokoschka's own comment: 'Ich richte an alle, die hier in Zukunft vorhaben ihre politischen Theorien, gleichviel ob links-, rechts- oder mittel-radikale, mit dem Schiessprügel zu argumentieren, die folgende Bitte, solche geplante kriegerische Übungen nicht mehr vor der Gemäldegalerie des Zwingers sondern etwa auf den Schiessplätzen der Heide abhalten zu wollen, wo menschliche Kultur nicht in Gefahr kommt. Ich wage nicht zu hoffen, dass mein Gegenvorschlag durchdringt, der vorsähe, dass in der Deutschen Republik wie in den klassischen Zeiten Fehden künftig durch Zweikämpfe der politischen Führer ausgetragen werden möchten, etwa im Zirkus Sarassani, eindrucksvoller gemacht durch das Homerische Geschimpfe der von ihnen "angeführten" Parteien.'—This manifesto I issued in the spring of 1920 after the German Communist Revolution had been defeated in Berlin, in the industrial districts and in Saxony, Bavaria and Hamburg. I saw the streetfighting of the workers, glamourised in the intellectual circles while the victims of the blunders of the Comintern policy were doomed to failure not only for theoretical reasons that the Social-Democrats considered the Communists to be the only real danger to them. Democracy had to bind its eyes while the counter-revolution of the united world-monopolies made Europe step by step safe against collective socialist doctrine and international creed which threatened to get the mass-support of the proletarised society of the West as well as in the East. Quite naturally German Social Democracy had to ask for foreign loans in order to rebuild its industry. No country with no capital invested abroad can live without exporting industrial products in exchange for foodstuffs and raw materials. Only Great Britain, as the international broker, lived on the interests from British capital invested abroad. Thus, in 1920, the combination of circumstances and events conditioned the birth of National Socialism in Germany, where the principle of rationalisation of the monopolies was adopted for the first time in its most dramatic form, challenging humanism. Whether rationalisation will allow recognition of the fact that the conservation of the human race is necessarily a condition, if only for the sake of preserving the economic prosperity of war industry and its future, will be left for consideration to these monopolies standing behind all capitalist governments.

[2] The mad Kokoschka.

143

became known as 'the story of the doll'. It was generally considered to be a horrible joke, but Kokoschka himself likes to refer to it as though it were a deed of valour. It undoubtedly had its serious aspect: it was the most tangible proof of the painful percussion which his sensitive brain had suffered through the upheavals of the times. The deliberate and the unintentional mingled curiously in this piece of folly which Kokoschka performed before the eyes of his astonished contemporaries. It represents the self-revelation of an artist whose life and art were always interrelated in an unusually high degree, and for this reason the story of the doll is of a paramount interest.

Kokoschka, still haunted by his experiences in pre-war Vienna as well as at the front, felt that all normal contact with human beings was unbearable. 'For years I could not physically stand the people who quietly conversed about their war experiences, machine-gunning, throwing hand-grenades into advancing phalanxes of living flesh, or bayoneting, while they themselves again having returned to their normal routine, went on living their sentimental lives. What shocked me was that criminals, as a rule, behave like other people, while eccentrics are an exception in their ranks as well.' Yet his was not the temperament to be contented in complete isolation. Particularly was his relationship with women complicated by the disappointments which had been the natural result of his exalted expectations. For his peculiar need he thought of an unusual remedy: he would have a doll made who would look like his ideal woman; she would be ever present, but silent and unobtrusive; on her he would heap his devotion and his care; she would be his creature, as 'Virginia' had been his daughter and his love during his starvation period in Berlin; but his doll, made of a more solid substance than his dream child, would also serve him as a model who never tired of sitting for his pictures. He began to invest his new idea with all the features of which his glowing imagination was capable; but he could not himself carry it out. Those of his women friends whom he asked to make him such a doll recoiled in horror at the monstrosity of the proposal. In the end he found an artist who lived in Stuttgart and declared herself ready to make the doll. The correspondence in which Kokoschka described this child of his desire has been preserved by Paul Westheim who published it under the title of 'Der Fetisch'.[1] They were accompanied by

[1] Published by Ullstein, Berlin (no date), in the collection of *Künstlerbekenntnisse* (Confessions of Artists).

XXXIX. VARIATIONEN ÜBER EIN THEMA
Drawing. 1921

XL. VARIATIONEN ÜBER EIN THEMA
Drawing. 1921

XLI. KARL KRAUS—II
1924-25

drawings, which indicated exactly how he envisaged certain details of execution. Once he even sent an oil painting to Stuttgart which represented the woman of his dreams. Westheim reprinted nine letters, of which some characteristic extracts are here translated. The first letter published contains the following passage:

. . . If you solve this task well and give me such an illusion that I can believe the woman of my imagination to live when I look at her and touch her, my dear Miss M., then I shall owe to your ingenuity and to your feminine sensibility what you may have guessed vaguely during our conversation.

I believe that you will have to make me a great number of figures to keep my heroine company. . . .

Please write and let me know for which part you need the next drawings. I implore you not to let yourself be distracted by anything, to employ your whole feminine imagination uninterruptedly for this work and to finish it in one go. Get feathers.

I am very, very intrigued.

The second letter, dated on the 8th August, gives technical instructions. More revealing is the next which follows:

20 *August* 1918

Dear Miss M., Yesterday I sent you through my friend Dr. P. a life-size picture of my beloved one, which I beg you to imitate nicely and, mobilizing all your patience and sensuality, to transpose it into reality.

Mind the dimensions of the head and of the neck, the chest, the hips and the limbs. And mind the contours of the body, for instance the line running from the neck to the back, the curve of the belly. The second, slanting leg I drew in only to let you see the shape from inside. . . . Please make it possible for the touch to enjoy those parts where fat or muscles suddenly give way to sinews, and where the bone penetrates to the surface, like the shinbone. . . . The head must be an entirely faithful representation; it shows exactly the expression of the face which I always desire and never meet. The belly and the stronger muscles on legs, back, etc., must have a certain firmness and substance. The woman is supposed to be about 35–40 years old. . . . The figure need not be able to stand. . . . Perhaps you can see me once more with the sketch when the skeleton is finished. In order that we should understand each other perfectly. . . . If

K   145

the drawing is not quite clear as to the position of a muscle, to a tension or a bone, it is better not to consult a book of anatomy, but rather to examine the place on your own body, which you must move with your hand until you have the feeling of it warmly and distinctly. Often hands and finger tips see more than eyes.

A few months later Kokoschka showed the first signs of impatience:

16 *October* 1918

. . . In the winter I shall move to Hellerau, here near Dresden, and I should be terribly glad to enthrone the princess of my fantasy there in my new dwellings.

. . . Please do not lose patience and continue to believe that you are doing me the greatest service by making with your hands the most seductive forms of all the feminine charms which I can imagine. Your hands may then be blessed.

The artist did not move to Hellerau, although he had given up his room at the Weisser Hirsch, packed his cases and placed them all in a cab which took him to that colony of Dresden's most eccentric intellectuals: on his arrival there he caught a glimpse of the powerful woman in whose *pension* he was to stay, and he was so terrified at the sight of the worthy lady that he turned back without alighting. Instead he went to Vienna, and from there he wrote a letter which is testimony to the obviously delicate state of his nerves:

10 *December* 1918

I cannot get the skin as I do not want to touch with my hand anything that is to be used for my fetish. You must get it yourself, otherwise I cannot believe in it, and that is so important.

And now the photos. At first I was quite taken aback by the uncanny, life-like appearance. . . . Hands and feet must still be articulated. Take your own hand as a model. Or think of a well-groomed Russian woman who is used to riding. And the foot should be that of a dancer. . . .

You must also remember that hand and foot are still attractive when naked, not plump, but nervous. The size should be such that one can put on an elegant shoe, as I have already bought a lot of beautiful underwear and clothes for this purpose. As to the head, the expression is very, very strange and should even be intensified, but all traces of the making should be ex-

146

tinguished as far as possible. Can the mouth be opened? And has it got teeth and a tongue? I should be happy.

The cut is good. When doing the eyes, do not try to stylise. Imitate your own lid, pupil, eye-ball, eye-corner, etc., as much as possible. The cornea could perhaps be glazed with nail varnish. It would be nice if one could shut the eyes.

You will not understand, my dear Miss M., that I should have been tortured for many years by letting those insidious real objects, such as cotton-wool, cotton, chiffon and whatever the names of those horrible things may be, obtrude in all their earthly concreteness, while now I hope to embrace with my eyes a being which is real, yet not real, dead, yet living spirit. I hope that you make rapid progress; I plan to go to Vienna in January; from there I hope to go to the mountains where I want to hide, to forget disgusting reality and to work. And as I can bear no living people but am often delivered to despair when alone, I beg you again to use all your imagination, all your sensitiveness for the ghostly companion you are preparing for me and to breathe into her such life that in the end, when you have finished the body, there is no spot which does not radiate feeling, to which you have not applied yourself to overcome by the most complex devices the dead material; then will all the delicate and intimate gifts of nature displayed in the female body be recalled to me in some desperate hour by some symbolic hieroglyph, or sign with which you have secretly endowed that bundle of rags.

Kokoschka never ceased to worry about the life-likeness of his doll, and was haunted by the fear that it might not fulfil his expectations after all.

23 January 1919

I am very worried about the face; the embroidery must be done in such a way that I do not notice the stitches, and the expression should be like a portrait. Please think of the best method of achieving this. If I should notice that it has been made artificially, if I should see a thread, I would be pained for the rest of my life. Although I feel ashamed I must still write this, but it remains our secret (and you are my confidante): the *parties honteuses* must be made perfect and luxuriant and covered with hair, otherwise it is not to be a woman but a monster. And only a woman can inspire me to create works of art, even when she lives in my imagination only. I count the days until she will be ready to greet me. . . .

147

Time dragged on, and still the doll was not finished. It was difficult in those days to obtain the material, and every new letter contained new instructions. The artist grew more and more impatient:

22 February 1919

I cannot live without my goddess one day longer than absolutely necessary, and I know of only one way for you to send her to me . . . and be assured that, whatever the doll may look like, it will be more dear to me and more of a refuge than the whole reality of today. . . .

Kokoschka was no longer satisfied with this correspondence and detailed instructions as to how he wanted his doll made. He prepared everything for her reception, and his preparations could not have been much more elaborate had he expected the arrival of a royal bride. At first he trained a surprised maid to wait upon a lady of distinction whose imminent arrival he announced to her in mysterious terms. Then he instructed a coachman to drive through the town in such a way that all the most important monuments could be shown, stopping here and there where the lady might like to rest, take the air or enter into a shop. He also had a box at the opera reserved for himself and his doll, from which she could see best and also be seen by a crowded house. And finally he invited his best friends to celebrate with him the arrival of his doll. The great day came, and the post delivered an enormous box which was to contain the realisation of the artist's dream. So full of expectation was he, so excited at the thought of the marvels which must emerge from the huge case that he could hardly wait for his friends to arrive; but he controlled his overwhelming desire to penetrate the secret of the box until at last they came, and the celebrations began. The air of mystery with which Kokoschka surrounded the box, and the half-embarrassed, half-complacent railleries of his friends were enhanced by the liberal consumption of wine, until they all demanded that the secret should be revealed. Kokoschka, triumphantly claiming that the lady whom they were now to see would prove to them that beauty and perfection were no vain dreams, opened the box. The anti-climax was terrible: from the careful packing emerged a monster, studiously constructed according to Kokoschka's most extravagant demands, exactly corresponding with his detailed orders, covered with the most delicate silks and skins, softly padded where softness was desired, movable

148

XLII. TOWER BRIDGE
1925-26

XLIII. THE MANDRILL
1926

in all its limbs, carefully painted and neatly dressed—yet a monster, ghostly in its faithfulness to life, grotesque in its life-lessness. Kokoschka was stunned. His dream had become literally true, only to die with its realisation. The doll, whom he had en-dowed with all the attributes of grace, attractiveness and the glamour of a love-thirsty heart, was still a doll. It was dead, comic and even less acceptable than the living women of whom he had despaired. Meanwhile his friends jeered aloud, and Ko-koschka grew enraged. The doll was seized and carried out of the house into the garden to be there buried. 'The whole party settled down by the water pond with its fountain and life-size China figures by Kändler in the middle, drank and tried to com-fort me while a famous quartet with their instruments and note-stands in the water went on playing classical music through-out the spring night under the blossoming magnolias. The orgy lasted until the next morning when criminal investigation police, warned by a passer-by that a woman had been stripped and murdered in that hidden place, put in an appearance and investigated the *corpus delicti* now in full daylight in the tulip field, where it had lain forgotten.'

This was, however, not the end of the doll. Kokoschka must have secretly taken her back to his house after all. He excused this with having read that a Buddhist service to comfort the spirits of broken dolls was introduced in Japanese schools as part of an educational reform after the first world war. 'Buddhism regards all things as living in spirit whose bodies have been sacri-ficed in service. For instance, a Sutra is read by a priest to calm the spirits of the broken needles of Singer sewing machines. How different this sounds compared with Christian civilisation taking the other turn and degrading human beings into "material" for strategical purposes. It would be more comprehensible if the warring governments would say prayers for the soul of the in-ternational armament combines instead of acting an unholy farce in front of a monument of an unknown soldier.'

For years there were rumours in Dresden that Kokoschka had been seen with the doll in public, mainly at gala-nights in the opera. At any rate she did serve him as a model, as he had in-tended from the beginning: the painting called *Woman in Blue* (No. 123) which was later bought by Director Posse for the Dres-den Gallery, was done from the doll. At least one preparatory drawing for this picture is known to be now in America.

If the story of the doll became the most notorious of the antics of 'the mad Kokoschka', it was not the only one. He was, in fact, incapable at this period of reacting rationally to anything. His friends told each other countless stories of his madness, which sometimes consisted in fantastic little extravagances, often only in the most irrational replies to ordinary questions, such as his answer to a questionnaire in a leading newspaper concerning the most suitable form of government. Kokoschka demanded that 'after the model of the beauty competitions which at that time dazed the victorious part of the world, a beauty queen should be elected under the system of general vote and the throne be offered to her, whereas the rest of the ruling should be done by the people, for the people.' As in the past, his reputation was partly due to his plays, which were now performed in various cities of the Reich. In June, 1917, the Albert Theater of Dresden put on his three early plays: *Mörder Hoffnung der Frauen*,[1] *Der Brennende Dornbusch* and an elaborated version of *Sphinx und Strohmann*, under the title *Hiob*; the author himself had produced these plays. 'And here, in order to economise in actors, which were few, and in material, of which there was none, I used for the first time the trick of painting minor parts and props not essential for acting on the background. This trick became the standing novelty in revues on the Continent and in the U.S.A. for many years.' In May, 1919, *Hiob* and *Der Brennende Dornbusch* were given at a matinée in Berlin, at Reinhard's Kammerspiele. 'I again produced my plays and designed the scenery. The result was, according to Reinhardt himself, the biggest row since the early days of Brahm. The police had to go on trying to separate the fighting audience in the street.' In April, 1920, the public of Frankfurt was introduced to *Mörder Hoffnung der Frauen* and *Hiob*. The same city was the first to see *Orpheus und Eurydice*, completed in 1918, performed in February, 1922. And some time between 1921 and 1925 the composer Hindemith put *Mörder Hoffnung der Frauen* to music; as an operatic play it was shown at Stuttgart and Frankfurt.[2] All four plays were also published in one volume by Paul Cassirer in 1919; *Der Brennende Dornbusch* was here dedicated to Käte Richter, and *Hiob* to Fritz Neuberger. The plays thus became accessible to a wide public throughout the Reich.[3]

[1] A new title for the former *Hoffnung der Frauen*.
[2] These dates are based on Paul Westheim's *Kokoschka* (1925), p. 88.
[3] The well-known German playwright Carl Zuckmayer records in *Second Wind* (1941), p. 141, how he started his stage career with Kokoschka's plays:

On the whole the last war years and the revolution period were times of great activity and growing acknowledgment for Kokoschka. In 1917 he illustrated a book for Victor von Dirsztay, *Das Lob des Hohen Verstandes*.[1] In that year he spent some time in Vienna where he drew portraits, including one of his mother. 1918 brought Westheim's biography, the first book on the painter published within the borders of Germany; in it Kokoschka was enthusiastically acclaimed as one of the most gifted of living artists. In the same year *Der Sturm* published some of his lithograph portraits in a series called *Die Schaffenden*.[2] Two years later, in 1920, Kokoschka was again in Austria's capital, where he made the acquaintance of the art historian Max Dvořak. Camilla Swoboda, the wife of Dvořak's assistant at the university, was the original of a magnificent series of drawings published in 1921 under the title of *Variationen über ein Thema*[3] (Plates XXXVII, XXXVIII, XXXIX and XL). Max Dvořak thought it worth while to write an introduction for the *Variationen*. And somewhat ironically, as though to crown his success, Kokoschka was now given the status of a Professor of the Dresden Academy of Art.

It was characteristic of the state of things artistic and intellectual in the new Germany after the revolution of 1918 that Kokoschka could be given official status: Oskar Kokoschka, who had been forbidden by the Austrian Ministry of Culture to teach at any public school and who had done everything possible to deserve his reputation as a madman and an anti-social being, was appointed to the professorship by the Government of the Republic of Saxony. This event seems to have taken place in or about 1919.[4] It meant very much to Kokoschka as an official

'All the more glorious by contrast were the theatrical evenings or theatre-like performances which we instituted in the suburbs of Heidelberg or excursion places in the vicinity. They became sensations, and soon the whole university in a body would appear wherever we staged one of the fantastic symbolic dramas of the painter Kokoschka. . . .'

[1] In praise of pure reason. Published by Kurt Wolff at Leipzig.

[2] Those who create.   [3] Variations on one theme.

[4] Westheim (1925), p. 88, reports that Kokoschka was called upon to teach at the Academy 'shortly before the revolution', thus implying the date of 1918. It seems unlikely, however, that the *ancien régime* would have supported such an appointment; moreover, Kokoschka himself holds that he was not at the Academy for more than four years, and he left Dresden in 1924. The catalogue of the Georges Petit Gallery exhibition (Paris, 1931) gives the date of 1920 for the appointment, but the *Cicerone* volume of 1919 records the event as taking place at the time.

acknowledgment as well as from a practical point of view: he obtained a large studio in the building of the Academy, from the windows of which he had a superb view over the River Elbe, its bridges and towers; at the same time he was given a house in Dresden's large park, the Grosse Garten, where he could live as a permanent guest of the government. This was one of the eighteenth-century pavilions which had served as homes for the mistresses of the kings of Saxony. This isolated retreat in the large garden where Kokoschka surrounded himself with his growing collection of fantastic objects, was ideal from every point of view. 'I was waited on by a pretty and capricious Saxon parlourmaid, Hulda, who belonged to the household of Director Posse. Her chief function consisted in producing a vacuum around me when I came home, in working a kind of hoover especially adapted for that purpose, into which she made disappear people who had angered me during the day, events that had oppressed me, nauseating sights, noises, smells, touches, until time and space and reality, originating action and motion with the help of the skeleton of our logical mind, had been swallowed up by her vacuum-cleaner. Where there is a will to cling to someone else's wishes, an alert child can change the face of the earth.'

Although he had actually gained nothing in respectability 'the mad Kokoschka' was now seen less and less in public and his notoriety consequently abated somewhat. He began a new life and even found that devoted and intelligent companionship which he had wanted for years: in 1921 a young Russian girl had come to Dresden, and she now became the woman in his pictures, a position which she kept for three years. Beside her blond, long-legged figure appeared that of a pretty brunette from Berlin who, although of a somewhat different, more precious type, was, for Kokoschka, a darker variation of the same woman. He liked to paint himself between these two women, creating the first of those three-figure compositions which he continued to favour even after the Dresden period.

The influence of his Russian friend was beneficial. The last year which Kokoschka spent in Saxony was more peaceful than those which preceded it, and entirely devoted to work. He spent his days in the Academy, but he had outgrown the pedagogical enthusiasm of his early years; he now gave little time to his students to whom he no longer was the good teacher he had been. He was far too obsessed by his own work to be able to devote much attention to others. He had always been little attracted by the company of fellow-artists, and he was even less interested in art students. In the Academy building he spent most of his time in his own studio. There he worked for many hours on end, returning home in a state of complete exhaustion. Although still young, he was in poor physical condition, and he needed hours of rest before he could eat, speak or take part in any other activities. And it is characteristic that even during those periods when he allowed himself distractions such as the episode with the doll, his travels or the production of plays, none of these was ever allowed to divert him from his work; they were rather necessary to him as a relief from over-absorption, and in the end they all led back to the one thing that really mattered: his painting.

For the development of Kokoschka's work the Dresden period was decisive. It was here that he finally emancipated himself from his Viennese background. Whether this was to the advantage of his art has often been disputed. But whatever the reception of his Dresden pictures, Kokoschka's later, mature style could never have evolved without the intervention of these experiments which were most closely linked with the German school of expressionism nor without his intense studies in the Dresden Gallery. 'Kaspar David Friedrich was the first European painter to reveal to me the spirit of pure landscape. He reminded me of Schubert's *Winterreise*, if not of the Buddhist approach to nature, of the Chinese of the past. As a daily visitor to the Dresden Gallery I was inspired by Vermeer's powerful and pure colour. There was Van Eyck as well with as much mystery of space and volume as man can possibly express. I stood in awe before my god. And finally there was my old love, the Japanese colour prints at the Kupferstichkabinett, bequeathed to the state by the German expert, Professor von Seidlitz, then retired, who had collected these treasures in Japan under Fenollosa's guidance.'

★ ★ ★

Kokoschka's one true war picture, the *Knight Errant* (No. 105; Plate XXIX), is dated 1915. It originated before the artist's first departure for the front. Stylistically as well as by its mental attitude the painting belongs distinctly to the second Vienna period, during which Kokoschka had been a romantic and dramatic artist and, more particularly, to the *Tempest* phase. The man in both pictures seems to have given himself up to elements

153

stronger than himself; in both he is torn by emotions which are as Romantic as they are of his day. As a composition the *Knight Errant* is unusual. As a self-portrait it is unique. It is the most imaginative of Kokoschka's pictures of himself, perhaps because he took it straight from one of his series of lithographs (*Der Gefesselte Kolumbus*). The young man is represented prostrate on the ground, in the middle of a landscape, wearing the blue armour in which he had depicted himself in his fans. His posture is that of one who abandons himself completely to the forces of nature, while his arms are opened in a gesture of desperate questioning, and his face is strangely contracted, as though in pain. On the sky flame the letters E S, which stand for Christ's appeal to God, *My God, why hast thou forsaken me*, and a tiny figure of Death bends down over the unhappy knight. Even without these letters the situation in which Kokoschka here showed himself would have been inevitably reminiscent of the Mount of Olives—just as his early poster had been a strange variation or the *Ecce Homo* theme: the *Knight Errant* is a picture of man, helpless and deserted, delivering himself into the hands of providence, praying for strength and guidance. This is one of Kokoschka's most sincere works and equally distinguished by its originality and depth of feeling. The brush work has that dynamic character which was typical of Kokoschka's paintings at this period, and which conveys the impression that the figures —the *Knight Errant* as well as those of the *Tempest*—are carried by a storm.

To the same year belong a portrait of a *Woman with Parrot* (No. 103), a nude whom he called *Susanne* (No. 102), a portrait of the *Princess Mechthild Lichnowsky* (No. 101), and a drawing of *Adolf Loos* (No. 106). He did also a second portrait of Dr. Schwarzwald (No. 107) whom he had already painted in 1911, and a series of lithographs representing *The Passion of Christ*. In the *Garden of Olives*, which belongs to this set, he represents himself as one of the two disciples of Christ, proving once more that he, like certain Old Masters, liked to identify himself with the characters of the Holy Story. These lithographs show Kokoschka on the verge of a new style: the beautiful flow of line which had been so characteristic of his earlier works and had culminated in the *Kolumbus*, is now breaking up, with the result that the representations have become less clear. Strong black-and-white contrasts, derived from the regular black hatching of the background, obscure the compositions. The *Passion* has only one feature in common with the *Kolumbus* and the *Bachkantate* — the striking, powerful gestures of the figures. And such a picture as *Villages in Saxony* (No. 108), finished in 1918, shows the same abandonment of the flowing line, the same breaking-up of the composition into many coordinated parts, in the field of painting. Lithographs as well as canvases of this time are further distinguished by brighter colours and an almost complete absence of symbolism.

A *Self-Portrait* of 1917 (No. 110; Plate XXX) shows a further development of these new characteristics. The artist faces us in this picture, his hand pointing to his own breast in a familiar gesture. Kokoschka usually portrayed himself in his favourite colour, the blue of the 1913 portrait and the *Double-Portrait*, but this time he wears a yellow coat: he was feeling ill and perturbed in 1917, and the cold, bright colour seemed to him expressive of his restless state. The hand which had applied the colours was nervous: it worked vigorously and swiftly, but with abrupt, erratic movements covering the surface with patches that seemed to have been applied quite unsystematically. The artist could not master his arm as before. The irritation which he felt he tried to overcome by a new 'staccato' style which he developed fully much later, in his travel landscapes. Thus this picture represents a step forward in Kokoschka's technique: even more than in his last Vienna paintings the drawn contour is here abandoned, and the composition, freed of the decorative line, relies entirely on the bodily structure which is achieved by the almost plastic application of colour. This *Self-Portrait* is completely devoid of the romanticism which distinguished Kokoschka's earlier pictures of himself; his look is one of inquiry, of insistent observation; this time he did not see himself as a hero in a story, but simply as a motif for a painting. The complete sincerity of this portrait is more moving than Kokoschka's former sentimentality.

The autumn of 1917, which gave birth to the yellow *Self-Portrait* as well as to that symphony in blue, the *Stockholm Harbour* (No. 111), was a very fruitful one. In the winter at Dresden, Kokoschka also completed one of his most revolutionary portrait-groups, the *Exiles* (No. 109). This painting, done at the Weisse Hirsch, shows his two friends, Käte Richter and Fritz Neuberger, seated before a landscape with bare trees, with the artist himself looking over the writer's shoulder. Here he is once more part of a story—for one may well say the *Exiles* represent a pictorial drama. The two figures in the foreground are posed in the most natural attitudes, the woman with her legs crossed, the bearded man resting his whole weight on his right elbow, yet they appear severely collected, shut up in themselves, with a distant, heavy gaze in their eyes. Nevertheless there is something that binds these two together: externally, it is the symmetry of composition, the even balance between the two halves of the picture, and the parallel gestures of arms and hands; internally, so to speak, it is the common mood of these two people, which is like an alliance in isolation. The head of the painter quite intentionally upsets the equilibrium of the composition and adds a disquieting note to the deep absorption of the two others. There is something strangely undefinable about the relationship of these three: the situation depicted seems to invite interpretation, and any one of a number of dramatic constructions might be placed upon it, but none is clearly indicated. Like so many of Kokoschka's best pictures, this one, although of particular persons and a particular occasion, is symbolic of a general human situation. The *Exiles* are two men and a woman who are excluded by the community, left to themselves and each other, burdened by an unknown fate which they have passively accepted. Our knowledge of the actual circumstances in which the picture was conceived allows of an interpretation less personal than might otherwise seem to be called for: these three people were among the few who took no part in the world's self-destruction, who looked on in horror, but helpless, paralysed, condemned to inactivity, and waiting. The impression of tension conveyed by this work derives in large measure from the artist's brush work, which has the same abruptness as in the yellow *Self-Portrait* and the same building-up of forms by brush-strokes that seem to conflict rather than to collaborate. Compared with Kokoschka's earlier portraits, this one offers a completely new solution to the problem of composition presented by the necessity of binding together three figures; the problem is met here, for the first time, by the conscious introduction of a note of disharmony into what would otherwise have been an harmonious, extremely balanced composition. But in common with earlier works this one presents abstractions from the individual figures who are characterised without any drawing of detail. The portrait-likeness is of secondary importance. The psychological situation conveyed by the expression of the faces and by the composition is what matters. Clearly the painter at this stage had ceased to be ruled by fear and pity, as he had been in his earliest

XLIV. THE TIGON
1926

XLV. PERSIAN CAT
1926

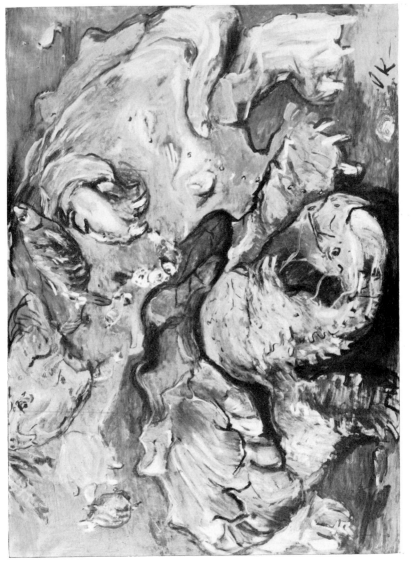

XLVI. GIANT TURTLES
1927

days, nor was he any more a prey to the passions which had torn him in the years before the war. This is a picture of resignation and suspense. The figures are of people who have been shaken by cosmic storms, and have emerged disillusioned, joyless, but dignified. It is a picture of modern man, representing not the many but those few whose fate it is to be lonely.

Only one parallel to the *Exiles* exists in the history of painting: Philipp Otto Runge's *Wir Drei*,[1] his self-portrait with his wife and brother of 1805, formerly in the Hamburg Kunsthalle;[2] there too we have three persons, isolated from the rest of the world, and linked by an intimacy which results from extraordinary circumstances; and the mood is the same one of intense concentration; but in Runge's picture the features of the individual portraits are predominant, and the landscape forms only an indistinct background, while Kokoschka's figures are more closely connected with their natural surroundings. It is interesting to note that comparable circumstances gave rise to both paintings: Runge like Kokoschka represented himself with two people who were very close to him, all three faced by a world in upheaval, torn by wars and revolutions. Each work expresses the artist's strong individualism, giving an impression of isolation and, consequently, of romanticism.

An earlier version of the same double-portrait—for there is no doubt that originally the *Exiles* was meant to be a double portrait of Fritz Neuberger and Käte Richter—may be seen in *The Rest on the Flight into Egypt* which had been included in Kokoschka's lithograph series of *The Passion*. The lithograph shows Käte Richter as the Virgin, holding the Child in her lap, leaning against her mule, while Fritz Neuberger appears as Joseph in the background. The pose of Neuberger in both representations is, in fact, almost identical.

At about the same time as the *Exiles* Kokoschka began another picture of his companions, which he called *Friends* (No. 113). A letter from the artist to Professor Tietze, in which he speaks of this new work, was partly reprinted in *Die Bildenden Künste*:[3]

'And so I now use as models the faces of people such as those who happen to have been holding out here with me for a long time and whom I know inside out, so that they torment me almost like nightmares, to build up compositions showing the

[1] We three.
[2] Burnt in the fire of the Munich Glaspalast in 1931.
[3] 1919, p. 251: 'Oskar Kokoschka's Neue Werke.'

struggle of man against man, their contrasts of one with another, like the contrast of hate and love, and in each picture I search for the dramatic accent that will weld the individuals into a higher unity. Last year I did a picture, the *Exiles*, that would interest you: and this year the *Gamblers*, which I started five months ago and which I am only now slowly finishing. It represents my friends playing cards. Each terrifyingly naked in his passions, and all submerged by a colour which binds them together just as light raises an object and its reflection into a higher category by revealing something of reality and something of its reflection, and therefore more of both. . . .'

These 'Gamblers', which he later called the *Friends*, were his companions at the Weisse Hirsch seated around a table: Käte Richter, this time in profile, her head kept highly erect, with a strangely changeable expression; the poet Hasenclever, in the centre, looking towards her with those dark pensive eyes which convey an impression of complete absorption, while his nervous, finely modelled head is resting on the back of his right hand; behind him, Neuberger and Iwar von Lücken are involved in one of those discussions which were the life-blood of the excitable little community; and in the foremost plane, with his back to the beholder, the painter himself is seated, recognisable at once by his long head. As a composition this group is not as well-balanced as the *Exiles*, nor is there any obvious connection between the five figures around the table. Some parts—such as the door with the indistinct figure of a servant, or the figure of the painter in the foreground—are not fully realised. Yet at the same time there are some wonderful parts in this painting: the melancholy poet, who sits in the middle so forlorn as though he neither saw nor heard the people around him, is a figure without any prototype or parallel in painting; and the brooding Neuberger as well as Lücken are unsurpassed in their penetrating characterisation. As a whole the picture, if still in existence, will one day be reinstated as a document of German intellectual life in 1917–18. It belongs to the series of group-portraits which was begun in nineteenth-century France. Courbet, in his *Atelier du Peintre* of 1855, had thus painted himself among his daily visitors; Fantin-Latour, in his *Hommage à Delacroix* of 1864, had shown himself thus surrounded by Whistler, Manet, Baudelaire and others. Renoir, in *Le Cabaret de la Mère Anthony* of 1866, had represented himself, Sisley and Lecour with a waitress grouped around a table. But more closely related to Kokoschka is

158

the work of a German, Hans von Marées: in a study for his Naples frescoes, preserved in the Elberfeld Museum, this painter had in 1877 portrayed himself and his friends, among whom was Adolf von Hildebrand, seated at a table, and the pose of one of these men, with his head supported by his hand and the absent-minded stare in his eyes, is not unlike that of Hasenclever in the *Friends*. Since Kokoschka knew Naples as well as Elberfeld, we may assume that he knew this picture. A faint, half unconscious recollection of Marées's work may have inspired his own composition. But as always he so transformed what he may have borrowed from tradition that the prototype becomes very remote, almost immaterial. More obvious and important is the fact that for this composition, too, Kokoschka had used one of his own earlier creations, the lithograph of *The Last Supper* from *The Passion* of 1916. The development of the idea was similar to that of the *Exiles*, which had also been based on one of the *Passion* lithographs. Of two of the heads, moreover, those of Hasenclever and Neuberger, he had made more than one study before: lithograph portraits of both are dated 1917, while another drawing of the young poet, showing him in exactly the same pose as in the painting, is dated 1918. The portrait-likeness is even greater in black and white. Hasenclever's finely shaped head, his dark eyes, his short, rebellious hair and protruding upper-lip are so sensitively rendered that one could almost believe that the skin twitches with life. Some of the nervousness in the painting was again due more to the painter than to his models: it lay in his handling of the brush as well as in his palette. Ludwig Justi, in the catalogue of the Berlin Nationalgalerie, has given an analysis of the colours used in the *Friends* which covers several pages[1]. Here it may suffice to say that almost every colour of the spectrum was used in this canvas without, however, producing an impression of brightness: the application of so much strong colour in uneven patches produced an effect of a general subdued atmosphere, which enhances the sense of tension ever-present just below the surface.

Two of Kokoschka's Dresden friends, Käte Richter and Walter Hasenclever, appear again in the *Lovers with Cat* (No. 118; Plate XXXI), which he painted in 1918. But portrait-like character hardly exists any more in this picture, which was rather an attempt to transfer movement on to canvas: movement

---

[1] *Führer durch die Nationalgalerie*, Berlin, 1931.

in support of the psychological action—a man's wooing of a woman.

The same intention, to represent movement, was realised in the *Hunting* scene (No. 115), which showed horses, riders and dogs gaily rushing through a landscape. As though painted solely for the purpose of the painter's relaxation this picture was unique in its unproblematic, purely idyllic conception. Like the *Tre Croci* (No. 90) of 1913–14 it showed that Kokoschka was a born landscape painter; but both pictures were only isolated instances of what he could do in a field which he did not find leisure to cultivate while he was still struggling with other, more intricate, psychological problems.

The gayer moods and occasional extravagances which, during those revolutionary years, alternated with Kokoschka's most problematic phases are expressed in his *Heathens* (No. 117), also completed in 1918. With a couple resting on green grass, the dark body of the man contrasting with the lighter skin of the woman in his arms, the content of this picture is a truly pagan lust for life. There is no trace here of the ecstasy, the almost mythological grandness of the *Tempest*: apart from purely technical problems there was here the desire to make physical things appear as physical and direct as could be done with colour on canvas. A similar picture was the *Summer* (No. 120), showing a single figure lying in a landscape.

Another two-figure composition, more symbolic in meaning, was *The Power of Music* (No. 119), which was several times repainted and renamed between the years 1918–19. The woman blows a horn and the man recoils and holds his hands to his ears in terror at the sound. This picture was a new variation of the struggle between the sexes which was at that time still foremost in Kokoschka's mind. To underline this symbolism the woman holds a flower in her hand, as though to indicate her ambivalence. Originally this painting had been named *Strength and Weakness*. Yet in spite of these efforts to give it a significant title the real point of the picture was its colour. Never before, and never since, did Kokoschka dare to use colour in such unmixed purity and almost vulgar contrast. The primary reds, blues and yellows are here applied like so many triumphant shouts, glaring and challenging. These colours are the vehicle of extreme passions and a manifesto of new theories on painting. *The Power of Music*, though perhaps not in itself a great work, was a milestone in Kokoschka's development.

XLVII. COURMAYEUR ET LES DENTS DES GÉANTS
1927

XLVIII. CHAMONIX—MONT BLANC
1927

For with this picture he finally took up the challenge of German expressionism eight years after his first acquaintance with this movement. When he had first seen expressionist pictures in Berlin in 1910, he had not been ready to embark upon a similar path, for he was still bound to the more æsthetic and delicate traditions of Austria. But now that his own mood had passed from timidity to despondency and even to a degree of violence, and that in his painting he had achieved emancipation from design, freedom of the brush and broader modelling, he was ready to become one of the leaders of the movement which surrounded him. Dresden was the native town of the Brücke group, and her galleries showed more or less the same works as those of Berlin. Saxon art collectors like Frau Ida Bienert filled their houses with the paintings of the Expressionists who were now at the peak of their vogue. These painters also contributed frequently to those same publications which reproduced Kokoschka's art. He had gradually learnt to appreciate the works of Corinth, Nolde and Chagall. He was far too open-minded to overlook the new possibilities they offered him. And as it was in his character always to want to surpass what he acclaimed in others, he painted a picture that was more consistent in its expressionism than anything the most advanced Expressionists had done. There is no doubt that the loud, symbolic colours, the lack of design and the excessive violence of *The Power of Music* were the outcome of Kokoschka's acquaintance with Nolde and some other Expressionists.[1] On the other hand it must be said that he himself had been an 'Expressionist' since he painted his first pictures in 1907–8. But while he had spontaneously devoted himself first to the profoundest aspect

[1] The artist himself sees the origin of his painting in a different light: '*The Power of Music* was the first painting of a series of compositions in which I expressed in my own way what I had admired in my youth in the revolutionary fresco painter of the Baroque, Maulpertsch. El Greco never appealed to my soul as much because the Spanish master was the last and most refined in a long chain, whereas with Maulpertsch begins a popular art of which Mathias Braun, the Tyrolean sculptor, is the best-known representative. Thousands of unknown artists from the Balkans to the Erzgebirge and farther north into Silesia, Poland and Ukraine, and from Vorarlberg to the mouth of the Danube gave the movement their fire and soul. It only died out with the first world war, when even the cheap popular colour prints, painted statues of St. Florian and Nepomuk, Holy Crèches and Christmas decorations, wooden soldiers and animals, merry-go-rounds, circuses, children's theatres, dolls, picture sheets, illustrated popular novels and a thousand other things, all became old-fashioned and were replaced by machine-made substitutes.'

L   161

of the new movement—its tendency to emphasise the internal, essential features of men and things—he had not originally been inclined to adopt the Expressionist technique of colourful planes and monumental design. This he tried for the first time in 1918.

The sensitive, the romantic and the witty Kokoschka seemed to be lost. But not for long; the *Woman in Blue* (No. 123), which he painted from his doll, a *Girl with Bird Cage* (No. 128) and a *Girl with Doll* (No. 127), all of 1919–20, were further examples of this same formally expressionist style. After this he returned to the symbolic story pictures which were so characteristic of his literary mind, and to the balanced harmonies of his landscape art. What he retained from that phase were a new monumental quality, a startling brightness of colour, and, for some time, the unusual proportions of expressionist figures, with the tendency to over-emphasise the human head.

The second of these new, monumental figure compositions— painted in 1921—was a picture of *Saul and David* (No. 146). Kokoschka had from time to time made drawings of religious subjects, such as *The Passion* of 1916, but he had not painted any biblical compositions since *The Visitation* (No. 52) and *The Annunciation* (No. 48) of 1910–12. In Germany, on the other hand, religious painting had been revived before the war by the Expressionists, particularly by Nolde and Corinth. And it is of Nolde that Kokoschka's *Saul and David* reminds us: the strong, contrasting colours, applied in big, unshapely patches, the uncouth figures, the inherent passion and the barbarism of this religious world were common to both artists. The head of Kokoschka's Saul is thrown back with an expression of mute despair almost like that of an animal. The head of the David is disturbing not only by its mysterious smile but also by the fact that it bears a woman's—the Russian girl's—features. Once more Kokoschka obviously takes the part of the unhappy, the suffering, and it was quite natural to him to express through feminine features the cruelty of the victor's triumph.

The intermingling of traditional and personal themes, which was particularly characteristic of Kokoschka, is most clearly found in his *Jacob, Leah and Rachel* (No. 147) of 1923. The problem of three-figure-composition was here solved in a new way: one of the two women is seated on the left, turned towards the right, in sharp profile; the man is seen on the other side of the picture, facing the front; these two form the same right angle which had been the basic structure of the double portrait of Dr.

162

and Frau Tietze (No. 15; Plate VII); but between Leah and Jacob stands Rachel, on whom the eyes of the two others are pensively resting, and whose hand Leah is holding in her two hands. Here again the fact that Jacob bears the painter's own features, while the two women were portraits of his Russian friend and the young beauty from Berlin, is immaterial from the point of view of this particular composition; in connection with the artist's whole development, however, it is worthy of note, for it shows that even when painting subjects of so general a character, he was always a portrait painter; that the individual, in other words, was his starting point, and the focus of his interest. The old urge to paint those persons who were his closest companions, was still alive in him; in Vienna he had painted straightforward, individualistic portraits of his friends; in his first Dresden years, his portraits were rather in the nature of types, and their general character was underlined by titles such as those of *Exiles* or *Friends*; now, from 1921 onwards, he represented his new friends in biblical rôles.

Another example of this new method was *Lot and his Daughters* (No. 159; Plate XXXII), also of 1923. This was another version of the three-figure composition, with the same models as had served for the *Jacob, Leah and Rachel*; but this time the solution of the problem of composition was both more original and more satisfactory: the man was represented seated, an emphatic silhouette above the two women in his arms, one naked, and the other, smaller one, clothed. The background with the River Elbe and one of Dresden's characteristic towers—as the painter saw it from his studio—is a further example of his reliance on his immediate surroundings and his attachment to local colour. The self-portrait in this picture with his characteristic long head, his broad nose and his lips, now slightly slanting on one side, was more easily recognisable than in the ape-like Jacob, more closely modelled from the painter's features, and more mature than in former works. The brush-work of both the *Lot* and the *Jacob* was broad, flat and regular: the nervousness of the war years had disappeared, the hand-writing was no longer excited, and the great intensity of earlier pictures had given way to a new serenity and an inclination towards clear, as it were architectural, composition. The variety of colour in the *Friends* was gone as well as the vivid contrasts of *The Power of Music*: instead there was a new beauty, a harmony of deeply glowing colours. The dark, warm reds and blues of *Lot and his Daughters* were comparable to the colours of old stained-glass windows, and reminiscent of the ready appeal of certain works of Kokoschka's Vienna years. This painting, with its perfect structure, its colour harmony, its melancholy mood and its manifold psychological implications, was typical of a new Kokoschka. Unfortunately it was lost in the fire that destroyed the Glaspalast of Munich. This is the more regrettable as the picture represented one of those peaks which Kokoschka's art reaches every few years—such as the *Forel* and *Else Kupfer* had been, or his *Double-Portrait* of 1913, and his *Exiles* of 1917.

A *Self-Portrait* (No. 152), accomplished in Vienna, shows Kokoschka in half-length and three-quarter profile, brush in hand and looking attentively at himself or, in effect, at the beholder. It is even less romantic in conception than the one he had done in 1917. It may, in fact, be called the most sober and impersonal of all his pictures of himself. In technique it resembles the *Jacob* and the *Lot*, with its broad, flat application of colour.

In addition two versions of a composition called *The Painter* (Nos. 160 and 164; Plate XXXIII), both obviously self-portraits, belong to this period. The first is a variation of the three-figure composition, again representing Kokoschka between two women. But there is a fourth figure in this canvas: the self-portrait on the easel, which Kokoschka is in the act of painting. Thus the solution of the old problem is again varied: there is a balance between the two women and the two men—even though one of these is only a picture in a picture, or a reflection of a reflection. The central figures are those of the painter and his Russian friend, whose smile seems to have had a particular fascination for him: even more mysterious than in the *Saul and David*, it is here full of a secret significance, expressing an unknown wealth of thought and controlled emotion. The face is round and broad-cheeked like that of a Slav peasant woman, while the strongly shaped nose and lips appear rather oriental, and the eyes, directed on the painter, are the chief vehicle of expression. Here once more the composition is open to manifold interpretation, while the title does not provide any clue as to the artist's real meaning.

The second version, painted in 1924, in Vienna, though more limited in its appeal because it suffers more from the impact of expressionism, is interesting for different reasons: it is an attempt to link the past with the present. The figure of the painter is

164

crude and heavy, painted with all the disregard of the external units of form, and with all the clumsiness of which German expressionism was capable: the portrait-likeness, although still faintly recognisable, is very remote, and the barbaric character of the mask-like head is strongly emphasised. The picture on the easel, which in the second version stands in the same position as before, is not this time a more or less realistic self-portrait: it recalls the spectre with hand pointing to a breast-wound which Kokoschka had painted in blood-red for the poster of the 1909 *Kunstschau*. The whole painting exclaims: 'This is my proof that I was an Expressionist in 1909, and this is how I paint now— more ruthlessly, more violently, more expressively than anybody else!'

Yet, it was precisely during those years of his extreme violence as a painter that Kokoschka began to develop that branch of his art in which he was to become most attractive, most generally acceptable and most objective: his landscape painting. Ever since he had occupied the academy studio with a magnificent view over the River Elbe, its bridges and a slender steeple overtowering the houses on the opposite embankment, he had been tempted to paint this panorama. He did, in fact, six or seven canvases of this subject, apart from the background of *Lot and his Daughters* which showed the same view, and of *Summer*. He probably started these paintings as a side-line, by way of relaxation from his figure compositions. But obviously the subject exerted an ever-growing fascination over him, in all the variety with which the different times of the day, the seasons of the year and his own moods endowed it. One version is hardly more than a sketch, indicating merely the position of the buildings on the far bank of the river; in another the standpoint was slightly transposed so that one of Dresden's bridges shifts to the left; in a third, a similar view is represented in the early spring, with the remains of snowdrifts on the river banks; in a fourth version the course of the river is followed further, to a point where a second bridge appears in the left background, and two steamers are seen in the foreground; yet another shows three horses being led through the water (No. 126). This last is the most important of them all, for in it the blue water and blue sky are most alive, its centre stripe of orange-coloured buildings most convincingly bathed in light and air; it is now in the Chicago Museum. But even in those canvases which Kokoschka himself considered as preparatory attempts he showed an extraordinary mastery of a subject—

165

townscapes—that was at this juncture, between 1922–24, relatively new to him. He applied to it all his new technique: the broad, square strokes of a brush dipped in bright colours, the flat, two-dimensional composition, the absence of outline drawing. There is a surprising sureness in the disposition of those plain, mosaic-like squares of colour on the canvas, in the perfect balance of the three stripes—water, embankment, and sky—and in the placing of the one tower that had to break the monotony of the line of buildings. There is even greatness in the straightforward, ever-changing and fresh approach to this relatively simple subject. Some of these views of Dresden are classical in their utter simplicity and natural harmony; yet a sense of dramatic tension is conveyed by the clustering old buildings on one side of the wide river, among which the church spire rises and seems to point one straight finger towards the sky. The subject 'Town on a River' has hardly ever been presented more perfectly. Although essentially modern in execution the river, the bridges and the spire in these pictures are of the same family as those painted by Jan Vermeer van Delft.

There was also a promise for the future in the vitality of the best versions. Thus the Chicago picture, with its cloudy sky and the multi-coloured reflections in the water, represented a transition from the more decorative, sketchy expressionist views to the dramatic impressionism of Kokoschka's later landscapes and town views.

During these years at Dresden, as at all periods, Kokoschka did some pictures of children. One of these was the portrait of *Gitta* (No. 142), the daughter of an art dealer and friend, which he painted in exchange for a Nô-mask, and another the *Girl with Doll* (No. 127). Here Kokoschka's inclination to underline any sweetness that might be inherent in his subject emerges even through the barbaric crudeness of this period. It is amazing how, in this work, he succeeded in producing the effect of soft roundness by those same bold brush-strokes, by the same colour patches which in other works resulted in harshness. The style of expressionism was on the whole unsuited to portrait painting, and consequently there are relatively few expressionist portraits in existence. These two portraits of children are interesting because they illustrate what possibilities nevertheless existed in this phase of art.

More interesting as exemplifying Kokoschka's development than attractive in itself is a *Mother and Child* (No. 139), in which an unpleasant note of sentimentality is added to the violence of colour and extreme simplification of design. Another version of the same subject, representing a woman seated, holding a baby in her lap, is one of a number of Kokoschka's experiments in the construction of monumental figures by means of strong colour only (No. 163). It is noteworthy that the 'Mother' motif in earlier years anticipated in *Blind Mother* (No. 75) and perhaps also hidden, unknown to the painter, behind all those pictures representing the figure of the leading, domineering woman, appeared now repeatedly in its most direct form.

★   ★   ★

Kokoschka's development as a draughtsman and illustrator followed the same lines as his development in painting. In 1917 he did a *vignette* and six plates for Victor von Dirsztay's *Lob des Hohen Verstandes*.[1] The restless, unhappy state of mind from which he was then suffering was clearly expressed both in the style and in the subjects he chose to illustrate: in the figure of a suicide hanging on a tree; in a bird with a human body; in a churchyard fantasy, with crosses and a figure howling over a skull; in the mad faces of a man and a woman posed like 'Aristotle and Phyllis'; and finally in the woman who, like some demon of vengeance, bears a sword. These were drawn with a hard, unwilling pen, apparently undisciplined and scribbling; yet there is form hidden, as it were, in these outlines and very sparse inner contours. The roundness of the pen-strokes corresponds closely with the hectic brush-strokes of the *Exiles* and the yellow *Self-Portrait*.

Of a similar, cartoon-like character were his *Hiob*[2] illustrations in black charcoal outlines with light grey shading. Over-large heads made the figures top-heavy, while their over-large hands and feet emphasised their expressive gesticulation. These *Hiob* drawings are very strongly reminiscent of certain Yiddish theatre scenes such as those of the Palestine Habima or the Moscow

[1] In praise of pure reason.

[2] Job. *Hiob* was the title which Kokoschka gave to a new version of his old play *Sphinx und Strohmann*. 'These *Hiob* drawings were a side-line of my activity as the producer of my own play. In my youth I had witnessed in Vienna the last period of the famous popular "Hanswurst" comedy, with Girardi leading in Nestroy's plays, which ended a tradition of a true people's art continuing in Vienna from the Middle Ages, while in Germany it had expired already in the days of the great classics.'

Yiddish State Theatre: they have the same grotesque picturesqueness, the same wide gestures, which are as expressive as any words, the same rhythmic movements and the same pathetic humour of people schooled in resignation. At that time Kokoschka could not have known either of these Eastern art centres; but it is possible that, when looking for a background suitable for his *Hiob* play, he remembered the Jewish milieu with which he must have been familiar in Vienna, where eastern and biblical traditions were still mixed with the squalor of modern lower-class life.

It was also in 1917—on the occasion of a short stay in Vienna —that Kokoschka made a portrait lithograph of his mother which ranks among his most beautiful works. So perfect in fact is the drawing that its genesis evades analysis. The head is seen in three-quarter profile to the left. With the eyes, clear and visionary, of youth, yet with the slack contours, indicated by certain lines around the chin, of an old woman, it seems ageless. The impact of heavy experiences borne with energy, even passion, has modelled the face of this obviously unusual woman. Great determination lies in her contracted forehead, her thin lips and her narrowed left eye. But her hair, sparkling with life, gives her an air of unruliness, almost rebelliousness. In this portrait of his mother Kokoschka did not allow himself any mannerism or stylisation: he just endeavoured to make it as truthful as he could. The result, although realistic, is not by any means academic naturalism: at this stage Kokoschka had mastered his material so completely that he could render any subject in an original, yet faithful manner. This head is outlined with a few sure, emphatic strokes around the most characteristic parts: the slope of the forehead, nose, chin, lips, eyelids and pupils; a few lighter strokes add eyebrows, the pouches under the eyes and around the chin, the lines near the corners of the mouth; some very slight touches mark the modelling of cheek and forehead: and lastly, an apparently deliberate, yet naturally organised criss-cross of very swift strokes renders the hair and accentuates a few characteristic places in the face, such as the angle between nose and eyebrow. This drawing has the perfection, objectivity and power of an Old Master. It bears comparison with Dürer's portrait of his mother which it rivals in combination of realism and artistic vision.

Portrait drawings, mostly translated into the medium of lithography, became one of Kokoschka's favourite genres. He did one of his father—not to be compared with that of his mother—and his own, as well as Hasenclever's and several of a young woman called *Coronna* in 1918. In 1919 followed one of *Lücken*, in 1920 that of the Dresden actress *Hermine Körner*; and more studies of young women, all published as lithographs under the title of *Die Töchter des Bundes*,[1] were finished in the same year. But the whole series culminated in the *Variationen über ein Thema*, also of 1920.[2]

Back in Vienna again for a short while in the summer of that year Kokoschka watched the young woman, who is the subject of these variations, while she listened to a Bach concert. And within a few weeks, during which he continued to study his new model, he made ten drawings of her, in which she appears in ten quite different moods, almost like ten different, but somehow related women. This is what Max Dvořák says in his preface to the *Variationen*: ' Kokoschka's cycle represents in ten variations the head of a young woman, or rather, it represents ten different pictorial visions, which were inspired by this head, but in which the individual impression that had constituted the starting point only plays the part of an accompanying melody, sometimes stronger, sometimes fainter, like a song heard from a distance. . . . Her ever-changing appearance derives neither from the discovery of new external features in the model, nor from changes caused by the influence of light and atmosphere, but from the inexhaustible variety and ceaseless flow of expression animated by a human soul, which is the real subject of these variations, as it is the essential basis of all human representation. Kokoschka follows here with feverish excitement spiritual transitions and fluctuations, as once artists of the Florentine Renaissance tried to discover laws of anatomy by illustrating various attitudes in a series of studies.'

The variety of expression of which one human face is capable is indeed portrayed in this series in a way such as had hardly been achieved before.[3] The model's actual features are completely subordinate to the studies in human expression. The

[1] The Daughters of the Covenant.

[2] Published by R. Lanyi, Vienna, 1921.

[2] Toulouse-Lautrec's *Elles* of 1896, ten lithographs, nine of which portray the same woman, can be considered as an attempt in the same direction, but the French artist was far more interested in the external features of his models, in their changing expressions during the various stages of awakening from sleep and of the female toilet than in psychological manifestations.

range is so wide that she appears now old and ugly, now young and attractive, even pretty. We have all observed similar changes in living people and therefore know that they exist. Not everybody, however, is capable of so many varying moods: concentration, tension, pensiveness, serenity, dejection. Kokoschka's model, by her high degree of sensitiveness, was particularly suited to such a study. The technical means used to produce the effect of change are so subtle as almost to defy analysis. Different viewpoints and poses, even differences in the arrangement of the hair, all contribute to the main purpose, the delineation of changes in facial expression. But the real differences are in the face itself, in the extent to which she opens her eyes, in their direction, and above all, in the position of modelling shadows. These are never quite alike, and it is mainly through their differences that the whole expression is modified. The means used here by the artist are purely those of line, and quite new. Although he seems to have had little regard for the actual features of his model and to have had no concern for portrait-likeness in the academic sense, the effect is life-like despite the extreme economy of line with which it is achieved. Beyond the outline of the head, and the position of eyes, nostrils and lips there is no drawing of detail; the face is modelled by shadows filled in with extremely quick strokes, like deliberate, untidy scribbles; but they are so placed as to emphasise precisely the most characteristic forms of the face, where grief had made hollows or smiles had engraved friendly lines. These scribbles are now like anatomical indications of muscles, now like symbolic rays and furrows. They create the character of these drawings. Only an artist who was absolute master of his medium could allow himself such revolutionary methods.

The *Variationen* (Plates XXXVII, XXXVIII, XXXIX and XL) may be said to comprise the essence of Kokoschka's art at that time. They certainly represent the culmination of his psychological studies. In his youth he had seen the expression of one dominating disposition in each human face, had conceived each one of his models as an actor in one rôle only. Now he had come to see countless moods in a single human being and had recognised the innumerable artistic possibilities in one face. After these *Variationen* he could hardly go any further in the exploration and representation of the human character.

More than anything Kokoschka had done before, these drawings showed that he had gradually fallen into a new mood himself: his exploring eye, which had in his early beginnings been influenced by a haunting compassion, and had later been turned in upon his own tempestuous emotions, was now guided by a new lyricism. Without losing any of his penetrating powers, with even an enhanced sensibility, Kokoschka had embarked upon the road towards a new objectivity: his abounding imagination was for once controlled by a realism more faithful in spirit than in detail and made possible by a gradually acquired virtuosity which gave him complete mastery of his craft. Where he had formerly been driven to work almost like one obsessed or in a trance, he was now able to canalise his creative impulse within the limitations imposed by calm observation and a masterful organisation of his material. But as yet he was capable of such detachment only in his drawings. His paintings, which always occupied by by far the greater part of his time, were more wildly experimental than ever, except in his landscapes which, like his drawings, give evidence of patient observation and have the same objective and unproblematic qualities. His brush achieved only gradually, and much later the same balanced mastery, his canvases the same broadness and depth, as these drawings. It is moreover interesting to note that it is always Kokoschka's graphic art which evidences most clearly the inherent continuity of his work, even when his paintings seem to lose themselves in a labyrinth of theories and experiments. This is true of the two periods within Kokoschka's career which have hitherto been least understood: the years from 1918–24, and those of the second world war. The link between Kokoschka's earliest portraits and his Dresden period can be traced through the *Variationen*, which have the psychological penetration of his earliest work as well as the new objectivity of approach and virtuosity in the application of new techniques.

After the *Variationen* Kokoschka did other portraits of women in the same manner, first drawing them in charcoal and then reproducing them as lithographs. Two of these, entitled *Recha* and *India*, both done in 1921, represent his Russian girl friend. Less elaborate in composition, and less surprising in expression than the *Variationen*, they are drawn with an even greater concentration on the main features of the head, particularly the eyes. Here even the hands, hitherto always used so effectively by Kokoschka as means of characterisation, are omitted. A few unflattering, but highly distinctive outlines, some light-grey shadows, large eyeballs and many vigorous strokes for

171

the hair compose these portraits which are more realistic, in the usual sense of the word, one might almost say more conventional, than Kokoschka's former drawings; it is, in fact, by the new economy of means employed in their production that they resemble the more familiar sketches of other artists. The outstanding quality of the *Recha*, however, which lies chiefly in the exquisite manner in which the neck rises out of the collar, in the sensitive drawing of the two slightly asymmetrical eyebrows, in the heavy gaze of the serious eye and in the beautiful curves of the hair, distinguishes it from other portrait drawings of the modern school.

★　　★　　★

Kokoschka's activity during his Dresden period was great as well as varied. In 1923 a new book by Victor von Dirsztay, *Der Unentrinnbare*,[1] appeared in Munich, illustrated with nine drawings by Kokoschka. As his paintings and drawings became well known to an ever wider public, his written works were welcomed with increased interest. Cassirer's publication of Kokoschka's plays in 1919 was one year later followed by a volume entitled *Die Gefährten*,[2] published in Vienna and Leipzig, which contained several of his early works, including the text of *Die Träumenden Knaben* of 1907; a poem of 1915, entitled 'Alos Makar'; the plays *Mörder Hoffnung der Frauen*, dated 1907, and *Der Brennende Dornbusch* of 1911; a *Spruch*[3] of the same year; a *Rätsel*[4] of 1915; a lecture given in 1911 under the title of *Vom Bewusstsein der Gesichte*;[5] and a *Schlusswort*,[6] also written in 1911. The volume was introduced by a poem by Albert Ehrenstein, addressed to Oskar Kokoschka. Most interesting among all these contributions is the essay *Vom Bewusstsein der Gesichte*. As autobiographical as many of Kokoschka's paintings, this piece of writing combines an introduction of general character, in which the painter acknowledges his debt to Amos Comenius and the great German classical authors (whom, characteristically, he refers to as 'humanists') and outlines his philosophy of life, with a symbolic tale about a red necklace. In that naïve, often involved but very vivid style which has always been at the painter's com-

[1] The Inescapable.　　　[2] The Companions. Genossenschaftsverlag.
[3] Saying.　　　[4] Riddle.
[5] Of the realisation of visions. Formerly printed in *Genius*, 1919, p. 39.
[6] Epilogue.

172

mand when writing, he tells here how the red necklace, a present from 'a formerly beloved woman', came back to his mind at the moment when, severely wounded in the war, he awoke from unconsciousness and felt: 'Apart from this necklace of stones which glow when held towards the sun, I have lost everything;' how, in the first letter he was able to write, he asked his mother to send him the necklace; how she, being unable to find it, was overcome by the fear he might not believe her and might think that she had purposely hidden the necklace to make him forget the woman 'who left me so much pain and this present'; how, at the very moment of his return, she upset a flower-pot: 'And among the broken pieces, at the very bottom, there was the cursed necklace! My mother, now quite changed, and myself, quite upset, picked it up from the ground: for the necklace stood for the fire which came from my love and died while I argued with my beloved one; until it destroyed me. . . . What appeared to me like hate, has remained preserved as love. . . . Had I to lose myself first, like the burning love, to find myself again with the help of a necklace? . . . After I had almost lost it, I now love to hold life, as much as I was once eager to clutch it.'

A symptom of the general and official acceptance which Kokoschka enjoyed during these years at Dresden was the fact that the Dresdner Künstlervereinigung in 1922 commissioned him to design a china plaque to be executed by the Meissen porcelain factory.[1] In his search for a suitable subject the painter resorted to one of those plays with words and pictures which he had invented in 1908, when he wrote his *Sphinx und Strohmann*: he drew an allegory of 'Anima' on one side, and one of the anagram 'Mania' on the other. 'Anima' was represented as an artist at work—as a self-portrait, of course, for to Kokoschka 'the artist' was always himself. 'Mania', on the other hand, was one of his old subjects: the struggle between man and woman seen here wrestling. Both scenes are executed in the emphatic style of the *Bachkantate*. This strange relapse into a stage the artist had left behind eight years earlier can be explained by his inexperience in a new technique. At the same time the solution of the problem of fitting an emblematic design of modern character into a circle is both individual and highly successful.

[1] Reproduced in *Das Kunstblatt*, January 1929, p. 16.

173

III. TRAVELS

THE LANDSCAPE PAINTER

In spite of his growing success Kokoschka's sojourn in Dresden came to an end very suddenly. Ever since he had been to Sweden in 1917 the painter had felt frustrated by his confinement within the frontiers of Germany and Austria, and in the course of seven years this feeling became unbearable. First the war, then the internal state of the Reich prevented him from escaping, and finally the inflation made travelling abroad impracticable. When the general state of affairs political and financial settled again, however, Kokoschka would stay no longer. He took his leave from Saxony in a way worthy of the title 'the mad Kokoschka' which the Dresdeners had given him: one evening he left a letter for the Director with the porter of the Academy, and when it was discovered next morning that the envelope contained his resignation, he had already left the country. He had gone to Switzerland, and with him was his Russian friend.

Kokoschka wanted to paint landscapes. But he did not intend to stay very long anywhere: he wanted to move, to see that the world was really open again, that he could go where he liked. The sensation of crossing freely into another country did not suffice to overcome his claustrophobia. He longed for an experience that would give him the long-missed feeling of being able to embrace the whole earth. He was driven to go high up in the mountains, where his eye could reach far and distances grew with every step. For this reason he and his friend settled in 1924 in the village of Blomay above Vevey on Lake Leman; and for the same reason Kokoschka has for twenty years—indeed up to the present—always chosen the highest point for his residence wherever he stayed—a top-floor room in the Savoy Hotel to paint the River Thames, and a slope of the Atlas Mountains to paint the African desert—and has always composed his landscapes so as to take in the widest possible view. It is from this high standpoint, which they all share, that they derive their characteristic breadth and wealth. For the *Tre Croci* of 1913–14 and to some extent also for his Elbe views of 1920–23, he had stood on the same level as the figures in his pictures; when he painted his views of *Lake Leman* (Nos. 168 and 169) in 1924, he occupied a position high up on a mountain slope, and the character of his pictures changed accordingly.

After five months on Lake Leman Kokoschka's stay there was interrupted as suddenly as was usual in his life: he received the news of his father's serious illness and hurried to Vienna. While he stayed with his mother after the death of his father, he was no less active than usual: a portrait of the composer *Arnold Schönberg* (No. 172), one of *Dr. Schwarzwald* (No. 173) whom he had already painted in 1911 and in 1915–16, one of the poet *Ernst Blass* (No. 179) and a new one of *Karl Kraus* (No. 180; Plate XLI) were the fruit of his few months at home. Painted in his broadest, most colourful style, of a massiveness that excluded all detail, these portraits represent a continuation of his latest Dresden phase. That portrait-like character was not necessarily an attribute of these pictures is testified by the following story told by one of Kokoschka's friends: asked for his opinion of the freshly begun portrait of Karl Kraus he replied 'It is one of those old prophets we know you can do. But it is not a portrait—it is not Kraus.' After some hesitation the painter admitted: 'You are quite right.' During the following night he locked himself up with his picture, and in the morning the likeness left nothing to be desired. It was no longer merely a spiritual one: in fact, this portrait of Kraus of 1924–25 resembles the sitter more than the one Kokoschka had done earlier. It shows Karl Kraus as he was best known to the greatest number of people: seated at his table lecturing, or performing one of those Offenbach operettas which, having adapted the text to his own purpose and interspersed it with his own satirical verses, but faithful always to the spirit of the author, he used to sing unaccompanied to a delighted public, with unsurpassable musical talent. He is seen as he was in his later years, lean and slightly bowed, with his beautiful eyes animated by a vitality which radiated from this physically so delicate man and affected all who came into contact with him, notwithstanding his air of complete withdrawal into an intellectual world of his own creation. The gesture of his hands in the picture is one he might have used to indicate the scenery when reading a play—one of those gestures by which he made every one of his spectators see what he saw before his inward eye. The eloquent eyes and hands of this second portrait of Karl Kraus

175

show clearly that Kokoschka in 1924–25, in spite of years of the crudest, most deliberately brutal and startling expressionism, had lost nothing of the sensitiveness which had distinguished the young Kokoschka of fifteen years earlier.

When these few portraits were finished, Kokoschka left Vienna, and started on a journey that took him through many countries and to the summit of his fame. These travels developed gifts which had remained dormant so long as his interest was focused on his personal life and his friends; his horizon widened through knowledge of foreign lands, the variety of nature and of people, and through contact with strange cultures which he had known from hearsay alone. And not least the opportunity which his travels afforded him of seeing works of art widely different from anything he had known before, and the new subjects, demanding entirely new methods, with which they confronted him, profoundly influenced his style. Briefly, his travels between 1924 and 1934 made of Kokoschka the landscape painter and dramatic Impressionist who is best known today.

In the autumn of 1924, when Kokoschka left Vienna, Adolf Loos was just going to Paris, and Kokoschka decided to accompany him, together with the painter Sebastian Isepp, who had once exhibited with him in the Hagenbund exhibition of 1911. All three being without any particular aim and, at least for the moment, without money, they accepted an invitation extended to them by some equally unprejudiced central-European artists to share an empty house in which everybody slept on the floor, wrapped up in blankets, and where they all felt as free as they desired. After a few weeks Kokoschka and Isepp moved to the old Hôtel Foyot, famous as a regular abode of celebrated artists and writers from Oscar Wilde to Rainer Maria Rilke. Here they stayed for some months during which Kokoschka sought out those things which he felt concerned him, or rather his art; he visited the museums and art galleries of Paris. The road to the Louvre became his daily pilgrimage. He worked little himself and enjoyed this leisurely life which did not, however, continue for long. One day an art dealer from Frankfurt, to whom he owed money, searched him out in his hotel and made a very definite proposal: he had taken for him an attic room in the Grand Hotel to which he removed the surprised artist, and he requested him to paint the view from his window, by way of repaying his debt. And Kokoschka set to work as he had been told.

176

XLIX. LYON
1927

L. EXODUS, COL DE SFA NEAR BISKRA
1928

LI. ARAB WOMEN
1928

It is difficult to establish whom Kokoschka met and mixed with in Paris. His Russian friend, whom he had left behind in Switzerland when he hurried to his father's deathbed, came from her new domicile in London to visit him. Nancy Cunard was another of his friends, as the portrait he did of her in 1924 testifies. He made many English contacts in the French capital. Naturally he knew Paris artists. They had heard of him and seen his graphic work long before he came to France, and they accepted him long before the critics or the French public understood him. Pascin was among those who drew him into their circle. He took part in their evening parties which usually began in some small café of the Quartier Latin and were continued in some flat or studio, where one sat and talked well into the small hours of the morning.

He absorbed many influences unconsciously. His art underwent a change—it became westernised. This happened in spite of many prejudices which he had brought with him from expressionist Germany: prejudices mainly against the current reign of 'good taste' in the arts as well as in daily life which embittered him just as it had driven him to opposition in the old Austria. Probably it is due to these prejudices that Kokoschka was not able to range himself with the fashionable artists of the day, and also that he remained such a solitary figure in modern European art. He had always made his own what fitted his purpose, and he did so in Paris. But more important than these individual influences were other factors. The varied scenery, with which Kokoschka became acquainted first in France and then on his further journeys, in its wealth and sun-bathed beauty, appealed to the painter's senses more strongly than anything he had known before and released in him those artistic faculties which had remained suppressed in the tense, comparatively cheerless atmosphere in which he had spent his earlier years. Further, he was deeply affected by the works of the impressionist school of which he saw many more in Paris than he had ever known before. There is no doubt that the towns and landscapes of the impressionist group contributed to Kokoschka's conversion to this genre. We know that he had done landscapes before, even with a fanatical persistence, as in Dresden where he painted the view of the River Elbe over and over again. But figure compositions had hitherto been his main subject, the task which he had taken most seriously. Since he began to travel he wanted to paint nothing but the scenery which surrounded him, and in each panorama he wanted to render the whole breadth of the world from which he had been excluded so long. He became obsessed by the desire to paint an *Orbis Pictus*, more colourful and wider in scope than that of Amos Comenius whose ideas had always had such fascination for him. This obsession kept him busy for ten years and drove him through three continents.

Kokoschka's methods changed with his ambitions. Discarding the monumental, often unshapely and problematic constructions of his Dresden period he re-introduced a more detailed design into his canvases. He did not, however, revert to the psychological art of his earliest years; his interest, directed inward for so long, turned now towards the outer world. Purely visual impressions became the new source of his art which had hitherto never been satisfied with the mere rendering of what his eyes saw. Interpretation, till then his main object, began to play a secondary part. Greater objectivity became characteristic of his work, although the strongly imaginative approach to his subjects as well as the unsurpassed virtuosity of his execution imbued his new paintings with the same individuality as had always distinguished them.

After some months in the French capital he began to explore the country. At first he went to Bordeaux, where he painted the cathedral and the theatre; then to Biarritz where he made a picture of the beach. A few months later, in 1925, he turned south, stopping at Avignon, Vernet-les-Bains, Aigues Mortes, on his way to Marseilles. He crossed the Spanish frontier and penetrated to Toledo, Madrid and Lisbon. In the same year he also went north to Amsterdam, where the firm of Cassirer, who were financing his travels, had opened a branch. In 1926 he came for the first time to London. The recollections of his English friends show that he travelled very much in style: he occupied a house in Park Lane, was served by a smart butler and a neat maid, and a hired car waited at his door to take him where he had to go. Later he moved to the Savoy Hotel from whose upper windows he was able to paint the river, *Waterloo Bridge* (No. 213), and his *Thames View* (No. 205). Excursions to Richmond and Dover also resulted in landscapes which he used at that time to finish in a day or two. The only portrait he painted in England seems to have been that of Adèle Astaire, now Lady Charles Cavendish. But in animals he had discovered a new subject that interested him as much as human models. He spent hours in the Zoo, first before a magnificent *Mandrill* (No. 207; Plate XLIII), then before the *Tigon* (No. 211; Plate XLIV), whose grotesque but awe-inspiring form he rendered in a picture of unique vividness. Some *Roes* (209), on the other hand, whom he watched in Richmond Park, retained in his canvas all the grace that is theirs in life. From London he seems to have gone to Berlin. One of his first works there was the picture of a *Persian Cat* (No. 212; Plate XLV), which concluded the series of animal pictures so magnificently begun in the Zoological Gardens of London. At night, in the Zoological Gardens of Berlin, he painted his *Giant Turtles* (No. 220). He also made a portrait of *Leo Kestenberg* (No. 214), who had become his friend in earlier days when, as a director of Paul Cassirer's publishing department, he had supervised the publication of Kokoschka's writings and graphic works and who was now Secretary of Music in the Ministry of Culture. Cassirer had died in the meantime, and his successors, Grete Ring and W. Feilchenfeldt, made efforts to strengthen the bond between the firm and the painter. In 1927 they arranged an exhibition of his portraits and animal pictures in their galleries,[1] where they had exhibited his landscapes two years before. The success with which these exhibitions met in Berlin was tremendous. But Cassirer's had still greater ambitions: they sent Kokoschka's works to Zürich, where they were exhibited in the Kunsthaus, and one year later, in 1928, to London where their exhibition in the Leicester Galleries attracted less notice than had ever been accorded to Kokoschka elsewhere. Meanwhile the painter, still travelling, had returned to France and added more French scenes to his work: *Lyon* (No. 218; Plate XLIX), *Annecy* (No. 216), *Courmayeur* (No. 217; Plate XLVII), *Chamonix-Montblanc* (No. 219; Plate XLVIII). But he wished to leave Europe. 'Wherever I went, I felt the same conditions leading to the same results, which I had experienced on the other side of the barricade. I could not regain confidence in the world I had known in my youth, and when I had visited the countries who had won the war I began to doubt whether peace would last very long. I wanted to live with the Mohammedans and quickly learnt some Arabic before I left Europe.' In 1928 he crossed the Mediterranean and began to explore Tunisia. From the Atlas Mountains he watched caravans, and from the slope of a hill he painted *Biskra: Exodus* (No. 224; Plate L). Once he was the guest of a French hermit who lived among the antique ruins of *El Kantara* (No. 223). From the monk's solitary cell high up

[1] Menschen und Tiere.

179

on a hill he painted that oasis of palm trees. To get a view over Tunis Market he climbed on to the flat roof of a grocer's dilapidated house which broke under his weight, with the result that he—or Cassirer's—had to pay for the whole shop to be rebuilt. By means of a cigarette lighter, which he presented to them, he persuaded two Arab women to sit for him. They belonged to a tribe of horse-breeders, and he accompanied the caravan for a month while their husbands travelled by railway—a means of transport considered far more thrilling by them than horseback. He also watched the building of a mosque and made the acquaintance of the Arab architect who 'looked like Michelangelo' but was completely illiterate. Kokoschka was fascinated by the contrasts in this African city: while he saw a bank being built in concrete with the most modern machinery, and yet never finished, the mosque was erected by natives who carried the building materials on their heads, while the Arab architect measured everything with a string. He was even more amazed when he saw 'Michelangelo' cover the interior of the cupola with exuberant decorations in one day. His interest won him the friendship of this master builder who took him up on the scaffold into his cupola; he also introduced him to the Marabout of Temacine. Kokoschka had no sooner seen this beautiful brown giant than he decided to paint a portrait of him. But this was not so simple as he had expected: the Marabout refused his request under the pretext that the Koran did not permit him to have his portrait painted. Kokoschka would not be deterred: he found out that it was forbidden only to make pictures that throw a shadow. In the end the Marabout yielded to his persuasion, and Kokoschka became a guest at his palace. 'I became a friend of that enlightened young prince who was a descendant from Muhammed's family. With this new friend and a Frenchman belonging to the Order of the Pères Blancs we carried on philosophical discussions which showed me the roots of decay in the scepticism of modern western civilisation and made me aware of the deep spiritual culture still alive in Arab philosophy: strengthening the soul with patience while nourishing the imagination and reason. In spite of all corruption, due to the subjugation of the Mohammedans, I found here again for the first time the magic world in which my soul felt at peace. I only know what it is to be homesick when I remember that time of my life.' His experiences at the Marabout's palace were very different from any he had encountered at previous sittings: he happened to start the picture during a period of fasting, when

LII. SIDI AHMET BEN TIDJANI, THE MARABOUT OF
TEMACINE
1928

LIII. VENICE, SANTA MARIA DELLA SALUTE WITH ROOFS
1928

the physical needs of mankind were utterly neglected in his new environment; as a result he was fed mostly on what he believed to be bad eggs and water in which he could see insects floating. As soon as the great fast was ended, however, he received an invitation to a festival of truly oriental splendour. The food was magnificent, and it was served by servants wearing white gloves.

Kokoschka's next journey took him to Istanbul and Jerusalem. His pictures of both these cities may be counted not only among his best works but among the most beautiful landscapes of our time (Nos. 232, 233; Plate LIV).

Kokoschka's permanent quarters through all these years were in Paris. But he never stayed there very long. Shortly after his return from the Near East, in 1929, he went northwards, to Ireland and Scotland.

But it was not long before he turned south again, this time to Egypt, where he painted the Pyramids (No. 235). In 1930 he was in Algiers where his *Algérienne au Tonneau* (No. 236) was done. His next journey took him to Italy, from where he brought the *Harvest at Anticoli* (No. 238; Plate LV). At this juncture his art dealer offered him a new travelling contract, but Kokoschka was longing to see his mother who was now very aged and in need of his support. Thus his journeys came to an end, at least for the moment.

The year 1931 was one of enormous success for him. Cassirer's had arranged a comprehensive exhibition of his works at the Kunsthalle of Mannheim, one of German's leading museums of modern art, which subsequently travelled to the galleries of Georges Petit in Paris. The French public, hitherto quite indifferent, was much impressed by this survey of Kokoschka's works. André Lhote gave voice to the general surprise in his article published in the *Nouvelle Revue Française*:[1] 'Le Parisien, isolé du monde par une conscience un peu trop haute de sa valeur, est appelé à l'ordre par cette exposition qui lui montre qu'au delà de ses frontières se cultive un art qui—est-ce possible —n'est pas uniquement Barbare! . . . Le jour du vernissage, des gens tombant de la lune, mais sympathisant tout de même, s'interrogeaient: "Qu'est-ce que vous pensez de ça?" . . . Ce délire clairvoyant, que j'appelai jadis "le coup de foudre", a produit des paysages magnifiques . . . *Lyon, Venise*, et *Richmond Terrace* qui nous émerveillent par leur organisation dynamique, leurs tons rares et intenses, et surtout par une harmonie chaque

[1] Quoted by Paul Westheim in *Das Kunstblatt*, Heft 5 (May), 1931.

fois renouvellée, ce qui nous change des tonalités toutes faites et des tableaux peints en séries pour être vendus "au numéro".'

After the spectacular success of the Paris exhibition Cassirer's thought that the time was ripe to launch Kokoschka as a permanent feature of the international art market—something like the Central-European counterpart of Picasso. Kokoschka, on the other hand, thought that his fame was now well enough established for him to be independent of all dealers. In 1931 their differences led to an open breach between them which received unusual publicity owing to the fact that both parties, in their disappointment, resorted to a public correspondence in one of Germany's most widely read newspapers, the *Frankfurter Zeitung*, where their mutual obligations and divergencies of opinion were discussed with as much wit as malice. Nevertheless, neither Cassirer's nor Kokoschka himself ever seriously regretted their long association.

★ ★ ★

The painter could look back on an enormous development. As soon as he had left Dresden behind and settled on the Lake Leman his view seemed to have extended, and a new element had entered into his art: none of his former landscapes—neither his very early works, nor his *Dresden* views nor even his *Stockholm Harbour*—had shown such breadth and depth as the picture he now painted of the Swiss lake: like a mighty diagonal the long, rather narrow lake cut across the canvas, with high mountains on the left bank and a flat stretch of land with houses on the right, and distant hills at the far end of the lake disappearing in mist. The varied colours of the sky reflected in the water give the scene its atmosphere and add new life to the impressive depth of the picture. Kokoschka was here already feeling his way towards a more impressionist method than he had employed before in order to convey the atmosphere he had been inclined to neglect, even though he had not yet been in Paris, where he was to take the opportunity of studying the works of the French Impressionists more closely than had ever before been possible for him.

When he passed through Italy in the same year, 1924, he applied similar methods to his view of Venice. His Canale Grande (No. 174) has not the same width and transparency as his *Lake Leman* (No. 169). But with its steamships and boats, the building on the left and the patchy sky, this picture shows Kokoschka sufficiently enterprising to tackle in his own way a subject as hackneyed and as romanticised as this. On this first stay in Venice he did not choose as subjects any of the magnificent palaces and picturesque passages for which the city is famous; neither the Piazza San Marco, nor the Giudecca, which every painter since the days of Canaletto had painted, attracted him; nor did he attempt to render the peculiar light of Venice, where water and air seem to merge into one another, producing those effects of mistiness or of flickering brilliance which had fascinated Turner, Whistler and Monet. His Venice is a city of modern, mechanised life, rendered with the same bright colours which he had adopted during his expressionist phase, and used in painting northern cities. What interested him at this moment was the quivering life and movement in the wide panorama and the odd contrast of motor launches hurrying to and fro between the marble-coloured, gothic façades. His picture of *Florence* (No. 167) is just as far removed from romanticism and the worship of historic monuments: rather sketchy in execution, its composition is a variation of that of his Dresden views: the embankment of the Arno with one church towering high above it and the hills behind is strongly reminiscent of the Elbe, and indeed less impressive. From these two Italian views one might judge that Kokoschka was less fascinated by his experiences there than would have been expected: a marked absence of the personal note, almost an indifference, is conspicuous in these works by a painter who could be so intensely personal, who would on occasion deliberately recast his subjects the better to fit the purpose his mood dictated. It is remarkable that some of his views of the most obviously picturesque, most paintable places in southern Europe were distinguished by the same sketchiness in technique, by the same apparent lack of enthusiasm: his pictures of *Avignon* (No. 185), *Aigues Mortes* (No. 182) and *Toledo* (No. 197) fall into the same category. Kokoschka was at this time most easily inspired by the dramatic contrasts in those towns where modern life pulsed between ancient buildings; or by landscapes of an inherently dramatic character. In Paris he chose one of the main centres of traffic for his subject, the *Place de l'Opéra* (No. 170; Plate XXXV); and he made the junctions of those arteries which cut through the city and seem to shape the big blocks of buildings within their curves the centre of his composition. But when he painted the *Tuileries* (No. 198) he emphasised the breath-taking width of this architectural miracle, treating it as a broad landscape, which is bounded by long rows of buildings on

183

two sides, with the Louvre Pavilions as corner-stones and divided by one straight avenue and many geometrical flower beds. Innumerable cars and human figures, drawn with the playful slightness of a Raoul Dufy, enliven this panorama. What primarily makes the *Tuileries* impressive and real is the bold spatial conception of the painting: the brilliant rendering of just those elements most characteristic of this particular scenery: its breadth and flatness, and the currents of life which so gaily animate the stifling pomp of the architectural layout and so utterly ignore the historic background of the scene.

When he went to Bordeaux Kokoschka, characteristically, painted the theatre with its classicist columns—a subject which another painter, more intent upon the usual picturesque effects, would hardly have chosen. Again it was the distribution of space, here clearly organised by two diametrically crossing avenues and the square, straight-lined building, that interested him. But when he painted the façade of *Bordeaux Cathedral* (No. 165) he was seized by a different impulse: as though the baroque forms, the bulges and recesses of the walls, the niches and statues had struck a chord in the breast of an artist whose descent from the Austrian Baroque has often been emphasised, he imbued this architecture with an almost organic life, made it rise and stretch and protrude, and painted it in colours—deep blues and greens and reds—whose glow seems to render something of the mysterious atmosphere which reigns in Catholic places of worship. Here too the usual, the most obviously effective approach—such as a complete frontal view—is avoided; instead, it is a corner of the building that is rendered, and seen from so short a distance that the steepness of its walls is emphasised; there is more detail in this picture than usual in this phase of Kokoschka's development, and a dramatic life that recalls the intense brush-stroke of his pre-war years.

One of Kokoschka's most successful pictures of these travel years is his *Marseilles Harbour* (No. 194; Plate XXXVI), now in the City Art Museum of St. Louis. While his views of Italy, Paris and Bordeaux might be considered sketchy, mere casual notes of visual impressions, this painting is as complete a composition, as well thought-out and balanced as it could be. The centre of the canvas, from the foreground to the background, is occupied by the basin of the harbour, its vertical direction accentuated by steam-boats that lie parallel to the banks; on the right and left this basin is enclosed by buildings, at the back by a lofty bridge.

3. DUCK SHOOTING (*1942-3*)

The blue surface of the water is quite calm, in contrast to the surrounding quays which are rich and alive with detail—small boats, shadows, moving figures. The firm, clear structure of this picture makes one conceive the basin of the harbour as an enclosed space of great depth. Two methods, as it were, are blended in a masterly manner in this canvas: the whole composition is based on a purely painter-like treatment of the large surfaces of water and sky, while the details closer to the frame are drawn in with a thin brush like a delicate design.

Similarly composed is a picture of *Monte Carlo* (No. 181), done shortly before or afterwards. Again the contrast between the smooth blue water and an accumulation of buildings at its border is the theme. But this time the houses are heaped together on a mountain on the right and on a lower hill at the back, while the foreground is half covered by an enormous bird—probably the first of those seagulls which later became one of Kokoschka's favourite motifs, almost a signature.

Quite different is the construction of Kokoschka's *Madrid* (No. 192), which reaches the high standard of *Marseilles Harbour* in its own way. This time the centre of the composition is the Puerta del Sol, from which several large avenues radiate. High buildings in the background again evoke the impression of an enclosed, definitely limited space, while horses and carriages move in the centre like a huge merry-go-round. Again it is not the ancient, historic Madrid, that caught the painter's eye, but a modern traffic point, which attracted him by its particular spatial character. The southern atmosphere of the city, like that of the *Bordeaux Theatre* (No. 176), is evoked by a combination of light colours, particularly bright red and green, which are thinly applied and seem to reflect a glaring sun.

An interest in spatial composition and in the contrast between natural elements—sand and sea—was also the starting point for Kokoschka's *Biarritz Beach* (No. 177). The magnificent sweep of the shore on the right leads deep into the background, though this time there are no diagonal or vertical lines to assist in producing the effect of depth. And on to the flat, yellow sand which gleams in the sun and is strewn with the mere suggestion of the figures of bathers, rolls the sea on the left in great, blue waves, like an immensely powerful but not hostile force. The grandeur in conception and execution of this view of a sandy beach is unequalled in the history of seascape painting.

London in 1926 saw Kokoschka at the summit of his development as a painter of cities. Not since the days of the French Impressionists and Whistler had the English capital been visited by a painter who portrayed it with so much individuality. Kokoschka's *Tower Bridge* (No. 200; Plate XLII), in composition not unlike *Marseilles Harbour*, but much wider and fuller of life, is perhaps the only picture ever painted that adequately conveys an impression of the peculiar character of London's dock area: boats cut across the river, cranes, spires and chimneys point innumerable fingers skyward. Noise, movement, activity and infinite variety are conveyed in a mysterious, undefinable way. Once more the only quiet element is the river that majestically wends its way through a mass of iron and bricks. Seen from a distance, the picture is quite clear and broadly painted; from rather nearer it appears to be composed of innumerable distinct, small strokes in every imaginable colour of the palette, but particularly light red, yellow, and green; and finally, if it is studied at quite close range, it can be plainly seen that every single stroke of colour represents one particular detail that can be identified —be it a roof, a glittering window or a distant steeple. Here indeed is a unity arising from diversity; harmony springing from boldness; and greatness from faithful observation of detail. Such a picture could only be painted by one who was enamoured of the spirit of the city which he could see better than anyone else because he was a stranger with well-trained and eager eyes.

Waterloo Bridge (No. 213) is another picture which shows that Kokoschka in his maturity was at his own best as a painter of cities and quite unrivalled in this field. The old bridge with its dark iron construction, a subject one would suppose to be utterly void of any æsthetic value, becomes at Kokoschka's hands a grandiose theme. It spans the river, measuring its great width by its arches under which pass steamers and motor boats, looking like a mighty iron bar that separates a light, airy city from the beholder. Once again innumerable, identifiable city buildings rise on both sides of the river, while the dome of St. Paul's Cathedral on the left over-towers the horizon. The sky is torn by bright-edged clouds through which strong rays of light penetrate to flood the city.

The river is the theme of the third work which Kokoschka completed in London, the *Great Thames View* (No. 205). In composition this painting is the most original of the three: it shows the river at its bend in such a way that it almost describes a circle, with three radiating bridges marking regular segments and the traffic on the Embankment running around its periphery. Cleopatra's Needle is in the foreground, and the towers of Westminster in the far distance. This time the atmosphere is misty and the background merely suggested.

It is difficult to give precedence to any one of Kokoschka's three great views of London. They have in common those qualities which were characteristic of the artist at this period: original approach, complete independence of such prototypes as he might have used—a fact which can be proved by comparison with Turner's, Whistler's, Monet's or Pissarro's views of London; vastness in conception; spiritualisation of the subject; and brilliance in execution. And in all three there is concentration on all that makes London's particular character which is captured and even intensified: the city which to many a visitor is a blackish-grey sea of houses, its river whose attraction is by no means so easily perceived as that of the Seine or the Danube, are endowed with vibrant life, with sweeping curves and fiery colours which excite curiosity and exercise irresistible fascination. Although very few Londoners at the time knew it, London had found its painter.

Richmond Terrace (No. 208) belongs in mood and style to the same kind of pictures as Kokoschka's *Hunting* (No. 115), of the Dresden period: it seems equally serene and light-hearted, painted for relaxation and sheer pleasure. Yet it gives further evidence of Kokoschka's mastery. The view over the green plain, extending from the Terrace to the distant city, contains neither architectural nor natural features that would form an obvious centre of interest for the composition; yet the painting, with its huge trees in the foreground and the river winding gently through the valley, is entirely satisfying.

Kokoschka's dramatic powers are illustrated most strikingly in his picture of *Lyon* (No. 218; Plate XLIX). This city can hardly be counted among Europe's beauty spots; yet Kokoschka made it the subject of one of his most superb pictures. He chose the most obviously paintworthy panorama of Lyon: the view over the River Saône, where it flows around the hill crowned by the church of Nôtre-Dame Fourvière. Once more what fascinated him was the form of a town fashioned by its river; once more he found grandeur in the massing of buildings on its banks and the slope of a hill. And here again, as in his *Monte Carlo*, he introduced an element of strong movement and of life with the six seagulls which wing across the sky.

187

When he arrived in the Alps, Kokoschka discovered a new and most tempting subject for his art. His inborn sense of drama could not but revel in the possibilities which these mountain valleys offered him, and it never even occurred to him to hesitate before the natural splendour that, unless mastered by an adequate brush, would inevitably produce an effect of bathos. There is no other painter living who could have undertaken successfully the task which Kokoschka set himself. Yet he succeeded completely: his *Chamonix* (No. 219; Plate XLVIII), as well as his *Courmayeur* (No. 217; Plate XLVII), evokes the sensations experienced only in these highest and most picturesque valleys of the Alps: the sense of elementary struggle between descending snowfields and climbing forests, between melting snow and penetrating stone; the impression of a beauty that terrifies by its very wildness; the distance of the mountain's foot, and the deceiving closeness of the summit; the transparency of the heights and the toy-like concreteness of the villages in the valleys. The feeling one sometimes gets in these alpine villages of being shut in by the mountains is the starting point of both paintings. The yearning for breadth and unlimited distance, that had guided Kokoschka's hand in his first travel pictures, had obviously been overcome: he now drew his mountain walls right up to the frame, hardly leaving space for even a narrow sky. And in so doing he came upon a new principle of composition. It is natural to compare these alpine landscapes of 1927 with his early *Winter Landscape*: with the *Winter Landscape* (No. 26) he for the first time felt the charm of mountain scenery and had discovered distance and a technique to render it; but one glance reveals how much he had since gained in feeling for space as well as in sense of contrast and power of composition. No longer did he draw in outlines with a timid brush. He modelled broadly with innumerable, well-placed strokes; behind the ragged mountain chains in his pictures one is aware of the others which unfold, range upon range, into distance without limit. They sink and fall down to the gabled houses that gather close around the little church whose tower rises trustingly towards the threatening majesty of the surrounding nature. And Kokoschka's achievement has the directness and fearlessness of one who was not embarrassed by the thought that for a hundred years hardly any painter of consequence had dared to venture upon the task of painting the Alps.

During the same journey Kokoschka stayed near the Lac

LIV. JERUSALEM
1929

LV. HARVEST IN THE SABINE MOUNTAINS (ANTICOLI)
1930

d'Annecy and painted a view of the lake, choosing once more a highly elevated viewpoint, probably above the village of Duingt. As though to prove his versatility the mood of this picture was very different from the other works Kokoschka had done in the same region. Its character is entirely lyrical, and suits perfectly the nature of the southern, almost Mediterranean scenery of this lake. The blueness and velvet smoothness of both lake and sky are rendered with a placidity most surprising in a painter who as a rule handled his brush with such intensity of feeling. In its own way this picture of the *Lac d'Annecy* (No. 216) is as lovely as Kokoschka's views of *Chamonix* and *Courmayeur*.

It was probably after the completion of these alpine views that Kokoschka made his last trip to Venice. This time he was attracted by one of its famous monuments: a room with a window over the Canale Grande confronted him with the façade and dome of *Santa Maria della Salute* (No. 228; Plate LIII), rising high above the old roofs that separated him from the church. He tried his hand again at an architectural subject and, characteristically, one of baroque style. What he had attempted in his picture of *Bordeaux Cathedral* (No. 165), three years before, he now achieved in consummate degree: he inspired the stones of which the church is built with life and made it, as it were, grow, move and breathe. Faithful in detail, he succeeded in rendering the impression of a powerful entity, of the baroque roundness and classic completeness conveyed by the building itself. In both the versions of the *Santa Maria della Salute* which he painted his approach was equally unconventional: in one he showed the building with its cupola cut off, laying all emphasis on the polygonal shape of its base and the canal that carries gondolas up to its steps; in the other the whole building is seen behind roofs, but leaning in the narrow angle in which the painter saw it from his house. This unusual aspect contributes to the liveliness of the picture in the same way as a distortion or over-emphasis may contribute to the liveliness of a portrait.

Insatiable hunger for picturesqueness and wide views drove Kokoschka to North Africa. In the footsteps of Delacroix, Matisse and Max Slevogt, he became a painter of the Near East. But Kokoschka painted Africa in his own way. Never had he been more independent, more inspired. The infinity of the desert endowed his brush with a sweeping broadness singularly appropriate to this scenery, for he found here that limitless spaciousness, that vastness in nature for which he had been hunting all

189

over the European continent. His *Biskra: Exodus* (No. 224; Plate L) is a landscape in which most other painters would have have found hardly enough subject-matter to interest them: merely a part of the desert as he saw it from a hillside, and separated from the beholder by a caravan of Arabs on horseback and camels, moving past in the foreground. These figures which in the work of any of the above-named three painters of the Orient would have been the backbone of the composition, the focus of interest, were only a subordinate animating element in Kokoschka's picture. His theme was the desert: the light sands under a sky that seemed clouded by a heat haze, formed by wind into ripples and waves like the sea, flattening out only in the distance where an indistinct horizon disappears in sun glare and sandy mist. This horizon is high, and the desert itself covers two-thirds of the canvas area. This fact together with the concentration of what little movement there is in the foreground produces an effect of unlimited depth. This painting has none of the dramatic tension of Kokoschka's northern landscapes: it reflects a mind in repose, collected and in possession of all those powers of artistic vision which distinguish the really great landscape painter from those who only just achieve the pedantic transposition on to canvas or paper of a piece of nature. The piece of reality which had inspired this work is still palpable before the beholder's eyes; but by discarding all encumbering detail and by endowing it with an atmosphere that his sensitiveness enabled him to experience in an unusual degree, the artist has made of it something more than a view seen from a particular point: *Biskra: Exodus* is a picture of the African desert in general, of the smallness of man engulfed in its vastness, of the mood which overpowers every visitor to these hot sands and of the slowness with which everything moves under the desert sun.

From a formal point of view *Biskra: Exodus* is composed on the same plan as *Marseilles* and *Tower Bridge*: the basin formed by Marseilles Harbour in the one, or the River Thames in the other, is here filled, as it were, with sand; but it is nevertheless present, again the centre of the composition, enclosed by the human figures in the foreground and the mountains on one side. It is almost certain that such a pattern of composition was applied unconsciously by the artist who, at the height of his powers, was far from experimenting or constructing in terms of geometry: his choice and transformation of subject was guided simply by his sense for pictorial completeness and effect. To round off his views in this way was as natural to him as it was to Vermeer to put his figures in a setting of furniture and walls of simple, straight lines, or to El Greco to make his heads elongated and their expression ecstatic. It is this unconscious formal element, combined with his inherent tendency to give even static objects the appearance of permanent motion, that justifies the classification of Kokoschka as a baroque artist.

The two cities which Kokoschka painted next—*Istanbul* (No. 232) and *Jerusalem* (233; Plate LIV)—showed a new stage in his development. He no longer took up a viewpoint in the centre of these towns; he moved right outside them and, from some elevated place, saw them as a part of the landscape that surrounded them. Clinging to the summit of a hill like its crown, or nestling deep in a valley of the heaving earth, they look as though Nature herself had formed them. Even the cupolas and minarets of *Istanbul* might be natural formations of the earth: and this impression is enhanced in the picture of *Jerusalem*, seen from the Jewish cemetery on the Mount of Olives; enclosed by its ancient walls, and set in the stony valley of a dried-up river, it might be a heap of stones among bigger rocks; yet it is clearly constructed as a living organism, around the Mosque of Omar, the architecture of which is clearly discernible in all its detail. The focus of the composition here is the city in the middle distance. Once more there is life and movement in the foreground—this time cows climbing heavily or resting among the rocks. The city itself appears fantastic like a mirage; yet almost every one of its buildings is clearly identifiable, and the whole cluster of buildings is unmistakably Jerusalem. This is perhaps the greatest of Kokoschka's paintings of towns. The spiritualisation here achieved invites comparison with another, more famous painting of a mountain city: El Greco's *Toledo* comes to mind quite naturally as one looks at Kokoschka's *Jerusalem*. Kokoschka may be said to have something of the spirit of the Old Master, who was incidentally greatly admired by the Expressionists; the temperament and emotionalism that distinguished El Greco, are also characteristic of Kokoschka, and Kokoschka has the same power of animating a natural scene as well as a human figure with the passions that fill his own mind.

Kokoschka's view of *Anticoli: Harvest in the Sabine Mountains* (No. 238; Plate LV), which he painted about the same time— perhaps on his way back from the East—is very different. Here life and movement, usually limited to a landscape's foreground,

191

spread across the whole picture surface; for what had fascinated the painter when he looked down from the Sabine Mountains, was the activity he perceived beneath him, the hundreds of animals—mostly oxen—moving round and round in circles as they turned the wheels to grind the corn, stamping and pulling and pushing ahead. And so Kokoschka painted the innumerable circles of working animals under a glaring sky, each one in a different stage of movement, and those in the distance no more than suggested by a few characteristic strokes with a light, colourful brush. The composition of this work, by its wealth of detail spread evenly all over the canvas and by its simple directness, recalls Pieter Brueghel, the Old Master whom Kokoschka always recognised as one of his teachers.

Kokoschka's interest in animals was by no means new: he had painted a *Cat* (No. 30; Plate IX) in his earliest years, and the dog on *Else Kupfer's* lap; the seagulls which he introduced in his landscapes were often indispensable elements of their composition; the *Persian Cat* (No. 212; Plate XLV) and the *Tigon* (No. 211; Plate XLIV) of 1926 were dramatisations, as it were, of animals, bringing out their preying character in a truly frightening degree, and making them appear almost monumental by their isolation; but the grace which distinguishes all animals is more apparent in the Richmond *Roes* (No. 209). In his later portraits, whenever the occasion permitted it, Kokoschka included animals, making of them double-portraits of a peculiar kind. His *Elsa Temary* (No. 215) of 1926–27 rests her elbows on a little dog, and *Adèle Astaire* (No. 201), in 1926, was portrayed with her big bull-dog as well as with her piano on which the score of one of her most popular songs lay open. But, parallel with Kokoschka's general development, the emphasis in his animal pictures changed in his later years: it was now no longer animals either as individuals or as symbols that fascinated him, but rather the infinite variety of movements and poses of which they are capable, and their appearance in the mass.

Kokoschka's portraiture too had changed considerably since his earlier years. It had gradually acquired the breadth of his landscapes, and the monumentality of his animal pictures. As he came to abandon the practice of drawing with his brush, and to use colour for broad modelling, he came also to abandon psychological description. He never lost, of course, his faculty for penetrating to the hidden personality of his models at a glance. But the pictorial aspect of men and women, their physique, now interested him more than had been the case in his youth. He no longer saw them as figures in a story, as interrelated members of a group. His youthful romanticism was gone. Instead he acquired a greater objectivity. The 'background-story', which his lively imagination still required, became a characteristic accompaniment only, relegated to its proper place in the background of his pictures. This phase of Kokoschka's portraiture, which started about 1925–26, still persists to this day.

The *Ernst Blass* (No. 179) of 1924–25, the portrait of the purblind poet seated on a sofa or easy chair, still has the heaviness of Kokoschka's Dresden figures. The *Nancy Cunard* (No. 166), slim and very simply dressed, her blond hair bobbed in the fashion of the immediate post-war years, sitting on her legs on the floor in a pose so characteristic of young English girls, with her hand supporting her long head, is painted with the lighter brush with which the *Tower Bridge* (No. 200; Plate XLII) was done, and consequently has none of the massiveness of earlier portraits, but on the contrary achieves some of the transparency and spirituality with which Kokoschka would have wanted to imbue this model. *Elsa Temary* (No. 215) is a nude, plain and simple, seated in a field, her legs pulled up and her head turned coolly upon the painter. To portray the roundness of her flesh was the obvious purpose of this picture. A masterpiece of its kind is the three-quarter length portrait of *Professor Leo Kestenberg* (No. 214). The stoutness of the seated man is magnificently depicted, his rotundity has definite pictorial character, the arms, legs, waistcoat and revers are clearly shaped, and the big features of the dominating head—his dark brows, heavy nose and thick lips—most characteristic of the man. His position in life—that of a State director of music—is indicated in one of those background scenes which Kokoschka at this time loved to introduce; a lady is seated at a piano in a large room, perhaps a concert hall—an interior that might or might not be taken into account in interpreting the portrait. From the rest of Kokoschka's work, however, it is clear enough that it was meant to add significance to the foreground figure, like the piano in *Adèle Astaire's*, or the battles in the background of Renaissance and Baroque warriors.

But the culmination of this development, at least in one respect, were Kokoschka's *Portrait of the Marabout of Temacine* (No. 226; Plate LII) and his *Arab Women* (No. 222; Plate LI): they were the purest transformation of human beings into pictorial matter, without any sacrifice in character-rendering.

Perhaps because he was dark and of a race so strange to the painter, the *Marabout* was for Kokoschka a subject to be approached in much the same way as a still-life or a landscape: his features did not betray very much of his real personality, his brown skin, so paintable in itself, masked the emotions and thoughts which often leave so clear an imprint on a white face. The half-length figure, clad in a wide, light garment, rises massive in its frame, the face under the turban impassive, impenetrable. Painted broadly like Kokoschka's African sands, this picture of the Marabout, seated against a neutral background, is unique both in Kokoschka's work and in modern art. It is monumental and mysterious as some statues of the Buddha or Rembrandt's *Man with a Golden Helmet*.

The picture of two *Arab Women*, equally picturesque, is different in character. It is carried out in a more calligraphic style, not unlike that of some of Kokoschka's earliest works, such as his *Auguste Forel*, and the sharp characterisation that results from this manner of drawing is almost cynical. The two young women, dressed in their national costume, sit side by side in a landscape with palm trees and tents, one of them playing with the cigarette-lighter which she had kept as a token of their friendship, and their faces as they watch the painter, betray the caution and mistrust that European peasant women would feel in a similar situation. But closely as they no doubt scrutinised him, his eyes were even sharper. There is more observation in this picture than can be put into words: it reflects the whole complex nature of these Arab women; their natural intelligence and their primitiveness; their timidity mixed with aggressiveness; their reliance on their mutual support and the presence of the husband in the background as well as their coquettish reserve; the fire within them is expressed in their dark eyes; they are fascinated like village children by an unfamiliar spectacle, but ready to run away at the slightest sign of danger. With the robes of Kokoschka's favourite colour, blue, this picture is decorative enough for an illustration for *1001 Nights*, and at the same time so faithful and exact that it might serve to illustrate an ethnographical treatise.

★   ★   ★

Before he returned to Vienna Kokoschka stayed once more in Paris in 1931–32. He painted a high arched bridge at *Nogent-sur-Marne* (No. 250). It was here too that he did a new *Self-Portrait*

12. MEIN LIED
1931

(No. 254), showing him in half-length with a cap, his features exaggeratedly crude. And it can perhaps be said that his career abroad was crowned by his participation in the Venice Biennale of 1932. It is reported that on this occasion the Duce reacted in much the same manner as the Archduke Franz Ferdinand had done in 1911. In view of official Fascist art this is not surprising. As a result the German press, which considered the exhibition of Kokoschka's works in the German Pavilion as tactless and almost a political *faux pas*, for the first time after many years once more attacked the painter.

Kokoschka's later Vienna period can be counted from 1931, when he first returned for a short stay, until 1934 when, following upon the Nazification of Austria, he moved to Czechoslovakia.

Since he had left his native country Kokoschka had become a famous man, and Vienna was one of the few art centres where he had not shown his work in recent years. Even when he returned he still bore a grudge against her inhabitants, for he could not forget the treatment that had driven him away twenty years ago. Nevertheless he settled down with his mother in his small house in the Liebhardstal, where the outskirts of the city meet the Vienna Woods. From here he painted the former Hapsburg capital, clustering around the spire of St. Stephen, in a valley surrounded by hills. As usual he worked incessantly. 'The city council of Vienna, at that time a socialist body, had asked me to paint a picture for the state-room in the town hall. They left the choice of the subject to me. As I could see and hear from my little house thousands of orphans playing happily on the opposite side of the valley, in the palace and park which before the revolution belonged to the archduke, I took my subject from them. I painted the *Wiener Sozialistische Kinderfürsorge* (No. 248) —the children's welfare of socialist Vienna. The idea I owe to a painting by Brueghel, showing children playing, which forms part of the most complete collection of Brueghel's masterpieces in Vienna's Kunsthistorisches Museum. The foreground was divided up into many groups of children playing the old games known to them and new ones taught to them. The middle groups showed the palace where they lived. The background offered a wide view of Vienna and the valley of the Danube fading out into the distance where the Alps rose with a steep slope from the Danube basin. As the foreground exceeded the other two in dimension, the painting seemed full of jubilant

LVI. MRS. M.
Drawing. About 1931

LVII. MRS. M.
Drawing. About 1931

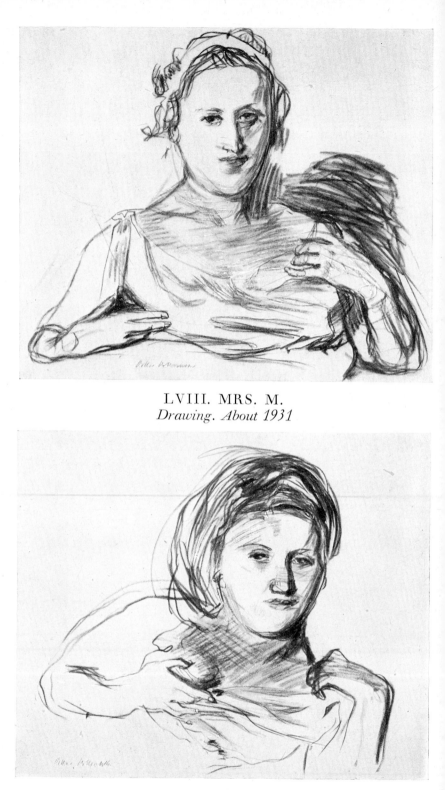

LVIII. MRS. M.
Drawing. About 1931

LIX. MRS. M.
Drawing. About 1931

children. It was my first picture with a political meaning. It was meant as a demonstration against the reactionary state of affairs under Chancellor Dollfus. The reactionary middle class was in conspiracy with their foreign equals. Partly due to the political pressure exercised by the League of Nations through the controller of Austrian finances, the Dutchman Van Terboven, later Gauleiter in occupied Norway, partly due to the clever play with democratic machinery, Dollfus became dictator with all the ruthlessness characteristic of an usurper of political power. But foreign powers took hardly any notice of his cruel policy of liquidation of socialism. They continued to pay tribute to him, to the "little martyr", after he was murdered by the Nazis. The democratic world possibly did not know about his gunning of workers who had only a few rifles, or of the deeds of his army chief Prince Starhemberg, destroying a group of the, then, most modern buildings erected in Europe for housing workers.'

At the beginning of that battle Kokoschka happened to be in Budapest. Over the wireless he heard the shrill voice of the little Chancellor, whom he hated with all his heart, proclaim: 'I give you one more hour, then the shooting will be continued.' This announcement was followed by music, a forced expression of the usual Viennese lightheartedness. Kokoschka, worried about his family, rushed back to Vienna. The capital looked like a military camp, and Prince Starhemberg's well-armed gangs ruled in the streets. Kokoschka found his mother in a state of excitement even worse than that of most other inhabitants: for four nights she stood at her window and looked at the fires, and she would not believe that it was by Austrians that the people of Vienna were shot. She did not long survive this upheaval in her world, and Kokoschka left the city where he had spent his youth, with the picture of his mother, looking down at the fires of Vienna, before his eyes. Before he went he received the news that his painting of *Vienna*, together with all other traces of the socialist régime, had been removed to an unknown place immediately after Prince Starhemberg's Heimwehr had stormed the town hall.

'Later the Austrian Government invited me to become the Director of the Arts and Crafts School, where I had once studied. I answered that I would accept under one condition: if my scheme of general reform of the educational system according to rational principles, which would guarantee peace, were accepted. In Prague I received the official regret on an open postcard—to save paper.'

197

But the city of his youth was to make another attempt at reconciliation after he had left it for good: to celebrate his birthday in 1937 his old friends arranged the first representative exhibition of his work there, in the rooms of the Oesterreichisches Museum für Kunst und Industrie. An extract from Carl Moll's introduction to the catalogue will show how Vienna now claimed Kokoschka as her son: 'You have been lost to your homeland. It reproaches you with avoiding it, you reproach it for looking the other way. Both reproaches are unjustified. It is not desertion to search the world, to live, work and add honour to one's homeland's name; and everywhere those who find it too difficult to look up will "look the other way". But it was Viennese friends with Josef Hoffmann and Adolf Loos at the head who, thirty years ago, prepared you to go out into the world. And your friends did not find the art through the man, nor the studio through the café, they found the man through his art; they felt your art and became your friends. It could not hurt you that, 25 years ago, you were not recognised but hotly rejected. What has happened to Gustav Klimt in Vienna, and what to Hans van Marées whom Munich also knew only from "looking the other way"? . . . Have the Parisians not actively attacked Manet's pictures, constantly rejected Cézanne's works? . . . Vienna lies in the periphery. Berlin has spoken for you, and Berlin was heard. Thus Berlin could also rob us of your work. But your work itself —without your recognising it—has remained Austrian. In your colour is your homeland's music. . . .'

IV. PRAGUE AND LONDON

THE POLITICAL ARTIST

A fast train took Kokoschka to Prague in six hours. Here everything was different. It had always been. Since a Hapsburg Emperor had suppressed Bohemia's independance more than 300 years ago[1] and had annihilated its Protestant aristocracy, the old Hussite land had become a Catholic country of quite provincial character, rich by the wealth of its soil and the industry of its inhabitants, but backward in its cultural development, which had been brilliant in Gothic times and the days of the Renaissance. The Czech language became almost a handicap; as all important posts in Bohemia were occupied by German-speaking officials and all administration was centred in Vienna, Czech was more and more neglected, until it was spoken by the common people only when they were alone with their compatriots. Most Bohemians were farmers; those who wanted to make a better career, study a science or be trained for a profession, had to learn German and go to Vienna, to acquire social standing as well as a means of livelihood. Thus, in the course of centuries, Bohemia had become a hinterland. It was only the Romantic movement, with its general encouragement of nationalism, which had revived the national consciousness of the Czechs. Their poets were the first to remind them of what they had lost and what was their due. They wrote in Czech, and they recreated the figures of Czech sagas and history. This movement, purely literary in its origin, was of enormous consequence: the revived national spirit of the Czech people never subsided again; on the contrary, it grew into a popular movement with a political leadership and aim. More and more Czechs began to consider their mother tongue, not as a means of communication with servants only, but as a language to be cultivated, spoken and even written. A Czech literature came to be born, never leading among European schools, but genuine, with an original flavour, and sufficiently developed to keep the Czech people in touch with the trend of European feel-

[1] In 1620.

199

ing and thought. During the nineteenth century a Czech school of painting arose in Prague, provincial it is true, but based on honest craftsmanship and popular tradition, and some of its masters were quite up to the standard of other, better-known romantic or naturalist painters. Czech writers, poets and historians produced works considered important enough to be translated into German, and the names of their authors—Palacký, Mácha, Havlíček, Vrchlický and Otokar Březina—have thus penetrated far beyond the frontiers of Bohemia. This development of the country's intellectual life could not but result in demands for a greater political independence: Czech politicians, forming a strong faction in Vienna's parliament, wanted to take their people's fate into their own hands. It was not until the collapse of the Hapsburg Monarchy in 1918 that this was achieved with Allied help. But as soon as the Republic of Czechoslovakia was established, the whole country awoke to new life. And within twenty years the little state ranked among Europe's most democratic, most advanced and prosperous countries.

When the train crossed the Austrian frontier into Czechoslovakia the view from its windows remained unchanging for some hours: the same deep, dark pine forests rose on both sides, and only gradually the wooded hills flattened into cultivated fields and rich meadows. Then, as far as the eye could reach, there was nothing but corn, interspersed with poppy fields that in mid-summer glowed with colour, divided by long, dusty lanes, with richly laden fruit-trees on both sides. There were many villages, their low farm-houses grouped around a pond on whose edges bare-footed peasant girls with bright handkerchiefs around their heads watched large herds of fat, noisy geese; there were few towns apart from those districts where the country's industry was steadily growing into one of international consequence. The one city in which modern life pulsed quickly without disturbing her ancient charm, was Prague. Anyone coming from Vienna had a feeling that he had left behind a city of ancient, unsurpassed splendour, a historic place, whose beauty was of the past, while the life still moving in its streets became sleepier and sleepier, only now and then roused to half-artificial gaiety, when the organisers of some festival remembered that the old place offered a magnificent stage for pageantry. To keep up the appearance that everything was not finished, that one was still alive, was the ambition of all Vienna. In Prague nobody wanted to revert to the past. Life was only just beginning. The place was ancient too, but the monuments of the past were regarded only as a natural background for development without limit in the future. The beauty of the old town had been known and sung by many visitors in the past. The Dane Herman Bang had called her 'The Golden City'. Rainer Maria Rilke, who spent his youth within her walls, never grew tired of praising her. Prague was indeed one of the three or four loveliest cities on the European continent. There is hardly any panorama that rivals the view from the banks of the Vltava to the hill that bears on its crown the Gothic cathedral of St. Vitus with its two noble towers, the enormous baroque palaces, built for emperors and archbishops, and picturesque medieval walls, while its slopes are covered with parks and terraces reminiscent of Italy. It rises out of a maze of narrow old streets and squares, unchanged for more than a hundred years, as they have crowded too close together to admit even one building to their picturesque abundance. Rough, steeply mounting pavements; bordering arcades of a southern character; narrow houses with overhanging upper-floors and coloured window panes; broad palaces with half-naked caryatids that grin down from both sides of the door; tiny bridges that span narrow channels; street markets under wide vaults; winding stairs and old trees: these make the old city into an enchanted place with which nobody could become intimate without a life-long familiarity. But on the other bank the modern city extends and, although at that time inhabited by hardly a million people, it offered all the advantages of modern city life. Here too were houses with steep stairs difficult to climb, where picturesqueness was bought at the price of modern comfort. But among these had been erected concrete buildings with wide glass fronts, banks, trading centres and hotels where interiors glittered with steel furniture. Prague's modern architects were very modern, and very good; they spoilt the aspect of the ancient town no more than the thronging traffic that squeezed through the narrow streets disturbed their style. The people of Prague liked physical comfort, and above everything they liked good, rich food. They were proud of their hams, their sausages, their beer. Some of their pastry shops enjoyed the reputation of being the best in Europe, and there sat the citizens, partaking of immense quantities of cake and whipped cream. Quite naturally they were not a slim race. But they were healthy, strapping, very athletic— their sports organisation, the 'Sokol', which dated back to the first days of national awakening in the nineteenth century, had

201

a branch in even the smallest towns—and their women were pretty, fair, with straight bodies and open faces. Robust, endowed with natural intelligence and musically very gifted, these people stood with both feet firmly planted on their country's soil. Prague derived her particular character from a middle-class of simple habits. The cultural life of the city rested in the hands of the intelligentsia which was also entrusted with the country's fortune: for almost every member of the government was a member of academic circles, a fact symbolised in the person of the Republic's first President, who was a former professor of philosophy and sociology. The Czech intelligentsia which had once taken directions from Vienna was now looking to Paris. Czechoslovakia's students went to France to finish off their studies whenever they could do so. Her artists were wont to spend considerable time in Paris, and her painters reflected all western art movements from cubism to surrealism. Prague's artists had two powerful organisations—the 'Manes', thus named after a dynasty of nineteenth century painters, and the Umělecka Beseda—which owned exhibition rooms, and each published a magnificently produced periodical. Outstanding among the cultural activities of the young state were its theatrical productions, which ranged from operatic performances to highbrow cabarets often of a political character; at a time when censorship had long muzzled all artistic activities in the neighbouring countries, Czechoslovakia's comedians and caricaturists enjoyed a liberty that permitted everything and was supported by an enthusiastic public. And stage experiments as well as musical performances gave outlet to the best artistic forces in the country.

★　　★　　★

Kokoschka liked Prague from the beginning but, severely disturbed by what he had seen happen in Vienna and by what he heard from Germany, he could not think of settling there. Surrounded by people who lived under the illusion of a false security, he could not but be aware of what went on beyond the frontiers of the small republic: the new régime in Germany appeared to him not only as a political disaster, but also as a declaration of war on his life's work, on him personally. The Führer had never made a secret of his opinions on art and his intentions to reform it, once he came to power. Art was, in fact, one of Hitler's favourite subjects. A general tendency to suppress all modern movements became noticeable throughout Germany as soon as the new régime was established: museum officials, who had identified themselves with an advanced art policy, and art critics and art historians who had encouraged extreme tendencies, had now to fight for the maintenance of their positions; art dealers, who had for years acted as the agents of modern artists, relegated their works to the back rooms of their galleries while a new kind of merchandise was exhibited in the show rooms; artists retired intimidated into complete isolation or made desperate efforts to conform to the new taste. But it was not until four years after the Nazi revolution that these developments reached a climax: in the summer of 1937 Adolf Hitler opened the Haus der Deutschen Kunst in Munich. His opening speech left no doubt about the fate of modern art in Germany. He declared that a turning point had been reached in the development of German artistic life. The collapse of Germany in 1918 had thrown up a lot of 'mud and dirt' to the surface, and general confusion in cultural life had followed. The Jews, by their control of the press, had used this confusion to destroy all remaining healthy instincts. Their slogans had made many uncertain in their judgment and intimidated all opposition. They had pretended that art was not racial but international. The phase 'modern art' had been invented. A new principle of an art that 'dated' had thus been introduced: every year had to produce its new art. Jewish art dealers had taken advantage of the public's cowardliness and offered the products of the newly created 'artists' for sale, while real masters were simply rejected as out of fashion. Old Masters were no longer appreciated. But, said Hitler, true art is eternal as an immortal revelation of the nation's deepest nature. During the years of the Weimar Republic there was a general conspiracy to suppress this true art in favour of the then leading 'artists'. But Germany will have a German Art, which will be eternal. A nation does not come and go with the years. Art is its eternal monument. Its judge will be the German people and their feeling. He wanted to 'see an art that takes account of our nation's racial composition and tends towards the same unification as our people. To be German is to be clear and true. German masters have always striven to be true. It is unfortunate that, during the Glaspalast fire in 1931, the works of German Romantic artists were burnt and not those of our "Moderns".[1] But we shall keep these "Moderns" as monuments of our nation's deepest downfall.

[1] Hitler was mistaken: some modern works, such as Kokoschka's *Lot and his Daughters*, were destroyed in the same fire.

I desire Germany's cultural regeneration. A suppressed nation must show its oppressors its values, the highest of which are its cultural achievements. Cubism, dadaism, futurism, impressionism etc. have nothing to do with our people. Works of art which cannot be understood by themselves will no longer find their way to the German people! A brilliantly beautiful type of man is growing up. And what are these modern art stammerers producing? Cripples and degenerates; women who can only horrify; men who are nearer to the animal state than to that of man; children who, were they to live, would be considered a curse! That is what these cruel dilettanti present as art to their contemporaries. Nobody can tell me that these artists see things in this way. I do not want to discuss whether they really see our people as decadent, whether they see the blue meadows, the green skies, yellow clouds. But in the name of the German people I forbid these unfortunates, who are obviously suffering from defective vision, to try to force their products upon their fellow men as real, or even as art. Either they are sincere: in that case they should be examined to see whether their defects are due to external causes or to heredity—which would raise the question whether further inheritance of such defects should be prevented. Or they have other reasons for insulting their nation with their humbug: and in that case their conduct must be regarded as an offence against the law. With the opening of this exhibition the cultural destruction of our nation has come to an end. We shall be indomitable in our fight against the last elements of cultural destruction. All those cliques of babblers, dilettanti and swindlers who support each other will be annihilated. These prehistoric art stammerers may return to the caves of their ancestors, there to sell their primitive international scribbling.'

While Hitler was thus introducing his art policy in the Haus der Deutschen Kunst,[1] in another building an exhibition of 'Degenerate Art' was shown to teach people what was in future to be rejected. Almost without exception all prominent modern artists were here represented. German museums and private collections had been ransacked to assemble the exhibits set out like a side-show, provided with labels explaining their character in a new light, quoting the prices supposedly paid for their acquisition and exhibited side by side with the works of mental patients. This exhibition, which drew 2,000,000 visitors in

[1] Hitler's speech is here summarised.

204

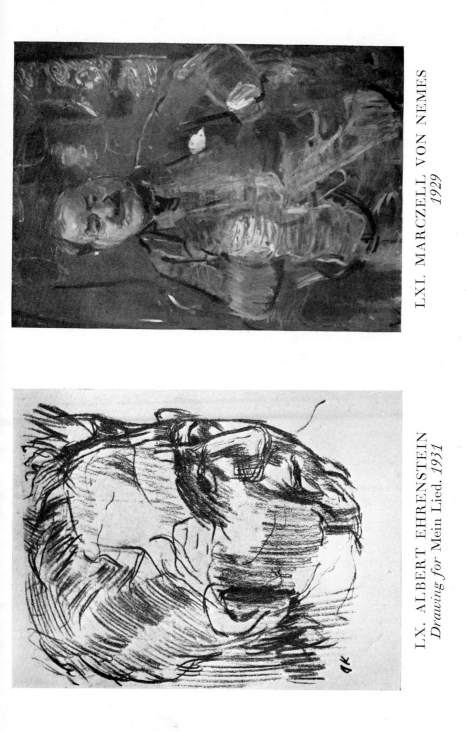

LXI. MARCZELL VON NEMES
1929

LX. ALBERT EHRENSTEIN
Drawing for Mein Lied. 1931

LXII. TRUDL, STUDY FOR DOUBLE PORTRAIT
1931

twenty weeks, contained eight works by Oskar Kokoschka. The *Tempest* (No. 98; Plate XXVI), removed from the Hamburg Kunsthalle, was its centre-piece. The *Exiles* (No. 109) and *The Duchess of Rohan-Montesquieu* (No. 38; Plate XVIII) were also included. As no catalogue was published, however, it is impossible at this moment to establish which other works by Kokoschka may have been selected. The small guide through the exhibition[1] contains, among its illustrations, the *Hasenclever* lithograph, reproduced opposite the drawing of a mentally defective.[2]

In contrast to most other artists who submitted quietly to this treatment, hoping for a more favourable development or prepared to bear any stigma rather than uproot themselves from their habitual surroundings, Kokoschka never suffered from the illusion that he could expect anything good from the Nazis. Even if they had let him live quietly in Germany or Austria, if they had forgiven him his past and closed an eye to his present activities, as they did in many cases where artists showed themselves willing to repent, he could not have done it: he would not deny his past; he could not change, either in character or in his method; he could not submit his individuality to a mass discipline that would have meant mental death. Kokoschka had not been the pupil and friend of Adolf Loos and Karl Kraus for nothing. He believed in human rights and cultural progress, but not in nationalism and dictatorships. Most of all, perhaps, he believed in his own art and what he still wanted to achieve. So he could only turn his back on Germany. He never made any attempt to return either to that country or to Austria while the Nazi regime lasted. Later events confirmed him in his attitude. All German museums were purged of his works—the fate of most of them remains unknown up to the present;[3] a few

---

[1] *Entartete 'Kunst'*. Ausstellungsführer. Verlag für Kultur und Wirtschaftswerbung, Berlin, 1937.

[2] It was Paul Schultze-Nanmburg, in his *Kunst und Rasse* (Munich, 1930) who first confronted a work by Kokoschka with works by mental patients.

[3] According to Dr. Hoffmann of the Reichsministerium für Volksaufklärung und Propaganda (speech delivered during the Gaukulturwoche 1938 at Naumburg), altogether 5000 paintings and 12,000 drawings, engravings and etchings were removed from public collections and confiscated by the state, 'to be dealt with according to an order from the Führer which is expected'. Only 125 of these were offered for sale by the Galerie Fischer, of Lucerne, on the 30th June, 1939.

may have been saved by some understanding museum official,[1] but a number of them may well have been finally destroyed. In November, 1937, Dr. Goebbels delivered a speech in which he repeated the Führer's principles that the state had to be the sole arbiter in art matters, as only 'the statesman' could decide what was good for the people. In the same year a book on *Säuberung des Kunsttempels*[2] by Wolfang Willrich was published in which Kokoschka, with reference to his early *Still-Life* (No. 4), was called 'the painter of the skinned sheep' (p. 21), while his *Heathens* (No. 117) was reproduced as an example of the scandalous acquisitions for public collections made out of public funds during the time of the Republic. After the occupation of Austria rumours penetrated to Prague that numerous paintings by Kokoschka had been destroyed by the Gestapo. The 'Exhibition of 20th Century German Art', held at the New Burlington Galleries in London in 1938, contained in fact a portrait by the artist which had been cut into four pieces, as a sign of disapproval, by the Vienna police on the 5th May of that year.

It is no wonder that Kokoschka was profoundly shaken by these events. His personal and his artistic pride were equally hurt. Together with all those who had fought the same battles he had been stigmatised as a swindler to be punished, or a mental defective from whom the public must be protected. Financial ruin, internment, sterilisation, had been decreed for him and his like by the Führer himself, when he spoke at Munich. His reaction was not as violent nor as rash as it would have been twenty years before: he published no reply, nor did he demonstrate his emotions in any other way. But he worried about the fate of his works in German hands. He began to manifest a more intense interest in politics than before and even let himself be tempted to take an active part.

'Although I had no official mandate to legitimatise my claims, I could not keep quiet. In lectures and articles in newspapers and magazines I tried to mobilise public opinion in favour of a revision of democratic thinking according to rational principles, instead of the rather immature, romantic and emotional attitude so far manifest in National politics. Logically I propagated my scheme of an international educational reform in that country which 300 years ago had borne the inventor of the only efficient

[1] The case of one museum director who tried to hide a work by Kokoschka in a neutral country is, in fact, known.

[2] Purge of the Art Temple.

method of mass-education, Jan Amos Komenský. The short-comings of national education in every country are due to the fact that, although Comenius's ideas had finally, 300 years after his death, been accepted by the civilised nations, no government so far had realised them in accordance with the true spirit of the inventor, whose aim was education to world-citizenship. This kind of propaganda among the peoples of the world would have opened their eyes, to the detriment of secret diplomacy. Not the invention of the "Bren-gun", but education in the true spirit of Comenius, could have saved Czechoslovakia and spared the world the total war.

'. . . The essential principle of his educational plan, translated into modern language, demands from World Democracy an in-ternational scientific control of mass education by a board of inter-nationally minded educational experts and scientists. Such a board of scholars, scientists and educational experts could not therefore be placed under the control of the functionaries of any single national state, but should have independent jurisdiction as a body responsible for the development of all international cul-tural intercourse for peaceful purposes on the principles of Mutual Aid. Its assemblies would be formally recognised by in-ternational law. It would see to it that science was taught in relation to its social relevance. Whereas Fascism or semi-religious Nationalism opens no new issues to mankind, a World Education Board, partaking even of something of the nature of a sovereign body, would be the greatest instrument ever forged in the in-terest of Democracy, and thus indeed a realisation of Komenský's highest aims. . . .' (From 'Comenius, the English Revolution and Our Present Plight' in *The Teacher of Nations*, Cambridge University Press, 1942.)

Amos Comenius and T. G. Masaryk were the two figures who captivated and held Kokoschka's imagination: their educational ideas inspired him with the faith that the evil he saw spread over the globe could have been prevented if only the youth born after the Great War had been brought up in a better spirit and, full of his old enthusiasm, he formed plans for a better, more human, a truly democratic education, which he repeatedly proclaimed in interviews and newspaper articles. He wanted Prague to become the seat of an international school in which children from all countries should be educated without consideration of race, nationality or religion; instead of being indoctrinated with mili-tary virtues, as was at this time the main educational aim in

207

some of Europe's greatest countries, they should be taught to work with their hands and to respect humanistic principles. Shortly after he had come to Czechoslovakia he had obtained permission to paint the aged Masaryk, and his pedagogic fervour was increased with every conversation he had with the great politician and humanist, who told him that he would consider the introduction of education on these lines the crowning of his own work.

Two years after his arrival in Prague the civil war broke out in Spain. Kokoschka passionately supported the republican side; he drew a portrait of *La Passionaria* (Figure 13), with a starving child in her arms, and a poster of a mother and child fleeing from bombing planes, inscribed 'Help the Basque Children!' It was also as a gesture with political meaning that he sought and obtained Czechoslovakian nationality: it was his reply to the Nazis, and at the same time an affirmation of his allegiance to the country from which his forefathers had come and which had now offered him hospitality. 'As a matter of fact it was the only decent thing to do in a world where you must possess a passport, or you do not exist for the authorities at all. It was suggested to me by President Masaryk who also took much trouble to translate the meaning of my name to me. In an old herbarium he showed me that in the Czech language my name means "Shepherd's Purse". When I asked why it is so called he said that a shepherd's bag usually contained medical herbs to cure his sheep, and this association pleased him.'

The full implications of the political events that were changing the face of Europe were plain to Kokoschka, although the majority of people were still living under the illusion that all was almost well; and owing to his clear understanding of what he observed he was thrown from one extreme mood into another: now he was roused to opposition and fighting spirit, trying to rally support for the most irrational campaigns; at other times he felt depressed and without hope, a state enhanced by his often failing health. On the whole, however, he was becoming an ardent socialist, and one might call him a communist, had he not always been too much of an individualist to join any party.

Externally Kokoschka's life in Prague was quiet. He had taken up residence in a big hotel in the centre of the modern city, and had on the top floor of a building on the embankment a studio with an extensive view from its windows over the River Vltava, the mountain with its castle and the old city. There he worked as steadily as ever. Few people were allowed to disturb him.

13. LA PASSIONARIA
1937

One of those privileged to see him here was his new muse, the student daughter of one of his friends, whose boyish head he drew innumerable times in charcoal and who looked after such of his affairs as he could not manage himself. He also took up again a painting begun ten years before in Dresden, *The Fountain* (No. 281), which represented his Russian friend in profile and himself in the background; he transformed her features into those of his new friend and added a nude in the centre, yet left it still unfinished.

Of all the men and women whose acquaintance he made during his four years' stay in Czechoslovakia, it was naturally T. G. Masaryk who made the greatest impression on him. The meetings of these two extraordinary men were not always as serious as one might expect. Kokoschka, who 'had the purpose to try to get his educational reform plans encouraged by the only living head of a state able to understand the importance of education for the protection of democracy', was introduced to Masaryk in the last year of his presidency. The old man had at that time had a stroke, from which he had fairly well recovered; his emaciated head was very pale; he kept his tall, thin body very straight and wore one arm in a sling. Kokoschka, who had met so many people of all kinds, was at first not a little shy when in the presence of this man who had already become a myth in his lifetime. He approached him with that air of modesty, timidity, even awkwardness which were half natural to him and half affected, but which never failed to work as a charm. 'I consider it a great honour to be allowed to paint your portrait,' he said, 'but I am afraid I will make a martyr of you. I cannot promise to be quick. But I might paint you while you are having your coffee, for instance—I must have black coffee myself anyway, and I would not dare to ask for it unless you had it too.' The ice was melted: the President laughed suddenly like a boy and retorted: 'I myself would like some coffee, but nobody gives it to me.' When pressed, Kokoschka said it would take him a month to paint this portrait. It took him two years. His visits to the President's country house at Lana near Prague were frequent during this period. He had been invited to stay at Lana but, perhaps afraid to forgo his independence, he refused to do so. Instead he travelled every time in the President's car to Lana and back again. At first the sittings lasted no more than a quarter of an hour and were attended by Dr. Alice Masaryk, the President's daughter, who had made it her task to watch over

her father's health. But Kokoschka's presence had such a beneficial influence on the old man that all restrictions were dropped
after a short while: he could stay longer and talk about anything
he or his sitter liked. He had now taken to addressing the President informally as 'Professor', and their conversation was accordingly freer. One of their favourite subjects was that of education
for democracy; no doubt the aged scholar and statesman often
smiled at the painter's enthusiasm, but he was nevertheless not
loath to express his own ideas. One of the historic figures of whom
he spoke to Kokoschka was Petr Chelčický, one of the leaders of
the Czech Reformation who had fought against the united powers
of State and Church. But while Masaryk had reservations concerning Chelčický's theories,[1] Kokoschka regarded him as the
greatest revolutionary. They agreed that his ideas could only be
realised if it were done in all countries at the same time. And
Kokoschka expressed his dislike of Luther whom he considered a
reactionary and nationalist.

Masaryk always liked to satisfy his own curiosity when he had
interesting visitors. When Kokoschka told him about his experiences in the war Masaryk asked him: 'Were you brave?'
Kokoschka replied: 'It is difficult to answer this question before
you have confessed to me: are you yourself courageous?' The
President told Kokoschka how he felt when he once got into the
middle of shooting during the revolution in Russia—a story that
has been retold by Karel Čapek in his *President Masaryk tells
his Story*.[2] 'There I was afraid,' he added. 'But it is easier to be
afraid and to continue to work in spite of it, than to confess that
one is afraid.' 'Now you look like a boy who steals apples—no,
like a dried, shrivelled apple with a million wrinkles!' exclaimed
the painter, who never neglected the real purpose of his visits.
He still insists that Masaryk had the 'most beautiful eyes in the
world' and that his charm was greatest when he was completely
informal and absorbed. 'He was a real aristocrat' is the highest
praise of the fervent socialist Kokoschka.

The portrait he painted of *T. G. Masaryk* (No. 263; Plate
LXVII) was perhaps the most ambitious work he had ever undertaken. 'I wish I could succeed in communicating something of
the radiation of this unique man. The individual human being,

[1] Masaryk's ideas about Chelčický and the relationship between State and
Church are explained in his *The Making of a State* (Allen and Unwin, 1925).

[2] P. 257 of the English translation published by George Allen & Unwin
in 1934.

subject to the passing of time, to personal fate and the process of ageing, is here overcome. Behind such a man one feels the whole of humanity. I believe biological laws exempt such a genius from their working. Such men need not be wrapped in cotton wool; they must be left alone; and they should be called upon to secure peace—for 15 millions will die if the guns go off again. . . . At an age in which others retire T. G. Masaryk has, through dangerous adventures and owing to his strange intellectual fate—a black-smith who became an academic teacher—founded a state for the nation which contributed the Komenský idea to the wealth of humanity. According to Komenský pictures are more suited to teaching than words; consequently a modern symbolical portrait shall serve our educational purpose. One in the old style would glorify imperialism or "domination" in general. Such conceptions have been outmoded by our democratic ideas. . . . Neither cloak nor crown, neither sceptre nor sword are attributes to charac-terise this President. I have seen no griffons, eagles, lions worship at his feet. While it would befit a dictator to be represented as a conqueror, holding a hand grenade and a gas mask, Masaryk conquers through pure humanity the best in our nature and exacts our love. At the President's side I paint Amos Comenius, his figure surrounded by the rays of the setting sun. Like a tablet of the law he holds up his *Orbis Pictus*, on which, instead of laws, the five natural indicators, the organs of the senses, are repre-sented. On the other side Prague—the castle, the old Charles Bridge, the river in which children bathe—is to be seen. By a representation of the burning of Huss in the background the days when prejudices become stronger than all reason, when all sense is perverted into nonsense are warningly evoked. Long is the line of T. G. Masaryk's spiritual ancestors, but the line of those who have fought against the spirit is just as long! I want to make it a historical picture; a picture that can be shown in schools, to teach the children that patriotic tasks as well as personal duties are united in humanism.'[1]

In another interview[2] he said more informally: 'He is a man of world stature, a European; I would like to be able to show him as I see him. Could I paint him as a statesman in a black coat with an order on his breast? No—it had to be an historical picture.'

[1] Translated from an interview quoted by Kurt John in the *Prager Tagblatt* of the 8th September 1935.

[2] Article by Dr. Palkovský in *New Yorské Listy*, 1941.

LXIII. DOUBLE-PORTRAIT: TRUDL THE AMAZON AND
TRUDL, MOTHERLY
1931

LXIV. TRUDL
1931

From these two interviews it becomes clear that Kokoschka, in his conception of the portrait, was guided by Comenius in a double sense: he wanted his picture to be symbolical, to tell a story and teach a lesson, and he wanted it to be a humanitarian lesson. He had thus progressed far beyond the stage when he had conceived the idea of an *Orbis Pictus* as a series of panoramas to represent the manifold aspects of the earth's countries in pictures. He could, in other words, no longer be called an impressionist painter. As in his youth, and yet in a new and very different sense, his visual impressions were no longer an end in themselves; they were made to serve a higher purpose: if they had formerly been used to express his emotions, they became now instruments for the expression of an intellectual system, of a moral conviction.

The portrait of T. G. Masaryk was but the first milestone on this new road chosen by Kokoschka. His deviation from the path of 'pure painting' will be regretted by those who do not conceive art as an instrument for the propagation of ideas. A painter who changes his ways as consciously as Kokoschka, however, would point out in his defence that *l'art pour l'art* is a relatively new conception. Kokoschka does, in fact, always evoke the example of Pieter Brueghel in this connection: 'Brueghel, from whom I learnt, painted symbolical pictures: the seasons, the games of children, Blind Man's Buff, bowling hoops, sack races; and he painted the childish games of the grown-ups: their orgies of eating and drinking, their superstitions, their wars and invasions, their soldiers eating their way through the countries, the tortures they have invented, and the Crucifixion.' And just as we today appreciated the Old Master's pictures not because of their subject-matter but because of their artistic qualities, so Kokoschka's later works, however charged with symbolism, can also be admired for their painterly qualities alone.

The portrait of *T. G. Masaryk* underwent several changes before Kokoschka considered it completed. Existing photographs of an early state show the President's face with dark, glowing eyes, which give his thin, white-bearded head a youthful fire; equally dark were the eyes of Comenius, who held up the volume inscribed *Orbis Pictus*. In its present form the figures have been moved closer to the beholder and have gained greater plasticity; one of Comenius's broad hands touches Masaryk's arm, as though to warn or remind him of something, while the cover of his book, ornamented with new pictures, is now headed *J. Amos Komen-*

213

sky—Via Lucis; the crucifix in the background is now turned towards the distant city, and the figure of a bishop has been added to the group; the face of the President, given another layer of colour, has lost its frailty and also its youthfulness, as well as some of its likeness to life: it has become an abstraction of what Kokoschka saw in Masaryk rather than a portrait. The erect pose of the old man, the long head that seems even longer because of the small pointed beard on his chin, the plain coat and the fine, long hands are immensely characteristic. But the face has been endowed with a broad monumentality and a soft vagueness which Masaryk's ascetic, intelligent and determined head certainly never showed: the features of T. G. Masaryk were in fact rather chiselled than modelled; and Kokoschka, who had so well understood the great man, who had been so impressed by the transparency and the vivacity of his appearance, had in the end only succeeded in creating what looks like Masaryk's ghost.[1]

The portrait of *T. G. Masaryk* was finished in 1936. In the same year Kokoschka painted one of himself (No. 280), wearing a red sweater and holding a stick in his hand; this picture has not been reproduced nor is its present whereabouts known. He also painted the portrait of *Herr Bloch-Bauer* (No. 279), an Austrian industrialist of Czech origin. He represented the elderly man, attired as a huntsman, with bright green waistcoat and high hat, seated in a forest, a gun on his knee.

Kokoschka's manner had greatly changed since his early days: there is no more drawing with the brush discernible in this portrait, and no apparent emphasis on psychology or even mood. Here the artist's interest has obviously been concentrated on the colouring—the yellowish green of the trees and waistcoat and the brown of the suit. Yet there is no lack of psychology: the old man's eyes are strangely sad, his mien thoughtful. It is not easy to instance the means by which the effect is produced, but it is partly due to the contrast between the sitter's attire and personality. What is most attractive about this picture is its unpretentiousness.

In the next year, 1937, Kokoschka did another self-portrait. This *Self-Portrait of a Degenerate Artist* (No. 282; frontispiece) was his reply to the condemnation his works had suffered in Ger-

[1] In 1944 the portrait was sold in New York. From the proceeds 4000 dollars were given by the artist to the newly founded 'Oskar Kokoschka Fund for War-Orphans of all Nations United in Liberated Czechoslovakia', under the trusteeship of the Czechoslovak Minister of Foreign Affairs.

many. It shows his head and shoulders and his two hands. Clad in a short-sleeved, open-necked pullover, his arms folded over his breast, he looks seriously straight at the beholder. Never before had Kokoschka scrutinised himself so earnestly: no trace of romanticism is left in this self-portrait, though it does not lack in self-dramatisation of a robust kind. His head is longer than ever, his nose broad, his lips crooked, and his eyes wide. A deep vertical line between his eyebrows contributes considerably to the strained expression of the face. Instead of softness, dreaminess, veiled emotions there is now a virile note of a somewhat scarred but brutal strength. The fierceness of the staring eye, the challenge of the whole pose is repeated and underlined in the figure of the stag visible in the landscape behind the painter's shoulder.

The painting produces an amazing effect of plasticity. Nothing would seem easier than to translate such a clearly shaped, big-featured face into clay. Kokoschka had, in fact, conceived a new ideal of representation: 'This time I tried to combine two contrasting aspects, different from the psychological point of view and different in the structural ideas as well, similar to the use of counterpoint in musical composition. That such processes are feasible in the arts which are nonsensically called "imitative" is manifest in the outstanding example of Michelangelo's late work, the *Pietà* in the Florence Duomo, where he combined three different actions and different ideas of form in one vision. This unfinished work opens in truth the period of art which we call the Baroque. If such terms as Cubism or Surrealism have any meaning, then here it can be found.'

At the same time problems of space fascinated him more and more; while he hardly ever spoke of colour or expression in his pictures he used to point proudly to this arm or that leg and to say: 'Do you see how much distance there is between this elbow and the hand? Do you understand that this figure sits further back than that?' Such problems may seem elementary to artists who have passed through an academic training; to Kokoschka, who had begun by discovering a completely new sphere of his own and had hardly heeded any conventions of perspective or composition, they became vital only when he matured completely.

This 'plastic' phase in Kokoschka's career had begun in the middle 'twenties. It is most clearly perceptible in his drawings of that time. He still liked to draw portraits in charcoal, but very differently now from what he had attempted, for instance, in his *Variationen* (Plates XXXVII–XL): then he had still been under the spell of 'expressionism', even though of his own brand; he had used the charcoal to translate facial lines, and most particularly those engraved by characteristic smiles or frowns, into calligraphic signs which thus reflected the sitter's psychological disposition. Now, as he became more and more detached and regarded his surroundings more and more objectively, he grew more intent upon the rendering of physical structure alone. He began to use his charcoal primarily to outline the shape of heads, to indicate the position of eyes, nose, lips, and then to fill in the shaded parts. On the whole his method was now much more conventional than that of a few years ago. Like his landscape art, his portraits became more sensuous. His shapes gained in roundness and lost in sensitiveness. But there was consummate mastery in the sparing use of line, in the restraint which enabled him to use unfilled spaces, in the sketchy indications of a swelling bone or of a shadow. Much detail is lacking or intentionally neglected in such drawings which were done out of artistic curiosity, but without the inquisitive, emotional frenzy of his beginnings. Nevertheless what little there is usually establishes very definitely the personality of the sitter.

After his return to Vienna in 1932 Kokoschka had already made the most formal use of his new method in his portraits of a little girl aged ten, named Trudl. The blending of heightened plasticity with his new symbolism which was beginning to emerge produced a strange effect which made the *Double-Portrait of Trudl* (No. 246; Plate LXIII) reminiscent of certain nineteenth-century pictures. Trudl is represented as though split into the two contrasting personalities of which, Kokoschka thought, her character was composed: as Diana, with a moon-sickle like a diadem on her forehead, and as a plain, motherly girl. The two images or, rather, the two girls, sit facing each other in a narrow space, thus showing not only two psychological aspects of one person but also the two physical aspects of one figure in one frame. In the past artists had frequently undertaken to paint one person's likeness from the front and in profile, right and left; the best-known example of this kind is Van Dyck's triple-portrait of *Charles I*, which was to serve as a model for Bernini's projected bust. It was always for some similar purpose that artists of the past represented one person, seen from several angles, in one canvas. But it was left to Kokoschka to conceive the strange idea that

216

one person could, in a finished picture, be divided into two different beings which confronted one another, enclosed in an interior.
This idea may be considered as a condensation, as it were, of the
one realised in his *Variationen* where he had, ten years before,
drawn one person in changing moods, as though under the lens
of a psycho-analytical film camera. Now he was satisfied with
two aspects, not only because his medium—oil colour—was by
its very nature a more final one, but principally because the
motives of movement and change were no longer of primary
interest to him: he had discovered two static, but contrasting
elements in one personality. As he had once, in his very early
paintings and plays, shown the contrast between two strange
elements, represented by man and wife, he was now observing
the contrast within each being. The struggle was now subdued;
but Kokoschka was still inclined to question Nature's harmony
and unity.

In Prague Kokoschka continued to execute figure compositions
in his newly acquired plastic style. It is very likely that *The
Fountain*, which he took up again after a lapse of ten years,
gained its roundness and depth at this stage. Another example
of Kokoschka's new ideal is a *Mother and Child* (No. 261), another
version of his old favourite theme. It is a long way from his early
Blind Mother (No. 75) with its emotional appeal, through the
monumental, colourful, fresco-like *Mother and Child* (No. 163)
of his Dresden period, to this picture which recalls Maillol by its
shape and its poise, and certain Old Venetian Masters by its dark
hues of brown and blue. This woman is full of healthy life, with
round cheeks and thick lips; a strong neck carries her proud
head: her face is animated by a soft carmine red, and all her
features seem to smile. Her right side is pushed forward as she
walks, while her right arm is crossing her body to hold the child
on her left. The trees in the background are of the same green
colour as the woman's clothes.

To depict human beings as part of a landscape had become
another of Kokoschka's favourite themes during these last years.
In Vienna he had thus painted his young friend Trudl with a
goat in the open air in a composition which he called *Pan* (No.
244). In Prague he finished two similar pictures, *The Garden
I: The Visit* (No. 266) and *The Garden II: Children and Goat*
(No. 267). All these are, at least for the present, lost.

In Czechoslovakia he also continued to paint pure landscapes.
During a journey to Moravska Ostrava he painted that city in

which, as once before in Biskra, it was the constrast between the ancient town and modern industry that attracted him. But most important are the panoramas of Prague, of which at least seven are known to exist. Some of these, in their breadth and depth, recall the most beautiful of his travel pictures. One, which was acquired by the Modern Gallery of Prague, represents a view most familiar to all those who know the Czech capital: the River Vltava, spanned by the old Charles Bridge with its pillars each crowned by a saint's statue, and the baroque cupola of a convent and square medieval towers in the right background. A boat is gliding over the water, and on the left the wall of a house with open windows closes the composition. The blueness of the water and sky, only here and there shot with pink tints, makes the whole panorama, romantic enough in reality, appear like a dream landscape of a celestial town. This favourite view, so often a subject for paintings, so hackneyed by engravings and post-cards, is here fresh and alive. The old city on the River Vltava had found its painter, a modern artist, who could appreciate its ancient beauty, who could feel and render the rhythm of the broad stream, of the arches of the bridges, and the enchanted spirit of its grey stones (No. 277).

Kokoschka haunted Prague seeking for its most picturesque corners, and he never tired of showing its varied aspects. It almost seemed as though all his travels had been merely pre-paration for what he was to achieve here. The city's character suited his temper, but he could hardly have portrayed it so com-pletely, had he not practised his eyes and his brush on such a variety of subjects beforehand. He had often imbued landscapes with dramatic movement as though the earth's forms were just taking shape before his eye, and Prague's soil seems to heave, fall and rise like the waves of a stormy sea, with monuments emphatically grouped on the crests. He had always moulded and kneaded the buildings under his brush, and in Prague every wall seems to be alive, every cupola to expand before the beholder's eye, every spire to rise like a flame. And from one of the heights that surround the city, its valley is seen stretching far away to the distant horizon which can be divined but not seen.

Kokoschka followed the course of the river to find new aspects of the old familiar corners. He climbed on the hills to overlook new parts of the town. He descended the narrow steps in the old city to catch a glimpse over a wall into an otherwise hidden park or Renaissance garden. He ascended remote heights, to see the cathedral on the castle mountain from new angles, its spires grouped in a different way. He painted the modern buildings, the chimneys and industrial installations of new suburbs as well as hitherto undiscovered corners of the old city. From his studio window he painted an unusual view (No. 270), which was to be one of his most successful, of the castle mountain with its cathedral rising on the right, while of the old Charles Bridge only two arches are visible; the river flows deep into the gap between the hills, its rushing waters hardly restrained from pouring over an island in its course; it is the river which shapes this composition. The houses around the church of St. Nicholas seem to dance. Reflections in the water are blue, purple, red, orange and yellow; the sky is afire with reds, yellows and greens. From the highest point of the cathedral's spire on the right the eye is led down surely to the left-hand corner, and from there again the course of the river guides it into immeasurable distances.

Some of these pictures, like that in the Prague Museum (No. 277), were executed with a painstaking brush, each stroke laid close to the next, so that reflections in the water are as clear and distinct as buildings on its banks; others were done in a more hurried, rather superficial manner. In the most perfect of them —for instance in the one which surveys the whole city from the slope of the castle mountain (No. 272; Plate LXX)—although a first glance seems to reveal just a vast sea of buildings, closer study shows that each is in correct place, and each familiar church, square or statue can be identified with certainty. Hung side by side these pictures of Prague would give as complete and faithful a rendering of the city as any film. And individually one or two of them, seen in isolation and closely scrutinised, will be found to have the quality of real portraits, not only faithful in detail, but also distinguished by that sensitivity to character and atmosphere with which Kokoschka is sometimes able to convey the essential yet most impalpable qualities of a human being or of a landscape.

★   ★   ★

Kokoschka had intended to make his home in Prague for a time at least. But his nature was always restless, and it was becoming increasingly apparent to him that he could not long remain in Europe. At the same time he felt bound to his new, self-chosen homeland, and its fate. He received an invitation to lecture at Mills College, California, which would normally have tempted him; even now he planned to follow it, but he could never make up his mind to go. Personal ties, political ideals and an undefinable fear of America (although he knew he had friends and fame there), each in turn prevented him from actually leaving. But unforeseen political events developed which brought the Nazi menace nearer and nearer: Germany laid claim to the Sudeten country, and after the Munich agreement of 1938 the Germans closed in upon the heart of Czechoslovakia. The tension in Prague became unbearable, the physical proximity of the Nazis, who had already shown themselves ready to kidnap and annihilate the inhabitants of small neighbouring countries whom they disliked to see at liberty, became a personal danger. Kokoschka felt that he was in a trap. All his friends endeavoured to persuade him to leave the country. And one day he could stand it no longer: improvising as usual, without any luggage or preparations, he went to the Prague airport. He had suddenly decided to fly to a country which the Nazis could not reach by land: the next plane that left Prague for London carried Kokoschka, his muse and an unfinished picture.

When Kokoschka arrived at Croydon aerodrome he and his companion between them had £10 in their possession. Kokoschka's suitcase contained a second suit and the most essential equipment for painting. Therefore the first thing he had to do was to deposit the unfinished picture, a bathing scene,[1] with an art dealer who was trusting enough to advance the artist some money on it. He was now a refugee, without means, in poor health and once more uncertain about the future. He remembered from his first stay in England, twelve years before, that to live well in this country one had to have a safe income—a consideration which fortunately could not affect his temper; a dirty boarding-house, later a furnished flat in Hampstead, with windows facing the Camden Town railway, and meals at Lyons's seemed at first a good enough exchange for the fate that had threatened him on the Continent. He was so cosmopolitan that he felt at home wherever he went. London, of course, was not Prague: the climate was difficult for a foreigner in poor health, and the light was hard for the eyes of a painter; materially life in this enormous city was not easy, even for those who could reckon on a regular but modest income; moreover the beauties of Lon-

[1] Now called *Summer* and the property of the National Gallery of Scotland (No. 284; Plate LXXI).

LXV. SELF-PORTRAIT WITH HAT
1934-37

LXVI. OLDA
Drawing. 1936

don were hidden away even from one who had known and appreciated them years ago—they had once more to be discovered; nor did he find in London the same friendliness, good living and broadmindedness of the town he had left behind. All streets here seemed dirty and noisy; all people were strangers, each living his own life, apparently unaware whether his neighbour was ill at ease, lonely or starving. Old friends were difficult to trace, new ones hard to acquire. But his position as an artist was what really mattered to Kokoschka; and this was once more as difficult as it could be. For twenty years he had been a famous man whose works were housed in the foremost collections of Europe. Now, at the age of 52, he had come to the one country where he had no name. England's art critics and connoisseurs looked exclusively towards Paris; of art east of the Rhine they knew nothing,[1] nor did they want to know anything, for in general they disapproved of expressionism and similar movements. Kokoschka's exhibition at the Leicester Galleries in 1928 had passed almost unnoticed. On the occasion of the 'Exhibition of 20th Century German Art' at the New Burlington Galleries in 1938 it had become clearer than ever that neither understanding nor interest for the new tendencies in Central European art existed in the British Isles. The daily press, generally speaking, had treated the exhibition as a sensation because it showed some of the works condemned by Hitler without, however, attempting to introduce the public to a completely unknown phenomenon. Only one or two of the critics mentioned the name of Kokoschka, who was represented by seven paintings and fourteen drawings. It therefore seemed that he would have to start the old fight all over again, the struggle for the support of individuals, for good prices and public recognition. He knew that it would be difficult; but fortunately he never suspected how unknown he really was in this country —how few people had ever heard of him, how small a proportion of these knew how to spell his name correctly, and how negligible was the number of those who had ever seen any of his work. But the directors of the leading museums received him well. Among dealers, only those who had come from the Continent and knew that they would get good prices for his works in the future were interested in him. The only private

[1] Mr. Clive Bell, in *Since Cézanne*, p. 7, writes thus: 'Though Paris is unquestionably the centre of the movement, no one who sees only what comes thither and to London—and that is all I see—can have much idea of what is going on in Germany and America.'

collections which included works by Kokoschka were again those that had been brought over by refugees. And some of his former friends, who had quarrelled with him years ago, now said that Kokoschka was finished, that he could paint no more, that he had long outlived his period of triumph. Even though he was luckily not aware of all this, Kokoschka felt his position to be precarious and his state of mind was far from cheerful. He had reason enough to be depressed. Although he had been in need before, he had never yet been restricted in his movements; he had been able to leave a country where he could not live for another. That was different now. His world had become very small. Many of his old friends, whom he met again, were now in the state of destitute refugees. The outbreak of the war in September, 1939, which severed his last continental ties, threatened to destroy finally the world he had known and, like any good European, had loved. Worst of all, London this time did not inspire him to work. At first he did only two portraits, both commissioned by a young Englishman, and a small picture of Prague that expressed his nostalgia. This poverty of achievement was decisive: it was clear to him that he must change his surroundings. He went to Polperro, the picturesque fishing village on the coast of Cornwall, where he settled down for the next nine months.

As always he was accompanied by his Czech friend. When he had first met Olda she had been a slim, boyish-looking and reticent girl who lived a sheltered life in the home of wealthy parents; she had studied law and modestly fulfilled her social obligations until she had made up her mind to devote herself entirely to her unusual friend, who often needed a nurse or a model and always a listener and a manager of his practical affairs. Under the strain of the last years' events she had become a mature and energetic woman, who had saved his life by forcing him to leave Prague and arranging his departure; she gave herself exclusively to the task of looking after the uprooted painter. Meanwhile she had become what he had seen in her when she was still undeveloped. Unusually tall and long-limbed, she had the classic profile, the regular, clear features and the poise of a statue; her beautifully shaped hands, her long legs and her usually immobile face were reminiscent of the perfectly built, powerful, and often somewhat masculine women of Michelangelo. What passed behind her smooth forehead it was impossible to guess: her facial muscles were hardly seen to move, her voice, which spoke English and German with the same hard, Slav accent, was never lifted. Quietly and methodically she went about the housework that she had taken upon herself, or sat listening at one side, sewing her frocks and serving Kokoschka's numerous visitors. After their arrival in London, which she knew from her student days, Kokoschka pretended to be a helpless stranger, and would not allow her to leave him a single moment: every visit, to gallery directors as well as to cocktail parties and bohemian dinners, they undertook together. The tall, broad-shouldered, tweed-clad painter, with slightly greying hair cut absurdly short, and ageless, monkey-like features, and the even taller young girl, who moved like a Pallas in tailor-made costumes and behaved towards him with the friendly calm of a sensible mother, became a familiar sight in the new circle which soon formed itself around Kokoschka. Those who saw them for the first time often remarked how surprisingly this man of over fifty and the girl who was not yet thirty, resembled one another in manner, speech and even in actual features, and how she would complete his sentences, to help his memory even when he spoke of something that had happened long before she was born. Those who had occasion to observe them more closely knew how utterly she had become Kokoschka's second self: how she had given up all interests but those that concerned him; how she had ceased to think for herself, unknowingly, in order to be able to follow his thoughts and fancies; how she unreservedly shared his political views and his opinions of people; how she sat up night after night to type his letters, his articles and the various versions of his new play *Comenius* on which he had begun to work soon after their arrival. Unobtrusive, without being self-effacing, she was always there. She watched over his health, his habits, his work. She took unpleasant duties off his shoulders, protected him when necessary. Even when he himself was so weak as to invite unwelcome visitors who took his time when he most wanted to concentrate or when the light was best for painting, she made good his mistakes, excused him and took all the blame for his ever-changing mind. After her parents had followed her into exile she divided her time between them and Kokoschka. But she had no other life of her own, nor did she desire one. Kokoschka absorbed her completely: for the essays which he was fond of writing he exploited her historical knowledge and her command of the English language; when owing to the political changes he became interested in China and was persuaded that the future would be governed from the East, she began to take Chinese lessons, in which she persevered with the stubbornness that was one of her characteristics; and whenever he felt a need to change his surroundings she moved with him to a new house or another part of the country. Uncritical, always practical, and unsurpassingly devoted, she made herself an instrument unhesitatingly at his service. He had long ago ceased to enjoy a bachelor's privileges and miseries. He was tired of adventures of any kind and intent only upon his work. In this new phase he was happy to have the companion who could best assist him.

In Polperro Kokoschka and Olda occupied an old cottage on the cliffs from which they could see the sea far below, a vast, ever-changing sky and seagulls everywhere. Kokoschka, gradually freed from the depression born of his recent experiences, set to work again as always when confronted with an inspiring subject. The landscape here, its ruggedness and romantic quality, appealed to his sense of picturesque beauty and natural grandeur. Living in it, breathing its atmosphere, smelling the sea, hearing the shrill voices of the sea birds by day and by night, and feeling the wind-carried foam against his skin whenever he stepped outside —he became, as it were, part of this landscape. He grew to know the place more intimately than most of the places he had painted, which he had seen only as panoramas from some height outside and above them. Olda, meanwhile, became part of the local population. She made her own experiments: in her small Cornish kitchen she baked the delicious and varied national cakes of her country—pastries shaped like half-moons, rings, cubes and pyramids, and filled with poppy seeds, ground nuts, plum jam, cream cheese—which she sold to the holiday makers and artists' households in Polperro. Her pastry shop was a success. Kokoschka, for his part, had one of his spells of inspiration. From his cottage he did watercolours of the sea, the cliffs, clusters of village houses, and others of the old corners and steps in the streets of Polperro; he also painted a picture of an enormous *Crab* (No. 294; Colour Plate 2) which lay rotting on the lawn in front of the cottage, while he still studied with amazement its 'ten legs that looked like a thousand'; lastly he painted one of the women whom he often saw sitting on the rocks and knitting, in a fanciful mood giving her a cat's head, a painting that he later called, in an effort to underline its symbolic meaning, *Private Property* (No. 290; Plate LXXV). Owing to this productivity and his new, healthy, settled life his mood improved considerably. After a short while he and Olda emerged from their isolation: they made friend with the sculptor Uni Nimptsch who lived in Polperro, were visited by the writer Rainer Heppenstall from London, who has since recorded their meeting in his novel *Saturnine*,[1] and by a young art lover and his sister, both of whom Kokoschka had painted (Nos. 291 and 292). These two leftish Tory youngsters amused Kokoschka as examples of a species whom he had never before met at such close quarters; he was also deeply grateful for the faithful enthusiasm of his young English admirer as well as sincerely delighted with the blonde, shy grace of his sister. The two were greatly entertained by Kokoschka's fantastic tales and elaborated recollections from a world that must have seemed utterly strange to them.

But the gaiety of those days was followed by one of Kokoschka's nervous spells. The winter of 1939–40 had been a period of suspense for the whole of Europe, and in Cornwall particularly, the war had seemed very unreal. But in the spring the German armies began to move, and soon they invaded one unprepared country after the other. Britain became suddenly foreigner-conscious. The wholesale internment of enemy aliens began and, of course, affected some of Kokoschka's oldest friends. These internments upset him beyond measure. He suspected animosity against foreigners, against himself, in the hitherto friendly people of Polperro. He began to feel threatened once more, surrounded by unsympathetic strangers. He and Olda packed their cases, locked up their cottage and left for London. There they took rooms in one of the biggest hotels in the West End. 'Here, among so many people, they cannot hurt me,' said Kokoschka. His fear was completely irrational, as there was not even a shadow of a suspicion that he would be treated as an 'enemy alien'. But he felt that the powers controlling the internment were the same dark, invisible but irresistible powers that organised wars, settled frontier disputes and managed passport questions, apparently with complete indifference to the effect on individuals, which had always been beyond the painter's comprehension. He was panic-stricken at what he saw happening here, to his friends, and it seemed to him a repetition of what he had seen on the Nazi-occupied Continent: the internment, without any chance of self-defence, of artists, scientists, intellectuals, democratically minded people on the ground merely that they belonged to a particular national group.

[1] Published in 1943, with a book cover by Kokoschka.

He could see no difference between here and there, between now and then. All at once he was again possessed by the old spirit that had driven him to fight hopelessly against the ruling authorities ever since his first public appearance. He wrote a reproachful letter to the Prime Minister and collected signatures in its support; in it he pointed out that the first opponents of the Nazi régime were treated as suspects by the Government of Britain, while English women fled to safety, taking their jewels and other wealth with them. Gradually he adopted more practical, but less spectacular methods: he sought the private intervention of influential personalities for the most urgent cases of interned refugees. His narrow hotel room was alternately an office where he dictated letters and a sick-room where he nursed his own breakdown. In this state he lived several weeks. But before long he was again sufficiently recovered and calm to wish for a more normal life. In the summer of 1940 he and Olda moved into a little house at St. John's Wood where he had a patch of green before his eyes, and once more they started a new life.

But always on the mantelpiece leaned Kokoschka's last picture of Prague, its blue burning fiercely like an exclamation; next to it, a photograph of his poster for the Spanish civil war, showing a bomber over Prague's castle. On the easel stood his *Summer* (No. 284; Plate LXXI), which he was once more repainting, or his *Crab* to which he was adding the finishing touches. At this time he was further experimenting with watercolours: he did the first of the flower-pieces which he was to develop to unsurpassed perfection.

Work was necessarily interrupted and fitful at this period: it was the time of the first air raids on London. The sirens went day and night, at the most unexpected moments. Soon there were few roads in the district which could not show one of those ominous holes which began to scar the face of London. Kokoschka's old house did not stand up too well to the bombing in the neighbourhood: big pieces of plaster were found on the floor every morning, and cracks in the walls seemed to widen almost before one's eyes. Before long Kokoschka and his wife felt they must put an end to this unsatisfactory state of affairs, and they decided to leave their quaint abode which, after a few months, had probably lost some of its charm, and to take an ordinary flat of more solid construction. The apartment they found, in a block of flats in Finchley Road, was very different in character: typical of middle-class flats, it consisted of a couple of narrow rooms, impersonally furnished, which barely allowed room for the easel beside a window giving on to a characteristic London back-view, over gardens and backs of other houses. There was little scope for Kokoschka's fancy in these surroundings—only the mantelpiece on which he crowded together things which appealed to him: wooden toys, photographs of negro nudes, coloured postcards from the British Museum showing Javanese masks and Chinese paintings, and odd souvenirs which his friends brought him. Here he lived for a few months, leading the quiet, regular life of a hard-working man. He painted as long as the light allowed, from morning till dusk, and during those hours he was inaccessible to would-be intruders.

More than ever Kokoschka now liked to express his opinions in writing. In October, 1941, the tercentenary of the visit of Comenius to England was celebrated in the Senate House of Cambridge University, and the addresses delivered there by President Beneš and various prominent scholars were published in a volume[1] together with some other contributions which included one by Kokoschka on 'Comenius, the English Revolution and our Present Plight'. As there is no need to quote extensively here from a recent English publication, a few sentences from it will suffice to give the gist of Kokoschka's ideas. After an historical introduction which gives proof of intimate knowledge of his subject, due to Kokoschka's long acquaintance with Comenius's work as well as to his conversations with President Masaryk, he turns to the situation of 1941: 'The resolve of the democratic peoples that this crusade against Fascism shall not again fade out in victory parades, but that it shall be succeeded by a long-lasting peace, can perhaps best be furthered by focusing attention on the problem of how to free the individual by removing the primary cause of his bondage, that is, education for national ends. . . . National-minded education still delivers its human product ready rather to die for his dogmas than to criticise them and live.' And he reverts to the ideas which he had frequently proclaimed in Czechoslovakia: 'The essential principles of his (Comenius's) plan translated into modern language demands from World Democracy an international scientific control of mass-education by a board of internationally-

[1] *The Teacher of Nations*. Addresses and Essays in Commemoration of the visit to England of the great Czech Educationalist Comenius, 1641. Edited by Joseph Needham, Cambridge University Press, 1942.

minded educational experts and scientists. Such was the plea
Jan Amos Comenius addressed to the conference of Breda (1667)
when the ideological wars of his time were ending. Three hundred
years later Democracy has before it the opportunity to set up a
World Education Board for the control of Schools apart from any
military settlements that may be made. . . . Whereas Fascism
or semi-religious Nationalism opens no new issues to mankind,
a World Education Board, partaking even of something of the
nature of a sovereign body, would be the greatest instrument
of world democracy, and thus indeed a realisation of Komenský's
highest aims.'

In January, 1943, Kokoschka expressed his views once more at
the opening of an exhibition 'The War as seen by Children' at
the Cooling Galleries in Bond Street. As this short speech has
only appeared in a small magazine, and as it contains some remarks on the painter's approach to his art, some extracts from it
are quoted here. Most of the children exhibiting were refugees
from Nazi oppression, and among them were German children.
Kokoschka took the occasion, after having saluted 'this group of
child-artists as a working model for an ideal human society of
the future', to dwell on one of his favourite subjects. 'There are
German children as well in this group. And I wonder whether
any one of those who, in order to restore a lasting world peace,
advocate the annihilation of the German people with their children and children's children, would be able to pick them out? . . .
Perhaps the thing to do would be for us to learn again our lesson
from these young survivors of the carnage. Maybe there are still
some stale ideas lingering in democracy. The dropping of prejudices rejuvenates one's own mind.' Then he comes back to
Comenius: '. . . something must have been generally wrong with
the European system of education for national ends, since it allowed two world catastrophes to happen within twenty years. Our
education has not taught us creative work, and it has been mainly
based on words. It is a sad thought that three hundred years ago,
at the Conference of Breda, which should have ended the ideological wars of that period, the Czech Jan Amos Comenius failed
to have adopted his international mass-education system which
would have guaranteed lasting peace. . . . I think in view of the
present children's art exhibition I do not without justification
refer to the inventor of true democratic mass-education, because
before their creations even he would not have had to exclaim:
"If youth only knew!" Age is not wisdom. As a grown-up artist

LXVII. T. G. MASARYK
1934-36

LXVIII. T. G. MASARYK, STUDY
1934-36

I am not wiser than the child. As I take their lesson to heart I understand even better what art means. There is no children's art, there are no different arts at all, there is only *art*, differing in physical means of creation such as sound, colour, plastic form, or in the psychological process of creation like the impressionist or expressionist approach to reality. We know that Madame Tussaud's wax figures are not works of art because they are only substitutes for people made without imagination. Most of the paintings in our dining-rooms are not works of art, although they are painted in oil by academic artists and represent things we today know only by hearsay. Nor have moralistic themes anything to do with art, otherwise preaching sermons would be reckoned among the arts. . . . A work of art cannot be enjoyed as something beautiful, wonderful, sweet like the good things we miss now on our dinner tables, nor can it be made useful to moral ends, or serve to educate people to national ends. War posters, army pictures and military music do not produce humanism, nor does Fascist production, on the other hand, account for barbarity. . . . You will have observed a picture of General de Gaulle done by a French child. Well, you see, a child's imagination is stirred by the thought of a liberator of his people as by a Robin Hood or an Uncle Tom in his cabin. Only the grown-ups muddle this inborn sense of justice with politics—they would perhaps do an Admiral Darlan instead. One characteristic feature of a true creator, as we learn from the child-artist, is the perception of meaning of things. One has to absorb in one's mind the kernels of things and drop the empty husks of words. Art is a spontaneous creation in which, to use a metaphor, the artist for a time gives himself up to his creation in the same way as a mother gives her life to her infant, as a child gives his love and tenderness to a toy. This toy may be a rough-cut piece of wood clad in rags. Art is the creation of a formerly non-existent reality by sensual means, a new order among things seen, heard, and touched by man. Cézanne has again taught our age that meaning of art. . . . The astonishing spirit of solidarity among children is derived from this love of creation, common to all children in the whole world, before they are spoiled by education. An uncreative child is an exception. Unfortunately the creative grown-up is also an exception. In our present-day society, alas, we all serve only destruction.'

Political writing and even public speaking has become a new habitual occupation of Kokoschka's. He has in recent years been almost exclusively preoccupied with political problems. This has

229

become increasingly evident in his painting: since the war, Oskar Kokoschka has become a painter of political pictures. The portrait of *T. G. Masaryk* (No. 263; Plate LXVII) was the first of this new series; but its symbolism was still of a general kind. The pictures which Kokoschka has painted in England are symbolic representations of topical events, or a painter's comments on political developments. When he deviates from this new line, when he paints a straight-forward landscape or a flower composition, it is done for relaxation. In his own eyes it is his political pictures which count for most among his current work.

★　★　★

During the 'Blitz' Kokoschka painted a new picture on the canvas he had brought with him from Prague (No. 284; Plate LXXI). It is another representation of human figures in natural surroundings and shows a bathing scene. A timid country girl, with a rosy, round face, a plump body and thick legs stands knee-deep in water, with hands crossed over her body; on the right a seated man stretches his naked feet in the grass before him; he is accompanied by a dog, alert and watchful; while on the left sits a second nude, slim and erect as only an English lady could sit, fishing in the stream. These figures are set in a summer landscape, with the narrow river flowing deep into the distance, and a cottage in the background. The idyllic subject is in perfect accord with its execution in fresh, bright colours: the strong, unbroken green of fields and bushes, the salmon-pink flesh tints, the blue of sky and stream. If proof were needed of Kokoschka's mastery it would be found in the two wonderfully painted still-lifes incorporated in the foreground: the bundle of clothes, with the hat on top, on the left, and the basket with a fish in it on the right. In the end Kokoschka added the Czech word for summer—*Zrání*—in the left-hand corner, above his usual signature. The picture, which had come to England under such extraordinary conditions, was to find a worthy home in the National Gallery of Scotland to which it was presented by President Beneš.

That the idyllic mood in which this picture was painted did not persist is demonstrated in Kokoschka's last picture of *Prague: Nostalgia* which followed upon the *Summer*. Entirely different from the panoramas which he had produced while he was actually in the Czech capital, it is a picture of Kokoschka's nostalgia for the lost city. This is a Prague dramatised and altered by recollection, a fantastic town which does not exist in reality,

230

and yet the Prague which lives in the memory of all Czechs: a
city of hills and cupolas and towers, of innumerable statues looking down on water, of ancient bridges spanning the majestic
river. The old Charles Bridge and the cathedral above the city
were correctly preserved in Kokoschka's memory. But apart from
these features the picture is an imaginative composition. Its blueness surpasses that of any other of the *Prague* views (No.
285). Its agitated water and clouded sky recall such dramatic
works by Kokoschka as his early *Tre Croci* (No. 90) landscape or
the dancing roofs of his *Santa Maria della Salute* (No. 228; Plate
LIII). A couple of emigrating lovers in the foreground add the
personal touch which Kokoschka has always liked to introduce in
his paintings. This picture of *Prague*, highly subjective and even
imaginative rather than realistic, and yet so genuine, may certainly be called an expressionist work *par excellence*: an existing
town has here been used, not as a model, as a *motif*, but as a
pretext for the expression of a highly individual emotion; its
chief architectural characteristics are used in this composition
much as the sound of bells, the murmuring of a flowing river, or
the songs of birds have been used by composers as realistic motifs
in their symphonies.

In Cornwall, in the autumn, winter and spring after his arrival
in England, Kokoschka was again able to set about painting a
great landscape, the first since he left Prague. Just as he used to
do many more or less sketchy pictures of the Czech capital, from
various points of view, before he produced one or two final versions of his *Prague* panorama, so here he went about sketching in
the English fishing village making a series of watercolours (No.
288; Plate LXXIII) and viewing his subject from various angles,
before he painted the one canvas which may be considered a con-
summation of those slighter works. Yet some of the watercolours
have themselves a freshness and finality which makes them, in
a more unpretentious way, perhaps even more attractive than
the big canvas. Steep rocks rising from the sea like groups of
rebellious stone giants; narrow lanes climbing uphill between
humble houses; walls over which the numerous boats on the
water of the little harbour are visible; seagulls that hover
shrieking under a clouded sky; and cats sitting on corner stones,
enjoying the sunshine; these are the subjects of the many watercolours executed with a vigour very different from the traditional
subdued atmosphere and delicate colour of English works in the
same medium. Even more revolutionary within the art tradition

of this country is Kokoschka's canvas of *Polperro* (No. 286; Plate LXXII). This picture may truly be described as an English landscape perceived by a foreign temperament. The colours alone are more vivid than the shades usually found on an English palette. They are even shrill in their intensity and reminiscent of the contrasts which are easily turned into harmonies by a southern sun. Yet this green is the colour that strikes the foreign traveller on his arrival in this island, though it may never strike an eye familiar with its brilliance. Kokoschka had, happily, if unknowingly, chosen a corner in which to stay and work to accord exactly with his own state of mind at that time: the torn, rocky coastline, the steep road curving round the bay, the sea and the sky so often troubled by furious winds, the shrieking seagulls and the boats accustomed to rough sailing were like a reflection of his own mood. The painted canvas might be of a volcanic landscape, and the innumerable irregular splashes which cover it might be foam from the sea blown over its surface by a storm. As a composition *Polperro* shows again Kokoschka's peculiar gift for choosing his viewpoint: while painters without number have for years tried their hands at the quaintest corners of the famous village, he took up his elevated position within the walls of his own house, from which he surveyed the entire panorama selected for his subject, and undeterred by the limitless extent of sea and sky made the most spectacular point—the rocky promontory jutting into the sea like an enormous hand with outstretched fingers—the centre of his composition. Kokoschka's *Polperro* is not the picturesque seaside village known to so many holiday makers. It is a fantastic edge of the earth where land and sea battle incessantly, a dramatic, almost cosmic setting seen through the eyes of an imaginative artist.

The picture of *Polperro* is nervous and disharmonious. That Kokoschka's state of mind was becoming more composed, however, and that he was rallying all his best forces, became obvious in the second painting which he undertook in Cornwall: the *Crab*, which must justly be counted among his masterpieces. The creature is shown against the background of the familiar Polperro scenery of the earlier painting, seen from a slightly different angle. It fills half the foreground; its shell is salmon-pink, but its claws are multicoloured, mainly red and blue; and as it crouches there broad and awkward, its legs spread out to embrace a maximum of space, its all too human expression recalls some bearded old man, or a troll or a prehistoric monster;

one can almost hear the moan it seems to utter. 'This is Chamberlain after Munich,' explains Kokoschka, 'he says "Uah! What have I done!"' ' On other occasions he declares that this is 'Hospitality'. He ridicules himself in the little figure swimming in the middle distance, who seeks refuge on the shores of England; this figure, hardly an integral part of the composition, is of no greater importance than the little man waving frantically to the lady in the poster, in the top left corner of Kokoschka's *Paris Opera* (No. 170; Plate XXXV)—a feature which Kokoschka added in an equally playful, but gayer mood to amuse his *valet de chambre*. This symbolism is interesting because it shows the direction in which the painter's mind was turning—how in these years he could not but introduce politics everywhere. It is certain, however, that the symbolic element was secondary. What first fascinated Kokoschka was the fantastic form of the crab, its colour and its landscape background. 'Such a creature, with its shell and its many legs, is like the invention of a madman! And yet its mechanism works perfectly,' he utters in amazement. The *Crab* is a piece of pure and consummate painting; its plaintive expression, whatever its interpretation, adds an emotional element which is emphasised by the dramatisation of the landscape. This is a picture of a sea-creature wrenched out of its element, magnificent in execution and colour, imaginative as a fairy tale, and moving by the sense of tragedy which the painter has instilled into it.

Tragic moods never held Kokoschka for very long, and the next picture he painted proves that he could be humorous too. It was not until he returned to London and became once more preoccupied with politics that he gave this work the title of *Private Property* (No. 290; Plate LXXV). Begun in Polperro, the scene it represents was one of daily occurrence: a woman sitting on the stones of the shore and knitting, with some cottages in the background, and an old woman stalking along leaning on her umbrella. The knitting women of Cornwall seem to have annoyed Kokoschka: the legs of his main figure, bare to the knees, are emphatically ungraceful, but as eminently characteristic as her whole pose; and the painter has given her the head of a cat that watches, with wide-open eyes and pointed ears, what goes on around her. There are some big fish on the sand in the foreground, and some mice playing on one of the boats in the middle distance. Obviously the cat is trying to keep her eyes on both these attractions at once. It is this very greediness which inspired

Kokoschka to give the picture its anti-capitalist title. There is something uncanny in the cat's watchfulness, as well as in its physical incongruity. But the fact that this cat has a woman's body, or this woman a cat's head, has aroused neither protest, nor even surprise, when the picture was exhibited—a proof that this fantastic creature is convincingly enough presented. The main colour of the picture is again the raw, bright green of the *Polperro* landscape. The most beautifully executed part is the still-life of fish in the foreground, one of those magnificent details which are found in each of Kokoschka's works and which always bear witness that he is unsurpassed not only in creative imagination, but also for purely painterly quality.

Back in London, Kokoschka's mind began once more to circle around the events of the near past and the fate of the Czech country he had had to leave so suddenly. The first picture which Kokoschka painted after his return to town was therefore a political comment: with satirical bitterness he called it at first *The Axes*; it expressed the idea that the four great European powers had contributed equally to the ruin of Czechoslovakia. The four partners—Hitler with a symbolic double-cross on his fool's cap, Mussolini, the British Lion with his tail curled up in the shape of a Pound Sterling sign, and France as a cat wearing Napoleon's three-cornered hat—have settled down to a roast chicken; but just as they start to carve it the bird, with a knife stuck in its back, flies off laying a red egg which bursts on the table, while the four table companions tumble back on all sides. Mussolini is choking with terror, Hitler screams with his mouth wide open, the Lion roars and the cat jumps under the table to watch mistrustfully what will follow. The red egg is as symbolic as the arrangement of the forks and knives on the table which form one axis between the dictators and another one linking the two democratic powers. But to make the picture's meaning quite clear the lion is resting on two big books inscribed '*In Pace, Munich*', and the panorama of a burning Prague looms in the background.

More outspoken than ever before, Kokoschka had here achieved a picture which could have no other meaning but the political one. When he painted it he had two examples in mind: that of Comenius, who had recommended teaching people through their eyes, and that of Pieter Brueghel, who had spoken to his contemporaries through his figure compositions. In this, his first purely political picture, which he finally called *The Red Egg* (No. 293;

Plate LXXVII), Kokoschka succeeded well enough in making himself clear, for its symbolism, if not understandable in all details, is supported by a masterly execution; nobody who saw the picture could misread the expression of the purple mask of Mussolini, and the blood-red egg is the obvious centre of the composition. Those who will not appreciate *The Red Egg* as a prophecy and as a personal confession, will at least agree that the conception is completely original and will admire the supple movement of the cat—this last version of Kokoschka's favourite animal—as well as the caricature of the gulping dictator.

During the 'Blitz' Kokoschka began and finished another picture, even more topical than *The Red Egg* which, by the course of events, had already become a piece of historical painting: *Alice in Wonderland* (No. 295; Plate LXXVIII), as he ironically called his representation of an air raid. The centre of this canvas is occupied by three air raid wardens with tin hats and gas masks who make the gestures of 'See no evil, hear no evil, speak no evil'. On their right is a baroque altar with a statue of the Virgin and Child, both headless as a result of bomb damage. On their left, as a counterpart to the Mother of Man, sits a terrified woman holding a baby with a gas mask. In the background the City, characterised by the Stock Exchange building, is burning and soldiers are marching. The 'Alice' in the picture is a nude in the foreground, who raises her hand in a pointing gesture, while one of the wardens points at her nakedness; she, however, is the one who speaks the truth, and she is therefore imprisoned behind barbed wire. 'Our Time' is the accusing inscription on the sheet of paper which one of the wardens holds in his lap, and 'INRI'[1] the other. In these new surroundings one can still recognise some of Kokoschka's old favourite figures: the mother, who holds her child to her breast, and the woman who through beauty and intuition, can see the light. From the point of view of composition the canvas is perhaps overcrowded. As a vision of a burning city it is still unsurpassed and in its splendour recalls the great landscapes of his travel period. The painting has been renamed '*Anschluss*'.

In the same year, 1942, Kokoschka got a chance to return once more to the painting of pure landscape. He received an invitation to visit an old Czech friend, the economist Professor Emil Korner, in Scotland. There, at Port William, he was again near the sea, and though this coast is not as rocky and romantic as in Cornwall,

---

[1] *Jesus Nazarenus Rex Judeorum.*

235

he found in its wide curve and in the cows grazing in the meadows an attractive subject. A couple of country women in the right-hand corner of his Port William painting are essential for the balance of the composition (No. 298). He also did innumerable small coloured-pencil sketches of animals, mostly cows, horses, sheep, in every imaginable posture, which prove how laboriously and seriously this experienced master of painting went about every new subject. Locked again in his London room, however, Kokoschka returned to his political fantasies. First he added a giant fish in the foreground of a half-finished seascape, which he had brought from Scotland. The fish opened a magnificently red mouth. A few days later it carried a plump female figure on its back, with the plainly recognisable features of Queen Victoria. Finally the fish was surrounded by drowning brown, yellow and white men, and itself devoured the arm of a first victim. The Queen held disapprovingly a little green frog in her hand, which obviously would not go into the shark's mouth willingly. 'Ireland,' the painter says, 'because in that country there are no other reptiles.' Kokoschka's imagination had been carried away by his anti-imperialistic tendencies: the *Loreley* (No. 296; Plate LXXIX), as he called this picture, is one of his less intelligible allegories. Nevertheless the monumentality of his unprepossessing Queen and the vastness of his storm-swept sea recall the imaginativeness and pictorial breadth of certain baroque compositions.

It was when he was painting this picture that Kokoschka confessed how he came to introduce political allegories even into his landscapes: 'What am I to do in this hole?' he said, referring to his London flat. 'I must invent subjects for my paintings. I am quite starved for something to *see*. When spring comes I feel how it stirs in me as in a migrant bird, and I become quite nervous: I must leave town and paint something real—a grasshopper or something. When I come back to town, the landscapes turn into political pictures. My heart aches, but I cannot help it. I cannot just paint landscapes without taking any notice of all that happens.' Once he has begun one of these symbolic compositions, however, he gets just as excited by his subject as he always does by a flower or a bird or the way in which a horse moves, and more enthusiastic than he could be as a painter of pure landscape.

More complex and involved than any of his previous works is a large canvas which, in 1943, he painted in a few weeks, for the special purpose of a 'Fight for Freedom' exhibition arranged by the Artists' International Association in bombed premises in Ox-

LXIX. PRAGUE IV: VIEW FROM THE SCHÖNBORN GARDEN
1934-37

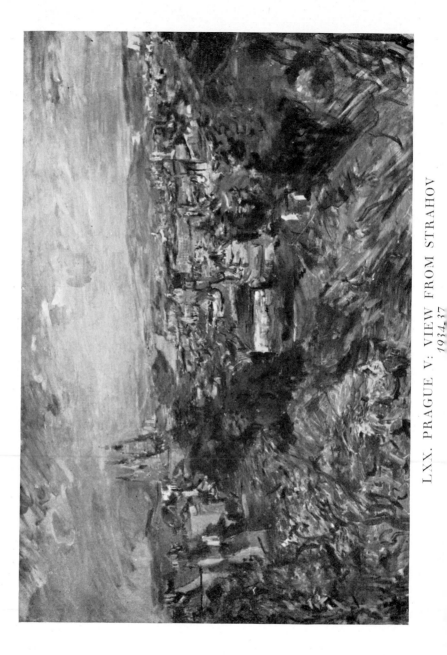

LXX. PRAGUE V: VIEW FROM STRAHOV
1934-37

ford Street. *What we are fighting for* (No. 301; Plate LXXXI) is the title of this composition which is meant to reflect conditions on the Continent. Outstretched on the ground lies a starved woman, her body reduced to a skeleton, her right hand still holding a bone which she has been chewing, while her left hand rests on the head of her child who embraces a rat, the only pet left alive in those starving regions. More bones are being produced by a curious machine—a symbol of modern armament industry—on the left, the wheel of which also turns the saluting hand of a Nazi in an eternal circle. On the right all the figures whom the painter considers as minor, but equally guilty, participants in the tragedy are crowded around a rickshaw: a French general in a gold-braided uniform; Dr. Schacht; Mr. Montagu Norman; and a 'representative of modern financial feudalism' with a coronet and a gas mask; sitting in the rickshaw is the stooping figure of Gandhi whose fast had stirred Kokoschka's imagination. Around the corner comes a fat bishop who with his left hand drops a coin into a Red Cross box, while his right blesses armies of marching soldiers who are held up by endless processions of refugees. In the centre the most prominent figure is a crucified human being marked as a Jew by a large 'P.J.'. In the foreground a bust of Voltaire smiles at the gruesome spectacles around it. 'Candide' is written across the base of the bust.

Crowded as this canvas is, it is not among Kokoschka's most successful compositions. There is too much to take in at one glance, but it certainly demands—and incites—the close attention which the propagandist Kokoschka wished to arouse. Moreover, it represents an unique effort by a contemporary artist to deal with the overwhelming problems offered by our time; for no other artist—except Picasso whose *Guernica* represents a similar effort in the same direction—has hitherto approached the subject of this war with the awareness that it is a war of ideas, and with the ambition to convey something of the complexity of the issues. To the reproach that the whole is not readily understandable it may be replied that this picture, like so many works of the past, and particularly of Kokoschka's admired master Brueghel, must be studied in detail before it yields its meaning. None will deny that such figures as the bird-like, emaciated Gandhi, the repulsive Dr. Schacht or the exhausted child with the rat in the centre are extremely convincing products of realistic observation as well as of constructive imagination. A work like *What we are fighting for* points again to the conclusion reached by Kokoschka's biographer Westheim on the evidence only of his earlier paintings, that Kokoschka may yet do his best work on a much larger scale and in the technique of mural painting.

What we are fighting for shows a terrifying, but quite understandable increase in the pessimism which had always had a place in Kokoschka's outlook. The Crucifixion in the middle-distance is certainly his saddest and most significant version of this theme which had first appeared in his *Passion* series during the first world war. Still more tragic is the development of his 'Mother and Child' motif: the original robust *Girl with Doll* becomes the headless Virgin and Child in the bombardment of the *Anschluss* (No. 295; Plate LXXVIII), and is finally transformed here into a skeleton-like corpse, struck down by starvation. This canvas is crowded with subjects which may at first sight appear disconnected, but each is linked with Kokoschka's earlier and earliest creations. And these roots of the symbolism of *What we are fighting for* in Kokoschka's own past give evidence that this painter, precisely because of his pictorial traditionalism, was a 'surrealist' long before the movement of surrealism or even its forerunner, dadaism, was established. His 'surrealism', however, is not limited to the coordination of symbolic objects: it is of a more spiritual nature and therefore just as independent as, in former days, his 'expressionism' had been. It consists in the persistent attempt to represent by pictorial language the world behind the object world. His inclination to penetrate below the surface first became apparent in the purely intuitive psychology of his earliest portraits. Even during the years of his greatest detachment, when he painted cities, landscapes and human figures for the sake of their pictorial aspect alone, he never ceased to imbue them with a dramatisation due to a strongly subjective interpretation. Now, having reached the conclusion that his art is to serve a tendentious purpose, he is far from becoming a history painter in the traditional sense of the word: he gives not objective representation, but pictures of his own conception, coloured by his political attitude. As his political creed arises from the same impulse that influenced his earliest artistic production —a genuine sympathy with human suffering—his development as a personality and as an artist is quite consistent.

Meanwhile Kokoschka has not abandoned portrait painting. His portrait of the former Soviet Ambassador in London, *M. Ivan Maisky* (No. 300; Colour Plate 4), is in fact more closely related to the works of his 'impressionist' period, during his years of

4. AMBASSADOR MAISKY (1942-3)

travel, than to any earlier or later phase: represented with the detachment of a cool observer, the statesman is as free from the sensitive emotionalism expressed in Kokoschka's earliest Vienna portraits as from the didactic intentions of the *T. G. Masaryk.* He is shown seated at his desk, writing, and just about to lift his eyes from his paper. Painted in broad, flat strokes of colour, the round head and the massive body are modelled with the brush rather than drawn in detail. Here the spatial depth, the plastic roundness achieved by the application of colour on canvas has been brought to an extreme. The figure of the model appears to have been built up like a piece of architecture, with the body and arms forming a base on which head and shoulders are heavily resting. A clever artistic device—the globe behind the ambassador's left shoulder—emphasises most unobtrusively the roundness of all contours. The light is concentrated precisely on that part of the globe where the realm of the U.S.S.R. lies. 'Western Europe seems just a little something on her borderline.' But it is not only the firmness of its pictorial construction that makes this portrait a masterpiece: it also gives another perfect example of Kokoschka's faculty of penetrating and spiritualising his subjects. The seriousness, dignity and importance of the personage in this picture would impress anybody immediately on seeing it, even without knowledge of the sitter's identity. Yet Kokoschka has this time permitted himself only a single symbolic attribute in the background which might give a clue to his position: behind the Ambassador's right shoulder stands a statue of Lenin, with arm raised in a familiar oratorial gesture. *Ambassador Maisky*, in its simplicity of composition, reserve of expression and economy of execution is one of Kokoschka's most brilliant and most mature works up to the present.

Kokoschka had from the beginning intended to present this work to the Soviet Red Cross, and he succeeded in raising £1000 for it which was given to the Stalingrad Hospital Fund. In a letter accompanying his gift he expressed his hope that it would help to heal the wounds not only of the heroic defenders of Stalingrad but of the wounded attackers as well, and that thus he desired to contribute something towards the stemming of the wave of hate with which the world was overflowing while the picture was painted. The portrait itself has been given by the buyer to the Tate Gallery.

★　　★　　★

From time to time all through his career, Kokoschka has done watercolours. The very earliest works of his we know, in fact, are drawings tinted with watercolour which he did during his student years. From the very beginning of his stay in England he turned again to this medium which had long been most popular in this country, and Kokoschka's recent watercolours must be considered among his major contributions to the art of the·present time.

The various views of Polperro, which started his superb English series of watercolours, were conceived and executed as studies for the major work in oils which he was at that time preparing. After his return from Cornwall in the summer of 1940, however, he began to paint flower-pieces in watercolours. He, who had completed many successful oil paintings of flowers, experimented like a beginner with the new medium, and he did innumerable sketches of sprays and bunches which his friends happened to bring him, before he was satisfied enough to show any of them to anybody. All through these recent years he has been doing flower-pieces. Originally they were undertaken because they were the only kind of studies from nature which he could indulge in the narrowness of a London sitting-room and, when he had familiarised himself sufficiently in this new sphere, he continued with them as a relaxation from his greater compositions and political paintings. But the perfection Kokoschka has reached in the use of his new medium raises these flower-pieces to the level of his most important and, particularly, his most readily enjoyable works. Each one is a masterpiece of its kind. The unusual gift of observation which has made Kokoschka an outstanding portrait painter, is now being applied to the study of the peculiar character of each flower: the human and often so humorous faces of the pansy, the lazy drooping of the peony, the stiff erectness of the lily and the radiant richness of the sunflower are rendered with the same sensitiveness as the passions and idiosyncrasies of nervous intellectuals and suffering women were in the past. No two of these many paintings are similar: they are as varied in composition as in colour. Now, an exuberantly rich bunch of summer flowers overflows from a round earthenware vase; now, delicate sprays are spread over the whole surface, with no apparent centre, like a blossoming hedge or a curtain of flowers. Some are remarkable for a delicate transparency, others for their robustness and vitality. All these plants are alive and real, none is merely decorative. Working with a light brush that hardly

240

LXXI. SUMMER
1938-39

LXXII. POLPERRO—I
1939-40

touches the paper, and never applying more than one wash of colour, Kokoschka leaves much paper uncovered; it is as though he had painted in a hurry but with trance-like sureness. How much work, how much seriousness of purpose has gone into these apparently light works becomes evident, however, on closer study: they are so full of detail that it is almost impossible to exhaust them; a half-hidden flower, an unfolding bud under a leaf, a grasshopper on a stem, a bird that peeps through the green thickness may not be seen at first, and something new remains to be discovered at every new inspection.

Flowers, though by far the most frequent, are not the only subject of Kokoschka's watercolours. From time to time he has done other kinds of still-life: fruit in a basket, or fishes in a basin, mainly, however, as studies for oil paintings and not as complete in themselves like the flower-pieces. Thus there is a version in watercolour of the fishes in the foreground of *Private Property* (No. 290; Plate LXXV). Some of the studies made for such an oil painting are finished enough to pass as complete works of art in their own right.

Apart from the flower-pieces and the preliminary studies there is another group of watercolour portraits of women who appear in this light, transparent medium as delicate and spiritualised as some of the flower-pieces. Far removed both from Kokoschka's early psychological studies and from his recent, more monumental portraits, they give just an impression of colours: brown hair against the white paper, dark eyes with a bright light, red lips and a few pink shades to indicate the moulding of the face. Utter economy could go no further than in these sketches in which each touch of the brush can be counted. Yet the result is a living and penetrating portrait: each one of these women is caught in a characteristic mood. The look of the eyes, whether naïve, sadly reflective or aggressive, conveys an idea of the whole personality. The inclination of the head expresses the disposition. And a faint indication of the clothes, the parting of the hair, a few pearls, a decolleté—reveal as much of the social status, and the background as is required. The psychological impact of these watercolour portraits is as astonishing as the solidity of structure here conveyed with such sparing means.

★ ★ ★

Certain characteristics are inherent in all of Kokoschka's works: the sensuality and the passion they express; their symbolism that has changed from personal allusions to general significance; the consciousness of the respective historical situations out of which they were born; their indebtedness to the artistic traditions of European and Eastern art which is frankly acknowledged and strangely combined with a revolutionising spirit; their tendency, in other words, to link the past with the present.

Kokoschka has enjoyed an equal measure of productiveness all through his life. He paints always with the same feverish intensity. His inexhaustible imagination could furnish whole generations of painters with motifs, and the virtuosity of his brush can keep pace with the fertility of his brain. His zest for life, for adventure is so harmoniously coupled with a gift for exact observation and contemplation that he is capable of both romantic and realistic pictures.

It is owing to these gifts of observation, to the capacity for realism as well as for dramatisation that Kokoschka has become the portraitist and the landscape-painter of our time. His men and women are individual as well as typical, familiar as well as mysterious. They live because Kokoschka has made of each of them a part of his own life, imbued each with the spirit he reads into them. And he treats animals, flowers and landscapes in the same way. They are all to him manifestations of the same life, that he loves even when he suffers under its burden. As he is a real artist each one of them communicates to us the fascination out of which it was born.

London, November, 1943.

14. POSTER: CHRISTMAS, 1945

APPENDIX

A PETITION

FROM

A FOREIGN ARTIST

TO

THE RIGHTEOUS PEOPLE

OF GREAT BRITAIN

FOR

A SECURE AND PRESENT

PEACE

Humbly tendered and signed
by

Oskar Kokoschka

Oskar Kokoschka
London, December 1945

245

I am indeed grateful that the opportunity for physical survival was offered to me in Great Britain when many an unfortunate friend of mine had been left behind in a Europe overrun by Hitler. Now, recovering from the first enthusiasm which has followed the defeat of Fascism, I pause for a moment of lucidity in which to find MY WAY BACK TO A CIVILISATION suspended during the war.

Nobody will forget that Great Britain stood alone against Totalitarianism before Soviet Russia had been invaded and the United States had joined in the war against the Axis. Victory on the battlefield had certainly depended on Great Britain.

I address to the conscience and human understanding of the hospitable people of this country some reflections evoked in a mind deeply apprehensive of certain theories now taking permanent shape in the post-war set-up. A refutation of such theories as are injurious to the principles by which creative man stands may be viewed unfavourably by those who are satisfied with the superficial aspect of a formal abolition of totalitarian rule. That the continent I had to flee is writhing under an almost lethal stroke, that the cultural soil from which I drew my spiritual resources, and from which my work as an artist had sprung to life, became barren due to the surrender of Europe to totalitarian ideas, must account for my possible, involuntary exaggerations.

My resolve to record the fact that during the time of my exile my mind has been moved is not in the hope of ensuring a change in public opinion. On the contrary, I am almost sure that the mere fact that most people would stare at the coming of a Last Judgment of their own making like visitors from the moon, proves that they do not know what they are doing. Indeed, as an artist, I have no thought of reforming others. I well know that at present the challenge to man's liberty is gaining momentum. It cannot be registered until its physical impetus has spent itself.

Great Britain was the only country to admit me when, as a 'degenerate artist', I had been deprived of civil rights in an Austria signed away to Hitler, and afterwards in Czechoslovakia where just previously I had been given full citizenship in spite of the fact that my mother-tongue was German. According to the official lists found in Prague after liberation, I was marked

246

out by the Gestapo as early as 1938 to be executed without trial on capture.

In this country I feel free to raise the question of the relationship of the individual to the community. Although it may appear to come from a somewhat unexpected quarter, an exiled artist's premonitions of further encroachment on man's liberty, even after victory, may not be thought wholly unfounded. The suffering world shouts the truth that man's efforts to find his way back to civilisation are paralysed by uncertainty. We are warned by high authorities, to whom it was quite clear that the common use of the shibboleth of Nationalism must confuse the issue of the war of liberation, of differing conceptions of freedom and democracy. During the war the idea of democracy gave a new hope to the despairing world. Today it must be frankly admitted that it does not.

How can a secure and present peace spring from those callous views on human life which became manifest at the gorgeous banquets at Potsdam, where the victors feasted among the unburied dead with rats roving in the ruins, refugees, suicides and starving children. Only the Secret Pacts were not revealed to the world. It possibly was as an act of mental self-preservation that the victors had to comfort themselves by taking the attitude of theatre-goers, who must not see the human beings on the stage of 'another world', with whom they must not identify themselves. But there is no war on at present. If now we fail to understand that the falling of the curtain entails deep spiritual problems, it will—as our own misfortune—blur the pattern of destiny for us and for posterity in this world of ours.

That reforms cannot be imposed on a largely unwilling society without overthrowing the framework of that society is a problem whose solution must elude the democratic politician (to whom it has been left to determine the nature of the peace to come) just as, at this stage, it eludes the economist and the technical and military expert.

For the creative man the problem is, first, to identify and define what darkens man's intellect; secondly, to set the mind free.

Due to the impact of totalitarian ideas there has arisen a recognised separation of two great worlds of inquiry, the study of the external world in the daily widening department of physical science, and the knowledge by which the working of the un-deviating regularity of the moral world can be traced. Totalitarian Government perfected a method for the psychological conditioning of human responses to leadership by propaganda. Democratic leadership has not yet begun, as it should, to improve upon totalitarian technique of thought-control by an uncompromising insistence on the vital connection between the action of external phenomena upon the mind, and the action of the mind upon these phenomena.

The basis of what is called the Sovereign State is the Sovereign Nation. The idea of national sovereignity is only an *a priori* construction in the international lawyer's textbook. Do not dare to ask the politician, the economist, the technical expert on production, the man of applied science, the educationalist or military expert, who are all in the service of the state, what they think to be the reality defined by the legal term of National Sovereignty. Here is a problem which is not easy to define for anyone who has not come under the spell of nationalist propaganda. Its effect on the mind is comparable to that of an *idée fixe*, to which the unhealthy mind erroneously attributes some part of physical reality as though it were an observable phenomenon. By giving power to a political obsession or hallucination the technical and military expert, the economist, or the politician expands the control of competitive industrialism.

Can we not throw some light on the nature of this idea of National Sovereignty, which has taken such a strong hold on the mind of the average modern adult, by the systematic application of the typological method of investigations? A method by which this delusion might be brought into line with such other peculiar sensations as are the empirical material of psychological enquiry.

* * *

First of all it ought to be generally realised that, whether we like it or not, and on whichever side of the barricade victory has found us stranded, A FALLACY IS BLURRING THE CLEAR DISTINCTION BETWEEN WHAT IS IN AND WHAT IS OUT OF THE MIND. It is the delusion of the uniqueness of mechanicalism that has made man apply mechanist conceptions to society.

In this transitory phase of democracy public opinion sides with the advocates of a peculiar method of mass-education which emphasises merely the logical operations of the mind on which progress is alleged to be based. This is a supposition for which, to say the least, no one has as yet brought forward any good evidence, since the supremacy of logics is not balanced any longer by cultural interests.

As an artist I am aware of a current tendency towards mental uniformity such as has never existed until now. This tendency threatens to circumscribe the originality of the individual mind. It induces man to subscribe voluntarily to elaborate systems of organisation which orientate him towards artificial ways of life completely divorced from his own true nature. The artist has no grounds for astonishment at the fact that, once man's actions cease to be the product of his volition, there can be no culture to create an epoch such as the world has known in the past; nor that, on the other hand, the destruction now operating wherever the creative mind manifests itself, has never been surpassed in the darkest ages.

Uniformity has warped imagination. Will it be left to the artist alone to seek the way back to civilisation amid this maze of incongruity which is the world today? Because vocationally he is not completely blinded to the æsthetic interest, he can never be made to believe that disparate details could be moulded into a homogeneous, harmonious and, as it should be, natural whole.

The training of the mind to analytic thinking isolates man. It was not the man of applied science who was victimised under totalitarian rule. I believe there is a tendency to magnify the advantage to democracy of the collaboration of scientific advisers from the countries once overrun by Hitler. As the events of the war move into the past it will be duly noted that in some democratic countries there is an effort to weld together the ideas of men who refused on principle to assist in building up the industrial and war-machine of the Third Reich (or who were discouraged to do so for other reasons), with those of scientists from the other side of the barricade kidnapped during the war or arrested at its end. Collaboration of men of applied science is encouraged irrespective of the fact that some of them refused to share secret scientific knowledge with those who, by their discoveries of synthetic processes, made it possible to immunise the Third Reich against blockade, or who, as pioneers in the development of aircraft and rockets, let loose the horrors of total war. Scientists are encouraged whose activity under the circumstances conditioning competitive industrialism leaves us no hope for Peace until the last competitor is removed.

In the attempt to invest the merely logical operations of the intellect with the authority which, in the cultural past, reasoning

249

shared with imagination, the artist sees the futility of wanting to shape society from an economic blueprint. Social planning is misleading when it denies the principle by which the creative man lives, i.e. that logical operations and imagination are complementary to each other in a well-balanced mind. This has led art to isolation, the artist to an 'ivory tower', to submission to commercial mob tastes. If people were not isolated by their very multiplicity of contacts, they would see in themselves that the loss of cultural interests results in a levelling down of standards. The great humanists of the eighteenth and nineteenth centuries observed that modern states represent loose aggregations of individuals bound to appeal to authority every time they feel a physical or spiritual need. As government is gradually gaining control over human activity the obligations of the individual to the state grow and citizens are progressively relieved from their obligations towards each other. Today, hardened in the battlefields, just as we can listen to appeals to help innocent children who are to die of hunger and cold in concentration camps and respond no longer, so we can become indifferent to our own emptiness, weariness, defeatism.

★   ★   ★

There is more than a grain of truth in the distrust with which the common man views the chances of the salvation of the world. It is due to the situation of society at present that, because we are indifferent to the state of things for which we do not feel responsible, we leave mankind to 'the atomic physicist who rummages in Nature's repository just like a burglar tackling the locks of a safe'.

The moral effect of the atomic bomb in Asia alone, a continent aflame as the result of the war of liberation, should make us reconsider the problem of HOW TO OUTLAW WHEN THERE IS NO LAW.

For the first time in the march of industrialism an agreement among governments has been announced in which emphasis is laid on the responsibility of instigators of 'crimes committed against humanity', including those 'committed against any civilian population before or during the war'. This agreement was the basis of jurisdiction at the Nürnberg trials. The fate of the atomic bomb is still veiled in secrecy. Our eyes are fixed on Dancing Death holding this devilish device, counting the hours of our life. The complete absence of any hope of peace-to-come is a characteristic feature of the technical structure of present-day civilisation.

In order to account for the chaotic state of affairs today, the causes leading to the last two world wars are explained as due to the perversion, by the defeated, of true nationalism into blind militarism. It has been rightly objected that the argument brought forward has been advanced with some inaccuracy. It may become merely incidental, as the events of social disruption move into history, whether the elimination of the Third Reich or of the Japanese Empire, and even a further reduction of the number of sovereign nations, will help to outlaw crimes against society as legitimate instruments of policy in competitive industrialism.

As there is no call for unification in a moral sense, the effect of competitive industrialism as an elementary dynamic force within the sovereign nations which are political and policed vehicles, must be as inevitable as a concussion between concurrent physical entities. It has been regretted that the atomic bomb, as the latest development of applied science in the field of war, has overstepped the growth of all moral sense in society. The scientists are not unaware themselves that something has happened which has altered the fundamental concepts of human life. They wish therefore that the odium for using the bomb should be transferred to the politician, who could use this horrifying discovery very effectively without dropping it on cities which cannot be protected against it. But in spite of their better knowledge of the fatal results the scientists will continue their researches. I see the man of applied science and his like as the prototype of the society to come, when individual experience can no more protect man from the repetition of his own errors.

★   ★   ★

It is more than a coincidence that the age of Mechanicalism began with the macabre mania for the Dance of Death. Then the Thirty Years' War opened an epoch of VOLUNTARY SUBMISSION TO FATE. Man's mind was to be reformed. The individual with imagination, human understanding, memory, the human being with sight and hearing, touch, taste and smell, was doomed to become an abstract term, a ghostly numerical fact systematically filed into economic statistics. In the early wars of industrial competition the first attempt was successfully made to force society to the acceptance of the gospel of political economics, which sees human industry as the working of a National Productive Machine.

In theory and in practice mutual aid between individuals is on the point of being outlawed. Collaboration between man and man, and cultural intercourse will be determined solely by an economic policy designed to lead to an ideal state, one in which the existence of mankind from birth to death, all lands and raw materials, indeed all human thought and activity would be uniformly controlled from one single political centre.

I wonder what made the rationalist borrow the symbol of Death, the hour-glass of running sand, from mythology? Life surrounded by Death! Could it have been the new invention, the mechanical device for counting the hours which was to replace the sundial? Till then the sun which rules the seasons of the year and the growth of organic life in the whole realm of Nature, had regulated a day's work as well. Was it the infernal tic-tac of machinery, this sound somewhat strangely associated with that of the beetle working invisibly in the old timber of a house as if within a coffin? People ceased to feel at home in their world once the old order has broken down and natural life has been sacrificed to the machine.

Current jokes tell about the peculiar attraction the watch exercises on the minds of pilfering soldiers who, in the course of their migration, are overrunning Europe at present. Today one ought to equip the Dancing Skeleton with a wrist-watch.

Whatever the rational foundation for accepting economic causes as an explanation of the complete reformation of the modern mind, the sceptic may think that, at least for the time being, only the economist profits by a play of words. It will be remembered that Jeremiah Bentham promised for the Economic Age 'the greatest happiness to the greatest number'. A too hasty application of uniform economic causes, while reflecting today's trend of thought, reveals, as one of the true causes of the greatest misery of the greatest number, the emotional readiness of an ever-increasing number of idealists of both the left and the right, to accept the fiction of the validity of physical laws in society, i.e. submission to determined fate.

★　　★　　★

Up to the sixteenth century the moral law was embodied in the SOCIAL HERITAGE carried on through the ages. In the continuity of a moral world the primitive democratic community unites

252

those who are alive, those who have passed away, and those who are to be born. Continuity is founded on human experience, collectively verified. A break in this continuity was regarded by religious doctrines as well as by positive law as a 'sin' against spiritual authority in the former and a 'crime' against secular authority in the latter. When great calamities befell mankind, when the abuse of power and the adoption of corrupt practice led to insurrections against petrifying social institutions and demanded the reformation of church or state, these movements were activated by the intellectual cohesion of the community. It is notable that, particularly in European history, this tendency was supernational. Because the authority of moral law was valid before that of Church and State in the relationship between the individual and the community, this spiritual heritage could be carried on, if necessary, outside of both.

The weakening sense of individual responsibility strengthens the superstitious belief that salvation can be found in a kind of super-state. There are animistic superstitions in the air, generalisations which make us think in terms of entities like National Sovereignty, Collective Responsibility, Collective Guilt. Whatever the riddle of the future, the human mind will be the guinea-pig in this experimental epoch. It will have to give the answer which the economic order has already assumed by forcing man into a prefabricated environment. The completion of an economic order depends on the renunciation of individual judgment. Physical power vitiates sound judgment.

From the beginning technical civilisation has worked under the assumption that the primary instinct of rearing a family in a natural environment, common to social man and animal, could be ignored. Economic theories lay emphasis on physical factors such as the concentration of production leading to phenomenal increase of urban population. We dare not draw the conclusion that the climax of the controlling process can only be reached by a decision for quantity against quality. Only in levelling down cultural standards can a uniformity of the mind be reached. Once the reality of national culture has lost the colour of life, has been stripped of its flesh and forced to spend its blood, it will be left as a skeleton in the cupboard of Materialist Philosophy.

From the time of the Roman Empire until the resistance movement of the last war we can see that, once the state had ceased to be an institution respecting the moral law of primitive democratic society, freedom has always been challenged by attempts to make an artificial social framework for an omnipotent arbitrary authority dispensing justice. Although as a policy it is un-European, the pernicious alliance of political power with metaphysical doctrines becomes a regular feature in empire-making. It is essentially the idea of oriental priest-kingship. When the political power of the Roman Empire was breaking up, Roman order and law became a matter for derision to the 'displaced' peoples of the day. Augustine, under the influence of the early Fathers of the Eastern Church, even tried to reform the Catholic Church, but he failed. This democratic institution resisted and condemned the doctrine of predestination as heresy. The church affirmed that there can be no order in this life unless the argument, *pro and contra*, can be adjusted to a reality. This reality must have a bearing on order *ex intima philosophia*.

All arguments, *pro and contra*, in the Hegelian version of the art of logics become, when completely exercised, equally accurate. Thus the disputes about the degree by which Democracy differs from Fascism resemble those of the Byzantine monks about the subtleties of the doctrine of predestination. All objections coming from contact with reality, prove the fallibility of the sophism which provides society with arguments that moral law can be had second-hand, and will only prolong our miserable belief in predestination. That the blowing up of the globe may soon be as easy as lighting a match makes the boasted rational approach more trustworthy to a logician stranded on some super or inhuman plane. Two thousand million people are now excited by the fashionable idea that Humanitas can be restored under the protection of the atomic bomb.

The nature of the justice to be administered must be tested by more than logic. We have a clear idea of what we mean by Sovereign Nation as a machine for producing National Wealth, and by Man as Labour. Is it enough? At least as an artist I cannot help thinking that it is not, even at the risk of being called a reactionary.

The individual in a static order was more fortunate in that his economic survival was not the dominant factor in his composite social pattern. Although our power of humanistic valuation is now much lower, we can still appreciate the energy thus freed for the creative work still to be seen in our museums. Now we can only analyse such isolated relics as we can analyse our psyches, we cannot contemplate, and therefore we necessarily miss the existential form of life of these men of the past who in their worldly doings bore themselves with their minds well composed.

I believe that the rosy prospects for Production and Distribution of National Wealth will never materialise, and I shall tell my reader why.

The Big Powers traded on the prevailing discontent with totalitarian rule by posing as liberators, just as Hitler traded on unemployment. Behold Democracy, a castle in the clouds wherein we cage all realities outside the limits of technical civilisation. In war, civilised man has acquired the outlook of a fly using the monuments of man's past culture as its target. As our age is in sole quest of the 'logically conclusive' proof of reality, cultural group-life seems to us as curious as the mysterious existence of an aborigine in his exotic pavilion in a world-fair. But materialist science cannot have it both ways. Human will is free to decide which way to take. It determines what takes place on the 'Other Side' (which is in fact in our own mind). Progress has changed man's world to a measureless field of ruins. The rationalist assumes the return of Freedom, Peace and Plenty as the result of world-wide acts of vandalism.

One of the aims of the United Nations Organisation is the sanctioning of force to support the rule of law. It hopes to make a democratic world in which the control of all human industry would be centred in the United Nations Organisation. Does such an economic pattern correspond to the needs of millions of shivering, hungry, homeless human souls? Are these doomed to accept the law of the strongest only because they were not united? Victory came as a result of a united war-effort. Does not the reality of recurring competitive wars prove the recurring failure of industrialised society in terms of peace? Any plan to provide for the united sanctioning of force to support the rule of law proves that nothing has been learned by experience, that the argument of Physical Law is still to be the negation of Moral Law.

Even the darkest ages of superstition religion never led man so far astray as to make him forget that his privileges corresponded to duties which a community owed to distant posterity. It will not be only for the absence of good manners that our puny bloated generation will be judged. We have condemned generations to come to pauperism. We came into the world as into a guest-house. We should leave it not worse than we found it.

Since the ignorant rationalist lost the fear of the devil he respects no moral law in the whole world. He thinks of this earth as his own property with which to do as seems proper to him. As he has learned nothing about the art of living and has no taste, beggar on horseback that he is, he does with the world as he will. He enters it helpless and fearful and consumes it to a burning fag's end.

★　　★　　★

While most people agree that as an egg becomes a chicken, the more eggs the more chickens; it is an irony that we become beggars in the degree in which the control of production progresses. There must be a short-circuit in modern logics. The scientist could not sort out of his fossils the progressive animal as the missing link in the biological process any more than economic theorists can draw out of the conjuror's hat the Four Freedoms of the Atlantic Charter with a concrete content. The reason is that the whole idea of progress is no more than a fiction. Once it has been taken for reality, it became a device to deceive people. It had its use in the heyday of Materialist Philosophy as an advertisement of the idea of the SURVIVAL OF THE FITTEST. If one looks round in the whole realm of man's creation—have not the varieties of fauna and flora suddenly been reduced to those with a bearing on supply and demand? Everything that grows above or rests beneath the surface of the earth has virtually altered its virtue. Even a seal which cannot balance a burning lamp on its nose has no chance of a job, nor the monkey who for a penny cannot fire a rifle to show children and soldiers what fun is. Man has altered his nature and become Manpower.

Before a new member is accepted by industrialised society he has to undergo the rite of initiation into mechanical thought. It is a painful process of mental transformation which does not succeed without a hard struggle by the normal victim of compulsory thought-control. Like the Chinese method of crippling women's feet in childhood, STATE-CONTROLLED EDUCATION AIMS AT A REFORMATION OF THE MIND. The lore of the survival of the fittest could not stand conclusive proof without a system of education to coordinate and control thought. In the early days of mass-schooling scepticism and resentment had to be aroused against what was called extravagance of the mind. Today it is

256

LXXIII. POLPERRO
Watercolour. 1939-40

LXXIV. POLPERRO
Watercolour. 1939-40

LXXV. PRIVATE PROPERTY
1939-40

called an insane delusion or even may be persecuted as 'Dangerous Thought'.

The perception of the world as a whole, as a spontaneous expression of a living existence, as a future coloured by multifarious culture, fecund imagination, wonder of the creative mind, is no longer thought of as the mark of mental health. But it takes an educationalist, a learned man, to enable a child to accept the belief that there are 'dead things'. Death has no meaning to that age-group which still feels the beat of cosmic reality. The unschooled child lives beyond the surfacial and contracted sphere. It has been proved in psychological research that, before the child's assent to our interpretation of reality as the logical continuity has been enforced by coercion, it had already acquired a knowledge of living continuity, the content of which can only be indirectly recorded by speech and print.

The reality of the primitive democratic society, now almost extinct due to the onslaught of industrialism, actually resembles the child's world more closely. The cultural means of primary social contact were founded on the development of 'primitive' man's senses, enabling him to take cognisance of faint indications which are beyond the range of our own senses. This knowledge was communicable and communicated in what can be called the documents of that cultural past where thought and form were not yet detached. These documents, which satisfied a now lost human need and taste, are collected as curios and kept in what have been called (with a slight wince) 'the storehouses of the imagination of the race', or National Galleries.

The industry of primitive society depended on a selective development of the human senses. It created the means of social contact, it favoured cultural progress as a refinement of manners, and by creating multifarious variety of satisfaction of desires raised the mental level. Conversely the 'knowledge' provided by industrial civilisation can be turned against the community and lead to biological regress.

If we are in doubt as to the right meaning of culture, our dictionary says that 'culture comes from cultivating the earth'. Thus culture becomes the wisdom of wisdoms because it produces food and table-manners; on mutual aid and social law is founded conviviality, i.e. society, you keep company with whom you share bread. A caveman could not have survived if he had been unable to rest for fear of being eaten for breakfast by a guest. Civilisation, on the other hand, is more intimately con-

R 257

nected with citizenship. The lawyer was once called the civilian. Civil law bound people into a 'state', the *polis*, or town, from where the countryside or a stretch of the coast could be controlled or policed. If the country produces food, a town produces merely money. Money on which one can live only if the control of the country or the sea is safely in the hands of the townspeople. Thus the progress of an abstract fashion of thinking about life, as a second-hand experience, is due to the gentlemen accustomed to what is called 'the world' whose lot had been cast in a town. Politicians, lawyers, magistrates, bankers, professors, or lay or ecclesiastical metaphysicians, have a natural weakness for the analytic approach towards culture or existential life. They divide entities into items and add them up again as a big sum of 'dead things'. With logics they bind together the torn limbs to form a new fictitious reality which can be controlled by pulling wires. Thus it progresses. But because these respectable gentlemen are firstly loyal citizens obeying the civil law, they cannot see that the dummy they take for progress is a mechanical continuity in which the living continuity of the moral world can never come to life. Civilisation must be unintelligible and appear a strange production in a much more narrow world than that on which experience had taught the rustic native to calculate.

As it has already been said, the intellectual cohesion of primitive society cannot be expressed by print or oratory exclusively. Nor can it be measured by the tools of scientific research. How the theory of the survival of the fittest gained its reputation, in spite of the fact that the past had to live without the national state-controlled education, has not even become one of the curiosities studied by anthropologists. How could these primitive people have developed their arts, crafts and habits without the existence of anything like a state? What made the hunter, fisherman, herdsman, the tiller of the soil survive? Who provided him with fire, tools, pottery, a house in which to rear the next generation? Who taught him to spin, weave, heal, grow flowers, dance, and make music, to create images from thought? All this was done by man's elementary need for conviviality. Even the rule of non-fraternisation, issued by the supreme leaders of democracy to the liberating forces, could not have been thought of without taking into account this general social need inborn in friend and foe alike. And it had to be cancelled because man's social instincts still prevail.

258

It was only since the theory of the progressive evolution of the species, based on competition for survival, was thought appropriate for the purpose of state-controlled mass-education, that the argument of thousands of years of continuity of social human life and the evidence of hundreds of thousands of years of social animal life was waived.

The static order was wrecked when Mechanicalism, setting out to explain Nature as being motivated according to the laws of physics, had also to invent a mechanical substitute for a living tradition in order to restore the equilibrium between the inner and the outer worlds. It requires a great degree of thoughtlessness to look on with indifference at the direction in which modern man's education is progressing. Mass-education seems to have lost touch with its practical and traditional purpose, i.e. to make man think of the ways by which the great Unknown —Time—can be filled or wasted.

In the Middle Ages the positive law still varied from one locality to another, but the authority of moral law was universal. Since industrialisation has extended over the whole globe and policing power rests with an increasingly smaller number of centres of political control, the moral codes change with the objectives of real politics whereas the positive law, in spite of its inflation, became more or less uniform. There will soon be hardly any human activity left which is not controlled by some regulation, no physical or spiritual need will be unrationed, no individual allowed to hold unauthorised thoughts.

★　　★　　★

I feel bound to meet possible criticism as to whether I have been cautious enough in testing such ill-omened speculations by sound logic. Unfortunately the drawbacks of Mechanicalism seem fully justified if the analogy between the ART OF LOGICS AND REALITY is once and for all established by the Dialectical Method. Dialectics may be called the art of judging based on rational thought. Rational thinking came to the fore during the Reformation. Since the parallelism of formal argument and Nature is believed not to contravene sound thinking and as thesis leads to antithesis, we may justly expect that the ideal of a man's own private world, on which the reformed thinker insisted, leads straight to the world-policed state. This would have to happen in order to forestall nihilism, which is the ultimate

259

synthesis. This is what we are trying to escape in our transitory phase of Democracy.

A world-police appears to be the only power defensible on the grounds of consistency when the 'Order of Charity' has totally broken down. When social service has no more practitioners, adepts or witnesses, sound judgment is impaired. In a 're-formed' world of one's own the mind is, naturally, unbalanced. Man is tempted to see reality in phantoms since he lost the sanity of his mind. Cunning and madness are now propelling unrestrained thought towards catastrophe at record-breaking speed. Are there not more and more willing to repay for sanctuary by the destruction of the rest of the world? Already rational man is willing to atomise the planet for the sake of the peace his soul has lost.

★   ★   ★

But this transitory phase of Democracy can be only of short duration. The apparent usefulness of transferring THE METHOD OF DOUBLE ENTRY ON TO THE MORAL PLANE will, in due course, cease with the unification of industrialised society under one single controlling power.

By speaking of Democracy and Fascism in terms of black and white we are caught by the fallacy of simplification. Simplification is used in physical science in the interest of classification. But in our case righteousness was up against Hitler, a bogeyman made of the same clay as the feet of Democracy. In dispensing law we forget how unreliable human evidence is when given by someone who had made up his mind beforehand. Still, it makes a great difference to see things as they are, and that something must be thus and not otherwise because we have the necessary evidence before our eyes. But we cannot see things as they are if we are prejudiced. It does not help to shake up reality and turn it upside down like a kaleidoscope.

Much political capital had been made out of the suffering of the victims of totalitarian rule. The Third Reich, with its colonies in Europe, Japan with its empire in China and the Pacific, the Italian Empire in North Africa, had to surrender unconditionally. The Big Powers will decide about their share in the world's zones of influence. At the time of writing, in Austria, the first country invaded by Hitler, these zones divide even Vienna.

LXXVI. PORTRAIT OF A YOUNG ENGLISHMAN
1940

LXXVII. THE RED EGG
1940-41

It is not my task to expose the fact that highly industrialised nations cannot rely only on their own resources. They must live by the sale of goods produced in excess of their own needs. More markets have to be opened and fought for, more soil commercialised, human industry more intensely controlled. It is a self-evident truth that in the progress of competitive industrialism every nation fights to become the arch-employer, the arch-planner, the arch-administrator and ruler, the arch-caucus boss and elected Herrenvolk. The history of the Colonial Empires beats everything that the Nürnberg Trials could reveal. Have we forgotten that the trade in human flesh flourished till the end of the nineteenth century? The history of rubber and oil cannot be whitewashed with all the white purity of the White Man. In the Middle Ages animals were brought before the court and accused of being possessed by evil spirits. What about putting Rubber and Oil on trial for the sake of justice?

Hitler's guilt was that he came too late. The course of colonial development, 'the years that the locust hath eaten', were over. Nevertheless there is some absurdity in his too early and abortive efforts to submit white people to experiments in colonial development. Though appearing less as a challenge to liberty to people used to methods of colonial development, this undertaking was understood as a challenge to the White Man. What happened to our neighbours may next time happen to ourselves. Hitler's guilt impinges embarrassingly on the principle of the racial superiority of the White Man. If there is going to be a 'Herrenvolk', it must be a 'righteous' one.

Hitler's raids on the prospering countries of peaceful people, concentration camps, wholesale expropriation, transfer of populations, mass-starvation as an atonement of collective guilt, forced labour in factory-plants by men, women and children as the brutal correlative of the more convenient method of recruiting coolies for plantations, the handling of human beings as if they were mere commodities or 'dead things', the hiring-out of prisoners of war, all this was previously unheard of in political relations among civilised nations. Such things could formerly be brought before the highest court of appeal, which was the consciousness of being a White Man. *It can't happen here* was the title of a best seller in the U.S.A. during the war. Now, when the attempt to make industrial 'plantations' promises to be successful, we remember that the challenge to liberty had nothing to do with the attempts to change the façade of

261

Democracy. Even the Nazi revolution in 1933 remained largely within a formal framework of legality. We can scarcely be further shocked.

★ ★ ★

It was obvious throughout the era of the industrialisation of society that the GROWTH OF SUBMISSIVENESS IN MODERN MAN MUST HAVE BEEN DUE TO FEAR. The stunned mind does not know how to search for the cause of its malcontent. The main purpose of controlled mass-education is to prepare for jobs in industrial production. But it does not provide a solid psychological foundation. Modern man had been left without a chance to adjust himself reasonably to the conditions of his environment. The Machine does not produce Culture. Consequently the man reformed to industrialism no longer desires even to search for the cause of his discontent.

If we read again the almost stale generalisations, slogans and charters which were never meant to be realised, we see the hopes of unhappy peoples raised in vain, since none of their victories have restored order. The ideals of national self-determination, a war to end wars, total war to make the world safe for democracy, etc., did not substitute anything for the moral law which society has lost. More particularly the lack of concrete peace aims in the last world war and the unexpected outbreak of peace have had the most disturbing effects on the smoothly running productive machine of the warring nations. The thoughtless squandering of the heritage of the past is now no longer opposed, but condoned by the people themselves. For the factory worker war had meant re-employment, for the soldier escape from drudgery, want and boredom, and the expectation of reward for bravery, the pleasures of unrestrained sex-freedom and loot. Only this our era of political economy has led to the growth of enormous standing armies, such fleets of ships and 'planes for the maintenance and concentration of policing power over man and his industrial activities.

Whatever the ideological subtleties, by which Democracy is seen to differ from Fascism, one fact emerges clearly; on both sides of the barricade there is an emotional willingness to submit to coercion; achieved from without on a physical, from within on a psychic plane. This willingness towards behaviourism, i.e. *Gleichschaltung*, is conditioned by the mind's loss of immunity against continual shocks. This would answer the question as to how totalitarian rule could be founded on the loyal support of the masses. All that was needed was to exploit the attitude of fear, created in the struggle for survival in industrialised society, into an *idée fixe*. Economic causes are seen to work in an irresistible logical manner. But, the spirit which animates the machine must be drawn from a deeper stratum of consciousness which can be reached only by much obscured sense-data, and where the day-dream of the tribal myth is still alive. It is not the kind of tribal myth which kindles the fire on the hearth. It is an unspeakable nightmare; thought without form, a mathematical version on the order of the schizophrene who makes his monotonous doodles in order to ban the empty horrors of a blackout.

The mobile equilibrium of intellectual interests as providing the cultural motives which shaped life, has become rigid. The intolerance of ideologies centred on economics makes it a question of life and death for everybody wholeheartedly to pretend to be united, in step with the rest in the march of progress. It would escape only a madman that, hourly, we step backward instead of forward. The propaganda for the master-plan uses the technique of making the individual doubtful of his personal *raison d'être*. The coming of the New Order fills us with such awe that it prompts no questioning of the moral credentials of its authority, which challenges even the political credo of progressive socialism of the past, which was the revolutionary doctrine of freedom for all.

'Man know thyself', the device of ancient Greek philosophy, has guided the European whenever he proved himself mature enough to realise that this, the power of reasoning, was all he had received from the hands of the Gods. The loss of free will to determine our own fate has led us into a dead end where we have no choice. We have to fit ourselves into the artificial master-plan of mechanical society in order to escape *bellum omnium contra omnes* or the Third Total War.

All sorts of feelings are mixed up in the mind of a banned artist who, during his life, has watched metaphysics turning the machine into a bogey with power to deform Man. Since the nightmare of the Third Reich has faded out, he feels bewildered, 'foreign' in the sense of being isolated in consciousness from the psychology of the mob.

Although the average man is not yet completely split-minded, we quickly forget that the seeing of phantoms appears normal once the mind is in disorder. We are no longer aware that under the unique guidance of Physical Law we have adopted the superstitious worship of Brute Force.

For instance, in the effort to outlaw war we all show faith in the creation of an international organisation, armed with such overwhelming force by the possession of the atom bomb that any nation which defied it would certainly be destroyed. This fate will be considered as God's judgment on the pride of Man. Where the rub comes is that some worthy man, on becoming the fountain and dispenser of divine justice, will, of necessity, have to be the judge in his own cause. This is because the law he dispenses is based on the possession of the atomic bomb. Article 99 of the Charter of the United Nations says: 'The secretary general may bring to the attention of the Security Council any matter which in his opinion may threaten the maintenance of international Peace and Security.' Apparently the world has become so small that to keep it rolling smoothly is being regarded as a one-man job. The job offered to the chief administrative officer is no less than to formulate future policy for the industrialised society of the whole world. What the Rationalists are up to is to enthrone a reformed Pope of the Economic order who is to claim the principle of infallibility in this critical phase when our society as a whole became out of joint. To take into one's mind the idea that it could be the task of one man to control all human activity, direct the productive machine of industrialised society, supervise the distribution of the raw materials of the world, and administer the political affairs of the whole world in order to secure Peace! It can only be fear of the Peace which has come, which will make the politicians, economists, technical and military experts delegate some of the power they hold to a superman in the name of the sovereign nations which they represent.

It all looks like an uproarious farce were it not already the affirmation of Nihilism. As the fallacy of fictive pluralities leaves its mark on both disguised and overt Fascism, this general secretary of the United Nations must be either an infallible superman dependent on divine inspiration, or he must be a stooge until such time as all hypocrisy can be dropped in the game of hard power-bargaining and appeasement as played by the Peace-makers. Do we not read of flying-trips to secret meetings in an ever-narrowing circle? Must the race for the sharing of the secret of the atomic bomb not end by the possession of the biggest cudgel by a single power, which can thus constitute itself as the uncontested dispenser of the Law of Physical Force?

★   ★   ★

It would seem that confusion arose in the early days of industrialism from the very attempt to increase knowledge about the resources from which 'national' wealth is built up. It is not mere coincidence that PROGRESS WAS THE IDEAL around which modern democrats have rallied. One can see in the Calvinist Doctrine of Predestination encouragement for the development of special abstract ways of thought. The popularity of the New National Church can be explained by the necessity of a strong faith which favoured the fixation of one's attention on one's own mind rather than on the interests and affairs of other people. In freeing those energies, formerly bound to doing 'good works', a one-sided mental training now allowed for a clear conception of certain mechanistic laws, in which modern man at present sees the attainment of the highest point human understanding can reach. The Rational Mind is less bound to Catholic traditions, norms and values, therefore the rationally thinking man is progressive.

But 'reformed' thinking must not necessarily be, as it is termed, democratic. Because the National Church was bound to the Representatives of the Sovereign Power of the Nation, moral appeals have to be used to support a *raison d'état*. The term 'democratic' lacks precision. Reformed moral law is of necessity positive law, i.e. regulations, because moral law cannot be other than the vision of catholicism, i.e. the continuity of the moral law preserved as the spiritual heritage of social man. Behind positive law stands the state police.

Progress is bound to continuity in arithmetical progression whereas, only by virtue of the spontaneous activity of the mind and by rebellion against mechanical tendencies, can complete changes be intimated of the habits and associations of the intellect. To continue the analytical approach, once it has reached the limits of usefulness, leads to uniformity and to petrification of the mind. The old argument against uniformity, that organs of the instinctive life of nutrition, digestion, procreation do not benefit by repetition would still be valid. The organs of vegetative life increase in size only, their duties are performed as completely in childhood as in middle age. Consequently it could

265

only mean existence in the dull monotony of a mathematical order were the functions of the organs of thought, vision, speech and hearing trained to progress forever in one direction. Individual experience springs from the spontaneous reaction of the psychic world to the physical world. It is only by changing aspects that we can compare one state of mind with another and so rectify previous errors. Individual experience protects man from repeating his errors.

True social process ought to be seen in the intellectual revolutions on which social revolutions are founded. The rise and fall of nations, the Protestant Reformation, and the progress of industrialisation are merely external events. For instance, our total world wars and dubious peace set-ups—short-lived intervals between wars—are the outward sign of a continuous mental revolution. The 'dynamic order' in the present experimental epoch is not a manifestation of order but rather of chaos. Similarly the plotting of the State against the Church of Rome, and the reverse, corrupting public moral and religion, were the first indications of the breakdown of the moral framework of the static order. The idea of Political Economy is closely connected with the Calvinist Doctrine of Predestination, with which this dynamic society started. It was conceived in an emergency which demanded immediate political action by the secular authorities against subversive elements in the state.

★　　★　　★

As soon as it was discovered where the shoe pinched, that is that unequal distribution of wealth happened to spring from the same source as social disturbance, political economy was raised to the status of a new science. THE METAPHYSICAL DOCTRINE OF PREDESTINATION IS NECESSARY TO THE CONCEPTION OF PROGRESS. The time had come for the economist to tell people that pauperism had to be accepted as a sort of miraculous act of the Deity. The belief might have been derived from analogy that Mechanics are somehow linked up with certain fixed laws governing the progress of industrialised society. And, just like the theologian, all that the economist had to do, in taking up the doctrine of Necessity as expressed in Mechanics, was to recast it into a paraphysical shape. He had to invent some mathematical masterplans, according to which each man might play his part in a way benefiting the community without power to decide what that part should be. Such master-plans are the vogue now

266

throughout industrialised society as a remedy against the cycle of recurrent economic crises.

The average intellect of men is probably always the same. It compelled the religious man of the seventeenth century to believe the most childish absurdities. But did not the Democratic and the Fascist Leaders alike tell us during the recent war that victory occurs on divine disposition, that God takes sides, that Providence gives victory to the Haves because the Have-nots are wicked?

In the field of inquiry into physics the *a priori* theory is a necessity by which the stability of events and uniformity of succession are accepted as a standard by the human mind. By it we may test reality and form judgments. It is tacitly understood that the theory or fiction is a working model which for practical purposes must always under precisely similar circumstances produce precisely similar results.

The notion of the wholeness of Mechanicalism with which the rationalist originally set out is guaranteed by the proposition that, as we never know the complete chain of antecedents causing events, it cannot be objected that they may not necessarily stand in the relation of causality to that which constitutes the phenomenal evidence. But whereas in physics it is not ignored that fictions are intimately bound up with the minds of men, metaphysics and political science stand for eternal truth in contradiction to the fact that minds of men change with the weather. Why should the invention of a new technical contraption involving considerable changes in the environment of society determine the fate of man? It was not industrialism which changed society, but the human mind, cowed and stunned by the unexpected destructive effects of the machinery it produced. It is already a matter of political faith not to dispute the fact that there are time-bound standards of truth. Belief in progress is uniformly shared.

Political economists are as intolerant as clergymen in their inability to admit that ideologies diametrically opposed to each other may be equally inaccurate. This would mean that not until rational man is allowed to be sceptical concerning the logical reasoning of his time—just as the protestant world became sceptical of the disputes of theologians—would it become possible to further man's welfare instead of his regress.

★   ★   ★

267

The true history of progress, that is to say, the development towards an industrialised society, could only be written when that scepticism, which resulted in the growth of religious tolerance in the seventeenth century, again openly dared to appear. If scepticism were still thinkable it might enable the historian to prove that industrialism itself was the process of mechanisation, acting in different direction in the external and the internal world. It was an effort to find a substitute for the WHOLENESS of organic life. This assumption would have to be verified by an examination of facts found at random but well proved— (such for instance as are published in *Eidetic Imagery* by Jaensch)—and by the investigation of certain particular aspects of the inner psychic life which are concerned with the building up of the world of perception.

The current fashion of interest in children's art may have been stimulated by the inability of the average adult to fit into an environment determined by mechanistic civilisation. Two world wars in one generation have made it only too obvious that mechanist theories, while inspiring man to progress in technique, have confused the issue. Without the psychological conditioning of human responses to environment society must be out of joint. It is no consolation that those moral norms and values, underlying the institutions through which the religious man had organised his life in the past, could not guarantee for ever the stability of society. But these values failed from the beginning of industrial revolution. Primitive democratic society quickly dies out once the machine-minded man passes through it. The last manifestations of cultural life in Europe, the ruins of the monuments of the Baroque age in catholic countries may in future tell of the deep rift in this present transitory phase of Democracy.

It is not only because æsthetic nature, proper to a moral perception of the world, cannot be revealed on the superficial physical plane; it is because we lack those values which relate individuals to the community that we penetrate into the inner psychic world with the hostile attitude of barbarians.

In its beginnings analytical psychology was to a large extent modelled on the science of mechanics. And it was rather from the clinical branches of this science, after the physicist's interpretation of psychic phenomena had overstepped the limits of its usefulness, that a recommencement of cautious relations with humanist philosophy recommended itself for practical pur-

LXXVIII. ANSCHLUSS: ALICE IN WONDERLAND
1942

LXXIX. LORELEY
1942

poses. In the pre-war German science of history and culture this *geisteswissenschaftliche* psychology was strongly emphasised. It promised to establish closer contact with cultural values which could not be taken into account in the civilisation in which we live.

Although this new knowledge cannot undo what looms large as the likely fate of modern man, it helps at least to reveal certain peculiar processes going on in the minds of children in this epoch of eclipsed individuality. Thanks to the typological method adopted in *Eidetic Imagery*, which asserts its claim to insist on a vigorously experimental procedure, a complete revision of an early psychological hypothesis concerning the building up of the perceptual world has taken place. According to the mechanist theory the primary, purely optic sensations in early childhood correspond exclusively to external stimuli and are only later in the course of mental development permeated with higher psychic processes. According to the experiments adopted for testing the validity of these assumptions, the development of sight with regard to spacial perceptions as well as to colour-vision is quite opposite. It was proved that the perception of depth is gradually lost in the adult in so far as it was connected with colour-vision, and, further, that the perceptional world of the average adult differs from that of the young child in that the optic sensations correspond more exclusively to the external stimuli and only in the imaginative type, which are the less normal cases of the research material, are they affected by associations with the inner psychic world. It is finally suggested that 'the ideal end-point of this mental development is not yet quite reached by the human species in the transitory phase of our civilisation'. Thus a purely sensational response in the field of sight would allow only a chaotic, lawless appearance of the world. Therefore it can be argued that the form of structure of reality as the adult now perceives it is a superstructure or a supporting structure, serving to obviate a loss in the perceptional mind. It would appear that under the impact of mechanist civilisation the wholeness of colour-vision is gradually lost and a readjustment of vision, dependent merely on the transversal retinal disparity, takes place. Vision is replaced by optical functions working according to the laws of perspective. Modern society obviously set great store on narrowing such issues to within the limits of a category of objectives which can be contacted in the analytic way. One obvious conclusion is, therefore, that progress can come only if the educational method, which is the mental reformation of the individual's mind, succeeds in breaking it into voluntary submission to a surfacial reality, wholly alienated from the irrational reality and divorced from the unchartered seas of imagination. The substitute surfacial 'reality' can now be measured and gauged by logical reasoning.

Without inner certainty about what it is, which in the cognitive terms of philosophy means the union of the conscious mind with the object, all efforts of the curious intellect must prove futile. This inner certainty need not necessarily be of a metaphysical nature. But it is a vain labour to attempt to recapture the wholeness of the perceptual world by analytic methods bearing with them the mechanist proposition. In this dilemma the psychologist, in the course of a nativistic conception, is forced to posit the mystery of the wholeness of the perceptual world as lying behind the reality from which the physical evidence of research is provided. He says that his method of research, which in principle denies the possibility of other worlds, cannot be applied to children who are too young to make verbal statements with respect to their psychic responses.

The empirical approach affirms that the eye, being anatomically a cerebral organ, has originally no other than a psychic content. Now this is exactly what the consciousness of wholeness means. The psychologist must maintain his 'nativistic' conception of colour-vision as an *a priori* statement, if he would not force us to assume that only the new-born child, when awakening from the slumber in his mother's womb, is in this blessed state of mind. Only at that moment are there no barriers between the inner and external worlds.

Thus we can see that biological science can no longer afford to ignore the fact that the property of living processes differs from that of mechanical processes in so far as life is always individual, always new. The psychologist uses the data of anatomical dissection, statistics, and the analytic method of physico-mechanical tests. If needed he introduces metaphysical speculations into his experiments. Life's wholeness is something irrational, real in a state of contemplation. Because life is inaccessible to theoretical conceptions, the scientist's argument leads us astray. To look for the true meaning of the idea of the union of the conscious mind with the object it would be necessary to remember that our world, if it is constructed only on our

270

analytical visual, tactual and auditory sense data, is a reality only in so far as it is wholly located in the realm of a time-bound mode of thought. Scientific truth is conditioned by mental environment. There is no infallibility of thought.

★   ★   ★

Nevertheless modern society took scientific statements for Gospel truth. In the educational direction of industrialised society they were not interpreted with the caution advisable. For example, the early biologist may have been biased by an assumption of a hostile nature, thus making amends for Adam's sin in Paradise. At the time the author of *The Evolution of the Species* could not have been aware that the dogma of HOSTILE NATURE is more profitable to the propaganda of industrial progress than appears on the surface. There was no contradiction or even inconsistency as regards economics, until the dialectic method evolved a metaphysical fraud. Just as the mental climate of a Sunday School may account for a peevish disposition nurturing a peculiar type of religious thought, so the human slavery in factories accounts for the neurotic mental condition and for the success of the theory of survival of the strongest.

Reformed thinking has certainly left man in no position of security in which he could be an impartial judge of his own doings. Having 'vertical' revelations, which are personal revelations from a Deity, as its starting-point, his judgment is one-sided. It consists of the inside view of personal wants. At the same time the mind is offended and dissatisfied with the aggressiveness of a civilisation which seems to decree that man is and always will be a stranger in the place where he lives.

The evidence of a mature civilisation is a philosophy which is not a dogma or theory but a collective method of selection that does not lose sight of the relation of what man builds around himself to his mind. The corresponding effect on manners is that civilised man does not war with Nature. The radical abandonment of man's spiritual heritage involves much more than we would dare to admit. As one cannot go outside oneself to look at one's self, one cannot observe how much reformed thinking has severed us from a perception of a humane world.

At present the most zealous evolutionist will not fail to notice that once philosophy ceases to be the perception of a humane world it becomes determined by the restrictions which every dogmatic belief carries.

271

is possible, but what is desirable within a given period of time. But the sophist method, which fishes in the lucky bag of words, has never been successful in the attempt to fix a permanent code of behaviourism. The man of the past could only temporarily be made to forget that reasoning leads no further than to the merely probable. Apprehension of reality beyond all understanding, which is part of every religious belief, assumes a spiritual continuity of Man from the past through the present into the future. As HUMAN CONSCIENCE it extends beyond the limit of individual consciousness. It is only when the warning conscience of the spiritual community, the voice of the suffering human nature, is silenced, that man stops to see things as they are and forgets what they might be.

This guiding principle of the search for truth has been changed into the conception of unconditional, eternal, scientific truth. But even from the scientific point of view this continuity of the living being is not contradictory to the validity of the laws of causation, which are understood as binding modern man. The content of the scientific theory of the hereditary pattern is the continuity of the being of the past, and the embodiment of the being of the future in everything living at present. This theory can be checked by schematic devices used by science for keeping account of the quantitative aspects of the surfacial phenomena. The fact that human decisions are related to the way things are shaped on the Other Side does not contradict the theory of Genetics.

In dealing with types in purely logical relation to each other, the conception of Absolute Truth is basic to the understanding of Laws of Physics, but it has no explanatory value beyond the field of mathematics. It was not the business of theologians in the service of the state to explain, how the use of a mere hypothesis about the nature of Absolute Truth could pervert the mind to mistake a fiction for an occult entity and a controlling agency which animates society. Metaphysics, this ghostly trail of bad conscience clinging inseparably to all economic theories is mystifying. Economists try to ease their conscience by explaining the mystery as the effect of the Industrial Revolution. But the puzzle is not solved by explaining intellectual tendencies through the introduction of the steam-driven weaving machine. Ill-defined as the agency is which is believed to motivate the mechanism of the economic order, it is capable of producing mechanical, not moral effects. As a matter of fact metaphysics had to serve as an emergency exit when the bag of mechanical tricks did not come off. To say today that the whole Industrial Revolution was merely a by-product of the enclosing of commons, and a quite unexpected one at that, would be risking offence of every school of economists!

The first climax of the industrialisation of society was reached when the crofters, becoming landless, besieged the towns, and the first employment policy had to be invented to counter the pressure. During the first mass-expulsions homeless people were concentrated in hastily fabricated camps, slums. With their want of jobs coincided the invention of the steam-driven weaving machine. Thus human industry had for the first time to be controlled from a centre of political power. There is no Employment Policy, not even the policy of the Dole or the Lend Lease, which does not affect ultimately the whole of the social structure, because it has to be paid for. Once social life has been interfered with, law and order must be maintained by brute force. Peace is neither wanted nor can it be created within the system of industrialism which has to look for markets. Right from the beginning this system grew at the expense of every individual affected and of every country in the world which has become the dumping ground of products it controlled. Labour makes Capitalism a bogey and vice versa. But the evil that inspired the wars of competitive industrialism was neither sheer exploitation nor was it a sign of a brutality 'innate' only in the German race. Markets have to be opened and fought for and industrial rivals removed.

Thus the missionary zeal in fighting for the glory of technical progress is inspired by bad conscience. One must not forget another fact, namely, that social pressure grew as the result of a simple cause. People living in filth, ignorance, and under the whip of the overseer, multiplied quicker than could be expected of populations in a natural social framework; paupers have no other source of pleasure. In a mathematically contrived growth of society it is not the loss of individuality or of quality *per capita* which will make the authorities feel deep consternation. As often as wars and economic crises threaten to thin out the ranks of the industrial army the falling birth-rate enforces necessarily more than legal measures to counter it. In advanced industrialism financial rewards and official honours are showered on exceptionally fertile mothers. Great publicity is given to the fact that they gave life to an abnormal number of children.

This becomes symptomatic of Democracy just as it had been of Totalitarianism.

To explain the breakdown of social order with the growth of spinning factories in England is as short-sighted as to accuse the shareholder that he acted in a perverted state of mind by investing capital in sheep-breeding just because it promised to pay. What he really did was to take advantage of the opportunity offered by the Enclosure Acts. On waste land one could rear sheep practically for nothing.

Whether enforced by capitalist or socialist policy, Enclosure Acts create paupers who have to be kept at arm's length from the well-ordered universe of the citizen possessing full civilian rights. But if we want to see in full the agency motivating the Industrial Revolution, another event must be re-examined which coincided with the first exodus of people from their soil in modern history. What in fact gave England the chance to give birth to industrialism was the effect of the Puritan's bible-reading. The dogmatic principle of 'Divine Selection' of the white and black sheep of Calvin's flock stimulated their practical interest in the tame, ruminant, woolly sheep. There is no doubt that Industrial Revolution is merely the by-product of the controversy of Free Will and Predestination.

We are used to accept as a sign of progress that the chains had been broken which bound man to the soil. But slavery had not been permanent in the static order. One of the most illuminating chapters of European history are the 'Peasant Risings', which end with the beginnings of the struggle for economic leadership: the 'religious' Thirty Years' War.

Something similar to the modern resistance movement united peasantry of many countries as often as the Church or the Barons attempted to challenge their freedom or to infringe on their traditional Rights and Privileges regarded as God-given. 'When Adam delved and Eve span, who was then the Gentleman?'

On the wave that swept away the moral law of the static order rode to power the maker of 'lawful' contracts. Gradually all over the world the *contrat social* of primitive Democracy was replaced by legal agreements. Their enforcement on man led to a psychological change in his mind. Instead of accepting the term 'Labour' as a landmark of social progress, as it is done, it would be more correct to see the nature of the change in the beginning of man's specialisation. Labour signifies a mental

276

LXXX. MARIANNE
1942

development which has not yet ended. Without a divinely inspired theory which legalises the order of industrial mechanism
man could not have been made into the legal property of another, or of others, or of a fiction, the Sovereign Nation, to whom
the sum of Man's Rights and Privileges has been transferred.
It is absurd that progress, imposed by the invention of labour-
saving machinery, should have made slavery legal. Indeed,
human flesh could be bought and sold merely by the virtue of
such 'lawful' contracts.

★   ★   ★

We stand on the threshold of a new age when it will be no
longer for the individual to decide THE MORAL PRICE which will
have to be paid for our adaptability to technical civilisation.
As we emerge from the second world war the by-products of the
wars of liberation may turn out even more surprising than the
afore-mentioned practical results of the Reformation. We will
find that a nexus is binding us to the ghostly vision of Europe
under Hitler, independent of whether one or the other highly
industrialised nation, or a block of nations, have won the war.
The winning of the war by Democracy cannot undo the fact
that the two world wars within thirty years have been longer
and more terrible than they should have been for the sake of
the continuity of 'legal' order in the orthodox sense. Not only
that particularly repulsive features of the Third Reich threaten
to become normal. It needed a Hitler to sanction the rule that
those who did not collaborate in his New Order got no rations
and starved, that populations could be transferred from one
country to another, that slave labour could be kept alive for
reasons of production, fed according to scientific schemes, housed
and clothed or, if not required, annihilated. To legally justify
the enforcement of Enclosure Acts on people in some liberated
countries just because they speak another language breaks new
legal ground. It has been almost the first and only act of policy
on which the Democratic governments agreed. The discrimina-
tion between nations as 'guilty' and 'not guilty' reveals more
than a fallacious process of reasoning destined to appease the
conscience. It is a disregard for the traditional method of lawful
proceedings which depend on satisfactory evidence. Crimes, even
in war, have to be committed by individuals. For crimes committed against humanity one can hang a man but not a 'guilty
Nation'. We shall at once see how steep has been the descent

277

from legal order when we remember the reaction of offended public conscience.

Under totalitarian rule modern Europe was united in an Underground movement, not wholly suppressed even in Germany where it sprang to life right in the beginning, as in Italy and Spain, in spite of hundreds of concentration camps and torture chambers. It is still remembered that the Fascist leaders have been officially recognised by Democratic governments as long as they claimed to have acquired power by constitutional means. The Underground Movement marshalled its secret forces when officially nothing was being done to prevent the rise of Fascism. It has been often regretted that there were no legal objections to those impostors who quite frankly and ruthlessly propagated and practised to the extent of physical extermination of their subjects the immoral policy of *Gleichschaltung*.

The secretiveness of the Peace-policy of democratic leaders was added to the demoralising effect of often promised and delayed military action. The disastrous counter-effects of a sudden change in war propaganda to racial lines of thought coincided with the breaking of the military power of the Axis. The final work of destruction beyond human power to repair may account for the demoralisation which left the task of liberation to physical force.

Continental famine, disease beyond human means to cure, sadist and masochist waves of mass-hysteria, savage national hate and maddening despair will be left behind in the whole of Europe. Part of our loss is the disturbed balance in moral accounts. Great parts of Europe can be described as gigantic Belsen camps. This is partly the consequence of political decisions for which the Peacemakers bear the responsibility. The sacking of countries already stripped by Hitler makes it quite obvious that civilisation ceases during a war. According to the code of unconditional surrender to Imperialism a country pays its ticket with physical bodies, goods, reparations, partition, and removal of all industrial equipment. But the artist, with the taste of the liberty of the past still on his lips, who gratefully remembers the enrichment of world's musical heritage by Germany's great contribution in the Thirty Years' War and in the Napoleonic era, regrets that the time of grace is over when a defeated country could work its passage by cultural reparations. What I want to stress is that, whatever the outburst of official oratory, Fascism has no potential existence in itself. The unemployed

278

man on the other side of the barricade, who became a collaborator in order to get or keep a job, has no innate 'racial' properties in which he differs from another man who did not yet have to live up to that decisive moment when individual responsibility must stand the test. It may be that in the very act of dispensing justice the humanitarian impulse is finally broken when unconditional surrender, confession of collective guilt, are taken more seriously than is due to slogans of the shivering moral war-propaganda.

When the Puritans put out the news that the white sheep are better than the black, they were not yet conscious that the fate of the 'Elected People' will depend on salesmanship. This war will not be the last war caused by unemployment, as it was not the first. The chronic recurrence of unemployment had still more enhanced the profession of the salesman. Virtue comes with success. From victories we have learned that it is profitable to sell the Gospel of the 'Elected People'. So far we have been successful in crediting to the Hun the sin of 'Racial Myth'. But now the skeleton has been let out of the cupboard. The moment has come to consider whether next time one can think of something better, for it must lead to the pulverisation of the globe even though the God of Battles be siding with us. Technical civilisation resulting in moral foulness in a world of suffering is where the religious past differs from our times. Democrats act according to the Racial Myth with a bad conscience. Fascists act according to what they profess and believe.

★　　★　　★

The control of industry has led to an extremely precarious position showing the inelasticity of the social framework. It makes it impossible to localise the process of disintegration as in the early days of the Enclosure Acts. LASTING PEACE is what we all want, at the expense of others of course. We are bored to death by the struggle for survival of the fittest because all conspires to deny us a chance. Daily the Big Powers denounce each other's fascist leanings. The little man in his turn is filled with the horrible fear that there will be no future opportunity. To the filth and sweat and blood and physical strain is added the pressure of this mental crisis. Fear is common to man and beast. The panic-ridden beast sinks to its knees before inescapable danger. Once this is past, it rises. The crouching slave of the economic order cannot rise again.

A mathematically contrived society leaves no emergency exit. A vast card-index system, identity cards, discs, fingerprints registered with the police, ration cards, pay books, are not only for the purpose of taxation, conscription, rationing, employment *per capita*. They contain the blueprint facts of the economic order. The card-index system has helped Himmler, the sinister genius of social engineering, not only to control society but to eliminate 'undesirable minorities' and to thin out resistance. He could not finish what he intended, in his own words, for the future of Germany: '. . . we are going over them thoroughly, selecting and crossing the most perfect surviving specimens.'

Why should Lasting Peace come out of a system which begins with invisible compulsion and completes in a ruthless logical way the elimination of social conditions under which freedom was effective in the past? This transitory phase of theoretical democracy is a biological process resulting in the uniformity of the mind. In spite of the national trappings in which the mannequin is dressed, it is the mask of man which is real to us. Machine-driven industry, which has replaced small local industries, uses standardised types of machinery, and produces the same standardised output in all the four corners of the world. Sweated labour is done in an uniform overall. Local culinary tradition, dependent on geographical conditions and climate, is going to be replaced by scientific nutrition. Nutrition in calories, based on statistical rationing sufficient or insufficient for survival, does not depend on the chances of the struggle of Disraeli's two nations within a state. It has become an instrument of international power policy. Hunger-blockade is no longer an instrument of war but continues after armistice. The soldier shares with the worker the detachment of the mind concerning the job he does. A soldier fears unemployment just as much as the civilian. Armies watch each other suspiciously across the frontiers. Although they dress uniformly in khaki battle-dress, soldiers remain old-fashioned. When we are uniformly prepared for a basic world language derived from initials, the time is ripe for the powdered eggs to become an omelette. But the soldier might yet spoil the show by pressing the button and bringing more fire, destruction and blood over the globe than modern man is able to imagine. Lasting peace is endangered by the soldier armed to the teeth. One or the other is bound to shoot in order to shoot first. Only the scientist in the service of the economic order possesses the vision of the uniqueness of Mechani-

5. CAPRICCIO (*1943*)

calism. He must decide its policy because he alone takes cognisance of 'dead things', numbers, materials, physical forces, as is required for the purpose of production for production's sake. He has freed himself completely from the feeling of ritual uncleanliness by which we all more or less still suffer in spite of ideologies calculated to atrophy our conscience. The scientist himself represents the type of man with a dying conscience whose agonies he studies in himself with a detached mind. He knows that the renewed structural adaptation will be conditioned by more than hot-house planning in industrial organisation.

The gap between the first objectives of the economic order and the individual had widened too much to be filled with the theories of fascism, socialism, or free enterprise of the United Nations. The universal unrest shows that it is futile for the democratic leaders to decide among themselves the way to take. The scientist alone has the means of testing the fever-curve of the wave of Messianism sweeping the ruins of the world. He has already warned us not to be squeamish when we learn about mass-production by the method of artificial insemination. Once neurotic group-life determines the policy of the future, there is no reason why science should not be called upon to prefabricate man, in order that he should fit into his prefabricated environment. Salvation coming from the homuncule out of the scientist's retort.

It only remains to re-examine certain possibilities suggested in the course of the development of the science of genetics. What we regard as the most important discovery, the splitting of the atom, has already been far surpassed in that specific branch of natural sciences. At present the scientist can say with authority, based on the findings of laboratory research, that the human chromosome contains the entire pattern of the man of the past. The method of scientific selection will allow to weed out of man what in his inheritance pattern has hampered the right functioning of modern society. The matter of scientific selection makes policy independent from the drawbacks of natural selection, which used to give the reformers sleepless nights. In a kind of Uriah's letter, written in the hereditary code-script of genetics, man can be made a reliable carrier of the plans of social engineers.

Once the biologist has fixed heredity on utility lines, 'the greatest happiness of the greatest number' is only a question of time necessary to produce by black magic the mind which bears no 'dangerous thought'. If the scientist is given the power to eliminate fear, Puritan prayer and thrift may see harmony return to the economic order. Even tyranny becomes superfluous once authority has nothing to fear from the people. If Nature is incongruous with economic order, the worse for Nature. The snag is that Nature has not allotted special physical laws for the United Nations, and others for the defeated Fascists. As I said before, there has been some confusion in the early days of Mechanisation. The confusion may be due to the particular version of Genesis, which starts with Man's upright walk. The evolutionist may have shared with other religious sects the pious wish to set the members of the progressive club above their fellow-men. But the Gospel of Free Thought has made us forget to see reality as it is. It has made us applaud the conjuror's trick while our Rights of Man were being stolen from us by pickpockets. The rights and traditional privileges of man were given to a figment of the mind, the Sovereign Nation without a body. Having avowed that over much of the conception of the National State there broods 'a horror of great darkness', let me point to the National Debt where alone reality and certainty attest their existence.

Now, when we see a homuncule coming out of the national cupboard, we may understand Industrial Revolution as well as Materialism as by-products of the dispute between Free Will and Predestined Fate. Submitting to fate, we can leave the fiction of the 'Evolution of the Species' to novels. The myth of the tree-climbing mammal tendered the industrial pioneers the very stuff for romance. They were in need of it after their ties with the cultural tradition had been so suddenly severed. In the iconoclastic purges all evidence of other spirits conjured out of the imagination have been hastily but methodically banned from life by the Puritan shepherds. The state of this blitzed world of ours has made us too apathetic even to suspect that the materialist was pulling a fast one by making us see as the primordial state of society the very chaos in which he landed us. Future policy of the biologist can do without the fiction of the National Product. It was no more than the fairy tale of the artificial cow that can be milked indefinitely and lives on sawdust thrown into its eyes.

The biologist demonstrates the saying that you cannot eat the cake and have it. He does not require metaphysics to build society on ant-instincts. The relativity of his truth is not incongruous with Dialectics, where in the process of reaching a rational attitude to reality the relativity of reason becomes a pre-supposition for reasoning. Nothing but the Three Rs for the homuncule!

In a moral state of the world the laws of causation led to a recognition of the moral law. In the world of a mechanist mind even the promise of the Four Freedoms enforces the Enclosure Acts.

Have we to close our eyes before the fact that the victory of the Big Powers is due to the supremacy of the British Navy added to the supremacy of the Soviet land army, and to the industrial output of the United States? All the oratory about justice, collective guilt and war to make the world safe for Democracy ought not to make us forget reality as it is. It is a waste of energy to listen to all the economist sects as numerous as were the theologian sects of the Byzantine monks. In the U.S.S.R. the will to return to a social framework previous to that of the Enclosure Acts, which meant the beginning of the control of human activities, has united 180 nations. All that is required of us is to RELEASE CONTROL, but we have lost the secret that was within ourselves.

Socialism existed before the Bible had been translated into the national tongues. The story of the suffering of the Son of Man has been communicable and communicated not alone by speech and print. The intellectual cohesion of society, imagination, allowed for a fourth dimension. Compassion and the perception of reality of the five senses could be compared with what was preached from the pulpit. The loss of compassion is perhaps the most regrettable by-product of the Industrial Revolution. When all these unkempt clowns of the Enclosure Acts were peeping through the windows, fear entered the heart of the Puritan. Thus he read the Bible as we read the paper, with a mind lacking compassion. What a different human face, when compared with that of the man of the blueprint age, is rendered by the artist before the Reformation! May we call him a mystic, he who ventured to portray the incarnation of Absolute Truth imagin-able to a religious man, while following a narrative of Christ's suffering with all the compassionate pity of a thoroughly human mind. It is from this world of primitive democratic society of the past that the spiritual echo comes to me through art. That is the reason why an artist does not need hints and clues from metaphysics to see what there is to be seen in future. It is also

283

the reason why I would like to reprint here a lecture delivered in Vienna in 1911, which was meant to persuade others to take cognisance of the phenomenon of reasoning. Already in the early epoch of materialism before the two world wars it seemed to me that society had not succeeded in doing so.

'L'état c'est moi' as the vest-pocket version of Democracy we owe to modern education. But the strange effect of enlightenment is that it made us unable to discover on the way to the polling-booth, that Dogmatism is always active as infallibility. Political power once vested in absolutism falls into no less irresponsible hands. Having sacrificed our loyalty, formerly given to noble princes—who in defence of the National Honour fought their own duels—to a modern faith in the Liberalism of modern Democracy, we have fallen between two stools. Uprooted as we are, we have to tolerate the fact that National Honour is left, by Chancelleries all over the world, to the ordeal of battle between nations instead of between these chairmen, who control production and distribution of National Wealth, thus actually governing our fate.

LXXXII. THE RIGHT HON. THE COUNTESS OF DROGHEDA
Unfinished. 1943-46

LXXXIII. OSKAR KOKOSCHKA
Photograph: Fleischmann

ON THE NATURE OF VISIONS

Translated by Hedi Medlinger and John Thwaites

The state of awareness of visions is not one in which we are either remembering or perceiving. It is rather a level of consciousness at which we experience visions within ourselves.

This experience cannot be fixed; for the vision is moving, an impression growing and becoming visual, imparting a power to the mind. It can be evoked but never defined.

Yet the awareness of such imagery is a part of living. It is life selecting from the forms which flow towards it or refraining, at will.

A life which derives its power from within itself will focus the perception of such images. And yet this free visualising in itself—whether it is complete or hardly yet perceptible, or undefined in either space or time—this has its own power running through. The effect is such that the visions seem actually to modify one's consciousness, at least in respect of everything which their own form proposes as their pattern and significance. This change in oneself, which follows on the vision's penetration of one's very soul, produces the state of awareness, of expectancy. At the same time there is an outpouring of feeling into the image which becomes, as it were, the soul's plastic embodiment. This state of alertness of the mind or consciousness has, then, a waiting, receptive quality. It is like an unborn child, as yet unfelt even by the mother, to whom nothing of the outside world slips through. And yet whatever affects his mother, all that impresses her down to the slightest birthmark on the skin, all is implanted in him. As though he could use her eyes, the unborn receives through her his visual impressions, even while he is himself unseen.

The life of the consciousness is boundless. It inter-penetrates the world and is woven through all its imagery. Thus it shares those characteristics of living which our human existence can show. One tree left living in an arid land would carry in its seed the potency from whose roots all the forests of the earth might spring. So with ourselves; when we no longer inhabit our perceptions they do not go out of existence; they continue as though with a power of their own, awaiting the focus of another consciousness. There is no more room for death; for though the

285

vision disintegrates and scatters, it does so only to reform in another mode.

Therefore we must harken closely to our inner voice. We must strive through the penumbra of words to the core within. 'The Word became flesh and dwelt among us.' And then the inner core breaks free—now feebly and now violently—from the words within which it dwells like a charm. 'It happened to me according to the Word.'

If we will surrender our closed personalities, so full of tension, we are in a position to accept this magical principle of living, whether in thought, intuition or in our relationships. For in fact we see every day beings who are absorbed in one another, whether in living or in teaching, aimless or with direction. So it is with every created thing, everything we can communicate, every constant in the flux of living; each one has its own principle which shapes it, keeps life in it, and maintains it in our consciousness. Thus it is preserved, like a rare species, from extinction. We may identify it with 'me' or 'you' according to our estimate of its scale or its infinity. For we set aside the self and personal existence as being fused into a larger experience. All that is required of us is to RELEASE CONTROL. Some part of ourselves will bring us into the unison. The enquiring spirit rises from stage to stage, until it encompasses the whole of Nature. All laws are left behind. One's soul is a reverberation of the universe. Then too, as I believe, one's perception reaches out towards the Word, towards awareness of the vision.

As I said at first, this awareness of visions can never fully be described, its history can never be delimited, for it is a part of life itself. Its essence is a flowing and a taking form. It is love, delighting to lodge itself in the mind. This adding of something to ourselves—we may accept it or let it pass; but as soon as we are ready it will come to us by impulse, from the very breathing of our life. An image will take shape for us suddenly, at the first look, as the first cry of a newborn child emerging from its mother's womb.

Whatever the orientation of a life, its significance will depend on this ability to conceive the vision. Whether the image has a material or an immaterial character depends simply on the angle from which the flow of psychic energy is viewed, whether at ebb or flood.

It is true that the consciousness is not exhaustively defined by these images moving, these impressions which grow and

286

become visual, imparting a power to the mind which we can evoke at will. For of the forms which come into the consciousness some are chosen while others are excluded arbitrarily.

But this awareness of visions which I endeavour to describe is the viewpoint of all life as though it were seen from some high place; it is like a ship which was plunged into the seas and flashes again as a winged thing in the air.

Consciousness is the source of all things and of all conceptions. It is a sea ringed about with visions.

My mind is the tomb of all those things which have ceased to be the true Hereafter into which they enter. So that at last nothing remains; all that is essential of them is their image within myself. The life goes out of them into that image as in the lamp the oil is drawn up through the wick for nourishing the flame.

So each thing, as it communicates itself to me, loses its substance and passes into the HEREAFTER WHICH IS MY MIND. I incorporate its image which I can evoke without the intermediacy of dreams. 'Whenever two or three are gathered together in My name, I am in their midst.' And, as though it could go out to men, my vision is maintained, fed, as the lamp is by its oil, from the abundance of their living. If I am asked to make all this plain and natural the things themselves must answer for me, as it were, bearing their own witness. For I have represented them, I have taken their place and put on their semblance through my visions. It is the psyche which speaks.

I search, inquire and guess. And with what sudden eagerness must the lamp-wick seek its nourishment, for the flame leaps before my eyes as the oil feeds it. It is all my imagination, certainly, what I see there in the blaze. But if I have drawn something from the fire and you have missed it, well, I should like to hear from those whose eyes are still untouched. For is this not my vision? Without intent I draw from the outside world the semblance of things; but in this way I myself become part of the world's imaginings. Thus in everything imagination is simply that which is natural. It is nature, vision, life.

OSKAR KOKOSCHKA.

287

LIST OF PAINTINGS AND DRAWINGS NOT CONNECTED WITH ILLUSTRATIONS[1]

1907–8

1. FRAU HIRSCH
   Canvas, 90 by 71 cm.
   Coll.: F. Wolff, Vienna.
   Exh.: Galerie Arnold, Dresden, 1925; Cassirer, Berlin, 1927; Kunsthaus, Zürich, 1927; Kunsthalle, Mannheim, 1931.
   Reprod.: Galerie Arnold exhibition catalogue, 1925, No. 3.

2. PORTRAIT OF AN OLD MAN
   Canvas.
   Coll.: Stadtmuseum für Kunst und Kunstgewerbe, Halle.
   Repr.: *Cicerone*, XVII, 1925, p. 982.

3. STILL-LIFE WITH PINE-APPLE
   Canvas, 110 by 80 cm.
   Coll.: Nationalgalerie, Berlin.
   Exh.: Kunsthaus, Zürich, 1927; Kunsthalle, Mannheim, 1931.

4. STILL-LIFE WITH TORTOISE AND HYACINTH
   Canvas, 87 by 114 cm.
   Coll.: Dr. Reichel, Vienna; Oesterreichische Galerie, Vienna.
   Exh.: Hagenbund, Vienna, 1911; Künstlervereinigung, Dresden, 1921; Kunsthaus, Zürich, 1927; Oesterreichisches Museum, Vienna, 1937.
   Reprod.: Oskar Kokoschka, *Dramen und Bilder*, 1913; Westheim, 1918, pl. 36; 1925, pl. 16; A. Faistauer, *Neue Malerei in Oesterreich*, 1923, pl. 30; catalogue of the Oesterreichische Galerie, Vienna, 1929, pl. 24.

5. THE TRANCE PLAYER
   Canvas, 84 by 65 cm.
   Coll.: Fritz Pollack, Frankfort-on-Main; Galerie Caspari, Munich; Schlesisches Museum der Bildenden Künste, Breslau.
   Exh.: Kunstschau, Vienna, 1909; Cassirer, Berlin, 1910;

[1] Only drawings reproduced in this book or elsewhere have been included in this list. The author will be grateful for the communication of additional information or corrections.

288

Hagenbund, Vienna, 1911; Galerie Arnold, Dresden, 1925; Cassirer, Berlin, 1927; Kunsthaus, Zürich, 1927; Kunsthalle, Mannheim, 1931; Galerie Georges Petit, Paris, 1931; Galerie Fischer, Lucerne, 1939 (Gemälde und Plastiken Moderner Meister aus Deutschen Museen).

Reprod.: *Kunst und Künstler*, VIII, 1909–10, p. 593; Oskar Kokoschka, *Dramen und Bilder*, 1913; Westheim, 1918, pl. 7; 1925, pl. 50; C. Einstein, *Kunst des 20. Jahrhunderts*, 1928, p. 426; G. Biermann, *Oskar Kokoschka*, 1929, pl. 1; H. Heilmaier, *Kokoschka*, 1929, pl. 1; Georges Petit exhibition catalogue, 1931, No. 1; Galerie Fischer exhibition catalogue, 1939, No. 63, p. 37.

1908

6. DR. CHRISOSTOMO
Canvas.

7. KARL KRAUS
Canvas, 100 by 74.5 cm.
Coll.: Private Coll., Neuss (Rhineland).
Exh.: Cassirer, Berlin, 1910; Hagenbund, Vienna, 1911; Kunsthaus, Zürich, 1927; Kunsthalle, Mannheim, 1931.
Reprod.: Oskar Kokoschka, *Dramen und Bilder*, 1913; Zürich exhibition catalogue, 1927, pl. III.

8. LANDSCAPE, HUNGARY (often called 'ITALIAN LANDSCAPE').
Canvas, 74 by 100 cm.
Coll.: Alfred Tietz, Cologne; Buchholz Gallery, New York.
Exh.: Cassirer, Berlin, 1925; Kunsthaus, Zürich, 1927; Kunsthalle, Mannheim, 1931; Galerie Georges Petit, Paris, 1931.
Reprod.: Westheim, 1925, pl. 1; C. Einstein, *Kunst des 20. Jahrhunderts*, 1928, p. 428; Zürich exhibition catalogue, 1927, pl. XV.

9. PORTRAIT OF A BOY
Canvas, 96 by 47 cm. (Plate V).
Coll.: Dr. Reichel, Vienna; Galerie Caspari, Munich; Galerie St. Etienne, New York.
Exh.: Hagenbund, Vienna, 1911; Cassirer, Berlin, 1927; Kunsthaus, Zürich, 1927; Leicester Galleries, London, 1928; Oesterreichisches Museum, Vienna, 1937; Art Club of Chicago, 1941; St. Etienne Gallery, New York, 1943.
Reprod.: Westheim, 1918, pl. 12; 1925, pl. 56.

About 1908

10a. ACROBAT SEEN FROM BACK
Drawing, 45 by 34 cm. (Figure 1).
Coll.: St. George's Gallery, London.

10b. THE ACROBAT'S DAUGHTER
Drawing, 45 by 34 cm. (Figure 2).
Coll.: Anton Walbrook, London.

11. HERR EBENSTEIN
• Canvas, 99 by 78.5 cm.
Coll.: Private Coll., Vienna; Hugo Simon, Paris; Christoph
Bernoulli, Bâle.
Exh.: Hagenbund, Vienna, 1911; Cassirer, Berlin, 1927;
Kunsthaus, Zürich, 1927; Leicester Galleries, London,
1928; Kunsthalle, Mannheim, 1931; Kunstmuseum,
Bâle, 1946.
Reprod.: Cassirer exhibition catalogue, 1927; Zürich ex-
hibition catalogue, 1927, pl. II; London exhibition cata-
logue, 1928; G. Biermann, *Oskar Kokoschka*, 1929, pl. 2;
H. Heilmaier, *Kokoschka*, 1929, pl. 3.

12. NUDE SEATED
Watercolour (Plate III).
Exh.: Galerie Arnold, Dresden, 1925; Buchholz Gallery,
New York, 1941.

13. NUDE SEATED
Watercolour (Plate II).
Coll.: Private Coll., London.

14. FIGURE BENDING FORWARD
Watercolour.
Coll.: Mrs. G. H. Putnam, St. Louis, U.S.A.
Exh.: Buchholz Gallery, New York, 1941.

1908–9

**15. PROFESSOR HANS TIETZE AND FRAU ERICA TIETZE-
CONRAT**
Canvas, 76.5 by 136.2 cm. (Plate VII).
Coll.: Professor Tietze, Vienna; Museum of Modern Art,
New York.
Exh.: Arts Club of Chicago, 1941; City Art Museum of
St. Louis, U.S.A., 1942.
Reprod.: *Magazine of Art*, Nov., 1945, p. 264.

16. PETER ALTENBERG
Canvas, 76 by 71 cm. Dated.
Coll.: F. Wolff-Knize, Vienna.
Exh.: Cassirer, Berlin, 1910; Hagenbund, Vienna, 1911;
Galerie Arnold, Dresden, 1925; Cassirer, Berlin, 1927;
Kunsthaus, Zürich, 1927; Gemeente Museen of Amster-
dam, Rotterdam, The Hague, 1927/8.
Reprod.: Oskar Kokoschka, *Dramen und Bilder*, 1913;
Cicerone, XI, 1919, p. 649; Landsberger, *Impressionis-
mus und Expressionismus*, 1920, pl. 15; *Cicerone*, XVI,
1924, p. 649; Westheim, 1925, pl. 52.

17. CHILDREN PLAYING
Canvas, 73 by 108 cm. Dated (Plate VIII).
Coll.: Adolf Loos, Vienna; Staatliche Gemäldegalerie,
Dresden; Theodor Woelfers, Malmö.
Exh.: Hagenbund, Vienna, 1911; Internationale Kunst-
ausstellung, Dresden, 1926; Cassirer, Berlin, 1927;
Kunsthaus, Zürich, 1927; Oesterreichisches Museum,
Vienna, 1937; Galerie Fischer, Lucerne, 1939 (Gemälde
und Plastiken Moderner Meister aus Deutschen Mu-
seen); Panama Pacific International Exposition.
Reprod.: Oskar Kokoschka, *Dramen und Bilder*, 1913;
Westheim, 1925, pl. 62; *Kunst und Dekoration*, LIX,
Oct., 1926, p. 116; *Cicerone*, XVII, 1926, p. 375; Bier-
mann, *Oskar Kokoschka*, 1929, pl. 8; *Magazine of Art*,
Nov., 1945, p. 261.

18. FRAU LOTTE FRANZOS
Canvas, 114.3 by 85 cm. (Plate VI).
Coll.: Mrs. E. L. Franzos, Vienna; Buchholz Gallery, New
York; Phillips Memorial Gallery, Washington.
Exh.: Hagenbund, Vienna, 1911; Kunsthaus, Zürich, 1927;
Arts Club of Chicago, 1941; City Art Museum of St.
Louis, 1942.
Reprod.: Hagenbund exhibition catalogue, 1911 (Detail);
Zürich exhibition catalogue, 1927, pl. IV.

19. ADOLF LOOS
Canvas, 74 by 93 cm. Dated.
Coll.: Adolf Loos, Vienna; Nationalgalerie, Berlin.
Exh.: Cassirer, Berlin, 1910; Hagenbund, 1911; Galerie
Arnold, Dresden, 1925; Kunsthaus, Zürich, 1927.

Reprod.: Oskar Kokoschka, *Dramen und Bilder*, 1913; Westheim, 1918, pl. 9; 1925, pl. 7; *Kunstwanderer*, 1./2., February, 1925, p. 191; Galerie Arnold exhibition catalogue, 1925, No. 4; G. Biermann, *Oskar Kokoschka*, 1929, pl. 4; L. Justi, *Von Corinth bis Klee*, 1931, pl. 67.

20. THE PAINTER HARTA
Canvas, 72 by 52 cm. Dated.
Coll.: A. Neufeld, Vienna; Cassirer, Berlin; Galerie Tannhauser, Munich; Hjalmar Gabrielsson, Göteborg.
Reprod.: Westheim, 1918, pl. 8; 1925, pl. 51.

About 1909

21. DR. STEIN
Canvas.
Coll.: Dr. Stein, Vienna.
Exh.: Cassirer, Berlin, 1910; Hagenbund, Vienna, 1911.
Reprod.: 'Die Kunst unserer Zeit,' exhibition, Vienna, 1930.

1909–10

22. CHILD WITH THE HANDS OF FATHER AND MOTHER
Canvas, 71.5 by 52 cm. (Plate XII).
Coll.: Leopold Goldmann, Vienna; St. Etienne Gallery, New York; Private Coll., Santa Barbara, California.
Exh.: Hagenbund, Vienna, 1911; Kunsthaus, Zürich, 1927; Arts Club of Chicago, 1941; St. Etienne Gallery, New York, 1943.
Reprod.: Westheim, 1925, pl. 53; Zürich exhibition catalogue, 1927, pl. VI; *Art News*, April, 1943, p. 23.

23. RITTER VON JANIKOWSKY
Canvas.
Coll.: F. Wolff-Knize, Vienna.
Exh.: Hagenbund, Vienna, 1911; Galerie Arnold, Dresden, 1925; Oesterreichisches Museum, Vienna, 1937.
Reprod.: Oskar Kokoschka, *Dramen und Bilder*, 1913; Oesterreichisches Museum exhibition catalogue, No. 6.

24. FRAU BESSIE LOOS
Canvas, 73 by 91 cm.
Coll.: Nationalgalerie, Berlin.
Exh.: Hagenbund, Vienna, 1911; Galerie Arnold, Dresden, 1925; Cassirer, Berlin, 1927; Kunsthaus, Zürich, 1927.

Reprod.: Westheim, 1925, pl. 8; *Kunst für Alle*, XLI, 1926, p. 153; L. Justi, *Von Corinth bis Klee*, 1931, pl. 68.

25. GUSTAV MEYRINK
Canvas.
Coll.: Harry Fuld, Frankfort-on-Main.

26. WINTER LANDSCAPE, DENT DU MIDI
Canvas, 79 by 116 cm. (Plate XIII).
Coll.: Wallraf-Richartz-Museum, Cologne.
Exh.: Hagenbund, Vienna, 1910; Sonderbund, Cologne, 1912; Kunsthaus, Zürich, 1927.
Reprod.: Oskar Kokoschka, *Dramen und Bilder*, 1913; Westheim, 1918, p. 14; *Kunst und Künstler*, 1921; A. Faistauer, *Neue Malerei in Oesterreich*, 1923, pl. 31; Westheim, 1925, pl. 61; Zürich exhibition catalogue, 1927, pl. XVI; G. Biermann, *Oskar Kokoschka*, 1929, pl. 5; *Cicerone*, XXI, 1929, p. 20.

1910

27. PETER BAUM
Canvas (Plate XIV).
Coll.: Cassirer, Berlin.

28. DR. RUDOLF BLÜMNER
Canvas, 80 by 57 cm.
Coll.: Herwarth Walden, Berlin; Cassirer, Berlin.
Exh.: Sturm, Berlin, 1910; Cassirer, Berlin, 1927; Kunsthaus, Zürich, 1927; Kunsthalle, Mannheim, 1931.
Reprod.: H. Bahr, *Expressionismus*, p. 136.

29. HUGO CARO
Canvas, 89 by 55 cm.
Coll.: Hugo Simon, Paris; C. Bernoulli, Bâle.
Exh.: Kunsthaus, Zürich, 1927; Kunstmuseum, Bâle, 1946.

30. CAT
Canvas, 42 by 70 cm. (Plate IX).
Coll.: Ida Bienert, Dresden.
Exh.: Galerie Arnold, Dresden, 1925; Cassirer, Berlin, 1927; Kunsthaus, Zürich, 1927.
Reprod.: Westheim, 1925, pl. 14.

31. RICHARD DEHMEL
Pen drawing.
Reprod.: Paul Wiegler, *Geschichte der Deutschen Literatur*, Vol. II, p. 265.

32. TILLA DURIEUX
    Canvas, 55.5 by 65 cm.
    Coll.: Private Coll., Krefeld.
    Exh.: Kunsthaus, Zürich, 1927; Kunsthalle, Mannheim,
    1931.

33. AUGUSTE FOREL
    Canvas, 71 by 58 cm.
    Coll.: Städtische Kunsthalle, Mannheim.
    Exh.: Cassirer, Berlin, 1910; Künstlervereinigung, Dres-
    den, 1921; Kunsthaus, Zürich, 1927; Kunsthalle, Mann-
    heim, 1931.
    Reprod.: Oskar Kokoschka, *Dramen und Bilder*, 1913;
    Westheim, 1918, pl. 13; *Kunst für Alle*, XXXIV, 1919,
    p. 393; Fritz Karpfen, *Oesterreichische Kunst*, 1923, pl.
    174; A. Faistauer, *Neue Malerei in Oesterreich*, 1923, pl.
    32; Westheim, 1925, pl. 58; *Kunst für Alle*, XLI, 1926,
    p. 153; Herbert Fürst, *Portrait Painting*, 1927, fig. 165;
    Zürich exhibition catalogue, 1927, pl. V; G. Biermann,
    Oskar Kokoschka, 1929, pl. 3; H. Heilmaier, *Kokoschka*,
    1929, pl. 4; *Das Kunstblatt*, 1930, Heft. 7; *Magazine of
    Art*, Nov. 1937, sup. p. 17; Sheldon Cheney, *The Story
    of Modern Art*, 1941, p. 402; *Magazine of Art*, Nov.,
    1945, p. 263.

34. ITALIAN WOMAN
    Canvas, 65 by 54 cm.
    Coll.: Kunstverein, Barmen.
    Exh.: Galerie Arnold, Dresden, 1925; Kunsthalle, Mann-
    heim, 1931.

35. KNIGHT, DEATH AND ANGEL
    Canvas, 60 by 76 cm.
    Coll.: Private Coll., Vienna.
    Exh.: Künstlervereinigung, Dresden, 1921; Kunsthaus,
    Zürich, 1927.

36. ELSE KUPFER[1]
    Canvas, 90 by 71 cm. (Plate XV).
    Coll.: Wolfgang Gurlitt, Berlin; Neue Galerie Nierenstein,
    Vienna; Museum, Stuttgart, 1927; Kunsthaus, Zürich.
    Exh.: Cassirer, Berlin, 1918; Künstlervereinigung, Dres-
    den, 1919, 1921; Galerie Arnold, Dresden, 1925; Cas-
    sirer, Berlin, 1927; Leicester Galleries, London, 1928;

[1] Kokoschka believes that he painted this picture in 1908.

294

Kunsthalle, Mannheim, 1931; Galerie Georges Petit, Paris, 1931.

Reprod.: *Der Blaue Reiter*, 1912; Oskar Kokoschka, *Dramen und Bilder*, 1913; Westheim, 1918, pl. 16; *Das Kunstblatt*, II, 1918, p. 248; Westheim, 1925, pl. 65; *Cicerone*, 1927, Heft 4; G. Biermann, *Oskar Kokoschka*, 1929, pl. 6; H. Heilmaier, *Kokoschka*, 1929, pl. 5; Georges Petit exhibition catalogue, 1931, No. 4.

37. PORTRAIT OF A MARQUIS

Canvas, 79 by 63 cm. (Plate XVII).

Coll.: National Museum, Stockholm.

Reprod.: *L'Amour de l'Art*, 1934, p. 450; *Magazine of Art*, April, 1935, p. 229.

38. THE DUCHESS OF ROHAN-MONTESQUIEU

Canvas, 95 by 50 cm. (Plate XVIII).

Coll.: Folkwang Museum, Essen; Paul E. Geier, Cincinnati, Ohio.

Exh.: Cassirer, Berlin, 1910; Galerie Arnold, Dresden, 1925; Cassirer, Berlin, 1927; Galerie Fischer, Lucerne, 1939 (Gemälde und Plastiken Moderner Meister aus Deutschen Museen); Cincinnati Art Museum, 1939.

Reprod.: Kokoschka, *Dramen und Bilder*, 1913; Westheim, 1918, pl. 11; Paul Ferdinand Schmidt, *Die Kunst der Gegenwart*, 1923, p. 102, No. 162; Westheim, 1925, pl. 54; H. Heilmaier, *Kokoschka*, 1929, pl. 2; H. Hildebrandt, *Die Kunst des 19. und 20. Jahrhunderts*, 1931, p. 374; R. Hamann, *Geschichte der Kunst*, 1933, pl. 1094; *Cahiers d'Art*, 1938, No. 1–2, p. 16.

39. COUNT VERONA

Canvas, 70 by 58 cm.

Coll.: Private Coll., Vienna.

Exh.: Cassirer, Berlin, 1910; Hagenbund, Vienna, 1911; Galerie Arnold, Dresden, 1925; Cassirer, Berlin, 1927.

Reprod.: Westheim, 1925, pl. 55.

40. HERWARTH WALDEN

Canvas, 100 by 68.5 cm.

Coll.: Mrs. Nell Walden, Switzerland.

Exh.: Cassirer, Berlin, 1910, 1927; Kunsthaus, Zürich, 1927; Leicester Galleries, London, 1928; New Burlington Galleries, London, 1938 (20th Century German Art).

Reprod.: Westheim, 1925, pl. 9.

41. WILHELM WAUER
Canvas, 95.5 by 55 cm.
Coll.: Private Coll., Munich.
Exh.: Kunsthaus, Zürich, 1927.
Reprod.: Zürich exhibition catalogue, pl. VII.

About 1910

42. FRAU KANN (Sketch)
Canvas, 70 by 50 cm. (Plate XI).
Coll.: St. Etienne Gallery, New York.

43. FRAU DR. K.[1]
Canvas, 99 by 73.7 cm.
Coll.: Dr. Reichel, Vienna; Buchholz Gallery, New York.
Exh.: Oesterreichisches Museum, Vienna, 1937; Buchholz
    Gallery, New York, 1941.
Reprod.: Westheim, 1918, pl. 17; 1925, pl. 66; Buchholz
    Gallery exhibition catalogue, 1941.

44. VERONIKA
Canvas.
Coll.: Dr. Reichel, Vienna.

1910–11

45. BOY SEATED
Watercolour.
Exh.: Galerie Arnold, Dresden, 1925.
Reprod.: Westheim, 1925, pl. 6; Galerie Arnold exhibition
    catalogue, 1925.

46. HERR VON FICKER
Canvas.
Reprod.: C. Einstein, *Die Kunst des 20. Jahrhunderts*, 1928,
    p. 427.

47. PAUL SCHEERBART
Canvas, 71 by 47 cm.
Coll.: F. Wolff-Knize, Vienna; Dr. Reichel, Vienna.
Exh.: Galerie Arnold, Dresden, 1925; Kunsthalle, Mann-
    heim, 1931; Oesterreichisches Museum, Vienna, 1937.
Reprod.: Oskar Kokoschka, *Dramen und Bilder*, 1913;
    Westheim, 1925, pl. 59.

[1] Kokoschka believes that he painted this picture in 1912.

296

48. THE ANNUNCIATION

Canvas, 82 by 122 cm.

Coll.: Carl Moll, Vienna.

Exh.: Galerie Arnold, Dresden, 1925; Kunsthalle, Mannheim, 1931.

Reprod.: *Zeitschrift für Bildende Kunst*, LIII, N.F., XXIX, 1917–8, Heft 4–5; Westheim, 1925, 15.

49. THE FLIGHT INTO EGYPT

Canvas, 55.5 by 68 cm.

Coll.: Private Coll., Vienna.

Exh.: Kunsthaus, Zürich, 1927.

Reprod.: *Genius*, 1920, p. 66; *Cicerone*, XVI, 1924, p. 223.

50. KNIGHT, DEATH AND ANGEL

Canvas, 86 by 75·5 cm.

Coll.: Stephan Kriser, Vienna; Hugo Simon, Paris; Ch. Bernoulli, Bâle.

Exh.: Galerie Arnold, Dresden, 1925; Kunsthaus, Zürich, 1927; Kunsthalle, Mannheim, 1931; Kunstmuseum, Bâle, 1946.

Reprod.: Westheim, 1918, pl. 18; 1925, pl. 60.

51. ITALIAN BOY

Wash drawing.

Coll.: Carl Moll, Vienna.

Exh.: Oesterreichisches Museum, 1937.

Reprod.: Oesterreichisches Museum exhibition catalogue, 1937, No. 55.

52. THE VISITATION

Canvas, 80 by 127 cm.

Coll.: Heinrich Meyer, Vienna; Carl Moll, Vienna.

Exh.: 'Ein Jahrhundert Wiener Malerei', Zürich, 1919; Galerie Arnold, Dresden, 1925; Kunsthaus, Zürich, 1927; Biennale, Venice, 1932.

Reprod.: Oskar Kokoschka, *Dramen und Bilder*, 1913; Westheim, 1918, pl. 20; 1925, pl. 63.

53. EGON WELLESZ

Canvas, 74 by 70 cm.

Coll.: Egon Wellesz, Vienna; Staatl. Gemäldegalerie, Dresden; Buchholz Gallery, New York.

Exh.: Cassirer, Berlin, 1927; Kunsthalle, Mannheim, 1931.

54. FRAU DR. SANDERS
Canvas, 82 by 56 cm.
Exh.: Galerie Arnold, Dresden, 1925.
55. PORTRAIT OF A CUSTOMS OFFICIAL
Canvas, 79 by 63 cm.
Exh.: Galerie Arnold, Dresden, 1925.
56. DR. SCHWARZWALD
Canvas, 90 by 65 cm. Dated on the back: 'ETATIS SUAE 40
AD 1911'.
Coll.: Städelsches Kunstinstitut, Frankfort-on-Main. Sold
by Galerie Fischer, Lucerne, 1939 (Gemälde und Plas-
tiken Moderner Meister aus Deutschen Museen).
Reprod.: *Zeitschrift für Bildende Kunst*, LIII, N.F. XXIX,
1917–8, Heft 4–5; Westheim, 1918, pl. 22; *Deutsche
Kunst und Dekoration*, XLIX, 1921–2, p. 34; *Cicerone*,
XV, 1923, p. 1118; Westheim, 1925, pl. 67; Galerie
Fischer exhibition catalogue, 1939, No. 66.

1912

57. DR. H. BURG
Charcoal drawing, 43.5 by 31.5 cm. Dated: 22. xi. 1912.
Coll.: Dr. H. Burg, London.
Reprod.: Oskar Kokoschka, *Dramen und Bilder*, 1913.
58. THE SINGER ENNEHJLEM
Canvas.
Reprod.: Oskar Kokoschka, *Dramen und Bilder*, 1913.
59. THE ACTOR ETTLINGER
Canvas, 68 by 56 cm.
Coll.: Private Coll., Vienna; Wallraf-Richartz-Museum,
Cologne.
Reprod.: Westheim, 1918, pl. 19; 1925, pl. 73.
60. KARL KRAUS
Charcoal drawing.
Coll.: Bohuslav Kokoschka, Vienna.
Exh.: Oesterreichisches Museum, Vienna, 1937.
Reprod.: Oskar Kokoschka, *Dramen und Bilder*, 1913.
61. THE DANCER NIJINSKY
Drawing (Plate XIX).
Coll.: Staatsgalerie, Vienna; Böhler Coll., Winterthur.
Reprod.: Oskar Kokoschka, *Dramen und Bilder*, 1913.

62. PORTRAIT OF A YOUNG WOMAN
   Charcoal drawing.
   Reprod.: Oskar Kokoschka, *Dramen und Bilder*, 1913.
63. THE REST ON THE FLIGHT INTO EGYPT
   Canvas, 55 by 67 cm.
   Coll.: Halle Coll., Vienna.
   Exh.: Galerie Arnold, Dresden, 1925.
64. SELF-PORTRAIT
   Canvas, 50 by 41 cm. (Plate XX).
   Coll.: Carl Moll, Vienna.
   Exh.: Cassirer, Berlin, 1927; Kunsthaus, Zürich, 1927.
   Reprod.: Oskar Kokoschka, *Dramen und Bilder*, 1913;
      Zeitschrift für Bildende Kunst, LIII, N.F., XXIX, 1917–8,
      Heft 4–5; Cassirer exhibition catalogue, 1927.
65. DR. JULIUS SZEPS
   Canvas, 74 by 59 cm.
   Coll.: Staatsgalerie, Vienna.
   Exh.: Kunsthaus, Zürich, 1927.
   Reprod.: Catalogue of the Staatsgalerie, 1929, pl. 25;
      Zürich exhibition catalogue, 1927, pl. IX.
66. THE ACTOR SOMMARUGA
   Coll.: Carl Nicolas, Berlin.
   Canvas.
   Reprod.: Oskar Kokoschka, *Dramen und Bilder*, 1913;
      Zeitschrift für Bildende Kunst, LIII, N.F., XXIX, 1917–8,
      Heft 4–5.
67. VENETIAN SCENE
   Canvas.
   Coll.: Koloman Moser, Vienna.
   Reprod.: Westheim, 1918, pl. 21; 1925, pl. 64.
68. ANTON VON WEBERN
   Drawing.
   Reprod.: Oskar Kokoschka, *Dramen und Bilder*, 1913.

1912–13

69. TWO NUDES; GREEN VERSION
   Canvas, 124 by 88 cm.
   Coll.: Dr. Reichel, Vienna; St. Etienne Gallery, New York.
   Exh.: Arts Club of Chicago, 1941; St. Etienne Gallery,
      New York, 1943.
70. TWO NUDES; PINK VERSION
   Canvas, 180 by 144 cm.

Coll.: Carl Moll, Vienna; Fritz Gurlitt, Berlin; Dr. Glaser.

Exh.: Galerie Arnold, Dresden, 1925.

Reprod.: Westheim, 1918, pl. 25; 1925, pl. 75.

71. SPOSALIZIO

Canvas, 104 by 62 cm. (Plate XVI).

Coll.: Dr. Reichel, Vienna; Mrs. E. L. Franzos, Washington.

Exh.: Galerie Arnold, Dresden, 1925; Kunsthaus, Zürich, 1927; Oesterreichisches Museum, Vienna, 1937; Arts Club of Chicago, 1941.

Reprod.: Oskar Kokoschka, *Dramen und Bilder*, 1913; Zürich exhibition catalogue, 1927, p. VIII; Gemeente Museen, Amsterdam, Rotterdam, The Hague, 1927–8.

1913–14

72. PORTRAIT OF A BEARDED MAN (HERR J. P.)

Canvas.

Coll.: Private, Vienna.

Reprod.: *Zeitschrift für Bildende Kunst*, LII, N.F., 7–8, Heft 4–5; *Kunst für Alle*, XLI, 1926, p. 153.

1913

73. ALFRED ADLER

Canvas, 100 by 70 cm.

Coll.: Private Coll., Vienna; Dr. Viktor von Klemperer, Dresden.

Exh.: Galerie Arnold, Dresden, 1925; Cassirer, Berlin, 1927; Oesterreichisches Museum, Vienna, 1937.

74. ALPINE LANDSCAPE, MÜRREN

Canvas, 70 by 95 cm.

Coll.: Cassirer, Berlin.

Exh.: Kunsthaus, Zürich, 1927.

75. THE BLIND MOTHER

Canvas, 95 by 65 cm.

Coll.: Dr. Reichel, Vienna.

Exh.: Galerie Arnold, Dresden, 1925.

Reprod.: Westheim, 1918, pl. 32; 1925, pl. 70; Galerie Arnold exhibition catalogue, 1925, No. 21.

76. DOUBLE PORTRAIT

Canvas, 100 by 90 cm.

Coll.: H. v. Garvens-Garvensburg, Hannover; Staatl. Gemäldegalerie, Dresden.

Exh.: Sezession, Berlin, 1913; Künstlervereinigung, Dresden, 1921; Galerie Arnold, Dresden, 1925; Kunsthaus, Zürich, 1927; Oesterreichisches Museum, Vienna, 1937.

Reprod.: Kokoschka, *Dramen und Bilder*, 1913; *Zeitschrift für Bildende Kunst*, 1913, XXIV, p. 281; Westheim, 1918, pl. 29; *Genius*, 1919, p. 43 (detail); *Ganymed* (Blätter der Marées-Gesellschaft), Vol. II, 1920, pl. facing p. 154; Westheim, 1925, pl. 13; Cheney, *A World History of Art*, 1937, p. 884; *A Primer of Modern Art*, 1939, p. 29.

77. GIRL SEATED
Canvas, 91 by 67 cm.

Coll.: Private Coll., Vienna; Dr. Rathenau.

Exh.: Galerie Arnold, Dresden, 1925; Cassirer, Berlin, 1927.

Reprod.: Westheim, 1925, pl. 39; Heilmaier, *Kokoschka*, 1929, pl. 6.

78. PORTRAIT OF A WOMAN
Canvas.

Coll.: Alma Mahler, Vienna; Folkwang-Museum, Essen.

Reprod.: Kokoschka, *Dramen und Bilder*, 1913; Westheim, 1918, pl. 28; 1925, pl. 12.

79. NAPLES IN A STORM
Canvas.

Coll.: Dr. Fritz Moll, Brieg; Private Coll., Munich.

Exh.: Cassirer, Berlin, 1919.

Reprod.: *Zeitschrift für Bildende Kunst*, LIII, N.F., XXIX, 1917–8, Heft 4–5; Westheim, 1918, pl. 15; *Kunst und Künstler*, 1919; Westheim, 1925, pl. 18; Einstein, *Kunst des 20. Jahrhunderts*, 1928, p. 429.

80. PORTRAIT OF THE PAINTER POINTING TO HIS BREAST
Canvas, 81.3 by 49.5 cm. (Plate XXI).

Coll.: Ludwig Fischer, Frankfort; Museum, Halle; Museum of Modern Art, New York.

Exh.: Künstlervereinigung, Dresden, 1921; Galerie Arnold, Dresden, 1925; Buchholz Gallery, New York, 1941; 20th Century Portraiture, Museum of Modern Art, New York, 1942; City Art Museum of St. Louis, 1942.

Reprod.: Westheim, 1918, pl. 31; *Genius*, 1919, p. 40;

Westheim, 1925, pl. 69; Biermann, *Kokoschka*, 1929, pl. 7; *Studio*, Vol. CXII, 1936, p. 243; Buchholz Gallery exhibition catalogue, 1941; *Time*, 10th Nov. 1941, p. 46.

81. F. WOLFF-KNIZE
Canvas.
Coll.: F. Wolff-Knize, Vienna.
Exh.: Oesterreichisches Museum, Vienna, 1937.

1913–14

82. BEARDED MAN (HERR H.)
Charcoal drawing.
Coll.: Private Coll., Vienna.
Reprod.: *Genius*, 1920, p. 64.

83. BARON DIRSZTAY
Canvas, 100 by 73 cm. (also quoted as 96 by 62 cm.).
Coll.: Cassirer, Berlin.
Exh.: Galerie Arnold, Dresden, 1923; 1925; Cassirer, Berlin, 1927; Kunsthalle, Mannheim, 1931.
Reprod.: *Cicerone*, XV, 1923, p. 740; Westheim, 1925, pl. 72.

84. ALBERT EHRENSTEIN or THE PRISONER
Canvas, 99 by 73 cm. (Plate XXVIII).
Coll.: Princess Lichnowsky; Suermondt Coll., Wiesbaden; Modern Gallery, Prague.
Exh.: Cassirer, Berlin, 1927.
Reprod.: Westheim, 1918, pl. 24; 1925, pl. 74.

85. SIX FANS
Paper and watercolour.
Coll.: Alma Werfel-Mahler.
Exh.: Oesterreichisches Museum, Vienna, 1937.

86. ROBERT FREUND
Canvas.
Coll.: Robert Freund, Vienna. (Lacerated by the Police of Vienna, Section II, H, on May 5th, 1938.)
Reprod.: Postcard published by Editions 'Deutsches Kulturkartell', Paris 6e.

87. HERR HAUER
Canvas.
Coll.: Städt. Kunstmuseum, Düsseldorf.

88. CARL MOLL
Canvas, 128 by 94 cm.
Coll.: Private Coll., Vienna; Staatsgalerie, Vienna.

Exh.: Galerie Arnold, Dresden, 1925; Cassirer, Berlin, 1927; Kunsthaus, Zürich, 1927; Biennale, Venice, 1932.

Reprod.: Catalogue of the Moderne Galerie, Vienna, 1929, pl. 26; *Kunst und Künstler*, 1929; Cheney, *A Primer of Modern Art*, 1939, p. 190.

89. SELF-PORTRAIT, PAINTING

Canvas, 107 by 70 cm.

Coll.: Private Coll., Berlin; Galerie Fischer, Lucerne.

Exh.: Cassirer, Berlin, 1927; Kunsthaus, Zürich, 1927; sold by Galerie Fischer, Lucerne, 1931.

Reprod.: Westheim, 1925, pl. 57; Zürich Exhibition catalogue, pl. 1; Thoene, *Modern German Art*, 1938, pl. 47.

90. TRE CROCI, DOLOMITES

Canvas, 82 by 119 cm.

Coll.: Prager, Munich; Staatsgalerie, Munich.

Exh.: 'Ein Jahrhundert Wiener Malerei,' Zürich, 1919; Künstlervereinigung, Dresden, 1921; Kunsthaus, Zürich, 1927; Kunsthalle, Mannheim, 1931; 'Entartete Kunst,' Munich, 1937.

Reprod.: *Zeitschrift für Bildende Kunst*, LIII, N.F., XXIX, 1917–8, Heft 7–8; Westheim, 1918, pl. 26; *Genius*, 1919, p. 227; *Katalog der Neuen Staatsgalerie*, Munich, 1921; Westheim, 1925, pl. 10; Zürich Exhibition catalogue, 1927, pl. XVII; Heilmaier, *Koskoschka*, 1929, pl. 7; *Magazine of Art*, Nov., 1945, p. 262.

1914

91. ARCHITECTURAL DRAWING—CREMATORIUM

Chalk drawing.

Coll.: Alma Werfel-Mahler.

Reprod.: Westheim, 1918, pl. 61, 62; 1925, pl. 133, 134.

92. DESIGN FOR CREMATORIUM—INTERIOR

Chalk drawing.

Reprod.: Westheim, 1925, pl. 134.

93. HERR BAUER

Canvas, 69 by 56 cm.

Coll.: Cassirer, Berlin.

Exh.: Kunsthaus, Zürich, 1927.

94. BROTHER AND SISTER

Canvas.

Exh.: Cassirer, Berlin, 1919.

Reprod.: *Kunst und Künstler*, 1919; Heilmaier, 1929, pl. 8.

95. LADY WITH FEATHER HAT
    Canvas, 55 by 40 cm.
    Coll.: Private Coll., Munich; Hugo Simon, Paris; Bernoulli
        Coll., Bâle; Buchholz Gallery, New York.
    Exh.: Cassirer, Berlin, 1927; Kunsthaus, Zürich, 1927;
        Kunsthalle, Mannheim, 1931; Kunstmuseum, Bâle, 1946.
    Reprod.: Westheim, 1925, pl. 71.
96. STILL-LIFE WITH CAT
    Canvas.
    Coll.: Franz Kluxen, Boldixum.
    Exh.: Künstlervereinigung, Dresden, 1921.
    Reprod.: Westheim, 1918, pl. 37; 1925, pl. 17.
97. ANTON VON WEBERN
    Canvas, 63 by 45 cm.
    Exh.: Galerie Arnold, Dresden, 1925.
98. TEMPEST (DIE WINDSBRAUT)
    Canvas, 181 by 219 cm. (Plates XXVI, XXVII).
    Coll.: Otto Winter, Gross-Flottbeck; Kunsthalle, Hamburg;
        Kunstmuseum, Bâle.
    Exh.: Sezession, Munich, 1914; Cassirer, Berlin, 1919;
        Kunsthaus, Zürich, 1927; Gemeente Museen, Amster-
        dam, Rotterdam, The Hague, 1927–8; Kunsthalle,
        Mannheim, 1931.
    Reprod.: *Deutsche Kunst und Dekoration*, 1914, XXXIV,
        p. 342; *Zeitschrift für Bildende Kunst*, LIII, N.F., XXIX,
        1917–8, Heft 7–8; Westheim, 1918, pl. 27; *Kunst und
        Künstler*, 1919; Woermann, *Geschichte der Kunst*, Vol.
        VI, 1922, pl. 198; Westheim, 1925, pl. 79; Meyer, *Lexi-
        kon*, 7. Aufl., IV, 1926, facing p. 273–4; *Kunst für Alle*,
        XLI, 1926, p. 153; Zürich Exhibition catalogue, 1927,
        pl. XVIII; *Magazine of Art*, Nov., 1945, p. 262.
99. TEMPEST, SKETCH
    Chalk drawing, 45 by 34 cm.
    Coll.: St. George's Gallery, London.
    Reprod.: Westheim, 1925, pl. 43.

1915

100. FORTUNA
     Canvas.
     Coll.: v. Garvens-Garvensburg, Hannover; W. Kahn-
         heimer, Berlin.

Exh.: Academy of Fine Arts, Berlin, 1922; Kunsthalle, Mannheim, 1931.

Reprod.: *Querschnitt*, 1921, p. 174; *Kunst und Künstler*, xx, 1922, p. 361; Einstein, *Kunst des 20. Jahrhunderts*, 1928, p. 433.

101. PRINCESS MECHTHILD LICHNOWSKY
Canvas, 110 by 85 cm.
Coll.: Princess Lichnowsky, Kuchelna.
Exh.: Cassirer, Berlin, 1927; Kunsthalle, Mannheim, 1931.
Reprod.: Westheim, 1918, pl. 30; 1925, pl. 77; Einstein, *Kunst des 20. Jahrhunderts*, 1928, p. 432.

102. SUSANNE
Canvas, 109 by 83.5 cm.
Coll.: Dr. Oskar Reichel, Vienna; Cassirer, Berlin.
Exh.: Kunsthaus, Zürich, 1927; Kunsthalle, Mannheim, 1931.
Reprod.: Westheim, 1918, pl. 33; 1925, pl. 78; Zürich Exhibition catalogue, 1927, pl. x.

103. WOMAN WITH PARROT
Canvas, 84 by 50.8 cm.
Coll.: Bernard Koehler, Berlin.
Exh.: Künstlervereinigung, Dresden, 1921; Kunsthaus, Zürich, 1927; Museum of Modern Art, New York, 1931 ('German Painting and Sculpture').
Reprod.: *Kunst und Dekoration*, XLVIII, 1921, p. 276; Westheim, 1925, pl. 76; New York Exhibition catalogue, 1931; Bulliet, *The Significant Moderns*, 1936, pl. 232.

104. WOMAN WITH PARROT, SKETCH
Charcoal drawing.
Reprod.: Westheim, 1925, pl. 44.

105. KNIGHT ERRANT
Canvas, 89.5 by 179.7 cm. (Plate XXIX).
Coll.: Dr. Oskar Reichel, Vienna; St. Etienne Gallery, New York.
Exh.: Arts Club of Chicago, 1915; Kunsthaus, Zürich, 1927; St. Etienne Gallery, New York, 1943.
Reprod.: Westheim, 1918, pl. 38; *Genius*, 1919, p. 42; Faistauer, *Neue Malerei in Oesterreich*, 1923, pl. 34; Karpen, *Oesterreichische Kunst*, 1923, p. 173; Westheim, 1925, pl. 80; Einstein, *Kunst des 20. Jahrhunderts*, 1928, p. 431.

106. ADOLF LOOS
Drawing, 64.5 by 48.5 cm.
Coll.: Kunsthaus, Zürich.
Reprod.: Frontispiece of *Adolf Loos zum 60. Geburtstag,*
am 10. Dezember, 1930 (Lanyi, Vienna).

107. DR. SCHWARZWALD, WITH BOOK
Canvas, 79 by 62 cm.
Coll.: von Garvens-Garvensburg, Hannover; H. Lange,
Crefeld.
Exh.: Cassirer, Berlin, 1918; probably Galerie Arnold,
Dresden, 1925; Cassirer, Berlin, 1927; Kunsthaus, Zü-
rich, 1927; Kunsthalle, Mannheim, 1931; Galerie
Georges Petit, Paris, 1931.
Reprod.: *Kunstblatt*, 1917, p. 4; Westheim, 1918, pl. 23;
Kunst und Künstler, 1919, p. 127; Faistauer, *Neue
Malerei in Oesterreich*, 1923, pl. 33; Karpen, *Oester-
reichische Kunst*, 1923, pl. 175; Westheim, 1925, pl. 68;
Einstein, *Kunst des 20. Jahrhunderts*, 1928, p. 434;
Heilmaier, *Kokoschka*, 1929, pl. 9.

108. VILLAGES IN SAXONY
Canvas.
Coll.: Freiherr Rudolph von Simolin, Berlin.
Exh.: Academy, Berlin, 1923.
Reprod.: Westheim, 1918, pl. 34; *Kunst und Dekoration*,
LII, 1923, p. 249; Westheim, 1925, pl. 81.

109. EXILES
Canvas, 94 by 145 cm.
Coll.: Private Coll., Berlin; Städtisches Museum, Halle.
Exh.: Cassirer, Berlin, 1919.
Reprod.: Westheim, 1918, pl. 39; *Die Bildenden Künste*,
1919, p. 249; *Genius*, 1919, p. 42; detail, p. 43;
Faistauer, *Neue Malerei in Oesterreich*, 1923, pl. 35;
Westheim, 1925, pl. 83; Einstein, *Kunst des 20.
Jahrhunderts*, 1928, p. 436; Biermann, *Kokoschka*, 1929,
pl. 10; Heilmaier, *Kokoschka*, 1929, pl. 10.

110. SELF-PORTRAIT
    Canvas, 78 by 62 cm. (Plate XXX).
    Coll.: Freiherr von der Heydt, Godesberg.
    Exh.: Cassirer, Berlin, 1918; Kunsthalle, Mannheim, 1931;
        Galerie Georges Petit, Paris, 1931.
    Reprod.: Westheim, 1918, pl. 1; *Die Bildenden Künste*,
        1919, pl. 256; *Genius*, 1919, p. 44; Westheim, 1925,
        Frontispiece; Einstein, *Kunst des 20. Jahrhunderts*,
        1928, pl. XXVI; Cheney, *A Primer of Modern Art*, 1939,
        p. 3; *The Story of Modern Art*, p. 404.

111. STOCKHOLM HARBOUR
    Canvas, 85 by 125 cm.
    Coll.: Hugo Benario, Berlin; U. Nimptsch, London.
    Exh.: Cassirer, Berlin, 1919.
    Reprod.: Westheim, 1918, pl. 35; *Die Bildenden Künste*,
        1919, pl. 253; *Ganymed* (Blätter der Marées-Gesell-
        schaft), Vol. II, 1920, facing p. 158; Westheim, 1925,
        pl. 82; *Kunst für Alle*, XLI, 1926, p. 153; Einstein, *Kunst
        des 20. Jahrhunderts*, 1928, p. 435; Biermann, *Ko-
        koschka*, 1929, pl. 12; Heilmaier, *Kokoschka*, 1929, pl.
        11; Cheney, *A Primer of Modern Art*, 1939, p. 88.

111a. SELMA LAGERLÖF. Lithograph.
111b. SVANTE ARRHENIUS. Lithograph.

112. ULTIMA RATIO
    Charcoal drawing.
    Reprod.: Westheim, 1918, pl. 51; 1925, pl. 109.

                        1917–18

113. FRIENDS
    Canvas, 100 by 150 cm.
    Coll.: Nationalgalerie, Berlin.
    Exh.: Cassirer, Berlin, 1919; Kunsthaus, Zürich, 1927;
        Kunsthalle, Mannheim, 1931.
    Reprod.: Westheim, 1918, pl. 40; *Die Bildenden Künste*,
        1919, p. 251; Westheim, 1925, pl. 84; Justi, *Von Corinth
        bis Klee*, 1931, pl. 69.

                        1918

114. THE ARTIST'S MOTHER
    Canvas.

Reprod.: *Die Bildenden Künste*, II, 1919, pl. 255; Bulliet, *The Significant Moderns*, 1936, pl. 234.

115. HUNTING
Canvas, 100 by 151 cm.
Coll.: Kunsthalle, Bremen.
Exh.: Cassirer, Berlin, 1919; Galerie Arnold, Dresden, 1925; Kunsthaus, Zürich, 1927; Leicester Galleries, London, 1928; Kunsthalle, Mannheim, 1931.
Reprod.: Westheim, 1918, pl. 41; *Cicerone*, XVI, 1924, p. 132; Westheim, 1925, pl. 85.

116. KATJA
Canvas.
Coll.: Private Coll., Elberfeld.
Reprod.: *Die Bildenden Künste*, II, 1919, pl. 252.

117. HEATHENS
Canvas, 75.5 by 125.5 cm.
Coll.: Stadtmuseum, Dresden.
Exh.: Kunsthaus, Zürich, 1927.
Reprod.: *Die Bildenden Künste*, II, 1919, p. 250; Westheim, 1925, pl. 31; Einstein, *Kunst des 20. Jahrhunderts*, 1926, p. 437.

1918–19

118. LOVERS WITH CAT
Canvas, 93.5 by 130.5 cm. (Plate XXXI).
Coll.: Hugo Benario, Berlin; Kunsthaus, Zürich.
Exh.: Kunsthaus, Zürich, 1927; Kunsthalle, Mannheim, 1931; Oesterreichisches Museum, Vienna, 1937.
Reprod.: Catalogue of Zürich exh., 1937, pl. XIX.

1918–20

119. THE POWER OF MUSIC
Canvas, 102 by 150 cm.
Coll.: Staatl. Gemäldegalerie, Dresden.
Exh.: Künstlervereinigung, Dresden, 1921; Oesterreichisches Museum, Vienna, 1937.
Reprod.: *Genius*, 1920, p. 65; Westheim, 1925, pl. 86; Heilmaier, *Kokoschka*, 1929, pl. 12.

120. SUMMER—WOMAN RECUMBENT
Canvas, 111 by 140.5 cm.
Coll.: Hermann Lange, Krefeld.

Exh.: Kunsthaus, Zürich, 1927.
Reprod.: Westheim, 1925, pl. 95; Einstein, *Kunst des 20.
Jahrhunderts*, 1926, p. 439.

1919

121. COUPLE AT A TABLE
Sepia drawing.
Reprod.: Westheim, 1925, pl. 46.

122. ORPHEUS AND EURYDICE
Canvas, 69.9 by 50.2 cm.
Coll.: James Simon, Berlin; St. Etienne Gallery, New York.
Exh.: St. Etienne Gallery, New York, 1943.

123. WOMAN IN BLUE
Canvas, 75 by 100 cm. Dated (on back) 'VI. 1919'.
Coll.: Staatl.Gemäldegalerie, Dresden.
Exh.: Künstlervereinigung, Dresden, 1921; Kunsthaus,
    Zürich, 1927; Kunsthalle, Mannheim, 1931; Gemälde
    und Plastiken Moderner Meister aus Deutschen Museen;
    Galerie Fisher, Lucerne, 1939.
Reprod.: *Die Bildenden Künste*, II, 1919, p. 254; *Kunst und
    Künstler*, XX, 1922, p. 44; Westheim, 1925, pl. 87.

124. STUDY FOR WOMAN IN BLUE
Coloured charcoal drawing.
Reprod.: Westheim, 1925, pl. 45.

1920

125. ELBE BRIDGE, DRESDEN—I
Canvas, 58.4 by 80 cm.
Coll.: Art Institute of Detroit, Michigan.
Exh.: Museum of Modern Art, New York, 1931.

126. ELBE BRIDGE, DRESDEN—II
Canvas, 81.3 by 111.8 cm.
Coll.: Staatl.Gemäldegalerie, Dresden; Buchholz Gallery,
    New York; Art Institute, Chicago.
Exh.: Internationale Kunstausstellung, Dresden, 1926;
    Arts Club of Chicago, 1941; City Art Museum of St.
    Louis, 1942.

127. GIRL WITH DOLL
Canvas, 90 by 78.7 cm.
Coll.: Dr. W. R. Valentiner, Detroit.

Exh.: Museum of Modern Art, New York, 1931.

Reprod.: Catalogue of Museum of Modern Art exh., 1931; *Magazine of Art*, Nov., 1945, p. 263.

128. GIRL WITH FLOWERS AND BIRD CAGE

Canvas, 129 by 84 cm.

Coll.: Cassirer, Berlin; Mrs. Adolph Mack, San Francisco, California.

Exh.: Galerie Arnold, Dresden, 1925; Kunsthaus, Zürich, 1927; Kunsthalle, Mannheim, 1931; Arts Club of Chicago, 1941.

Reprod.: Westheim, 1925, pl. 34.

129. MOTHER AND CHILD, HEAD AND SHOULDERS

Canvas, 51 by 60 cm.

Coll.: Private Coll., Berlin; Benno Elkan, London.

Exh.: Kunsthaus, Zürich, 1927; Gemeente Museen, Amsterdam, Rotterdam, The Hague, 1927–8; Kunsthalle, Mannheim, 1931.

Reprod.: *Kunst und Künstler*, xx, 1922, p. 50; Faistauer, *Neue Malerei in Oesterreich*, 1923, pl. 37; Westheim, 1925, pl. 88.

130. PORTRAIT OF WOMAN WITH OPEN MOUTH

Chalk drawing.

Reprod.: Westheim, 1925, pl. 124.

131. OLD WOMAN (MRS. LANYI)

Chalk drawing.

Reprod.: *Kunst und Künstler*, xx, 1922, p. 49; Westheim, 1925, pl. 122.

132. SELF-PORTRAIT

Charcoal drawing. Inscribed: 'Im 34. Jahre Oskar Kokoschka, Wien, Oktober, 1920.'

Coll.: Dr. F. Goldschmidt and Dr. V. Wallerstein, Berlin.

Reprod.: *Querschnitt*, 1921, p. 248; *Kunst und Künstler*, xx, 1922, p. 40; Westheim, 1925, pl. 115.

133. STILL-LIFE WITH MASK

Canvas, 50 by 60 cm.

Exh.: Galerie Arnold, Dresden, 1925.

134. WOMAN AND SLAVE

Canvas, 78 by 97 cm.

Coll.: R. Lanyi, Vienna; J. v. Sternberg, Hollywood.

Exh.: Galerie Arnold, Dresden, 1925.

Reprod.: *Kunst und Künstler*, xx, 1922, p. 45; Galerie Arnold exhibition catalogue, 1925, No. 35; Westheim,

1925, pl. 89; Faistauer, *Neue Malerei in Oesterreich*, 1926, pl. 36.

155. THE ARTIST'S BROTHER BOHUSLAV
Drawing. Inscribed: 'Bruder Bohuslav K.'
Coll.: B. Kokoschka, Vienna.
Reprod.: *Kunst und Künstler*, XX, 1922, p. 46.

About 1920

136. DRESDEN
Watercolour.
Exh.: Galerie Arnold, Dresden, 1925.

137. THE PHOTOGRAPHER HUGO ERFURTH
Ink drawing.
Exh.: Kunsthaus, Zürich, 1927.
Reprod.: *Ganymed*, III, 1921, p. 148.

138. GIRL SEATED WITH HER KNEES CROSSED
Watercolour.
Exh.: Galerie Arnold, Dresden, 1925.
Reprod.: Galerie Arnold exhibition catalogue, 1925.

139. MOTHER AND CHILD
Canvas, 110 by 70 cm.
Coll.: Mrs. Ursula Elkan, New York.
Exh.: Galerie Arnold, Dresden, 1925.

140. NUDE, LIFTING HER ARMS
Pen drawing.
Reprod.: Westheim, 1925, pl. 20.

141. PORTRAIT OF TWO MEN
Canvas.
Coll.: Dr. Carl Georg Heise, Lübeck.

1921

142. GITTA
Canvas, 85 by 60 cm.
Coll.: Dr. V. Wallerstein, Berlin.
Exh.: Kunsthaus, Zürich, 1927; Gemeente Museen, Amsterdam, Rotterdam, The Hague, 1927–8; Kunsthalle, Mannheim, 1931; Carnegie Institute, International Exhibition, Pittsburg, 1933.
Reprod.: *Kunst und Künstler*, XX, 1922, p. 47; Westheim, 1925, pl. 90; *Magazine of Art*, XXVI, 1933, p. 536.

143. PORTRAIT OF A GIRL
   Chalk drawing.
   Reprod.: Westheim, 1925, pl. 130.
144. PORTRAIT OF A NUDE GIRL
   Chalk drawing.
   Reprod.: Westheim, 1925, pl. 123.
145. PORTRAIT OF A WOMAN
   Chalk drawing.
   Reprod.: Westheim, 1925, pl. 129.
146. SAUL AND DAVID
   Canvas, 166 by 105 cm.
   Exh.: Künstlervereinigung, Dresden, 1921; Galerie Arnold, Dresden.
   Reprod.: Arnold exhibition catalogue, 1925, No. 36; Westheim, 1925, pl. 91.

1921–23

147. JACOB, LEAH AND RACHEL
   Canvas, 150 by 164 cm.
   Exh.: Cassirer, Berlin, 1923; Galerie Arnold, Dresden, 1925.
   Reprod.: Westheim, 1925, pl. 36.

1922

148. GIRL WITH CAP
   Watercolour.
   Reprod.: Westheim, 1925, pl. 25.
149. TWO WOMEN
   Canvas, 120 by 80 cm.
   Coll.: Cassirer.
   Exh.: Galerie Arnold, Dresden, 1925.
   Reprod.: Galerie Arnold exhibition catalogue, 1925, No. 37.
150. THE RIVER ELBE, DRESDEN—III
   Canvas, 80 by 120 cm.
   Exh.: Galerie Arnold, Dresden, 1925.
   Reprod.: Galerie Arnold exhibition catalogue, 1925, No. 39.
151. THE RIVER ELBE, DRESDEN—IV
   Canvas, 65.5 by 95 cm.
   Coll.: Private Coll., Dresden.
   Exh.: Kunsthaus, Zürich, 1927.
   Reprod.: Westheim, 1925, pl. 93.

152. SELF-PORTRAIT WITH BRUSH
Canvas, 110 by 70 cm.
Coll.: Kunsthütte, Chemnitz.
Exh.: Galerie Arnold, Dresden, 1925; Kunsthaus, Zürich,
1927; Kunsthalle, Mannheim, 1931.
Reprod.: Westheim, 1925, pl. 40; Galerie Arnold exhibi-
tion catalogue, 1925, No. 38; *Cicerone*, XVII, 1925, p.
839; Zürich exhibition catalogue, pl. XI; Biermann,
Kokoschka, 1929, pl. 9; Heilmaier, *Kokoschka*, pl. 15.

153. DR. VIKTOR WALLERSTEIN
Watercolour.
Coll.: Dr. Viktor Wallerstein.
Reprod.: Westheim, 1925, pl. 26; Einstein, *Kunst des 20.
Jahrhunderts*, 1926, pl. XXVII.

1922–23

154. THE RIVER ELBE, DRESDEN—V
Canvas, 70 by 110 cm.
Coll.: Mrs. Nothmann, London; M. Sarachi, London; Miss
Diana King.
Exh.: Leger Galleries, London, 1941; Redfern Galleries,
London, 1943.

1922–25

155. HERSELF
Canvas, 100 by 80 cm.
Exh.: Internationale Kunstausstellung, Dresden, 1926.

156. HIMSELF
Canvas, 115 by 80 cm.
Exh.: Internationale Kunstausstellung, Dresden, 1926.

1923

157. THE RIVER ELBE, DRESDEN—VI: AUGUSTUSBRÜCKE
Canvas, 65 by 95 cm.
Coll.: Mrs. Kaden, Gloucestershire.
Exh.: Galerie Arnold, Dresden, 1925; Kunsthaus, Zürich,
1927; Kunsthalle, Mannheim, 1931.
Reprod.: Zürich exhibition catalogue, 1927, pl. XX; Heil-
maier, *Kokoschka*, 1929, pl. 13.

313

158. THE RIVER ELBE, DRESDEN—VII—(WITH A STEAMER IN
      THE FOREGROUND)
   Canvas.
   Exh.: Galerie Arnold, Dresden, 1923.
   Reprod.: *Kunst für Alle*, XXXIX, 1923, p. 302; Westheim,
      1925, pl. 94.
159. LOT AND HIS DAUGHTERS
   Canvas, 175 by 110 cm. (Plate XXXII).
   Coll.: Hugo Benario, Berlin; burnt in Munich Glaspalast
      fire, 1931.
   Exh.: Galerie Arnold, Dresden, 1925; Kunsthaus, Zürich,
      1927; Gemeente Musea, Amsterdam, Rotterdam, The
      Hague, 1927–8; Kunsthalle, Mannheim, 1931.
   Reprod.: Westheim, 1925, pl. 92; Einstein, *Die Kunst des
      20. Jahrhunderts*, 1926, p. 440; *Kunst für Alle*, XLI,
      1926, p. 153; Biermann, *Kokoschka*, 1929, colour plate.
160. THE PAINTER—I
   Canvas, 85 by 130 cm. (Plate XXXIII).
   Coll.: Richard von Kuehlmann.
   Exh.: Cassirer, Berlin, 1923; Galerie Arnold, Dresden,
      1925; Kunsthaus, Zürich, 1927; Gemeente Museen,
      Amsterdam, Rotterdam, The Hague, 1927–8; Leicester
      Galleries, London, 1928; Kunsthalle, Mannheim, 1931;
      Galerie Georges Petit, Paris, 1931; Oesterreichisches
      Museum, Vienna, 1937.
   Reprod.: *Kunstblatt*, VII, 1923, p. 130; Westheim, 1925, pl.
      96; *Kunst für Alle*, XLI, 1926, p. 153; Biermann, *Ko-
      koschka*, 1929, pl. 11; Heilmaier, *Kokoschka*, 1929, pl. 14.
161. THE PERSIAN (WOLFGANG GURLITT)
   Canvas, 96 by 62 cm.
   Coll.: Wilhelm Holzmann, Berlin.
   Exh.: Cassirer, Berlin, 1927; Kunsthaus, Zürich, 1927.
162. THE SLAVE
   Canvas, 101 by 80.5 cm.
   Exh.: Kunsthaus, Zürich, 1927; Kunsthalle, Mannheim,
      1931.

About 1923

163. MOTHER AND CHILD
   Canvas, 120.6 by 81.3 cm.
   Coll.: Dr. W. R. Valentiner, Detroit.

164. THE PAINTER—II

Reprod.: Westheim, 1925, pl. 3.

165. BORDEAUX CATHEDRAL

Canvas, 80 by 60 cm.

Coll.: Nationalgalerie, Berlin.

Exh.: Cassirer, Berlin, 1925; Galerie Fischer, Lucerne, 1939; Gemälde und Plastiken Moderner Meister aus Deutschen Museen.

Reprod.: Westheim, 1925, pl. 99a; Lucerne sale catalogue, 1939, No. 64.

166. NANCY CUNARD

Canvas, 116 by 73 cm.

Coll.: Ida Bienert, Dresden.

Exh.: Cassirer, Berlin, 1927; Kunsthaus, Zürich, 1931; Galerie Georges Petit, Paris, 1931.

Reprod.: Zürich exhibition catalogue, 1927; pl. XII; *Kölnische Zeitung*, October, 1928; Heilmaier, *Kokoschka*, 1929, pl. 16.

167. FLORENCE

Canvas.

Coll.: Kunsthalle, Hamburg.

Exh.: Cassirer, Berlin, 1925; Oesterreichisches Museum, Vienna, 1927.

Reprod.: Westheim, 1926, pl. 98; Biermann, *Kokoschka*, 1929, pl. 14.

168. LAKE LEMAN—I

Canvas, 64 by 95 cm.

Coll.: Städtisches Museum, Ulm; Galerie Fischer, Lucerne, 1939 (Gemälde und Plastiken, Moderner Meister aus Deutchen Museen); sold by Paul E. Geier, Cincinnati.

Exh.: Kunsthaus, Zürich, 1927; Leicester Galleries, London, 1928; Kunsthalle, Mannheim, 1931; Cincinnati Art Museum, Ohio, 1939.

Reprod.: Westheim, 1925, pl. 37; *Kunst für Alle*, XLI, 1926, p. 153; Zürich exhibition catalogue, 1927, pl. XXI; Biermann, *Kokoschka*, 1929, pl. 13; catalogue of Lucerne Sale, 1939, p. 39, No. 69.

169. LAKE LEMAN—II

Canvas, 120 by 81 cm. (Plate XXXIV).

Coll.: Museum der Bildenden Künste, Leipzig; Oesterreichische Staatsgalerie, Vienna.

Exh.: Akademie der Bildenden Künste, Berlin, 1924; Kunsthaus, Zürich, 1927; Kunsthalle, Mannheim, 1931.

Reprod.: *Kunst für Alle*, XXXIX, 1924, p. 303; Westheim, 1925, pl. 97.

170. PARIS, THE OPERA

Canvas, 80 by 115 cm. (or 62 by 117·5 cm.) (Plate XXXV).

Coll.: Kunsthalle, Bremen; Buchholz Gallery, New York.

Exh.: Cassirer, Berlin, 1925; Galerie Arnold, Dresden, 1925; Kunsthalle, Zürich, 1927; Leicester Galleries, London, 1928; Kunsthalle, Mannheim, 1931.

Reprod.: Westheim, 1925, pl. 38; Galerie Arnold exhibition catalogue, 1925, No. 48.

171. PARIS, ROOF OF THE OPERA

Canvas, 65 by 50 cm.

Exh.: Kunsthaus, Zürich, 1927.

172. ARNOLD SCHÖNBERG

Canvas, 99 by 75 cm.

Coll.: F. Wolff-Knize, Vienna.

Exh.: Cassirer, Berlin, 1927; Kunsthaus, Zürich, 1927.

173. DR. SCHWARZWALD—III

Canvas, 100 by 74 cm.

Coll.: Private Coll., Berlin.

Exh.: Galerie Arnold, Dresden, 1925; Cassirer, Berlin, 1927; Kunsthaus, Zürich, 1927; Carnegie Institute, Pittsburgh, 1930.

Reprod.: *Kunst und Künstler*, 1925, p. 249; Bulliet, *The Significant Moderns*, 1936, pl. 235.

174. VENICE, BOATS NEAR THE DOGANA

Canvas, 75 by 95 cm.

Coll.: Staatsgalerie, Munich.

Exh.: Cassirer, Berlin, 1925; Galerie Arnold, Dresden, 1925; Galerie Georges Petit, Paris, 1931; Oesterreichisches Museum, Vienna, 1937.

Reprod.: Westheim, 1925, pl. 99; *Kunstwanderer*, 1925, 1./2. Februarheft, p. 191; *Zeitschrift für Bildende Kunst* (*Monatsrundschau*), March, 1925, p. 129; Biermann, *Kokoschka*, 1929, pl. 15; *Kunstblatt*, XIV, 1930, p. 215.

175. VIENNA, COTTAGE

Canvas, 66 by 90 cm.

Coll.: Cassirer, Berlin.

Exh.: Kunsthaus, Zürich, 1927.

176. BORDEAUX, THE THEATRE[1]

Canvas, 81 by 118.

Coll.: Nationalgalerie, Berlin.

Exh.: Cassirer, Berlin, 1925.

Reprod.: Westheim, 1925, pl. 106; Einstein, *Die Kunst des 20. Jahrhunderts*, 1926, p. 442; *Kunst für Alle*, 1926, XLII, p. 36; Heilmaier, *Kokoschka*, 1929, pl. 21; *Deutsche Kunst und Dekoration*, LXVII, 1930, p. 89; Justi, *Von Corinth bis Klee*, 1931, pl. 70.

177. BIARRITZ, THE BEACH

Canvas, 77 by 101 cm.

Coll.: Cassirer, Amsterdam.

Exh.: Cassirer, Berlin, 1925; Kunsthaus, Zürich, 1927; Leicester Galleries, London, 1928; Kunsthalle, Mannheim, 1931; Stedelijk Museum, Amsterdam, 1945–6.

Reprod.: Zürich exhibition catalogue, pl. XXIII.

178. BIARRITZ, ROCKS

Canvas, 81 by 113 cm.

Coll.: Private Coll., Berlin.

Exh.: Cassirer, Berlin, 1925; Kunsthaus, Zürich, 1927; Leicester Galleries, London, 1928.

179. THE POET ERNST BLASS

Canvas, 80 by 120 cm.

Coll.: Cassirer, Amsterdam.

Exh.: Internationale Kunstausstellung, Dresden, 1926; Cassirer, Berlin, 1927; Kunsthaus, Zürich, 1927; Galerie Georges Petit, Paris, 1931; Kunsthalle, Mannheim, 1931.

Reprod.: Einstein, *Die Kunst des 20. Jahrhunderts*, 1926, p. 438; *Kunstwanderer*, April 1926; Heilmaier, *Kokoschka*, 1929, pl. 19; Georges Petit exhibition catalogue, 1931, No. 17.

180. KARL KRAUS—II

Canvas, 65 by 100 cm. (Plate XLI).

Inscription on the back: '*Der Sessel, auf dem Karl Kraus für dieses Bild gesessen ist nach der letzten Sitzung auseinandergefallen 7.II.25 und musste der Tischler gerufen werden.*' Further: '*Aus dem Schiffbruch der Welt Jener, die mit Brettern oder Barrikaden vor der Stirn geboren sind, hast Du eine Planke zu einem Schreibtisch geborgen.*'

[1] Generally, but incorrectly known as 'Die Börse'—'The Stock Exchange'.

'(The chair in which Karl Kraus sat for this picture collapsed after the last sitting, and the joiner had to be called in.' And: 'From the ship-wreck of the world of those who were born with boards or barricades before their foreheads, you have saved a plank to be used for a writing table.')

Coll.: Eva M. Röder, Lugano.

Exh.: Cassirer, Berlin, 1927.

Reprod.: Cassirer exhibition catalogue, 1927.

181. MONTE CARLO

Canvas, 80 by 115 cm.

Coll.: Städtische Galerie, Frankfort-on-Main; sold by Galerie Fischer, Lucerne, 1939 (Gemälde und Plastiken, Moderner Meister aus Deutschen Museen; Museum, Liège.

Exh.: Cassirer, Berlin, 1925; Musée Moderne, Brussels, 1946.

1925

182. AIGUES MORTES

Canvas, 73 by 100 cm.

Coll.: Mrs. Adolph Mack, San Francisco.

Exh.: Kunsthaus, Zürich, 1927; Leicester Galleries, 1928.

Reprod.: Westheim, 1925, pl. 99d; Biermann, *Kokoschka*, 1929, pl. 19.

183. AMSTERDAM, KLOVENIERSBURGVAL

Canvas, 62 by 85 cm.

Coll.: Kunsthalle, Mannheim.

Exh.: Cassirer, Berlin, 1925; Kunsthalle, Mannheim, 1931; Galerie Georges Petit, Paris, 1931.

Reprod.: *Cicerone*, XIX, 1927, p. 413; Biermann, *Kokoschka*, 1929, pl. 20; Heilmaier, *Kokoschka*, 1929, pl. 20.

184. AMSTERDAM, NIEUWE MARKT (OR MONTALBAANSTOREN)

Canvas, 61.5 by 83.5 cm.

Coll.: Kaiser-Wilhelm-Museum, Krefeld; F. Simon.

185. AVIGNON

Canvas, 61 by 81 cm.

Coll.: Dr. Oskar Reinhart, Winterthur.

Exh.: Cassirer, Berlin, 1925, Kunsthaus, Zürich, 1927; Biennale, Venice, 1931; Oesterreichisches Museum, Vienna, 1937.

186. NUDE IN LANDSCAPE NEAR AVIGNON
Canvas, 38 by 45 cm.
Coll.: W. R. Valentiner, Detroit.
Exh.: Kunsthalle, Mannheim, 1931; Galerie Georges Petit,
Paris, 1931.
Exh.: Kunsthaus, Zürich, 1927.
Reprod.: Zürich exhibition catalogue, 1927, pl. XXIV.

187. BERLIN, PARISER PLATZ
Canvas, 77 by 110 cm.
Coll.: Private Coll., Krefeld.
Exh.: Kunsthaus, Zürich, 1927; Akademie, Berlin, 1928.

188. FLOWERS IN A WINDOW
Canvas, 70 by 100 cm.
Coll.: Private Coll., Düsseldorf.
Exh.: Kunsthaus, Zürich, 1927.

189. THE LADY'S-MAID
Canvas, 76 by 56 cm.
Coll.: Cassirer, Berlin.
Exh.: Kunsthaus, Zürich, 1927.

190. LISBON, STREET SCENE
Canvas, 38 by 46 cm.
Coll.: Private Coll., Frankfort-on-Main.
Exh.: Kunsthaus, Zürich, 1927; Kunsthalle, Mannheim,
1931; Galerie Georges Petit, Paris, 1931.

191. PARIS, LOUVRE
Canvas, 73 by 100 cm.
Coll.: Cassirer, Berlin; Buchholz Gallery, New York.
Exh.: Kunsthaus, Zürich, 1927; Leicester Galleries, Lon-
don, 1928.

192. MADRID, PUERTA DEL SOL
Canvas, 67 by 98 cm.
Coll.: Max Glaeser, Eselsfürth; sold by Galerie Fischer,
Lucerne.
Exh.: Cassirer, Berlin, 1925; Kunsthaus, Zürich, 1927;
Kunsthalle, Mannheim, 1931; Galerie Georges Petit,
Paris, 1931; 20th Century German Art, New Burlington
Galleries, London, 1938.
Reprod.: Westheim, 1925, pl. 99, 1; Heilmaier, *Kokoschka*,
1929, pl. 18; *Kunst und Dekoration*, LXVII, 1930, p. 83.

193. MARSEILLES—I
Canvas, 73 by 100 cm.
Coll.: Hugo Simon, Paris; Bernoulli, Bâle.

Exh.: New Burlington Galleries, London (20th Century German Art), 1938; Kunstmuseum, Bâle, 1946.

Reprod.: Einstein, *Kunst des 20. Jahrhunderts*, 1926, p. 144*a*.

194. MARSEILLES—II

Canvas, 73 by 100 cm. (Plate XXXVI).

Coll.: Buchholz Gallery, New York; City Art Museum, St. Louis, Missouri.

Exh.: Cassirer, Berlin, 1925; Kunsthaus, Zürich, 1927; Kunsthalle, Mannheim, 1931; Galerie Georges Petit, Paris, 1931; Arts Club of Chicago, 1941.

Reprod.: Westheim, 1925, pl. 99*f*; *Bulletin of the City Art Museum of St. Louis*, December, 1942, p. 33; *Magazine of Art*, May, 1942, p. 184; *Art in Progress*, New York, 1944, p. 49.

195. PORTRAIT OF P.G.

Canvas, 65 by 50 cm.

Coll.: Cassirer, Berlin.

Exh.: Kunsthalle, Mannheim, 1931; Galerie Georges Petit, Paris, 1931.

196. SELF-PORTRAIT WITH HAT

Pen drawing. Dated.

Reprod.: Westheim, 1925, p. 99, 1.

197. TOLEDO

Canvas, 67 by 101·6 cm.

Coll.: Margarete Oppenheim, Berlin; Lilienfeld Galleries, New York; Private Coll., New York.

Exh.: Cassirer, Berlin, 1925; Kunsthaus, Zürich, 1927; Leicester Galleries, London, 1928; Kunsthalle, Mannheim, 1931; Galerie Georges Petit, Paris, 1931; Biennale, Venice, 1932; Galerie St. Etienne, New York, 1943.

Reprod.: Westheim, 1925, pl. 99*h*; Biermann, *Kokoschka*, 1929, pl. 17.

198. PARIS, JARDIN DES TUILERIES

Canvas, 81 by 115 cm.

Coll.: Cassirer, Berlin.

Exh.: Cassirer, Berlin, 1925; Kunsthaus, Zürich, 1927; Leicester Galleries, London, 1928.

Reprod.: Westheim, 1925, pl. 99*c*; Zürich exhibition catalogue, 1927, pl. XXII.

199. VERNET-LES-BAINS

Canvas, 88·5 by 116 cm.

Coll.: Elmer Rice, New York.

Exh.: Kunsthaus, Zürich, 1927; Leicester Galleries, London, 1928; Kunsthalle, Mannheim, 1931.
Reprod.: Westheim, 1925, pl. 99*i*.

1925-26

200. TOWER BRIDGE
Canvas, 76 by 128 cm. (Plate XLII).
Coll.: Kunsthalle, Hamburg; Galerie Fischer, Lucerne, 1939 (Gemälde und Plastiken Moderner Meister aus Deutschen Museen); sold by Joseph von Sternberg, Hollywood.
Exh.: Cassirer, Berlin, 1925; Kunsthaus, Zürich, 1927; Leicester Galleries, London, 1928; Kunsthalle, Mannheim, 1931.
Reprod.: Hanfstaengl, Munich, Coloured Reproduction and postcard; *Kunst und Künstler*, 1925; *Kunstblatt*, 1926, Heft 1, p. 1 (colour plate); *Kunst und Künstler*, XXIV, 1926, p. 166; Biermann, *Kokoschka*, 1929, pl. 18; Heilmaier, *Kokoschka*, 1929, pl. 17; *Cicerone*, 1929, XXI, p. 20; *Kunst und Dekoration*, 1930, p. 89; *Kunstblatt*, February, 1931 (colour plate); H. Hildebrandt, *Die Kunst des 19. u. 20. Jahrhunderts* (Handbuch der Kunstwissenschaft), 1931, pl. XVII (colour plate); Lucerne sale catalogue, 1939; Cheney, *A Primer of Modern Art*, 1939, p. 16.

1926

201. ADÈLE ASTAIRE (LADY CHARLES CAVENDISH)
Canvas, 96 by 131 cm.
Coll.: Cassirer, Amsterdam.
Exh.: Cassirer, Berlin, 1927; Kunsthaus, Zürich, 1927; Gemeente Museen, Amsterdam, Rotterdam, The Hague, 1927-8; Leicester Galleries, London, 1928; Kunsthalle, Mannheim, 1931; Galerie Georges Petit, Paris, 1931.
Reprod.: Cassirer exhibition catalogue, 1927; *Berliner Tageblatt*, 5th February 1927; *Cicerone*, XIX, 1927, p. 125; Georges Petit exhibition catalogue, 1931; *Kunst und Künstler*, 1931, XXIX, p. 178.

202. DOVER
Canvas, 76.5 by 127 cm.
Coll.: Reinhardt Galleries, New York; Private Collection, England.

Exh.: Kunsthaus, Zürich, 1927; Leicester Galleries, London, 1928; Museum of Modern Art, New York, 1931 ('German Painting and Sculpture').

Reprod.: Einstein, *Die Kunst des 20. Jahrhunderts*, 1926, p. 443; Zürich exhibition catalogue, 1927, pl. XXVI; *Cicerone*, XXI, 1929, p. 19; Biermann, *Kokoschka*, 1929, pl. 25; Heilmaier, *Kokoschka*, 1929, pl. 22; *Deutsche Kunst und Dekoration*, 1930, LXVII, p. 86; *Kunst und Künstler*, 1931, p. 190; Museum of Modern Art exhibition catalogue, 1931.

203. FLOWERS IN A VASE
Canvas, 55 by 75 cm.
Coll.: O. Hirsch, Frankfort-on-Main; C. Sarachi.
Exh.: Kunsthaus, Zürich, 1927.

204. FLOWERS IN AN OPEN WINDOW
Canvas, 73 by 100 cm.
Coll.: Private Coll., Frankfort-on-Main.
Exh.: Kunsthaus, Zürich, 1927; Leicester Galleries, London, 1928; Kunsthalle, Mannheim, 1931.
Reprod.: Hanfstaengl, Munich, Coloured postcard.

205. LONDON BRIDGE (GREAT THAMES VIEW)
Canvas, 90 by 130 cm.
Coll.: Paul Cassirer, Berlin; St. Etienne Gallery, New York; Albright Art Gallery, Buffalo.
Exh.: Kunsthaus, Zürich, 1927; City Art Museum, St. Louis, 1942.
Reprod.: Biermann, *Kokoschka*, 1929, p. 27; *Beaux-Arts*, 7th April, 1939, p. 4; *Magazine of Art*, Nov. 1945, p. 265.

206. LONDON EVENING (SMALL THAMES VIEW)
Canvas, 61 by 91 cm.
Coll.: Countess Auersperg.
Exh.: Internationale Kunstausstellung, Dresden, 1926; Kunsthalle, Mannheim, 1931; Galerie Georges Petit, Paris, 1931.
Reprod.: *Cicerone*, 1926, XVIII, p. 375; *Kunst und Künstler*, 1931, XXIX, p. 191.

207. THE MANDRILL
Canvas, 127 by 101 cm. (Plate XLIII).
Coll.: Cassirer, Amsterdam.
Exh.: Cassirer, Berlin, 1927; Kunsthaus, Zürich, 1927; Leicester Galleries, London, 1928; Kunsthalle, Mann-

heim, 1931; Galerie Georges Petit, Paris, 1931; Stedelijk Museum, Amsterdam, 1945–6.

Reprod.: Cassirer exhibition catalogue, 1927; Leicester
Galleries exhibition catalogue, 1928; Biermann, *Kokoschka*, 1929, pl. 21; *Cicerone*, 1929, XXI, p. 20; Georges
Petit exhibition catalogue, 1931, No. 19; *L'Amour de
l'Art*, 1934, p. 450.

208. RICHMOND TERRACE
Canvas, 90 by 130 cm.
Coll.: V. v. Klemperer, Dresden.
Exh.: Academy, Dresden, 1927; Leicester Galleries, London, 1928; Galerie Georges Petit, Paris, 1931; Oesterreichisches Museum, Vienna, 1937.
Reprod.: *Kunst für Alle*, XLII, 1927, p. 355; *Kunstblatt*,
1928, p. 195 (colour plate); Biermann, *Kokoschka*, 1929,
pl. 24; Georges Petit exhibition catalogue, 1931; Hanfstaengl, Munich, colour reproduction.

209. ROES
Canvas, 130 by 89 cm.
Coll.: Cassirer, Amsterdam; Mrs. Katzenellenbogen, Santa
Monica, California.
Exh.: Cassirer, Berlin, 1927; Kunsthaus, Zürich, 1927;
Biennale, Venice, 1932; Oesterreichisches Museum,
Vienna, 1937.
Reprod.: Cassirer exhibition catalogue, 1927; Biermann,
Kokoschka, 1929, pl. 23.

210. ROSES
Canvas, 116 by 81 cm.
Exh.: Kunsthaus, Zürich, 1927; Galerie Matthiesen, Berlin,
1927.
Reprod.: Zürich exhibition catalogue, 1927, pl. XIII;
Kunst und Künstler, 1927.

211. THE TIGON
Canvas, 96 by 129 cm. (Plate XLIV).
Coll.: Private Collection, Czechoslovakia.
Exh.: Cassirer, Berlin, 1927; Kunsthaus, Zürich, 1927;
Leicester Galleries, London, 1928; Kunsthalle, Mann-
heim, 1931; Galerie Georges Petit, Paris, 1931.
Reprod.: Zürich exhibition catalogue, 1927, pl. XXVIII.

212. PERSIAN CAT
Canvas, 90 by 125 cm. (Plate XLV).
Coll.: Robert Tannahill, Detroit.

Exh.: Cassirer, Berlin, 1927; Kunsthaus, Zürich, 1927; Leicester Galleries, London, 1928; Kunsthalle, Mannheim, 1931; Galerie Georges Petit, Paris, 1931.

Reprod.: Heilmaier, *Kokoschka*, 1929, pl. 23; *Kunstblatt*, February, 1931.

213. WATERLOO BRIDGE

Canvas, 89 by 130 cm.

Coll.: R. Loeb, Berlin; Herriot Collection, Paris.

Exh.: Internationale Kunstausstellung, Dresden, 1926; Kunsthaus, Zürich, 1927; Leicester Galleries, London, 1928; Kunsthalle, Mannheim, 1931; Galerie Georges Petit, Paris, 1931.

Reprod.: Dresden exhibition catalogue, 1926; *Kunst für Alle*, 1926, XLII, p. 137; Zürich exhibition catalogue, 1927, pl. XXV, *Le Arti Plastiche*, November, 1928; *Cicerone*, XXI, 1929, p. 20; Biermann, *Kokoschka*, 1929, pl. 26; Georges Petit exhibition catalogue, 1931, No. 24; *Westermanns Monatshefte*, No. 846.

1926–27

214. PROFESSOR LEO KESTENBERG

Canvas, 127 by 102 cm.

Coll.: Leo Kestenberg, Tel Aviv.

Exh.: Akademie der Bildenden Künste, Berlin, 1927; Kunsthaus, Zürich, 1927; Leicester Galleries, London, 1928; Kunsthalle, Mannheim, 1931; Galerie Georges Petit, Paris, 1931; Biennale, Venice, 1932; Oesterreichisches Museum, Vienna, 1937.

Reprod.: Zürich exhibition catalogue, 1927, pl. XIV; *Kunstblatt*, VI, 1927, p. 208–9; Biermann, *Kokoschka*, 1929, pl. 22; Heilmaier, *Kokoschka*, 1929, pl. 24; *Kunst und Künstler*, 1931, XXIX, p. 193.

215. ELSA TEMARY

Canvas, 96 by 130 cm.

Coll.: Hermann Lange, Krefeld.

Exh.: Cassirer, Berlin, 1927; Kunsthaus, Zürich, 1927; Kunsthalle, Mannheim, 1931.

Reprod.: Cassirer exhibition catalogue, 1927; Zürich exhibition catalogue, 1927, pl. XXVII; Heilmaier, *Kokoschka*, 1929, pl. 26.

216. LAC D'ANNECY—I
 Canvas, 70 by 91 cm.
 Coll.: St. Etienne Gallery, New York; Mrs. Maas, Santa
 Monica, California.
 Exh.: Cassirer, Berlin, 1927; Leicester Galleries, London,
 1928; Kunsthalle, Mannheim, 1931; Galerie Georges
 Petit, Paris, 1931.

217. COURMAYEUR ET LES DENTS DES GÉANTS
 Canvas, 89 by 130 cm. (Plate XLVII).
 Coll.: Marcell von Nemes; Buchholz Gallery, New York;
 Phillips Memorial Gallery, Washington.
 Exh.: Leicester Galleries, London, 1928; Kunsthalle,
 Mannheim, 1931; Galerie Georges Petit, Paris, 1931;
 Arts Club of Chicago, 1941.
 Reprod.: *Deutsche Kunst und Dekoration*, LXVII, 1930,
 p. 82 (colour plate); *Kunst und Künstler*, XXIX, 1931,
 p. 185.

218. LYON
 Canvas, 97 by 130 cm. (Plate XLIX).
 Coll.: Mrs. E. Katzenellenbogen, Santa Monica, California.
 Exh.: Cassirer, Berlin, 1927; Leicester Galleries, London,
 1928; Kunsthalle, Mannheim, 1931; Galerie Georges
 Petit, Paris, 1931; Oesterreichisches Museum, Vienna,
 1937; Stedelijk Museum, Amsterdam, 1945–6.
 Reprod.: *Kunstblatt*, XII, 1928, p. 192–3; Biermann, *Koko-
 schka*, 1929, pl. 30; Heilmaier, *Kokoschka*, 1929, pl. 28;
 Deutsche Kunst und Dekoration, 1930, LXVII, p. 87;
 Georges Petit exhibition catalogue, 1931, No. 31; *Kunstblatt*, February, 1931; Vienna exhibition catalogue, 1937,
 pl. 16.

219. CHAMONIX-MONTBLANC
 Canvas, 90 by 130 cm. (Plate XLVIII).
 Coll.: Marcell von Nemes; Helmuth Lütjens, Amsterdam.
 Exh.: Cassirer, Berlin, 1927; Leicester Galleries, London,
 1928; Kunsthalle, Mannheim, 1931.
 Reprod.: *Kunstblatt*, July, 1928, p. 198; Leicester Galleries
 exhibition catalogue, 1928; Biermann, *Kokoschka*, 1929,
 pl. 29; Heilmaier, *Kokoschka*, 1929, pl. 29; Georges
 Petit exhibition catalogue, 1931, No. 28.

220. GIANT TURTLES
 Canvas, 91 by 121 cm. (Plate XLVI).

Coll.: Fritz Rothmann, Berlin; Private Coll., England.

Exh.: Kunsthaus, Zürich, 1927; Kunsthalle, Mannheim, 1931.

221. FRITZ WOLFF

Canvas, 110 by 87 cm.

Coll.: Private Coll., Vienna.

Exh.: Kunsthaus, Zürich, 1927; Gemeente Museen, Amsterdam, Rotterdam, The Hague, 1927–8; IV. Ausstellung der Vereinigung Bildender Künstler, Wiener Sezession (Kunstchau), 1929.

Reprod.: Vienna exhibition catalogue, 1929.

1928

222. ARAB WOMEN

Canvas, 89 by 130 cm. (Plate LI).

Coll.: Marcell von Nemes; Paul Cassirer, London.

Exh.: Leicester Galleries, London, 1928; Kunsthalle, Mannheim, 1931; Galerie Georges Petit, Paris, 1931; Oesterreichisches Museum, Vienna, 1937.

Reprod.: Biermann, *Kokoschka*, 1929, frontispiece (colour plate); Heilmaier, *Kokoschka*, 1929, pl. 32; *Deutsche Kunst und Dekoration*, 1930, LXVII, p. 84; *Kunst und Künstler*, 1930–31, XXIX, p. 179; Georges Petit exhibition catalogue, 1931, No. 33; Vienna exhibition catalogue, 1937, No. 17.

223. EL KANTARA

Canvas, 89 by 130 cm.

Coll.: Cassirer, Berlin.

Exh.: Leicester Galleries, London, 1928; Kunsthalle, Mannheim, 1931.

224. EXODUS, COL DE SFA NEAR BISKRA

Canvas, 89 by 100 cm. (Plate L).

Coll.: Max Warburg, New York.

Exh.: Leicester Galleries, London, 1928; Galerie Georges Petit, Paris, 1931; St. Etienne Gallery, New York, 1943.

Reprod.: *Kunstblatt*, July, 1928, p. 197; Biermann, *Kokoschka*, 1929, pl. 31; Heilmaier, *Kokoschka*, 1929, pl. 30; *Deutsche Kunst und Dekoration*, 1930, LXVII, p. 88.

225. LAKE LUCERNE

Canvas, 63.5 by 78.7 cm.

Coll.: Francesco von Mendelssohn, New York; Buchholz Gallery, New York; Mrs. Carlos Weinberg, Washington.

226. SIDI AHMET BEN TIDJANI, THE MARABOUT OF TEMACINE
Canvas, 97 by 130 cm. (Plate LII).
Coll.: Marcell von Nemes; Städtisches Museum, Halle.
Exh.: Leicester Galleries, London, 1928; Kunsthalle, Mannheim, 1931; Galerie Georges Petit, Paris, 1931.
Reprod.: *Kunstblatt*, July, 1928, p. 196; Leicester Galleries exhibition catalogue, 1928; Biermann, *Kokoschka*, 1929, pl. 32; Heilmaier, *Kokoschka*, 1929, pl. 31; *Deutsche Kunst und Dekoration*, 1930, LXVII, p. 85; Georges Petit exhibition catalogue, 1931, No. 32.

227. TUNIS MARKET
Canvas, 86 by 128 cm.
Coll.: Marcell von Nemes; Paul Cassirer; Private Collection, London.
Exh.: Kunsthalle, Mannheim, 1931; Galerie Georges Petit, Paris, 1931; Exhibition of Modern German Art, Museum of Fine Arts, Springfield, 1939.
Reprod.: Kunstblatt, February, 1931, p. 40.

228. VENICE, SANTA MARIA DELLA SALUTE WITH ROOFS IN THE FOREGROUND
Canvas, 90 by 116 cm. Dated (Plate LIII).
Coll.: Mademoiselle Lindauer, Paris.
Exh.: Leicester Galleries, London, 1928; Akademie der Bildenden Künste, Berlin, 1929; Galerie Georges Petit, Paris, 1931; Biennale, Venice, 1932.
Reprod.: Georges Petit exhibition catalogue, 1931, No. 27; Biermann, *Kokoschka*, 1929; Heilmaier, *Kokoschka*, 1929, pl. 27; *Kunst und Künstler*, 1931, XXIX, p. 183; Read, *Art Now*.

229. VENICE, SANTA MARIA DELLA SALUTE—II
Canvas, 73 by 100 cm.
Coll.: Private Coll., Paris; Fr. Arnold, Zürich; Hermann Lütjens, Amsterdam.
Exh.: Leicester Galleries, London, 1928; Oesterreichisches Museum, Vienna, 1937.

1929

230. DOLCE BRIDGE, SCOTLAND
Canvas, 71 by 91 cm.
Coll.: Paul Cassirer, London.
Exh.: Kunsthalle, Mannheim, 1931; Galerie Georges Petit, Paris, 1931.

231. FINTHORN RIVER, SCOTLAND
Canvas, 71 by 91 cm.
Coll.: Paul Cassirer, London.
Exh.: Kunsthalle, Mannheim, 1931; Galerie Georges Petit,
Paris, 1931.

232. ISTANBUL
Canvas, 80 by 110 cm.
Coll.: Private Collection, Czechoslovakia.
Exh.: Kunsthalle, Mannheim, 1931; Galerie Georges Petit,
Paris, 1931.
Reprod.: Georges Petit exhibition catalogue, 1931; *Kunst-blatt*, February, 1931, p. 34; *Kunst und Künstler*, 1931,
XXIX, p. 181.

233. JERUSALEM
Canvas, 80 by 128 cm. (Plate LIV).
Coll.: Detroit Institute of Arts, Detroit, Michigan.
Exh.: Kunsthalle, Mannheim, 1931; Galerie Georges Petit,
Paris, 1931; Arts Club of Chicago, 1941; City Art Museum
of St. Louis, 1942.
Reprod.: Georges Petit exhibition catalogue, 1931, No. 41;
Kunstblatt, February, 1931, p. 41; *Magazine of Art*,
August, 1939, p. 480; *Catalogue of the Detroit Institute
of Arts* (*Paintings and Sculpture Illustrated*), 1943, pl.
128; *Magazine of Art*, Nov. 1945, p. 265.

234. MARCELL VON NEMES
Canvas, 135 by 95 cm. (Plate LXI).
Coll.: Moritzburg, Halle.
Exh.: Akademie der Bildenden Künste, Berlin, 1929;
Galerie Georges Petit, Paris, 1931.
Reprod.: *Weltkunst*, November, 1930; Georges Petit ex-
hibition catalogue, 1931, No. 36.

235. THE PYRAMIDS
Canvas, 87 by 128 cm.
Coll.: Glaeser Coll., Eselsfürth.
Exh.: Kunsthalle, Mannheim, 1931; Galerie Georges Petit,
Paris, 1931.
Reprod.: *Kunstblatt*, February, 1931; *Kunst und Künstler*,
1931, p. 192.

236. ALGERIENNE AU TONNEAU
   Canvas, 80 by 100 cm.
   Coll.: Mme Wanda Kofler, Paris; Marcel Fleischmann,
      Zürich.
   Exh.: Kunstmuseum, Lucerne, 1937; Exhibition of 20th
      Century German Art, London, 1938; Museum of Modern
      Art, New York, 1939; Buchholz Gallery, New York,
      1941.

237. FISHES ON THE BEACH, DJERBA
   Canvas, 69 by 100 cm.
   Coll.: Paul Cassirer, Amsterdam.
   Exh.: Kunsthalle, Mannheim, 1931; Galerie Georges Petit,
      Paris, 1931.
   Reprod.: *Kunstblatt*, February, 1931.

238. ANTICOLI: HARVEST IN THE SABINE MOUNTAINS
   Canvas, 81 by 116 cm. (Plate LV).
   Coll.: Bob Gesinus Visser, Paris; Marcel Fleischmann,
      Zürich.
   Exh.: Kronprinzenpalais, Berlin (no date); Kunsthalle,
      Mannheim, 1931; Galerie Georges Petit, Paris, 1931;
      Exhibition of 20th Century German Art, London, 1938;
      Museum of Modern Art, New York, 1939; Golden Gate,
      San Francisco, 1940; Buchholz Gallery, New York, 1941;
      Wassar College, Poughkeepsie, New York, 1941.
   Reprod.: *Kunstblatt*, February, 1931, Frontispiece; *Kunst
      und Künstler*, XXIX, 1931, p. 187.

239. SWEDISH WOMAN
   Canvas, 82 by 117 cm.
   Coll.: Paul Cassirer, Amsterdam.
   Exh.: Galerie Georges Petit, Paris, 1931.

240. ANNECY—II
   Exh. Kunsthalle, Mannheim, 1931.

About 1930

241. SANTA MARGHERITA
   Canvas, 73 by 92 cm.
   Coll.: St. Etienne Gallery, New York.
   Exh.: Arts Club of Chicago, 1941.

242. LIGURIAN LANDSCAPE
Canvas.
Coll.: Paul Cassirer, Amsterdam.

1931

243. FLOWERS
Canvas.
Coll.: F. Wolff-Knize, Vienna.
Exh.: Oesterreichisches Museum, Vienna, 1937.
244. PAN (TRUDL WITH GOAT)
Canvas.
Coll.: Franz Kochmann, Dresden.
Exh.: Biennale, Venice, 1942; Oesterreichisches Museum,
Vienna, 1937.
245. TRUDL
Canvas. Dated (Plate LXIV).
246. DOUBLE-PORTRAIT: TRUDL THE AMAZON AND TRUDL,
MOTHERLY
Canvas (Plate LXIII).
Coll.: Franz Kochmann, Dresden.
Exh.: Biennale, Venice, 1932.
247. TRUDL, STUDY FOR DOUBLE-PORTRAIT
Charcoal drawing (Plate LXII).
248. VIENNA, VIEW FROM WILHELMINENBERG
Canvas, 92 by 136 cm.
Coll.: Historisches Museum der Stadt Wien (Rathaus).
Reprod.: *Josef Strzygowski-Festschrift*, 1932, pl. 60.

About 1931

249. MRS. M.
Red chalk drawing, one of a series of about twenty (Plates
LVI, LVII, LVIII, LIX).
Coll.: Paul Cassirer, London.
Exh.: Buchholz Gallery, New York, 1938.

1931–32

250. NOGENT-SUR-MARNE
Canvas, 61 by 91.4 cm.
Coll.: French Art Galleries, New York, 1938,
Exh.: Buchholz Gallery, New York, 1941,

251. STARFISH
Canvas.
Coll.: Staatl.Gemäldegalerie, Dresden.
Exh.: Biennale, Venice, 1932.

252. VIENNA
Canvas, 56 by 76 cm.
Coll.: St. Etienne Gallery, New York.
Exh.: Girls' Club of Chicago, 1941; St. Etienne Gallery,
New York, 1943.

253. TWO WOMEN RECUMBENT
Canvas.
Exh.: Biennale, Venice, 1932.

1932–33

254. SELF-PORTRAIT WITH CAP
Canvas, 97.8 by 71 cm.
Coll.: O. Eisler; Mrs. Löw-Beer, Epsom.
Exh.: Allied Artists' Exhibition (British Council), London,
1942; Dublin, 1942.

255. PORTRAIT OF ROB GESINUS VISSER WITH DOG
Canvas.
Coll.: Consul Visser, Cuba.

256. PORTRAIT OF BOB GESINUS VISSER IN A HAMMOCK
Canvas.
Coll.: Consul Visser, Cuba.

257. MRS. VISSER WITH CAP
Canvas.
Coll.: Consul Visser, Cuba.

258. MRS. VISSER WITH VASE
Canvas.
Coll.: Consul Visser, Cuba.

1933

259. MISS BETTY, RAPALLO
Canvas.

1933–34

260. FLOWER STILL-LIFE WITH ANTIQUE HEAD
Canvas, 80 by 65 cm.
Coll.: St. Etienne Gallery, New York.
Exh.: Arts Club of Chicago, 1941; St. Etienne Gallery,
New York, 1943.

261. MOTHER AND CHILD
Canvas, 60 by 74 cm.
Coll.: Mrs. Jaray-Bondi; M. Chatin Sarachi, London.

262. PRAGUE I: VIEW OF ISLAND IN THE VLTAVA
Canvas.
Coll.: Private Coll., Prague.

1934–36

263. T. G. MASARYK
Canvas, 94 by 128 cm. (Plate LXVII).
Coll.: Dr. Hugo Feigl, New York; Private Collection.
Exh.: International Exhibition of Painting, Carnegie Institute, Pittsburgh, 1936; Buchholz Gallery, New York, 1938; Arts Club of Chicago, 1941; Czechoslovak Contemporary Art, Demotte Gallery, New York, 1942.
Reprod.: Thoene, *Modern German Art*, 1938, pl. 45; *Magazine of Art*, November, 1938, p. 656.

264. T. G. MASARYK, STUDY
Chalk drawing.
Reprod.: *The Spirit of Czechoslovakia*, Vol. III, No. 4, 29th March, 1942, p. 29.

1934–37

265. MORAVSKÁ-OSTRAVA
Canvas.
Coll.: Ladislav Jerie, Moravská-Ostrava.

266. GARDEN I: THE VISIT
Canvas.
Coll.: Lida Palkovská, Prague.
Exh.: Oesterreichisches Museum, Vienna, 1937.

267. GARDEN II: CHILDREN AND GOAT
Canvas.
Coll.: Zádra Coll., Moravská-Ostrava.

268. FRAU KNIZE
Canvas.
Coll.: Ladislav Jerie, Moravská-Ostrava.

269. PRAGUE II: VIEW OF STRAHOV
Canvas.
Coll.: Lida Palkovská, Prague; Phillips Memorial Gallery, Washington.
Exh.: Oesterreichisches Museum, Vienna, 1937; Inter-

national Exhibition of Painting, Carnegie Institute,
Pittsburgh, 1938; City Art Museum of St. Louis, 1942.
Reprod.: Catalogue of Carnegie Exhibition, 1938, pl. 26.

270. PRAGUE III: ANOTHER VIEW FROM THE STUDIO
Canvas, 45.7 by 71 cm.
Coll.: Hugo Feigl, New York.
Exh.: Demotte Gallery, New York, 1942.

271. PRAGUE IV: VIEW FROM STRAHOV
Canvas (Plate LIX).
Coll.: Private Coll., New York.
Exh.: St. Etienne Gallery, New York, 1943.

272. PRAGUE V: VIEW FROM THE SCHOENBORN GARDENS
Canvas, 81 by 100 cm. (Plate LXX).
Coll.: Paul Schmolka, Prague; Hugo Feigl, New York.
Exh.: Oesterreichisches Museum, Vienna, 1937; Demotte
Gallery, New York, 1942.
Reprod.: Vienna exhibition catalogue, 1937, No. 10.

273. PRAGUE VI: MALÁ STRANA FROM THE VILLA KRAMAŘ
Canvas.
Coll.: Müller Coll., Vienna.
Exh.: Oesterreichisches Museum, Vienna, 1937.
Reprod.: Thoene, *Modern German Art*, 1938, pl. 46.

274. PRAGUE VII: NEAR THE NATIONAL THEATRE
Canvas, 81 by 100 cm.
Coll.: Hugo Feigl, New York.
Exh.: Demotte Gallery, New York, 1942.

275. PRAGUE VIII: THE CHARLES BRIDGE IN THE BACKGROUND
Canvas.
Coll.: Hugo Feigl, New York.
Reprod.: *Prager Presse* (Sonntagsbeilage), No. 46.

276. PRAGUE IX: VIEW OVER THE VLTAVA RIVER WITH
CHARLES BRIDGE AND HRADŠANY
Canvas.
Coll.: J. B. Neumann, New York.
Reprod.: Cheney, *The Story of Modern Art*, 1941, p. 403.

277. PRAGUE X: KARLŮV MOST (CHARLES BRIDGE)
Canvas.
Coll.: Hugo Feigl, Prague; Museum of Modern Art,
Prague.
Exh.: Oesterreichisches Museum, Vienna, 1937; Inter-
national Exhibition of Painting, Carnegie Institute,
Pittsburgh, 1938.

Reprod.: Vienna exhibition catalogue, 1937, No. 8; *Emporium*, Vol. XXXVI, 1937, p. 445; *Studio*, Vol. CXV, January, 1938, p. 36.

278. SELF-PORTRAIT WITH HAT
Canvas, 48 by 35.5 cm. (Plate LXV).
Coll.: Private Coll., New York.
Exh.: St. Etienne Gallery, New York, 1943.

1936

279. FERDINAND BLOCH-BAUER
Canvas.
Coll.: F. Bloch-Bauer, Vienna; Kunsthaus, Zürich.
Exh.: Oesterreichisches Museum, Vienna, 1937.

280. SELF-PORTRAIT WITH STICK
Canvas.
Coll.: Ladislav Jerie, Moravská-Ostrava
Exh.: Oesterreichisches Museum, Vienna, 1937.

1936–38 (begun 1921–24)

281. THE FOUNTAIN
Canvas, 165 by 150 cm.
Coll.: Buchholz Gallery, New York.
Exh.: International Exhibition of Painting, Carnegie Institute, Pittsburgh, 1939; Arts Club of Chicago, 1941.
Reprod.: Catalogue of Carnegie Exhibition, pl. 92.

1937

282. SELF-PORTRAIT OF A DEGENERATE ARTIST
Canvas, 85 by 110 cm. (Colour Plate 1).
Coll.: Emil Korner, Port William.
Exh.: New Burlington Galleries, London (Exhibition of 20th Century German Art), 1938.

1938

283. BATHER: NUDE SEATED
Canvas (unfinished).

1938–39

284. SUMMER
Canvas, 67.3 by 87.7 cm. Inscribed 'Zrání' (Maturity) (Plate LXXI).
Coll.: National Gallery of Scotland, Edinburgh.

Exh.: London Gallery, London, 1939; Wertheim Galleries, London, 1939.

Reprod.: *London Bulletin*, January-February, 1939 (first state); *Near Writing and Daylight*, 1945, pl. 152.

1939

285. PRAGUE XI: NOSTALGIA
Canvas.
Coll.: The Hon. Michael Croft.

1939-40

286. POLPERRO—I
Canvas, 60 by 85.8 cm. (Plate LXXII).
Coll.: Tate Gallery.
Exh.: The Tate Gallery's War Time Acquisitions, National Gallery, 1942.
Reprod.: *The Listener*, 6th March, 1941; *The Burlington Magazine*, May, 1942.

287. POLPERRO—II
Canvas, 60 by 85 cm.
Coll.: Private Collection, England.

288. POLPERRO
Watercolour, 32 by 50 cm. (Plate LXXIII).
Coll.: The Hon. Michael Croft.
Exh.: Works by Polish and Czechoslovak Artists, Oxford, 1942.

289. POLPERRO
Watercolour, 35 by 55.5 cm. (Plate LXXIV).
Coll.: The Hon. Michael Croft.
Exh.: Works by Polish and Czechoslovak Artists, Oxford, 1942.

290. PRIVATE PROPERTY
Canvas, 63·5 by 76 cm. (Plate LXXV).
Coll.: Private Coll., London.
Exh.: Leger Galleries, London, 1941.

1940

291. PORTRAIT OF A YOUNG ENGLISHMAN
Canvas (Plate LXXVI).
Coll.: The Hon. Michael Croft.

292. PORTRAIT OF AN ENGLISH GIRL
Canvas.
Coll.: The Hon. Michael Croft.

1940–41

293 THE RED EGG
Canvas, 63.5 by 76 cm. (Plate LXXVII).
Coll.: Czechoslovak Government.
Exh.: Leger Galleries, London; Artists' International, 1942.
Reprod.: *Studio*, January, 1942, p. 22.

294. CRAB
Canvas, 63.5 by 76 cm. (Colour Plate 2).
Coll.: Lady Knott; Major Beddington-Behrens.

1942

295. ANSCHLUSS: ALICE IN WONDERLAND
Canvas, 63.5 by 76 cm. (Plate LXXVIII).
Coll.: Private Coll., London.
Exh.: Berkeley Galleries, London, 1942; St. George's
Galleries, London, 1945.
Reprod.: The Austrian 22nd June Committee in 'Aid of
Russia', London, 1942.

296. LORELEY
Canvas, 63.5 by 76 cm. (Plate LXXIX).
Coll.: Private Coll., London.

297. MARIANNE
Canvas, 61.5 by 76 cm. (Plate LXXX).
Coll.: Private Coll., London.

298. SCOTTISH COAST
Canvas.
Coll.: Madame Aubard; Cathleen, Countess of Drogheda,
C.B.E.
Exh.: Polish and Czechoslovak Artists, Oxford, 1942.

1942–43

299. DUCK SHOOTING
Canvas (Colour Plate 3).
Coll.: Major Beddington-Behrens, London.

300. AMBASSADOR MAISKY
Canvas, 102 by 76 cm. (Colour Plate 4).
Coll.: Tate Gallery.

Exh.: War Artists' Exhibition, National Gallery, London, 1943.
Reprod.: *The Studio*, December, 1943, p. 176.
301. WHAT WE ARE FIGHTING FOR (Plate LXXXI).
Canvas, 117 by 152 cm.
Coll.: Private Coll., London.
Exh.: Artists' International Association, Oxford Street 1943.
Reprod.: *New Writing and Daylight*, 1945, pl. 153.

1942–45

302. THRENODY
Canvas, 71 by 66 cm.
Coll.: Major Beddington-Behrens.

1943

303. CAPRICCIO
Canvas, 63.5 by 76 cm. (Colour Plate 5).
Coll.: Private Coll., London.
304. HUNTERS
Canvas, 63.5 by 76 cm.
Coll.: Private Coll., London.
305. LANDSCAPE WITH SHEEP, SCOTLAND
Canvas, 63.5 by 76 cm.
Coll.: Private Coll., London.
306. MINONA
Canvas, 58 by 62 cm.
Coll.: Lida Palkovská.
307. PORTRAIT OF CATHLEEN, COUNTESS OF DROGHEDA, C.B.E.
Canvas, 101 by 77·5 cm.
Coll.: Private Coll., London.

LITHOGRAPHS AND DRAWINGS FOR ILLUSTRATIONS

1908[1]

JAGDBUCH. Illustrated by Kokoschka.
Publ.: Wiener Werkstätte, Vienna.
DIE TRÄUMENDEN KNABEN. By Kokoschka, with coloured lithographs (Plate I).
Publ.: Wiener Werkstätte, Vienna.
Reprod.: *Kunstblatt*, I, pp. 306/308; II, 367/370; *Deutsche Kunst und Dekoration*, XXIII, pp. 52/53; *Zeitschrift für Bildende Kunst*, N.F., Vol. XXIX, 1917/8, Heft 4/5; Westheim, 1918, pl. 42; 1925, pl. 100; *Magazine of Art*, Nov. 1945, p. 262.
POSTER, Kunstschau Wien. Self-portrait in two colours.
POSTER, Kunstschau Wien. Pietà.

1909

POSTER, Kunstschau Wien. 'Ver Sacrum', figure of a girl.

1910

20 ZEICHNUNGEN
Publ.: Sturm Verlag, Berlin.
1. Adolf Loos (Figure 3).
2. Herwarth Walden (Figure 4).
3. Paul Scheerbart.
    Reprod.: Westheim, 1918, pl. 44; 1925, pl. 11.
4. Richard Dehmel.
    Reprod.: Paul Wiegler, *Geschichte der Deutschen Literatur*, 1930, Vol. II, p. 265.
5. Alfred Kerr.
6. Yvette Guilbert (Figure 8).
7. Mörder Hoffnung der Frauen.
8. Mörder Hoffnung der Frauen (Figure 6).
9. Mörder Hoffnung der Frauen (Figure 7).
10. Kindsmörderin.
    Reprod.: Westheim, 1918, pl. 43; 1925, pl. 101.
11. Himmlische und irdische Liebe.
12. Schlangenzeichnung.
13. Wintergarten, Archie A. Goodale.

[1] Dates refer to the year of publication.

14. Die schöne Rollschuhläuferin (Figure 9).
15. Der Erstbeste darf der süssen Lilith das Haar kämmen.
16. Gesindel in der Sternennacht.
17. Friss Vogel oder stirb.
18. Belauscht.
19. Mann mit Goldstück.
20. Ausruhende Tänzerin.

LEVIN LUDWIG SCHÜCKIN
Publ.: Der Sturm, Berlin.

1910–12

HERR VON GARVENS. Red lithograph.

1910–16

MENSCHENKÖPFE
Publ.: Sturm Verlag, Berlin.
1. Rudolf Blümner.
2. Richard Dehmel.
Reprod.: Paul Wiegler, *Geschichte der Deutschen Literatur*, 1930, Vol. II, p. 265.
3. Gertrud Eysoldt.
4. Yvette Guilbert.
5. Alfred Kerr.
6. Karl Kraus (Figure 5).
7. Mechthild Lichnowsky.
8. Adolf Loos.
9. Paul Scheerbart.
Reprod.: Westheim, 1918, pl. 44; 1925, pl. 11.
10. Herwarth Walden.
11. Nell Walden.
12. Claire Waldorf.

1911

POSTER, Der Sturm, Berlin. The same self-portrait as the one used for the Kunstschau, 1908.
Reprod.: Westheim, 1925, pl. 2.

About 1911

POSTER, Akademischer Verband für Literatur und Musik, Vienna. Figure composition.

TUBUTSCH (Figure 10). By Albert Ehrenstein. Illustrated in
1911 by 13 drawings. (Discussed in *Der Sturm*, November
1911.)

Publ.: Georg Müller, Munich.

Reprod.: Kokoschka, *Dramen und Bilder*, 1913; Westheim,
1918, pl. 2; 1925, pl. 4, 5.

1913

DIE CHINESISCHE MAUER. By Karl Kraus, illustrated by 8 drawings.

Publ.: Leipzig.

Reprod.: *Zeitschrift für Bildende Kunst*, N.F., XXIX, 1917/18,
Heft 4/5.

WOLFGANG GURLITT

KARL KRAUS

Publ.: Graphisches Kabinett J. B. Neumann, Berlin.

DER GEFESSELTE KOLUMBUS. 12 lithographs illustrating play by
Kokoschka (Plate XXII, XXIII, Figure 11).

Publ.: Fritz Gurlitt Verlag, Berlin.

Reprod.: *Zeitschrift für Bildende Kunst*, N.F., XXIX, 1917/18,
Heft 4/5; Westheim, 1918, pl. 45, 46; 1925, pl. 102, 103.

1914

BACHKANTATE: OH EWIGKEIT DU DONNERWORT
11 lithographs illustrating Bach's Cantata (Plate XXIV, XXV).

Publ.: Fritz Gurlitt, Berlin; Book form in 1918.

Reprod.: *Zeitschrift für Bildende Kunst*, N.F., XXIX, 1917/18,
Heft 4/5; *Cicerone*, XI, 1919, p. 273; Westheim, 1918, pl. 6,
48, 49; 1925, pl. 24, 104, 105, 106; Einstein, *Die Kunst des
20. Jahrhunderts*, 1926, pl. 444.

ALBERT EHRENSTEIN

Publ.: as frontispiece of Ehrenstein's *Dem Ewigen Olymp*, Leipzig, 1921; frontispiece of Ehrenstein's *Mein Lied*, Berlin,
1931.

1915

DER HELDENSCHREI

Lithograph illustrating Ehrenstein's poem 'Die Welt möcht ich
zerreissen' in *Zeitecho: Ein Kriegstagebuch der Künstler*, Heft
10, p. 139; four further lithographs in Heft 20, pp. 297, 299,
303, 305.

Publ.: Graphik Verlag, Munich.

1916

EMMY HEIM

Lithograph, dated.

Publ.: Gesellschaft zur Förderung deutscher Kunst des 20. Jahrhunderts, Berlin.

Reprod.: Westheim, 1918, pl. 47; 1925, pl. 107.

JUDENTOCHTER

Coloured lithograph, used as cover for poems by H. Walden.

ADOLF LOOS

Lithograph.

THE PASSION OF CHRIST

Lithographs. 1. The Last Supper. 2. The Mount of Olives. 3. The Taking of Christ. 4. The Crown of Thorns. 5. Crucifixion. 6. Resurrection.

Publ.: Paul Cassirer, Berlin.

Reprod.: Westheim, 1918, pl. 52; Die Bildenden Künste, Vol. IV, 1921, pl. 233; Tietze, Deutsche Graphik der Gegenwart, 1922, pl. 10; Westheim, 1925, pl. 52; Catalogue of Galerie Arnold exhibition, Dresden, 1925, p. 42; Bulliet, The Significant Moderns, 1936, pl. 233.

THE ANNUNCIATION

Lithograph.

THE REST ON THE FLIGHT INTO EGYPT

Lithograph.

Reprod.: Westheim, 1918, pl. 3; 1925, pl. 21.

1917

THE ARTIST'S MOTHER

Lithograph, inscribed 'Zeichnung nach meiner Mutter' and 'Meiner lieben Mama zur Feier des 70. Lebensjahres'.

Reprod.: Westheim, 1918, pl. 59; Kunst und Künstler, XXIII, 1920, p. 67; Westheim, 1925, pl. 59.

HIOB

14 lithographs illustrating Kokoschka's play.

Publ.: Paul Cassirer, Berlin.

Reprod.: Westheim, 1918, pl. 4, 53, 54; 1925, pl. 23, 110, 111.

WALTER HASENCLEVER—I

Lithograph, profile to the right.

Reprod.: Westheim, 1925, pl. 28; Catalogue of Galerie Arnold exhibition, Dresden, 1925, p. 34; Wiegler, Geschichte der Deutschen Literatur, Vol. II, 1930, p. 844; Guide through the exhibition 'Entartete Kunst', Munich, 1937, p. 31.

Blue lithograph, reproduced in *Kunstblatt* (Liebhaberausgabe), 1917, Heft 10.

FRITZ NEUBERGER

Lithograph.

Publ.: Paul Cassirer, Berlin.

Reprod.: Westheim, 1918, pl. 55; *Kunst und Künstler*, 1919, Westheim, 1925, pl. 112; Einstein, *Die Kunst des 20. Jahrhunderts*, 1926, p. 445.

LOB DES HOHEN VERSTANDES. Book by V. v. Dirsztay, with 7 illustrations by Kokoschka.

Publ.: Kurt Wolff, Munich.

ULTIMA RATIO. Dated.

Reprod.: Westheim, 1918, pl. 51; 1925, pl. 109.

1918

WALTER HASENCLEVER—II

Lithograph, head resting on hand. Dated.

Publ.: Paul Cassirer.

Reprod.: Westheim, 1918, pl. 56; 1925, pl. 116.

THE ARTIST'S FATHER

Lithograph, dated.

Publ.: Paul Cassirer, Berlin.

Reprod.: Westheim, 1918, pl. 60; 1925, pl. 114.

CORONNA—I

Lithograph, dated. Profile to the left.

Publ.: Paul Cassirer, Berlin.

Reprod.: Westheim, 1918, pl. 58; 1925, pl. 118.

CORONNA—II

Lithograph, dated. Almost frontal.

Publ.: Paul Cassirer, Berlin.

Reprod.: Westheim, 1918, pl. 57; 1925, pl. 117.

O. EICHELKAMP

Lithograph.

Publ.: Paul Cassirer, Berlin.

LITTLE GIRL

Lithograph.

Reprod.: Westheim, 1925, pl. 119.

ORPHEUS

5 lithographs.

About 1918

LIBERTÉ, EGALITÉ, FRATRICIDE
Coloured lithograph.

1919

VIER DRAMEN, cover design for new edition of Kokoschka's plays.
IWAR VON LÜCKEN
Lithograph.
Reprod.: Westheim, 1925, pl. 120.

1920-22

DIE TÖCHTER DES BUNDES
10 lithographs: 1. Esther. 2. Deborah. 3. Hagar. 4. Miryam.
5. Naëmi. 6. Ruth—I. Reprod.: Westheim, 1925, pl. 28.
7. Ruth—II. Reprod.: Westheim, 1925, pl. 49. 8. Ruth—
III. Reprod.: Westheim, 1925, pl. 132. 9. Hefa. Reprod.:
Westheim, 1925, pl. 47. 10. Recha. Reprod.: Westheim,
1925, pl. 125.

1920

HERMINE KÖRNER
Lithograph.
Reprod.: Westheim, 1925, pl. 121.

About 1920

MAX REINHARDT
Lithograph, large and small version.
Reprod.: Westheim, 1925, pl. 35.

1921

TILLA DURIEUX
Lithograph, full face.
Reprod.: Westheim, 1925, pl. 27.
OMNIA VANA
Lithograph.
Reprod.: Westheim, 1925, pl. 131.
POSTER, Sommerausstellung der Künstlervereinigung, Dresden.
Coloured lithograph, self-portrait with heraldic flowers.
VARIATIONEN ÜBER EIN THEMA
10 chalk drawings, reproduced in collotype (Plates XXXVII,
XXXVIII, XXXIX, XL).

Publ.: Richard Lanyi, Vienna. Introduction by Max Dvořak.
Reprod.: *Die Bildenden Künste*, IV, 1921, pp. 97–101; Westheim, 1925, pl. 127, 128.

About 1921

TILLA DURIEUX
Lithograph, profile.

INDIA
Lithograph.
Reprod.: Faistauer, *Neue Malerei in Oesterreich*, 1923, pl. 38; Westheim, 1925, pl. 126.

MARIA ORSKA
Lithograph.

1923

MAX LIEBERMANN
Lithograph.
Reprod.: Westheim, 1925, pl. 19.

DER UNERTRINNBARE, or DER DOPPELGÄNGER
Novel by Viktor v. Dirsztay, with 9 illustrations by Kokoschka.
Publ.: Munich.

1923–24

MATTHÄUS PASSION
About 50 chalk drawings, made for reproduction, but never published.

1924

POSTER, Kunstsalon Wolfsberg, Zürich (Kokoschka exhibition).
Lithograph in two colours, self-portrait seen from two angles.

PAUL WESTHEIM
Lithograph.
Reprod.: Westheim, 1925, pl. 19.

1925

MACH DIE TÜR ZU, ES ZIEHT
Text by Bohuslav Kokoschka, illustrated by Oskar Kokoschka.

1931

MEIN LIED
Poems by Albert Ehrenstein, 8 illustrations by Kokoschka (Plate LX; Figure 12).
Publ.: Ernst Rowohlt, Berlin.

1937

POSTER FOR THE BASQUE CHILDREN
Lithograph, showing mother and children, panorama of Prague
in the background, bomber above. Inscribed 'Pomozte Bas-
kickým Dêtem!' (Help the Basque Children!)
Publ.: Prague.

LA PASSIONARIA
Etching, made for a poster (Figure 13).
Reprod.: *Zeitspiegel*, London, 1942.
Publ.: Prague.

1945

POSTER: REMEMBER THE CHILDREN OF EUROPE WHO WILL STARVE
THIS WINTER (Figure 14).
Publ.: London.

WORKS BY KOKOSCHKA, NOT LISTED ABOVE

1907–8

SELF-PORTRAIT
Clay, painted with colours, signed.
Coll.: Adolf Loos, Vienna; Blanche Bonestall, New York.
Exh.: Kunstschau, Vienna, 1908.
Reprod.: *Kunstblatt*, January, 1929, Heft 1, p. 17.

MEDAL WITH SELF-PORTRAIT
Relief, over Liszt portrait.
Coll.: Nell Walden, Ascona.
Reprod.: *Kunstblatt*, January, 1929, Heft 1, pl. 18.

DAS GETUPFTE EI
'Bewegliche Lichtbilder' (lantern slides).
Produced in 'Fledermaus'.

1920

PLAQUE, inscribed 'Anima' on the obverse and 'Mania' on the
reverse; porcelain, produced at Meissen for the Dresdener
Künstlervereinigung.
Reprod.: *Kunstblatt*, January, 1929, Heft 1, p. 16.

BIBLIOGRAPHY

THE WRITINGS OF OSKAR KOKOSCHKA[1]

Die Träumenden Knaben. Poem. Vienna, 1908; Leipzig, 1917.

Wintergarten. Berlin (*Der Sturm*, 1910, p. 207).

Nach der Verurteilung zum Tode geschrieben. Berlin (*Der Sturm*, 1910, p. 291).

Dramen und Bilder: HOFFNUNG DER FRAUEN, SPHINX UND STROHMANN, SCHAUSPIEL (later renamed DER BRENNENDE DORNBUSCH). Leipzig, Kurt Wolff Verlag, 1913.

DER GEFESSELTE KOLUMBUS. Berlin, Fritz Gurlitt, 1913; 'Neue Bilderbücher', III/6, 1916.

Alos Makar. Poem. In *Zeitecho, Ein Kriegstagebuch der Künstler*, 1915, Heft 20.

Vier Dramen: ORPHEUS UND EURYDICE, DER BRENNENDE DORNBUSCH, MÖRDER HOFFNUNG DER FRAUEN, HIOB. Berlin, Paul Cassirer, 1919.

Vom Bewusstsein der Gesichte. (A story, not identical with a lecture held by Kokoschka in Vienna under the same title.) Munich, Kurt Wolff Verlag, in *Genius*, 1919, p. 39.

Der Fetisch (Letters). In *Künstlerbekenntnisse* (ed. Paul Westheim), Berlin, Ullstein Verlag, ca. 1923 (not dated).

Die Schale. Berlin (*Das Kunstblatt*, 1923, p. 129).

Geschichte der Schmiedin. Eine Legende, Berlin (*Das Kunstblatt*, February, 1931).

Autobiographie. Vienna (*Der Wiener Kunstwanderer*, November, 1933, No. 10).

Comenius, The English Revolution and our Present Plight. In *The Teacher of Nations.* Cambridge University Press, 1942, p. 61.

The Baroque Art of Czechoslovakia. London (*The Burlington Magazine*, November, 1942).

The Portrait in Past and Present. London (*Apropos*, March, 1945, p. 18).

---

[1] The titles of plays are printed in capital letters, those of articles and other short pieces in italics. Dates refer to the year of publication.

BOOKS ON OSKAR KOKOSCHKA

Paul Stefan: *Oskar Kokoschka*. (Introduction to *Oskar Kokoschka: Dramen und Bilder*.) Leipzig, Kurt Wolff Verlag, 1913.

Paul Westheim: *Oskar Kokoschka*. Potsdam-Berlin, Gustav Kiepenheuer Verlag, 1918.

Paul Westheim: *Oskar Kokoschka*. Berlin, Paul Cassirer Verlag, 1925.

Hans Heilmaier: *Kokoschka*. Paris, Ed. G. Crès & Cie ('*Les Artistes Nouveaux*'), 1929.

Georg Biermann: *Oskar Kokoschka*. Leipzig-Berlin, Klinkhardt und Biermann, 1929 (Vol. 52 of '*Junge Kunst*').

ARTICLES AND NOTES ON OSKAR KOKOSCHKA

BIERMANN, GEORG. 'Oskar Kokoschka.' *Cicerone*, XXI, 1929, pp. 19–24.

BORN, WOLFGANG. 'Neue Bilder von Oskar Kokoschka.' *Deutsche Kunst und Dekoration*, 67, 1930, p. 83.

BORN, WOLFGANG. 'Oskar Kokoschka and his Time.' *Bulletin of the City Art Museum of St. Louis*, December, 1942, p. 32.

BURCHARD, LUDWIG. 'Neue Bilderbücher' (Die Bachkantate). *Cicerone*, XI, 1919, p. 273.

DÖBLIN, ALFRED. 'Oskar Kokoschka's Tubutsch.' *Der Sturm*, 1911, p. 751.

DONATH, ADOLPH. 'Kokoschka in Dresden.' *Der Kunstwanderer*, February, 1925, p. 190.

DVOŘAK, MAX. 'Variationen über ein Thema.' (Introduction.) Vienna, Richard Lanyi, 1921.

EHRENSTEIN, ALBERT. 'Oskar Kokoschka.' *Zeitecho, Ein Kriegstagebuch der Künstler*, 1915, Heft 20.

EHRENSTEIN, ALBERT. 'Oskar Kokoschka' (poem and essay). *Menschen und Affen*, Berlin, Ernst Rowohlt, no date (after 1925), p. 107.

GEORGE, WALDEMAR. 'Kokoschka and Max Beckmann.' *Creative Art*, April, 1931, p. 459.

GEORGE, WALDEMAR. 'Humain, Trop Humain . . .'. *Beaux-Arts*, 7th June, 1939, p. 4.

GROHMANN, WILL. 'Galerie Arnold: Oskar Kokoschka.' *Cicerone*, XVII, 1925, p. 149.

GRÜNER, FRANZ. 'Oskar Kokoschka.' *Die Fackel*, 28th November, 1911.

HAUSENSTEIN, WILHELM. 'Über Kokoschka.' *Kunst für Alle*, XLI, 1926, p. 153. (*Die Kunst*, LIII.)

HILLER, KURT. 'Oskar Kokoschka.' *Der Sturm*, 1910, p. 151.

KÜHLMANN, R. v. 'Zu den Landschaften von Oskar Kokoschka.' *Das Kunstblatt*, 1926, Heft 1.

KÜNSTLER-ZEDAIK, W. 'Der Aufbau von Oskar Kokoschka's Bild "Wien vom Wilhelminenberg".' *Joseph Strzygowski-Festschrift*, Klagenfurth, 1932.

MANN, THOMAS. 'Oskar Kokoschka.' *Der Wiener Kunstwanderer*, November, 1933, No. 10.

MICHAELIS, KARIN. 'Der Tolle Kokoschka.' *Das Kunstblatt*, December, 1918.

NEUMEYER, ALFRED. 'Oskar Kokoschka.' *Magazine of Art*, November, 1945, p. 261.

POGLAYEN-NEUWALL, S. 'Aquarelle und Graphik von Oskar Kokoschka in der Neuen Galerie.' *Cicerone*, XVI, 1924, p. 729.

SCHEFFLER, KARL. 'Oskar Kokoschka.' *Kunst und Künstler*, XVII, 1919, p. 123.

SCHEFFLER, KARL. 'Kokoschkas Landschaften.' *Kunst und Künstler*, XXIX, 1931, p. 190.

SCHMIDT, P. F. 'Oskar Kokoschka.' *Feuer*, I, 1919/20, p. 745.

SCHÜRER, OSKAR. 'Zwei Moderne Porträts.' *Cicerone*, XI, 1919, p. 738.

SPRENGLER, J. 'Kokoschkas Bühnendichtungen.' *Hochland*, XIX, 1921/22, 2nd part, p. 670.

TESAR, E. L. 'Der Fall Oskar Kokoschka und die Gesellschaft.' *Die Fackel*, 1st April, 1911.

TIETZE, HANS. 'Oskar Kokoschka.' *Zeitschrift für Bildende Kunst*, N.F., XXIX, 1918, p. 83.

TIETZE, HANS. 'Oskar Kokoschkas neue Werke.' *Die Bildenden Künste*, II, 1919, p. 249.

TIETZE, HANS. 'Oskar Kokoschka.' *Der Ararat*, II, 1921, p. 219.

TIETZE, HANS. 'Oskar Kokoschka.' *L'Amour de l'Art*, 1934.

WALLERSTEIN, VIKTOR. 'Die Neuen Werke Oskar Kokoschkas.' *Kunst und Künstler*, XX, 1922, p. 43.

WEIGERT, H. 'Kokoschka-Ausstellung in der Galerie Arnold,' *Zeitschrift für Bildende Kunst*, LXIII, March, 1925, Heft 11/12 (Monatsrundschau, p. 129).

BOOKS CONTAINING MATERIAL ON OSKAR KOKOSCHKA

Bahr, Hermann, *Expressionismus* (Munich, Delphin Verlag), 1920.

Brockhaus, Der Grosse, x, 1931.

Cheney, Sheldon. *Expressionism in Art* (New York), 1934.

Cheney, Sheldon. *A World History of Art* (New York), 1937.

Cheney, Sheldon. *A Primer of Modern Art* (New York), 1939.

Cheney, Sheldon. *The Story of Modern Art* (New York), 1941.

Einstein, Carl. *Die Kunst des 20. Jahrhunderts* (Propyläen-Kunstgeschichte, Berlin), 1926, 1931.

Encyclopædia Britannica, 14th edition, 1929.

Faistauer, A. *Neue Malerei in Oesterreich* (Zürich, Leipzig, Vienna), 1923.

Forel, Auguste. *Out of my Life and Work* (London), 1934.

Glaser, Curt. *Graphik der Neuzeit* (Berlin), 1922.

Gurlitt, F. *Das Graphische Jahr* (Berlin) I, 1921.

Hamann, Richard. *Geschichte der Kunst* (Berlin, Knaur), 1933.

Hildebrandt, Hans. *Die Kunst des 19. und 20. Jahrhunderts* (Handbuch der Kunstwissenschaft) (Potsdam, Wildpark, Verlag), 1931.

Justi, Ludwig. *Von Corinth bis Klee* (Berlin), 1931.

Karpfen, Fritz. *Oesterreichische Kunst*, 1923.

Kürschners Deutscher Literatur-Kalender auf das Jahr 1926.

Landsberger, Fritz. *Impressionismus und Expressionismus* (Leipzig, Klinkhardt und Biermann), 1920.

Meyers Lexikon, 7th edition, IV, 1926.

Read, Herbert. *Art Now* (London), 1933.

Rössler, A. *Kritische Fragmente* (Vienna), 1918.

Sauerlandt, M. *Die Kunst der letzten 30 Jahre* (Berlin, Rembrandt Verlag), 1935.

Scheffler, Karl. *Geschichte der Europäischen Malerei vom Impressionismus bis zur Gegenwart* (Berlin), 1927.

Schmalenbach, Fritz. *Kunsthistorische Studien: Grundlagen des Frühexpressionismus* (Bâle), 1941.

Schmidt, Paul Ferdinand. *Kunst der Gegenwart* (Neubabelsberg, Akademische Verlagsgesellschaft Athenaion), 1922/3.

Schultze-Naumburg, Paul. *Kunst und Rasse* (Munich), 1930.

Sydow, Eckardt von. *Die deutsche expressionistische Kultur und Malerei* (Berlin, Furche Kunstgaben, II), 1920.

349

Szittya, E. *Malerschicksale; Vierzehn Porträts* (Hamburg), 1925.

Thoene, Peter. *Modern German Art* (London, Penguin Books, Ltd.), 1938.

Thieme-Becker, A. *Allgemeines Künstlerlexikon*, XXI (Leipzig). Article by H. Tietze, 1927.

Tietze, Hans. *Deutsche Graphik der Gegenwart*, 1922.

Walden, Herwart. *Expressionismus—Die Kunstwende* (Berlin), 1918.

Walden, Herwart. *Einblick in die Kunst* (Berlin), 1925.

Waldmann, Emil. *La Peinture Allemande Contemporaine* (Paris, Ed. Crès), 1930.

Willrich, Wolfgang. *Säuberung des Kunsttempels: Eine kunstpolitische Kampfschrift* (Berlin, J. F. Lehmann), 1937.

Woermann, Karl. *Geschichte der Kunst*, VI (Leipzig), 1922.

MAGAZINES CONTAINING REFERENCES TO, OR ILLUSTRATIONS OF, WORKS BY OSKAR KOKOSCHKA

ART NEWS, April, 1943, p. 23.

ART QUARTERLY, Detroit, Summer, 1941 (W. R. Valentiner, 'Expressionism and Abstract Painting').

LE ARTI PLASTICHE, November, 1928.

DIE BILDENDEN KÜNSTE, II, 1919, p. 249 (see Tietze); III, 1920, p. 65, 67, 69; IV, 1921, pp. 97/101, 233.

BLÄTTER FÜR GEMÄLDEKUNDE, VI, 1911, p. 173 (Th. v. Frimmel, 'Wiener Kunstbriefe I: Die Jungen im Hagenbund').

DER BLAUE REITER, III, 1912.

BULLETIN OF THE MINNEAPOLIS INSTITUTE OF ARTS, May 17, 1941 (J. B. Neumann, 'Who is Who in Modern German Art').

THE BURLINGTON MAGAZINE, May, 1942 (see THE WRITINGS OF OSKAR KOKOSCHKA).

CAHIERS D'ART, 1938, 1/2, p. 16 (Will Grohmann, 'L'art contemporain en Allemagne').

CICERONE, XI, 1919, pp. 259, 273 (see Burchard); XII, 1920, pp. 385, 421, 641/9; XV, 1923, pp. 392, 740, 783, 1117 (S. Schwabacher, 'Moderne Bilder im Städel Neubau'); XVI, 1924, pp. 130, 217, 729 (see Polgayen-Neuwall), 1031; XVII, 1925, pp. 149/51 (see Grohmann), 841, 983, 1138; XVIII, 1926, pp. 34, 204, 375, 396, 743; XIX, 1927, pp. 34, 90/93, 124, 221/3, 383; XXI, 1929, pp. 19/24 (see Biermann).

DEUTSCHE KUNST UND DEKORATION, XXIII, 1908, pp. 50/53
(J. A. Lux); XXXII, 1913, pp. 244, 246; XXXIII, pp. 364, 368;
XLIII, pp. 6, 8, 10; XLV, pp. 322, 327; XLVIII, pp. 84, 276, 278;
XLIX, p. 34; LII, pp. 249, 254; LIX, p. 116; LXVII, p. 83 (see
Born).

EMPORIUM, XXXVI, 1937, p. 445.

DIE FACKEL, 9th April 1910 (Karl Kraus).

GANYMED, II, 1920, p. 150 (W. v. Alten, 'Die Kunst in Deutsch-
land'), p. 159 (C. Moll, 'Die Möglichkeiten Wiens'); III, 1921,
p. 148.

GENIUS, I, 1918, pp. 40/5, 227; II, 1919, pp. 63/66 (H. Tietze,
'Jung-Oesterreichische Malerei'), 71, 73.

HORIZON, Vol. XIII, No. 73 (January, 1946), p. 57 (Augustus
John, 'Fragment of an Autobiography').

JAHRBUCH DER JUNGEN KUNST, IV, 1923, pp. 269, 354, 362.

DIE KUNST, XXXIX (KUNST FÜR ALLE XXXIV), 1919, pp. 384,
393; XLIX (KUNST FÜR ALLE XXXIX), 1924, pp. 34, 303;
LIII, (KUNST FÜR ALLE XLI), 1926, pp. 153/61 (see Hausenstein); LV (KUNST FÜR ALLE XLII), 1928, pp. 36/7.

KUNST FÜR ALLE (see DIE KUNST).

KUNST UND KÜNSTLER, VIII, 1909/10, p. 593 (Franz Servaes);
X, 1912, p. 511; XVII, 1919, p. 123 (see Scheffler); XVIII, 1920,
p. 67; XIX, 1921, p. 372; XX, 1922, p. 40, 43 (see Waller-
stein); XXIII, 1925, p. 249; XXIV, 1926, pp. 93, 164, 166;
XXV, 1927, p. 272; XXVII, 1929, p. 477; XXIX, 1931, p. 360
(A. Basler, 'Deutsche und Schweizer in Paris').

DAS KUNSTBLATT, 1917, I, pp. 211, 289/316; 1918, pp. 367/370;
1923, pp. 129/132, 193/8; 1926, January, February, April,
December (see Kühlmann); 1928, p. 197; 1929, pp. 16/18;
1930, March, May, July, December; 1931, January (prices of
paintings by Kokoschka), February (see THE WRITINGS OF
OSKAR KOKOSCHKA).

DER KUNSTWANDERER, 1924/5, pp. 190/1 (A. Donath).

LONDON BULLETIN, January/February, 1939.

MAGAZINE OF ART, 1933, p. 536; 1935, p. 229; 1937, p. 17
(sup.); 1938, p. 656; 1939, p. 480; 1945, p. 261.

NEUE BLÄTTER FÜR KUNST UND DICHTUNG, I, 1918/19.

DIE NEUE DEUTSCHE GRAPHIK, XIX, 1920, pp. 73/6 (G. Hart-
laub).

PICTURES ON EXHIBIT, November, 1941, p. 22.

DER QUERSCHNITT (MARGINALIEN DER GALERIE FLECHTHEIM),
I, 1921.

STUDIO, January, 1938, p. 36; January, 1942, p. 22; December, 1943.

DER STURM, 1910, p. 166 (Else Lasker-Schüler); 1911, pp. 671, 710 (Else Lasker-Schüler, 'Briefe aus Norwegen').

WELTKUNST, November, 1930.

ZEITSCHRIFT FÜR BILDENDE KUNST, N.F., XXIII, 1912, p. 229 (P. F. Schmidt); XXIV, 1913, p. 287 (Ewald Bender, 'Deutsche Kunst um 1913'); XXIX, 1918, pp. 83/97 (see Tietze); XXXIV, 1925 (Monatsrundschau), p. 129 (see Weigert).

Public Collections are listed under the names of cities, private collections under the names of their owners. All numbers refer to the list of Kokoschka's works.

z

INDEX

The figures in *italics* refer to illustrations. Titles of works are translated into English, except those which appear printed under lithographs, over plays or other publications.

357